UNHOLY GRAIL

THE OPERATIONAL LEVEL OF WAR
Edited by Michael Krause, Deputy Chief of US Army
Center for Military History, and Andrew Wheatcroft

The Operational Level of War series provides for a theory of armed conflicts
in the present and the immediate future. Unlike many theories, it is
not rooted in abstractions but the practice of war, both in history and
the immediate past.

The books in the series all contribute to the clearer understanding of
the potentials and the dangers of war in the 1990s.

The key contribution of the operational theory of war is to provide a
link between strategy and tactics, a connection which is of unique
importance in modern warfare.

Other titles in the series include:

THE FRAMEWORK OF OPERATIONAL WARFARE
Clayton R. Newell

UNHOLY GRAIL

The US and the wars in Vietnam, 1965–8

Larry Cable

London and New York

First published 1991
by Routledge
11 New Fetter Lane, London EC4P 4EE

Simultaneously published in the USA and Canada
by Routledge
a division of Routledge, Chapman and Hall, Inc.
29 West 35th Street, New York, NY 10001

Set in 10/12pt Palatino
by Hope Services (Abingdon) Ltd
Printed and bound in Great Britain by
Biddles Ltd, Guildford

British Library Cataloguing in Publication Data
Cable, Larry E.
Unholy grail: the U.S. and the wars in Vietnam, 1965–8
1. Policies of United States government
I. Title
959. 70432

Library of Congress Cataloging in Publication Data
Cable, Larry.
Unholy grail: the U.S. and the wars in Vietnam, 1965–8 / Larry Cable.
p.   cm.
Includes bibliographical references and index.
ISBN 0–415–05043–X
1. Vietnamese Conflict, 1961–1975 – United States. 2. Vietnamese
Conflict, 1961–1975 – Aerial operations, American. I. Title
DS558.C35   1991
959.704′3 – dc20   90–47819
CIP

ISBN 0–415–05043–X

CONTENTS

MAPS

INBRIEF

War exists first as an idea. Before men and materiel are assembled, long before the fear and exhilaration of combat, very long before the consequences become apparent, war exists as an idea in the minds of policy makers and military commanders alike. The conceptualizations of war which exist in the minds of those who make and execute national security and foreign policy will in large measure govern the outcome of war. Bad concepts assure a bad outcome. Material strength and technological sophistication or human courage and suffering cannot redeem a faulty idea.

Policy makers must conceive of a goal for the war, the political purpose for which it is being fought. Policy makers and generals must define victory, the referent against which success or failure might be gauged. Generals must have a theory of victory, the way in which the war will be fought. These three elements must be internally coherent, consistent over time, consensually accepted and, most importantly, relevant to the realities which emerge on the ground.

For some countries in some wars, for example the United States in the Second World War, the fixing of a goal, the defining of victory and the development and refinement of a theory of victory are accomplished easily and accurately. In other wars, for example the Korean War, the task is made more difficult by the nature of the war itself. In the Korean War, unlike the Second World War, the national survival or core values of the United States were not at risk. There had been no attack on American territory which served to rally political will. There was no sense of moral crusade against evil. Indeed, the Korean War, being a limited war in support of policy, made the mobilization of crusading zeal and its concomitant, a requirement for total war and total victory through the enemy's unconditional surrender, undesirable.

The Vietnam War was a limited war in support of policy. In this it resembled the Korean conflict. However, the Vietnam War differed in character from its immediate predecessor. It combined aspects of conventional and guerrilla war. It mixed insurgency with partisan conflict. It had a chameleon appearance as its character changed several times between 1964 and 1968. As a result, the formulation of a goal, the definition of victory and the development of a theory of victory placed greater demands upon the policy makers and military commanders of the Johnson Administration.

Policy makers and senior military commanders must constantly monitor the feedback from the war provided by the intelligence mechanisms available them. This feedback is critical to the assessment of success and provides the basis for modifying policy and its means of implementation. It is not enough that the intelligence product be timely, accurate and relatively unambiguous. The policy makers and military commanders must be willing and able to abandon or to modify failed theories of victory and operational concepts. An administration and its senior military command must have the intellectual courage to see things the way they are. Additionally, the administration and its military commanders must have the moral courage to act upon knowledge regardless of personal consequences. The Vietnam War placed intense demands upon the Johnson Administration civilian officials and military officers in these areas.

The intellectual construct of war, its goals, its definitions and theories of victory must take into account the nature of allies and enemies alike. Proper consideration must be given to their goals, definitions and theories of victory. It must not be assumed that the allies and enemies of the United States have identical interests, hierarchies of values and needs or share an interchangeable calculus of rationality. There were three direct participants in the Vietnam War other than the United States and its junior partners, Australia, New Zealand and the Republic of Korea. These were South Vietnam, the Viet Cong and North Vietnam. The Johnson Administration was challenged by the requirement that each of these be understood as a separate entity with its own goal, definition and theory of victory.

The intellectual constructs of the Johnson Administration and the senior military commanders, as well as the ways in which these were implemented, evaluated and modified are the main focus of this book. There are heroes and villains, but more to the point there is wisdom and witlessness. This is a record of perceptions and ideas and their consequences for those who fight.

Shortly before the first American ground combat forces arrived in South Vietnam a quarter century ago, two US military advisors were crouched close to the wall of a Buddhist tomb in Quang Tri Province. It had been one of those little nature walks where nothing had gone quite right. Now, in one of those lulls which happen without rhyme or reason in every firefight, one asked the other, 'Why the hell are we here?' The reply was as accurate as it was unsatisfying, 'Damn if I know, but if I ever find out, I'll pass the word.' This book, like its predecessor, *Conflict of Myths: The Development of American Counterinsurgency Doctrine and the Vietnam War*,[1] represents an attempt to partially answer that question.

This work focuses on the intellectual constructs of the Johnson Administration. It looks not so much on the systems and processes of decision making and policy formulation as it does on the ideas which drove the war. What did the Administration think the nature and character of the war was? How did it and its military commanders intend to fight and win the war? How was intelligence used to modify policy and implementation? Where were intellectual and moral courage to be found and where were they absent? By design this work is based almost exclusively on archival materials ranging from Combat After Action Reports to CIA studies to minutes of meetings and memoranda. Much of the material is drawn from the Lyndon Baines Johnson Presidential Library.

A great debt is owed by me to the staff of that excellent outpost of the National Archives and Records Service. Dr David Humphrey, Ms Lynda Hanson, Ms Irene Parra, and the others who made my research both possible and more fun than it should have been are models of the profession of archivist.

Larry Cable
Wilmington, NC
April 1990

1

THE VAST VOID

The 553rd session of the National Security Council on 27 July 1965 started at 5:45 p.m. The meeting lasted only a little while. Its consequences would linger for decades. Those attending, including President Johnson, Secretaries Rusk, McNamara and Fowler, Admiral Raborn, the Director of Central Intelligence, National Security Advisor McGeorge Bundy, General Earle Wheeler, Chairman of the Joint Chiefs of Staff and such key aides as John McNaughton, the Assistant Secretary of Defense for International Security Affairs (ASD/ISA) were anxious to get through the ceremony quickly since they had a meeting with the Congressional leadership of both parties scheduled for 6:30 p.m. There was only one item on the agenda. The matter was a formality; the meeting was a ritual approving decisions already made.[1]

Like actors in an overly rehearsed play, the senior policy makers of the United States delivered lines already too well-known, long since drained of passion and content. They spoke for the distant audience of history or, perhaps, they participated in a liturgy commemorating an important moment of state and nation.

The single subject presented was the deployment of significant additions to the US ground forces already in combat in South Vietnam. A very precise plan of incremental increase had been provided by the Secretary of Defense.[2] Its content and hopes, if not its implications, were well understood by all. The only disagreement noted in the forty-minute meeting was between Secretary of State Dean Rusk and Secretary of Defense McNamara. It came over a map showing the amount of territory controlled by the Viet Cong. Rusk thought it represented an overstatement; McNamara argued the opposite, that the map understated Viet Cong domination.[3] Agreement on the main matter was quick and unanimous. The NSC assented to a policy that in many ways was a blank check. The military commanders in South Vietnam would be supplied with the men and materiel they believed necessary for the achievement of American policy goals. According to the minutes of Bromley Smith, Executive Secretary of the National

1

Security Council, 'There was no response when the President asked whether anyone in the room objected to the course of action decided upon.'[4]

The Congressional leadership meeting following was attended by the majority and minority leaders of both House and Senate as well as such key figures as Hale Boggs, Bourke Hickenlooper, Carl Albert and Mike Mansfield. There was scarcely more dissent among the Congressmen than there had been within the Administration. The Speaker of the House echoed the thoughts of many.

> I don't think we have any alternatives. Our military men tell us we need more and we should give it to them. The lesson of Hitler and Mussolini is clear. I can see five years from now a chain of events far more dangerous to our country.[5]

The Republican House minority leader, Gerald Ford, raised some minor questions and objections regarding the increase in the draft calls and the manner of funding, but agreed overall with the decision to increase the number of US troops in Vietnam. Senator Dirksen of Illinois, the very well-known Republican minority leader, raised the issue of apathy within the American public. 'Tell the country we are engaged in a very serious business. People are apathetic.'[6] Senator Mike Mansfield agreed, but urged an important cautionary note:

> Whatever pledge we had was to assist SVN in its own defense. Since then there has been no government of legitimacy. We ought to make that decision every day. We owe this government nothing – no pledge of any kind.
>
> We are going deeper into war. Even total victory would be vastly costly. Best hope for salvation is quick stalemate and negotiations. We can not expect our people to support a war for 3–5 years. What we are about is an anticommunist crusade. Escalation begets escalation. [emphasis in original][7]

July 27 was the day of ritual, the moment of official approval by Administration and Congress. All the real discussion concerning the increased, even open-ended, commitment to South Vietnam had occurred during a series of meetings held between 21 and 26 July 1965.

From the first of these conferences on 21 July, it had been evident that, with the very obvious exception of the Under Secretary of State, George Ball, all the participants were quite optimistic about the military and political effects of augmenting the US troop presence in South Vietnam and enlarging the American campaigns of aerial attack on North Vietnam and the network of trails and tracks through Laos believed to be so important for the infiltration of men and supplies from North Vietnam into the South. Ambassador Henry Cabot Lodge and US

Information Director Carl Rowan, both pessimistic about the ability of the South Vietnamese government to gather and retain support, or even to maintain itself against the threat of a *coup*, believed that the US military effort could create real stability in the country by blunting the Viet Cong threat. Only George Ball dissented. He resisted the attraction of the military option, telling the President, 'I would not recommend that you follow McNamara's plan.'[8]

Lyndon Johnson, his instincts reinforced by a series of CIA reports, was concerned that the North Vietnamese could match any US escalation and that the greater US ground-force numbers would translate into greater loss of American life. He was reassured by General Wheeler on both counts. The JCS Chairman stated: 'The more men we have, the greater the likelihood of smaller losses.'[9] The General welcomed the possibility of the North Vietnamese attempting to match the US in the escalation game with evident relish. 'This means greater bodies of men – which will allow us to cream them.'[10]

That afternoon the President's doubts were reflected by the careful hearing he gave George Ball's pessimistic prognosis of US prospects. Ball's doubts, as he had expressed in a memorandum circulated to the senior members of the Administration, were based upon a conviction that bombing North Vietnam would not accomplish American political objectives and that the addition of ground combat forces to bombing would not enhance the prospects. He believed that once the decision to send additional ground combat forces to South Vietnam was made, it would be virtually impossible to reverse.[11] Ball's judgment was well advised. The prestige of great power once invested could not easily be retrieved. Once American blood had been spilled, its loss must be redeemed by successful prosecution of the war.

In his mind these considerations were reinforced by his perception that the current South Vietnamese government was inherently unstable and lacked popular support. As he had earlier, the Under Secretary urged that the United States issue a virtual ultimatum to the Saigon government requiring fundamental political and economic reforms as the price for continued assistance. These reforms would be calculated to force the South Vietnamese into negotiations with the NLF.[12] Ball believed that the American military had no realistic chance of 'winning' in Vietnam. He had concluded the strengths of our weapons and organizations were not applicable to the 'jungles and rice paddies' of a 'rotten country.'[13]

Ball's arguments were countered by McGeorge Bundy and Dean Rusk, both of whom believed that an American withdrawal from South Vietnam would have strong and adverse effects upon the status and influence of the United States throughout the world. American irresolution would be seen by allies and enemies alike as a failure of political will and an abdication of leadership. Rusk concluded that the entire strategy of containment would be placed in peril if the United States lacked firmness of purpose in Vietnam. 'If the communist world finds out we will not pursue our commitment to the end, I don't know where they will stay their hand.'[14] This argument, along with the Munich analogy expressed by Ambassador Lodge, carried the day against Ball.[15]

When the discussions resumed the next day, 22 July, George Ball was excluded while the Service Secretaries and the Joint Chiefs of Staff were included. The discussions centered on the various military options. Navy Secretary Paul Nitze took the lead, arguing that were the United States 'to acknowledge that we couldn't beat the VC, the shape of the world will change.'[16] He invoked history. 'In the Philippines and Greece, it was shown that the guerrillas lost.'[17] After this grave oversimplification of historical experience which was of dubious relevance, he advised that more troops should be sent without delay. This advice was echoed by all the Service Secretaries and Chiefs. The same degree of unanimity was shown when Air Force Chief of Staff McConnell told the President that the air strikes in North Vietnam, Operation ROLLING THUNDER, had not been as effective as had been hoped, 'because we are not striking the targets that hurt them.'[18] Wallace Greene, the Marine Corps Commandant, was the only service chief willing to assign some numbers to the amount of men and time it might take for the US to secure its most immediate goal, restoring security and internal stability to South Vietnam. He thought it would take 500,000 men and five years, but only if the industrial base and infrastructure of North Vietnam were to be attacked heavily and Cambodia blockaded, preventing its use as a base for infiltration.[19]

After four hours of discussion a consensus emerged. An increased US ground presence directed against the most effective enemy units coupled with a more efficient application of US airpower against the North should serve to bring about negotiations. There was real fuzziness about the goal of any future negotiations. The potential for and political ramifications of a 'Yugoslavian solution' were discussed at length. It was unclear how the emerging South Vietnamese political culture would affect negotiations. Whether American policy interests and domestic public opinion could accept the appearance of a Laotian-style neutralization of South Vietnam was considered but left unresolved. There were many uncertainties and ambiguities concerning the substance and appearance of negotiations alike. The fuzziness of goal and difficulties of defining policy success were put to one side as general agreement emerged on an overall theory of victory. The use of military coercion upon North Vietnam and their presumed proxies, the Viet

Cong, coupled with the promise of negotiations, was seen as the correct strategic mix to accomplish hazy ends. The President summarized:

> We have got to keep peace proposals going. It's like a prizefight. Our right is our military power but our left must be peace proposals. Every time you move troops forward, you move diplomats forward. I want this done. The generals want more and more and go farther and farther. But State has to supply me with some too. We need Ernie Pyles out there interviewing soldiers who can tell how proud they are to do their duty.[20]

The air war over North Vietnam, in particular the introduction of Soviet surface to air missiles (SAM), was the topic considered on the 26th. These missiles could present a real threat to the ROLLING THUNDER missions. As the SAM sites indicated the presence of Soviet personnel, an attack upon the positions could provide diplomatic complications to the United States. It was argued by Clark Clifford that attacks against the SAM batteries would be a powerful demonstration of American resolve. The failure to remove the missile threat would preclude the option of destroying high-value North Vietnamese industrial targets. The President was convinced, 'TAKE THEM OUT. [emphasis in original]'[21]

Over the course of four days much discussion was given to SAMs, the necessity of prosecuting the air war over the North more efficiently, the need to provide the ground combat and support forces requested by General William Westmoreland, the Commander, US Military Assistance Command, Vietnam (COMUSMACV) and the certainty that guerrillas could be defeated by conventional ground and air forces. Little discussion occurred on the subjects of South Vietnamese political, social and economic difficulties. No real consideration was given to the nature and legitimacy of the obvious political disaffiliation in the South. No attention was paid to the character of the war itself.

Despite these considerable deficiencies, a policy goal had been defined, stabilizing South Vietnam to the point that there was no imminent danger of collapse to external invasion or internal subversion. A definition of victory had emerged, bringing the Viet Cong and the North either to a tacit ending of the war or to the bargaining table. A theory of victory emphasizing the traditional American belief, 'fire-power kills,' had been reified. Other than George Ball no one had questioned the relevance of either goal or method to the realities as they had developed on the ground in South Vietnam. This was only to be expected when the shared intellectual heritage of the conferees is considered.

The consensus emphasizing the application of air power to the North and increased US ground combat operations in the South at the expense of less lethal and disruptive options had emerged so easily and with so little opposition or genuine debate largely because the Johnson Administration officials, both military and civilian, shared a common intellectual heritage. This common heritage was composed of a matrix of collective experience, a bipolar world view which saw the hidden hand of the Kremlin behind all political violence directed against the status quo and a generous appreciation of US military capabilities. As a result of this mental baggage carried into the decision-making process there was an automatic predilection to perceive the deteriorating situation in South Vietnam as being a particular type of conflict, partisan war, requiring a particular type of military response.[22]

American military strategists, policy makers and defense intellectuals had consistently misconstrued the lessons of the several protracted guerrilla wars in which the US had been either a direct participant or a very interested observer. Since the end of the Second World War the US had been immediately involved in three such wars: the Greek Civil War, the guerrilla component of the Korean War and the Huk Insurrection. It had been a secondary participant in the French Indochina War and an interested observer in the Malayan Emergency. Knowledge of other guerrilla conflicts such as the Algerian War and Mau Mau Uprising was far less complete. Further in the past but still exercising influence over the common American perceptions were the various partisan resistance movements of the Second World War and the prolonged struggle in China between the Kuomintang and the Communists. Misunderstandings, misperceptions and misapprehensions had combined to give Americans the view that all these conflicts were partisan wars and that insurgent guerrilla war was not possible.[23]

Partisan war and insurgency represent profoundly different forms of war, even if both share guerrilla tactics and organization. In the partisan war, the guerrillas operate as armed auxiliaries to a conventional force. They depend upon this force acting as an external sponsoring power, for supplies, intelligence, missions and ultimate victory. The partisans constitute a preparatory unit; the conventional armed forces of the external sponsoring power must ultimately act as the decisive force. Insurgents are the armed expression of political discontent and disaffiliation arising organically from conditions within society as a result of the actions of the government under attack. Insurgents in the main rely upon their own exertions for supplies, intelligence, manpower and the other necessities of war. They set their own agenda and goals. Ultimately, they must look to themselves and the society they claim to represent for victory or defeat. While an insurgent organization might attempt to internationalize a conflict and might seek material or other assistance from an external source, it will not allow the vitiation of its agenda or goals. The external power is the auxiliary of the insurgent. Quite obviously, the two disparate forms of war require fundamentally different types of counter. Similarly, to confuse the two, to fuse the two into a single amorphous mass as did the American strategists and policy makers represented a major intellectual error with many significant ramifications.

From the American perspective insurgency was an impossibility. All guerrilla conflicts within any country were presumed to be of the partisan variety. Even if a conflict started as a pure insurgency the American presumption was that it would be quickly captured by an external sponsoring power and become a partisan war. There were no exceptions.[24] This view acted synergistically with the nature of US military doctrine.

The doctrine of an armed service, be it ground, air or naval, might be best understood as its theory of victory, its concept of war and how to win it. Doctrine emerges from several sources, the self-interpreted historical experience of the service, its understanding of the most likely opponent, the strengths and weaknesses of the social, political and economic infrastructure which supports the service and technological developments. Of these the most important are the historical and the perceived nature of the most likely war. American ground doctrine was well rooted in the Clausewitzian formulations developed nearly a century and a half earlier. In particular, doctrine for land warfare emphasized the destruction of the enemy's armed forces in the field in decisive combat. Air doctrine as developed from the American experience in the Second World War stressed the exhaustion of the enemy's will and capability through the progressive destruction of high-value industrial and infrastructure targets and the weakening of the enemy's armed forces in the field through interdicting the lines of communication and supply.[25]

From 1946 to the time of the decisions on Vietnam in 1965, the primary threat seen by the writers of US ground and air doctrine was general war between the Soviet bloc and the American-led western alliance. Leaving aside nuclear attacks upon the heartlands of the major opponents, the most critical locale was seen as the central front of Europe where land warfare would be both geopolitically threatening and extremely destructive. Effective deterrence required a credible war-fighting capacity as exhibited in doctrine, training, equipment and organization. Army doctrine was predicated on the need to prepare for mechanized and armored combat against a similarly configured enemy on the presumptively nuclear battlefields of Germany. Air Force doctrine, while not so exclusively driven by the Fulda Gap focus, did give significant attention to the interdiction of Soviet supply lines using nuclear munitions. All other missions and threats were subordinate to the clash of nuclear-capable alliances in Europe.

In common with most armed forces at most times, US ground and air doctrine was oriented toward capitalizing upon perceived strengths rather than upon attempting to identify and exploit weaknesses within the enemy. The American strengths were those of heavy firepower, both ground- and air-delivered, high mobility by tracked vehicles and helicopters, and communications systems of a highly advanced sort. These capabilities were developed and refined so that widely dispersed forces could be rapidly and effectively concentrated against the enemy's armored and mechanized formations without providing a lucrative target for nuclear weapons. By the early 1960s the organizations and equipment necessary to implement the doctrine of heavy firepower and high tactical mobility coordinated by a sophisticated communications system were in place and had been tested by numerous field exercises. By the early 1960s the Tactical Air Command had procured the aircraft and munitions and developed the doctrine necessary to execute line of communication (LOC) interdiction and infrastructure strike missions. Intellectual and budgetary limitations alike required the command structures of both Army and Air Force to assume that the doctrine, forces and equipment developed for use in Europe against an armored, mechanized and nuclear-capable opponent would work equally well against guerrillas in the bush of Asia.

While it is scarcely credible that the civilian policy makers of the Johnson Administration had pored over the field manuals and similar official statements of the Services' theories of victory, it is legitimate to assume that these theories constituted much of the basis for the advice and briefings given by the military as well as for the specific operational concepts and plans developed by the Joint Chiefs of Staff and commanders in the field such as COMUSMACV. It was quite likely that the civilian planners within the Department of Defense, including those within the Office of the Secretary of Defense (OSD) and the Assistant Secretary of Defense for International Security Affairs (ISA), the office with the most immediate and pervasive responsibility for US efforts in Southeast Asia, would be familiar with the doctrine governing everything from posture statements and budget requests to specific operational plans. It is not necessary simply to rely upon assumption or hypothesis concerning the familiarity of senior Johnson Administration figures with the essential theories of victory, for all the major officials had played games in 1964 and 1965.

The games they had played were war games developed and operated by the Joint War Games Agency of the Joint Chiefs of Staff. These simulations came in many types and sizes covering all the likely modes and venues of conflict, including guerrilla wars in Southeast Asia. Of particular relevance were two, SIGMA I–64 and SIGMA II–64 played in April and September 1964.[26]

In the SIGMA I game it was assumed that direction and support of the Viet Cong insurgency lay with the North Vietnamese and that the US/SVN responded with 'tit-for-tat' military actions against the North. After a number of diplomatic preliminaries, the US escalated the air war over the North by striking economic targets. This provoked strong declaratory policy statements from the USSR and the Peoples' Republic of China (PRC) in support of North Vietnam as well as an increase of material support from Moscow. The sinking of a Soviet ship in Haiphong harbor by American aircraft placed the US on a collision course with both the PRC and the USSR. World opinion turned hostile to the US. At this point the game was terminated for review despite the conviction held by the blue (US) team that the storm could be ridden out and that the situation in the South was improving. At the conclusion of the game the director offered a cautionary note underscoring the uncertainties involved in the use of air power as an instrument of coercion.

> A political/military game – while useful in delineating certain problem areas, communication difficulties, possible bargaining ploys and in fostering rapport between interested agencies – is scarcely a conclusive medium for evaluating such things as North Vietnamese ability to withstand military pressures. However, both the RED [North Vietnamese] and YELLOW [PRC] Teams had reservations concerning the efficacy of air strikes in causing the DRV [North Vietnam] to cease direction and support of operations in RVN [South Vietnam].[27]

In the critique which followed the game's indecisive conclusion, the blue team, which included such senior Administration policy makers as McGeorge Bundy, John McNaughton, John McCone, General Maxwell Taylor, General Curtis LeMay and George Ball, maintained that their side had possessed the initiative and had enjoyed the greater success when the game had been terminated. If there had been faults, these were undertaking escalation too slowly and failing to properly mold public opinion. The blue team argued that their red opponents had behaved in an un-Vietnamese fashion, implying that a more accurate mimicking of the North Vietnamese would have made blue's success all the more obvious.[28] No one questioned the assumption that the North was directing the war in the South. No one questioned the use of air strikes against line-of-supply targets. No one questioned the absence of any efforts to improve the legitimacy, efficiency or military competence of the South Vietnamese.

The SIGMA II game was similar to its predecessor but had as an additional complication the assumption that both North Vietnam and the Peoples' Republic of China were directly supporting and directing the Viet Cong. Following US air attacks on the North and the introduction of American ground combat forces and logistics units into South Vietnam, organized units of the Peoples' Army of Vietnam (PAVN) were infiltrated into the South and the Chinese planned the movement of forces into the North. This development was posited despite the often demonstrated historical antipathy between China and Vietnam. Further US vertical escalation of the air war caused the Chinese to escalate horizontally by introducing forces into Laos. In the final move the blue team saw its only viable options were further vertical escalation within Vietnam and Laos or the execution of a general air war against PRC. The game was terminated at this point.[29]

It should be noted that the game was biased to underscore one major American apprehension based on the Korean War experience – the entrance of Chinese forces into the conflict. Factoring out the skew introduced by this quite unlikely eventuality, the game underscored problems with the use of air power. It was widely agreed that interdicting supply lines would be quite difficult, which implied that the best use of air strikes would be against infrastructure and economic targets in North Vietnam. However, it was generally accepted that attacks on Northern population centers was the most likely way of prompting further Soviet and Chinese support for Hanoi. There was some skepticism regarding the ability of bombing to undercut the political will of the North Vietnamese to continue the war. The challenge to American planners was to balance the military requirement of interdicting supplies and eroding political will with the diplomatic necessity that the PRC and USSR not be given an inducement to enter the war.[30] The blue team, which once again contained such key people as McGeorge Bundy, John McNaughton, John McCone and the new Chairman of the JCS, Earle Wheeler, was divided on the question of how effective air power would be against a low-technology, low-supply-requirement enemy. Perhaps the answer to the implicit conundrum, how to destroy the lines of supply to a force that needed no supplies, was to force the enemy to use more supplies.

Overall, the effect of the war games had been to reinforce several sets of beliefs and preconceptions within the common intellectual heritage: the linkage between the Viet Cong in the South and Hanoi, the linkage between Hanoi, Beijing and Moscow, the potential utility of air power despite implicit risks involved in its employment. The war-gaming experience would have exposed the senior policy makers both to the doctrine of the services and to an informal, yet powerful briefing on the services' self-assessment of capabilities thanks to the interaction of the players and the action teams comprised of field-grade officers.

The nature of the war-games scenarios in which the South Vietnamese were strangely absent save as a strategic equivalent of Banquo's ghost and in which non-military concerns such as preemptive reforms, internal propaganda, civic affairs and the difficulties of nation-building were entirely absent would have confirmed the pernicious and specious thread within the common intellectual heritage that military force alone was sufficient to counter the insurgent threat. The war games also would have confirmed in the minds of the policy makers the correctness of their presupposition that the calculus of values and needs within the North Vietnamese government mirror-imaged that of the United States. This allowed policy makers in Washington to assume that their counterparts in Hanoi practiced the 'least-worst' model of decision making.

This concept, which had permeated nuclear strategy for a decade, held that a rational actor when faced with alternative courses of action, each with its own reward and risk, would choose, not the one with the maximum reward, but the one which promised the least penalty, the least-worst outcome. This model might be true in some conditions, but it was imprudent to assume that a government whose historical trajectories, hierarchy of values and priority structure were poorly understood by the American administration, but were certainly quite different from those obtaining in the US, would follow its dictates.

In short, the SIGMA I and SIGMA II games had both reflected and reinforced all of the incorrect lessons learned by the US planners from previous guerrilla wars. The participation of the senior policy makers from the Johnson Administration had assured that these would be reified by those responsible for guiding US interests through the ever worsening situation in South Vietnam.

A second reason for the speedy and easy consensus in July for the potentially open-ended expansion of troop deployments was the very simple fact there was no visible alternative except a retraction of the American presence. With the exception of George Ball no member of the Administration could contemplate retraction with equanimity. American credibility and Communist containment seemed to be at stake in South Vietnam.

Most of the members of the Johnson Administration present for the July 1965 discussions had lived with the spectre of a Communist takeover of Southeast Asia since they had come to Washington with President Kennedy four-and-a-half years earlier. They had been governed by the March 1961 perception conveyed by the CIA that the leaders of Asian nations had believed that 'if the US had given the anti-Communist elements bold and prompt support, the Laotian crisis would not have reached serious proportions.'[31] The argument of Laos had been reinforced by the course of events in South Vietnam.

Although the 'domino theory' had been declared dead thirteen months earlier in a memorandum from Dr Sherman Kent, the Chairman of the Board of National Estimates, to the President, its conclusion regarding the result of the successful domination of South Vietnam by Hanoi continued to be unsettling to the Administration.

> Aside from the immediate joy in the DRV over achievement of its national goals, the chief effect would be upon Communist China, both in boosting its already remarkable self-confidence and in raising its prestige as a leader of World Communism. Peiping has already begun to advertise South Vietnam as proof of its thesis that the underdeveloped world is ripe for revolution, that the US is a paper tiger and that local insurgency can be carried through to victory without undue risk of precipitating a major international war. The outcome in South Vietnam and Laos would conspicuously support the aggressive tactical contentions of Peiping as contrasted with the more cautious position of the USSR. To some degree this will tend to encourage and strengthen the more activist revolutionary movements in various parts of the undeveloped world.[32]

To the President's men and to the President, Dr Kent's assessment seemed to promise that the failure to secure a stable and non-Communist South Vietnam would open a veritable flood of guerrilla wars of national liberation with endless opportunities for Soviet and Chinese mischief. The vision of chronic instability in the still decolonializing areas of the world with its attendant implications for the global balance of power was apocalyptic.

Reinforcing the effect of the conclusion was Dr Kent's cautionary note that the 'loss' of South Vietnam would be 'profoundly damaging to the US position in the Far East' because Washington had 'committed itself persistently, emphatically and publicly to preventing Communist takeover' of the country.[33] The failure would 'seriously debase the credibility of the US will and capability to contain the spread of communism elsewhere in the area.'[34] The dike of containment would have been breached, perhaps irretrievably. Considering the perceived nature of the stakes in South Vietnam, to do nothing more or to retract from what had been done was clearly unacceptable.

An extensive study done by the Defense Intelligence Agency (DIA) and released on 1 December 1964 reinforced the more pessimistic implications of Dr Kent's assessment.[35] It established

> The ultimate objective of the VC, in concert with the Communist leadership of North Vietnam, is the reunification of Vietnam under the control of the government in Hanoi (presumed to be

part of a larger plan whereby Hanoi expects to gain control over all of former French Indochina: Vietnam, Laos and Cambodia).[36]

This analysis would have reinforced the general acceptance of the war as a partisan conflict. It would have underscored the danger of a Viet Cong success in undermining the integrity of the doctrine of containment and it reinvoked the spectre of the falling dominos. DIA exhibited the typical uncertainty as to the importance of North Vietnamese support. In one section, the VC were portrayed as pure insurgents using captured weapons and internal resources, while in another, the cruciality of infiltrated men and supplies and the complex network of supply routes was demonstrated.[37] Intelligence ambiguity of this sort allowed the consumer to choose what best fitted his predilections rather than being forced to accept the interpretation which accurately described the reality on the ground no matter how unpleasant.

The Johnson Administration, in common with most, worked from an action-oriented imperative, take charge and get ahead of the crisis. This characteristic, coupled with the fact that US policy makers inaccurately saw the war in South Vietnam as a partisan guerrilla conflict, assured that the only visible solution to the obviously worsening situation in the South was increased use of US military, air and naval force. Once this choice had been made, the effectiveness of its implementation was governed by the appropriateness of the American doctrine and the quite inflexible juggernauts created to its specifications.

A final reason for the quick and clean consensus was simple institutional and intellectual inertia. The solution to the South Vietnamese problem had always been construed to exist with military force despite ritualistic genuflections before various non-military initiatives.

This trajectory had been established by General Maxwell Taylor's report to President Kennedy in November 1961.[38] This widely circulated document had placed responsibility for the insurgency upon Hanoi thus defining it, without significant evidence, as a partisan war with DRV as the external sponsoring power. In his report the General argued that at some time in the future the US would have to 'impose upon Hanoi a price for participating in the present war which is commensurate with the damage being inflicted on its neighbor in the south.'[39] Taylor had noted that while there are many political, social and economic problems, the 'first vicious circle is military.'[40] In order to deal with this military vicious circle, General Taylor and his team had made a wide variety of recommendations which encompassed both overt and covert US options including the use of air and ground combat forces. General Taylor and his team had concluded that without military actions which can secure stability and an absence of armed threat to the population, political and economic pre-emptive reforms would be meaningless.

Roger Hilsman, the Director of the State Department's Bureau of Intelligence and Research (INR) had attempted to counter the military priority but ultimately his recommendations for civic action, psychological operations, nation-building and carefully limited use of large unit combat operations had come to nothing as a result of the failure of his pet project, the Strategic Hamlet program.[41] The Hilsman theme had been echoed by Secretary of Defense McNamara and General Taylor who were going through a brief period of de-emphasizing military measures in October 1963.[42]

Early in the Johnson Administration the flow of the intellectual currents definitely and finally had set in favor of giving priority to the military solution. Maxwell Taylor had started the trend by again identifying North Vietnam as the root of the problem.[43] The CIA had sounded a very loud alarm bell in February 1964 which seemed to provide support for Taylor's contention.[44] General Taylor was joined in his position by Secretary of Defense McNamara and McNamara's fertile idea man, ASD/ISA John McNaughton, by March 1964.[45] By the time of the Gulf of Tonkin Incident the military focus had become well defined with the introduction of air attacks on North Vietnam simply serving as confirmation.

Further affirmation of military priority had come with the Viet Cong attacks upon American air bases and personnel billets. These gave rise to the Administration's lengthy consideration of using US ground troops to protect the bases and provide a highly mobile strategic reserve for employment against particularly threatening guerrilla main forces as well as the commencement of the sustained air campaign against North Vietnamese military and infrastructure targets, Operation ROLLING THUNDER.[46] With American troops on the ground in the South and American aircraft over the North the Administration had placed both the lives of troops and the prestige of a nation at risk. It is small wonder that consensus to give the commanders in South Vietnam a virtual blank check was so swift in coming.

Final impetus for quick consensus had come from the state of play in South Vietnam during the three months since the marines and paratroops had gone 'down south.' Steady deterioration had been demonstrated by the Central Intelligence Agency weekly and monthly reports entitled 'The Situation in Vietnam.'[47] The arrival of US troops and the continuation of aerial operations against North Vietnam and the presumed lines of supply through Laos had not had any demonstrable, positive effect. In a review of the preceding year dated 29 June 1965, the Agency noted that the Viet Cong was more capable of mounting regimental-strength attacks at the end of the period than it had been at the beginning. The CIA analysts credited US air power as the critical factor in preventing the defeat of heavily engaged units of the South Vietnamese Army (ARVN), but concluded that air attacks had not adversely affected the movement of supplies from the North or weakened the pro-Viet Cong posture of Hanoi and might well have had just the opposite effect.[48] The arrival of US troops had exercised no impact upon the situation in the South except to increase the security at certain US air bases.[49]

It was certain that the demonstrations of US resolve and commitment to South Vietnam had not served to stabilize the chronic political chaos in what passed for a central government in Saigon nor to increase the perceived legitimacy of that government. The CIA was quite pessimistic regarding the future of the government; the impression was one of impending collapse at the center.[50] The instable governmental situation was of particular concern as it provided a perfect opportunity for the Viet Cong to make advances militarily and for its political arm, the National Liberation Front, to extend its governmental control over a greater area.[51]

The situation had not changed for the better by June 1965 as Maxwell Taylor had reported in an extensive assessment on the 5th.[52] While not stating in so many words that the situation had become so desperate that only massive American intervention could retrieve it, that implication screamed from between the lines as he underscored in stark terms the perceived strength of the Viet Cong, and the apparent decision by Hanoi to 'respond to the growing commitment of US military resources by employing the Viet Cong, reinforced by PAVN, in intensified operations in the South.'[53] Taylor's assessment dovetailed well with a somewhat earlier special memorandum from the Board of National Estimates to McGeorge Bundy in which Sherman Kent had concluded that further Viet Cong victories over the summer would result in an increase in Communist momentum, but, 'if a major VC military effort this summer is generally repulsed, the Viet Cong position would suffer substantially with a corresponding increase in GVN morale and popular support'.[54]

The question of what effects would result from an increased US ground-force commitment had been considered in a series of assessments performed by the CIA between 10 June and 20 July 1965. The conclusions drawn by the Agency's analysts were somewhat ambivalent. While it was believed that the introduction of greater numbers of American ground combat troops would initially raise South Vietnamese morale, this would be counterbalanced by a willingness of ARVN to allow the US to carry the burden of combat.[55] The Agency's conclusion regarding the effect upon the Viet Cong was not at all optimistic, arguing that the US buildup 'would not alter VC/DRV determination to prosecute the struggle.'[56] In another assessment also dated 10 June, the agency had considered several different option packages available to the United States and concluded that one of these, Option D, limiting the committed American forces to a package of 70,000 men and placing priority 'on a program of political, social and economic action for South Vietnam' provided the best opportunity to assist the Saigon government in establishing its legitimacy. This approach avoided the danger of providing ARVN with an excuse to see the US as taking over the war while demonstrating to the Viet Cong and Hanoi that the US was willing to run increased political risks.[57]

The day before the senior policy level meetings on Vietnam were scheduled to begin, the CIA had issued a SNIE on the probable reactions to a major US escalation.[58] The Agency concluded that both the Viet Cong and North Vietnam would be able to cope with the contemplated increase in American ground strength and air activity.[59] In keeping with previous patterns of behavior, unaffected by the escalating Sino-Soviet dispute, Moscow and Beijing would provide increased economic and material assistance including air defense systems, but would not send troops despite the very truculent Chinese rhetoric.[60] No assessment had been requested or offered concerning the effect upon the South Vietnamese government, armed forces or people of introducing 175,000 American personnel over the next three months.

The CIA had concluded on a pessimistic note. Nothing attempted by the US had yet worked. The situation in South Vietnam was desperate, but there was little reason to believe that the escalation would prove any more efficacious. Weighing against the cerebral waffling of the Agency analysts was the argument of the senior military commanders.

The Joint Chiefs of Staff consider that the ground forces situation requires a substantial further build-up of US and Allied forces in the RVN at the most rapid rate feasible on an orderly basis.

The Joint Chiefs of Staff consider that air action against North Vietnam should be intensified to include increased armed reconnaissance of LOCs and strikes against militarily important targets. Such action is necessary to reduce DRV capabilities to support the VC and PAVN, further punish the DRV and further establish US intent to prevent a communist seizure of SVN.[61]

The JCS call had been reinforced within days by a dispatch from General William Westmoreland which put forward a crisp request for additional forces buttressed by an outline of his operational concept for their employment in high-mobility, heavy-firepower offensive combat operations against the enemy's main forces. He had underscored the urgency of his request and the saliency of his operational concept by concluding that the Viet Cong were destroying ARVN battalions faster than they could be replaced and that ARVN commanders 'do not believe that they can survive without the active commitment of US ground combat forces.'[62]

Ambassador Maxwell Taylor had concurred, presenting an exercise in impressive-appearing but not particularly relevant statistical thaumaturgy which purported to demonstrate the correctness and urgency of the troop request.[63] By the end of June even the current strongman of the Saigon military government had directly and urgently requested more US troops behind whom the government and ARVN might regroup.[64]

In opposition to the CIA's assessment that nothing done by the US had yet proved effective and that there was no compelling reason to believe that the contemplated escalation would prove any different there was the urgent request for more troops and air power from the Joint Chiefs of Staff, COMUSMACV and the head of government in South Vietnam. By the time McNamara prepared in early July for another of his rapid-motion visits to South Vietnam, it had become clear that he was completely predisposed to accept the necessity of major increases in the US air and ground efforts as he telexed the Embassy and COMUSMACV that the 'main purpose' of the trip was to discuss precise numbers and scheduling of deployments.[65] Upon his return, McNamara, who had not yet met a force strength increase he didn't like, had strongly recommended an increase of US ground troop strength to 175,000 men with the understanding that an additional 100,000 might be necessary in early 1966. In addition, he had recommended that the air-strike rate in the North be gradually increased from 2,500 sorties per month to 4,000.[66] Such matters as pacification, economic stabilization and governmental development were relegated to the subsidiary category of 'other actions.'

The situation was one of extreme crisis as indicated by a long and pessimistic cable from Ambassador Taylor and the senior Country Team which had been relayed to the President by McGeorge Bundy on 13 July 1965.[67] The Viet Cong were getting stronger. The South Vietnamese government was becoming increasingly factionated. The South Vietnamese people were war-weary and defeatist. ARVN was on the ropes. The conclusion warned, 'an acceptable negotiated settlement' could come about only after the intensity of the war on the ground in the South and in the air over the North had been increased and maintained 'for an indeterminate period.'[68]

In crisis, with conflicting advice and time-sensitive demands, policy makers fall back on instincts, the instincts of shared intellectual heritage, shared perceptions of capabilities, a shared view of the stakes at risk and a shared desire to act, a shared need to assure that no later charges of passivity in the face of national danger might be levied. American credibility and Communist containment were in the balance, even the CIA had indicated that; the honor of the United States embodied in numerous, uncompromising expressions of declaratory policy was in hazard.

It was a time to be bold, a time to rely upon the military and its theory of victory. It was a moment to suppress doubts, stand up, hook up and leap into a vast and uncertain void.

2

PLOTTING THE QUEST

Plans more than troops, planes and tanks are necessary for fighting a war. Plans that are relevant to the realities as they develop on the ground and employ the military instruments in a correct way as part of an overall program of political, social, economic, intelligence, psychological and military measures are necessary for winning a war. The decision whether or not to go to war in Southeast Asia was not the central intellectual task confronting the Johnson Administration and its military command structure. The central task, the most important intellectual process, was determining the purpose for which war was to be waged, against whom it was to be fought, how it was to be conducted and how the United States would know if it was winning or not.

Between spring 1964 and early fall 1965 the Administration's policy makers, both civilian and military, had to ask and answer several interlocking questions: what should be the purpose of fighting, where should we fight, against whom should we fight, how will we know if we are winning or losing, and how do we intend to win? It was necessary that all these questions be asked and answered in a way which was internally consistent, coherent and which reflected an accurate understanding of the situation developing on the ground in Southeast Asia both as to its internal dynamics and its implications for American national interests in the region for any commitment of American military force to have the potential of yielding a positive result.

In any war, to ensure that military operations usefully serve a policy purpose as well as to assure that ground and air operations are properly and effectively integrated into the total mix of implementation media, it is essential that the administration establish the goal toward which all efforts are directed, define success or victory and provide or approve an overall theory of victory. These three elements must be coherent with one another, consistent over time, understood by all subordinate commanders and planners and, most importantly, relevant to the realities which have developed and continue to develop within the proposed operational venue.

A close scrutiny of military history argues powerfully that without the existence of a well-delineated goal, a definition of victory against which the progress of military operations can be assessed by decision makers and a theory of victory which is predicated upon a candid and realistic appraisal of the strengths and weaknesses of all combatants, defeat has been far more likely than victory. The goal, definition and theory of victory must be coherent with one another and, without being rigidly dogmatic, consistent over time. It must be possible to modify one or another of the elements if it becomes evident that events are not taking a desirable course. The process of establishing the goal, defining victory or success and establishing a theory of victory must be of a catholic enough nature to assure that the realities on the ground are recognized, the goals, definitions and theories of the other combatants understood, and the military assets and liabilities of each properly appreciated. Unduly expansive goals, vague and overly elastic definitions or a 'can do' theory of victory have usually resulted in failure. A fundamental intellectual failure in conceptualizing the war cannot be redeemed by the courage or blood of men. It cannot be rectified by mere weight of munitions or prowess in the technologies of war.

An interventionary power enters a conflict not of its own making. It is therefore necessary to fully understand the goals and theories at work in the war if the intervention is to have a real chance of success. In South Vietnam, the United States was acting as an interventionary power in support of a status quo regime threatened by domestic insurgency and the possibility of either conventional or guerrilla invasion. This was an uncomfortable role for the nation to play. It was a difficult role if the policy makers did not understand that the local belligerent had their own goals, definitions of victory and theories of victory. It was an untenable role if the policy makers failed to understand that these factors might or might not be compatible with those of the United States.

South Vietnam, the Viet Cong/National Liberation Front and North Vietnam were the primary parties to the conflict; their definitions of victory or defeat and their goals served to constrain the freedom of the United States to impose its own schemata with any legitimate expectation of success. The Johnson Administration was obliged to recognize that the multi-party conflict in which it was immersing the United States arose from cultural, social, economic and political factors which were endogenous to the region and governed by regional historical trajectories. This recognition must not simply be a matter of rhetorical genuflection; it must be acted upon as a central factor in policy formulation and execution. The obligation was unmet. The recognition was not made.

The underlying assumption of the American policy makers since the commencement of the South Vietnamese insurgency in 1959 and the formation of the NLF in Hanoi in 1960 was that the goals of the VC/NLF and North Vietnam were identical: the formation of a federated or unified Communist state under the direction of Hanoi.[1] It followed that their definitions of victory would be identical: the removal of any strong, anti-Communist government in Saigon and its replacement by a neutralist-oriented regime which would end the American presence, seek negotiations with the united DRV/VC front and allow South Vietnam to come under Hanoi's domination. From the perspective of Washington, the theory of victory followed by the Viet Cong and their North Vietnamese sponsors was simply that of the Communists in China: a protracted guerrilla conflict gradually weakening the capability and political will of the target government until it collapsed by combining a program of increasing military potency with a coordinated program of psychological warfare and political subversion.

As the United States had viewed the conflict for some time as a partisan war, it had assumed that the primary enemy was North Vietnam and that without support and direction from Hanoi the Viet Cong would be reduced to the status of annoyance readily handled by the police forces of the South. Thus it had been presumed that Saigon's primary goal should be the deterrence of conventional cross-border invasion by North Vietnam with a subordinate goal of reducing the attractiveness of guerrilla warfare. The definition of victory would be negative in nature, the absence of invasion and serious internal political violence. From the US point of view the appropriate theory of victory for the South Vietnamese government coupled the development of an American-style general purpose ground combat force equally capable of suppressing guerrillas and defending the borders with the implementation of reforms in land ownership, the development of efficient, honest government and the creation of liberal, pluralistic, free-market institutions.

These assumptions, based upon an intellectually skewed misinterpretation of American experience with insurgent warfare, constituted a comfortable but misleading exercise in mirror-imaging. The possibility that the Viet Cong had been independent actors before 1965 was simply overlooked, despite the long-standing inter-regional antipathies and rivalries which had characterized Vietnamese history. North Vietnam prior to 1965 had been quite preoccupied first with the problems of consolidating a new state born of long war and later with the disastrous consequences of Ho Chi Minh's ill-considered policy of agricultural collectivization which had been exacerbated by several years of poor harvests. The probability that it was beyond the capacity of the North to provide more than rhetorical assistance to the Southern insurgency was never seriously considered.

The likelihood that the South Vietnamese government and society were not able and eager to emulate or adopt American institutions was never envisioned. The chance that the Saigon government and the South Vietnamese elite would behave like the Kuomintang in the Second World War was not examined. It was never contemplated that Saigon would act from a conviction that the US would fight the war for reasons of its own, deciding as a result to stand back from the conflict, conserving strength for the postwar environment, and refusing to lessen its status or privilege through accepting American-sponsored pre-emptive reforms.

American policy makers did not attempt so much to understand the goals, definitions and theories of victory which arose organically within the conflict as to impose upon the belligerent those of an American manufacture. Without a real working awareness of the organic goals, definitions and theories, it was impossible for the US policy makers to take proper advantage of American strengths and limit American weaknesses. It was also impossible for the policy makers to become aware of the changes in the character of the war which occurred in 1965 following the first American escalation and again in late 1966 after the weight of the US effort had affected North Vietnamese political will. The nature of the intellectual process underlying the formulation and execution of American policy was essentially projective. We projected goals, definitions and theories on the other parties and acted as though these were the only possibilities. It was to be an American war whether the other parties accepted the contention or not.

Between early 1964 and late summer 1965, the Johnson Administration, including the military command structure, acted like a committee of architects engaged in designing a building that must be constructed using a well-established and limited set of materials. The committee complicated its task by arbitrarily changing the size of the lot, refusing to believe reports on the nature of the soil at the building site – sand, mud or rock – and willfully ignoring the local building and zoning codes. Further difficulties arose from a chronic inability of the committee members to decide where to put the bathroom or whether to build of wood or brick.

From March 1964 when Secretary of Defense McNamara drafted the report to the President which served as the basic architecture of the increasing US involvement in Vietnam, there was a degree of confusion and a real lack of consistency within the Administration about American goals in Southeast Asia. To Secretary McNamara in March 1964 the goal of American policy in Southeast Asia was simple.

We seek an independent non-Communist South Vietnam. We do not require that it serve as a Western base or as a member of a

22

Western Alliance. South Vietnam must be free, however, to accept outside assistance as required to maintain its security . . . (including) police and military help to root out and control insurgent elements.[2]

As a penumbra to this statement, the Secretary invoked the 'domino theory' which held that most of Southeast Asia would fall to Communist domination should South Vietnam succumb and averred that the South Vietnamese situation constituted a major test of American ability to counter the Khruschev doctrine of support for wars of national liberation.

McNamara's narrow statement of goal, but not the more expansive containment context, was reflected in the National Security Action Memorandum (NSAM) adopted at the 17 March 1964 NSC meeting and officially disseminated the next day. This document, which should have been considered authoritative by all members of the Government, defined the US goal to be the maintenance of a stable, independent South Vietnam.[3]

At the time of the Gulf of Tonkin Resolution a draft justification of the Resolution circulated among the senior Administration officials. In it three goals of US policy in Southeast Asia were presented. Only one, the preservation of Laos and South Vietnam from Communist domination was completely endogenous to the region. The other two, reassuring Pacific Rim countries of our continuing interest and generally reinforcing the doctrine of containment around the world were less related to Vietnam than to the general policy stance of the United States.[4]

The inclusion of Laos was in itself confusing since Secretary McNamara had made it clear in March 1964 that Laos was considered to be a buffer area useful for interdiction operations but of no real importance on its own.[5] Shortly after the Gulf of Tonkin Resolution, American policy treated Laos not as a country whose independence and territorial integrity were to be maintained as a portion of the American goals in Southeast Asia, but as an area for conducting operations in support of South Vietnam. Laos was less important than the cooperation of the Laotian government so the US and South Vietnam could conduct air and ground operations directed against the presumed infiltration routes from North Vietnam to the South.[6] Walt Whitman Rostow, the Director of the State Department Policy Planning Council, had accurately warned in a June 1964 memo to Assistant Secretary of State William Bundy 'there was no common assessment as to our operational objectives.'[7]

If that warning had been correct in June, it was even more apposite by November. There were two conflicting statements of US goals written that month by key second-echelon policy makers. In the first ASD/ISA John McNaughton, joined notionally by Bill Bundy, held that the US goals in South Vietnam were the enforcement of containment and the maintenance of US prestige generally.[8] Assistant Secretary Bundy, writing on his own, but with the concurrence of Maxwell Taylor, Dean Rusk, Robert McNamara, John McCone, Earle Wheeler and McGeorge Bundy, defined US goals in a far less expansive manner: to end North Vietnamese support for and direction of the Viet Cong, to reestablish an independent, secure and pro-west South Vietnam and to maintain the security of the other non-Communist Asian nations.[9] Bundy's statement of goal became US policy on 2 December 1964 when President Johnson approved a top secret policy memorandum to that effect and issued instructions to Ambassador Maxwell Taylor based upon the new policy.[10]

The policy memorandum was approved and issued by the President following a meeting with the Executive Committee which included all the senior members of the Administration. It should have ended the ongoing confusion over US goals in South Vietnam.[11] It did not. In March 1965, at the time the first US ground combat troops were going ashore in South Vietnam, John McNaughton reflected upon the still deteriorating situation in the country. He defined US goals:

> 70% – To avoid a humiliating US defeat (to our reputation as a
>   guarantor)
> 20% – To keep SVN (and adjacent territory) from Chinese hands
> 10% – To permit the people of SVN to enjoy a better, freer way of
>   life.[12]

By July, McNaughton had slightly rephrased the statement, but the thrust remained unchanged.

> 70% – To preserve our national honor as a guarantor (and the
>   reciprocal: to avoid a show-case success for Communist
>   'wars of liberation.')
> 20% – To keep SVN (and then adjacent) territory from hostile
>   expansive hands
> 10% – To 'answer the call of a friend,' to help him enjoy a better
>   life
> ALSO – To emerge from crisis without unacceptable taint from the
>   methods used.[13]

McNaughton was out of synchronicity with the presidential statement of goals, but his more expansive statement of goals was a sign of impending change. Over the next year, without meetings and votes, without presidential memoranda, McNaughton's goals were adopted in practice by Administration officials generally. In this way they became national policy goals in Vietnam.

The process of adoption was unclear, but the expansive nature of the chief goal, the preservation of national honor, was of a sufficiently unrestricted nature to justify the escalating ground and air wars. A broader, more unconditional goal required more resolute and robust action to achieve it.

Confusion and inconsistency plagued the development of an American definition of victory. This was an important area of difficulty, as without a clear, consistent and relevant definition of what might constitute success and failure, measurement of success or failure in accomplishing the goal became impossible. Secretary McNamara did not establish, nor apparently employ, a definition of victory in the 13 March 1964 report. Not until late November 1964 did any member of the Administration present a coherent definition of victory. Walt Whitman Rostow in a memorandum to the Secretary of State suggested the following as a measure of final American success in Southeast Asia:

> The touchstone for compliance should include the following: the removal of Viet Minh troops from Laos; the cessation of infiltration of South Vietnam from the North; the turning off of the tactical radio network; and the overt statement on Hanoi radio that the Viet Cong should cease their operations in South Vietnam and pursue their objectives in South Vietnam by political means.[14]

His definition of victory was buried deep in a memorandum which focused upon the potential threat posed by the PRC which had recently completed its first nuclear weapon test, but Rostow's effort was the first and remained one of the very few attempts to define victory.

John McNaughton, also writing in November 1964, suggested a set of standards for North Vietnamese and Viet Cong behavior that taken in aggregate would define a complete American victory.

(4) DRV must stop training and sending personnel to SVN and Laos.
(5) DRV must stop sending arms and supplies to SVN and Laos.
(6) DRV must stop directing military actions in SVN and Laos.
(7) DRV must order VC and PL to stop their insurgencies.
(8) DRV must stop propaganda broadcasts to SVN.
(9) DRV must remove VM forces and cadres from SVN and Laos.[15]

These, plus four other, more tentatively expressed results such as North Vietnamese assuring that the Viet Cong and Pathet Lao stop all operations, turn in arms and surrender for amnesty or expatriation, constituted the most unrestricted definition of victory offered in the early period of American involvement and represented the most ambitious statement of US policy.[16]

On the eve of the troop deployment decision, McNaughton again drafted a list of indicators which taken together would constitute a definition of American victory.

1 VC attacks stop.
2 VC terror and sabotage at low level.
3 DRV/VC infiltration at low level.
4 US bombing of North Vietnam stops.
5 Independent GVN (hopefully pro-US).
6 GVN functions in almost all of SVN.
7 No major Red gains in Laos.
8 No significant Red gains in Thailand.
9 PAVN forces (not regroupees) withdrawn.
10 VC practically disbanded.
11 US removes combat forces.
12 US continues AID to SVN.
13 DRV propaganda continues.
14 'Revolutionary' GVN domestic program.
15 Local and national elections promised.
16 NLF permitted as political party.
17 GVN & DRV members of UN.[17]

The Assistant Secretary remained the source of the most ambitious and unlimited definitions of victory, but this was consistent with his understanding of US goals in the conflict which were the most global and absolute.

Also writing in early July 1965, Assistant Secretary of State William Bundy was much less clear on his definition of victory. In a long memorandum, Bundy allowed the inferential definition of a US victory to be Hanoi's tacit ending of direct control and support of the insurgency in the South but maintaining a covert political apparatus in South Vietnam.[18] This would be an inconclusive and unsatisfying end to the war but, in Bundy's view, was 'the only avenue which offers real promise of obtaining an ultimate non-Communist South Vietnam, without Hanoi feeling that it must go all out in a military context.'[19] Bundy's narrowly drawn definition flowed from his relatively limited goal in South Vietnam. A limited goal was best served by limited means seeking a limited victory. The definition of victory advanced by Bundy demonstrated his understanding of this.

In his recommendation of 20 July 1965 for additional troop deployments, Secretary McNamara accepted the core of John McNaughton's definition of victory.[20] At least implicitly, the McNaughton definition was accepted at the series of meetings leading up to the formal authorization of 27 July 1965. Despite the priority given by the McNaughton definition to the ending of Viet Cong attacks as the most important single indicator of US victory, the thrust of the war effort had been and would continue to be the air attacks against North Vietnam. This constituted an inconsistency which would return to vex both implementation and assessment of policy. The McNaughton definition of victory while not unchallenged over the next two years continued to serve as a major standard for the measurement of American success just as his expansive understanding of the American goals at stake in the region continued to reflect a broad consensus over the same period.[21]

The overarching US theory of victory had been established in skeletal form in the 13 March 1964 McNamara report. The Secretary of Defense had seen correctly that it would be necessary for the South Vietnamese government to undertake a number of military, political, economic and social reforms so as to legitimize its position, mobilize popular support and prepare itself to prosecute the war in a more efficient manner. In these areas of endeavor, the US role would be one of advice and support. The Secretary believed that internal reforms and American military advice and assistance would not be enough to bring success. Because of the North Vietnamese sponsorship, the US would probably have to do more to keep South Vietnam free of Communist domination.

It might be necessary for the US to become directly involved as a counterweight to North Vietnam. There were three ways in which this might be done with relatively low risk and cost to the US: border control actions, retaliatory actions such as 'tit-for-tat bombing strikes' and 'graduated overt military pressure.'[22] The obvious instrument for these three options would be US aircraft. By the end of March the political–military planning process at the National Security Council level demonstrated that the interdictory, retaliatory and coercive use of US air power against North Vietnam occupied a high priority.[23]

Following the first 'tit-for-tat' retaliatory air strikes after the Gulf of Tonkin incident and the Viet Cong mortar attack upon the US air base at Bien Hoa, John McNaughton began formulating a theory of victory relying upon the use of US air power against North Vietnam. It was his intention that American air efforts would directly and positively affect the stability of the South Vietnamese government and the effectiveness of ARVN in the field. It was his belief that American air attacks could degrade the combat effectiveness of the Viet Cong by slowing the flow of infiltrated men and supplies from the North. An ongoing American air effort would improve the morale of the Southern government while reducing that of Hanoi by showing the willingness of the US to run military risks and implying the will to escalate the commitment further. Ably employing the Goldilocks gambit, McNaughton put forth three options of which the clearly preferred course of action was the one he entitled 'Progressive Squeeze and Talk.'

> Present policies plus an orchestration of (a) communications with Hanoi and (b) a crescendo of additional military moves against infiltration targets, first in Laos and then in the DRV and then against other targets in North Vietnam. The scenario should give the impression of a steady deliberate approach. It would be designed to give the US the option at any point to proceed or not, to escalate or not and to quicken the pace or not. These decisions would be made from time to time in view of all relevant factors.[24]

He elaborated this option depicting three distinct escalatory phases starting with US armed reconnaissance strikes against infiltration targets in Laos, escalating to include US/VNAF strikes against infiltration-oriented targets in southern North Vietnam and concluding with full, direct attacks against the infrastructure and industrial targets of North Vietnam, potentiated with aerial mining of the ports and the imposition of a naval blockade.[25]

One of the major appeals of McNaughton's theory of victory was the apparent ease and precision with which air power could be managed. Ground combat was messy, imprecise and difficult to control. Air operations suffered from none of these deficiencies. A management-oriented Secretary of Defense and a politically sensitive President would have found the use of air power quite attractive as it held the promise of quick effectiveness, low losses and precise central control. All of these features would have recommended McNaughton's 'Progressive Squeeze and Talk' option to the Administration when it was circulated in final form in late November.[26]

In November 1964 McNaughton was not the only figure in the Administration considering a theory of victory based upon air strikes against the North. In the State Department, Tom Corcoran sent a memorandum to Michael Forrestal, the Special Assistant to the Secretary of State for Vietnam. In this tightly reasoned document Corcoran argued for

> the use of the strongest U.S. military resources against the most marked DRV vulnerabilities in a manner which would leave it possible for us to discontinue operations if they did not work out and at the same time minimize the risk of high casualties . . . coming out of any ground operations in Laos.[27]

Corcoran's operational concept centered on a sustained campaign of heavy air attacks on North Vietnamese infrastructure and industrial targets. It would be justified to press and public as a program of broad reprisal for Viet Cong operations with the intention of 'building up the greatest strain upon their governmental machinery.'[28] Forrestal forwarded the memorandum in mid-November to Assistant Secretary of State William Bundy with a very favorable endorsement in which he characterized Corcoran's memorandum as the able articulation of an idea with which he had been wrestling for some time.

Whether Mike Forrestal knew it or not, he had sent the Corcoran memorandum with its well-developed theory of victory and operational concept to just the right man at Foggy Bottom. William Bundy had been groping toward the same concept in a lengthy draft memorandum a month earlier. Under the heading 'Option B' Bundy had argued for

> systematic air attacks on North Vietnam (plus aerial mining of key harbors) starting with infiltration related and other directly military related targets and proceeding to include major communications and economic targets although stopping short of civilian population on any major scale.[29]

Bundy had an 'Option E' which was similar but more limited, stopping as soon as the North entered into negotiations.[30] In this respect it closely resembled McNaughton's 'Option B' entitled 'Fast/Full Squeeze.'[31] The similarity between McNaughton's theory and that of Corcoran by way of Forrestal and William Bundy might be understood as the result of informal, and therefore unrecorded, conversations or, more simply, as the consequence of shared intellectual heritage. A theory of victory which employed air strikes to erode the material capability and enervate the political will of the North Vietnamese government to continue the presumed direction and sponsorship of the Viet Cong was emerging from the second echelon of both the Department of Defense and the State Department to claim the support of the senior policy makers.

'Progressive Squeeze and Talk' with minor modifications was presented to the Johnson Administration's top level in a memorandum from William Bundy to the President on 30 November 1964.[32] The Bundy document was the only item on the agenda for the 1 December meeting of the Executive Committee. Present were the President, Vice President, Secretaries Rusk and McNamara, both Bundys, John McCone, John McNaughton and Ambassador Taylor. The manuscript notes show that the President gave approval to the 'Progressive Squeeze and Talk' option, but indicated that initiation of the program would have to wait until various political preconditions had been met.[33]

All of the preconditions had been met by 8 February 1965 following the US air strike upon the barracks complex at Dong Hoi, North Vietnam in retaliation for a Viet Cong attack on US facilities and personnel in Pleiku. In an annex to a memorandum to the President on 7 February 1965, McGeorge Bundy provided a modified version of the

'Progressive Squeeze and Talk' package which he called 'sustained reprisal.'[34] In common with its predecessor, the 'sustained reprisal' concept focused upon a continuous, gradually escalated campaign of air attack on North Vietnam. As Bundy commented, his approach merged quickly with Phase II of McNaughton's original design. Its escalatory nature would be understood by Hanoi and its bloc supporters which constituted an acceptable risk.[35] Unlike 'Progressive Squeeze and Talk,' the 'sustained reprisal' theory did not address the relationship of coercion with the possibility of diplomatic talks.

At a meeting of the NSC on 10 February 1965 attended by the Congressional leadership, President Johnson used carefully chosen language in responding to a question from Republican House minority leader Ford. The President stated that the US would no longer limit itself simply to retaliating for specific VC attacks.[36] Under the President's innocuous words lay the reality that he had already authorized the execution of Phase II of McNaughton's 'Progressive Squeeze and Talk' option as agreed at the ExComm meeting of 1 December. This authorization had been given only minutes before the Congressional leadership had arrived for the NSC briefing.[37] Within the minds of the Administration's decision makers, there must have been some confusion as to what exactly was being implemented. Had approval been given to the McNaughton formulation which considered the aerial campaign as a means of coercing North Vietnam, and through Hanoi, the Viet Cong to negotiations? Or had the President authorized the execution of McGeorge Bundy's 'sustained reprisal' theory which made no mention of negotiation? The two operational concepts were identical in all salient respects except for the role of negotiation. For McNaughton's concept to work, there must be periodic unconditional pauses during which negotiations might be sought. In the Bundy concept there was no such requirement. If the ultimate attractiveness of the air war was its seeming potential for careful central management, this critical area of ambiguity would be a serious detriment. From the very beginning the tactical expression of the air-oriented theory of victory, Operation ROLLING THUNDER would be dogged by true confusion as to what it was supposed to achieve and how progress was to be measured.[38]

This confusion – and the importance of negotiations – was recognized by late June 1965 as shown in an early draft of Secretary McNamara's recommendations for increased US military operations in Vietnam.[39] Of three options discussed, the one preferred by the Secretary was to increase direct American military pressures against Viet Cong and North Vietnamese alike while 'at the same time launch[ing] a vigorous effort on the political side to get negotiations started.'[40] Unfortunately, Secretary McNamara overlooked the difficulty of coordinating the effects of bombers and diplomats.

There were continuing questions concerning the primacy given by the Administration's theory of victory to purely military actions and the necessary concomitant that pacification, governmental reform, nation-building and even the reforging of ARVN had been relegated to lesser importance. Maxwell Taylor spoke for the entire senior echelon of the Administration when he responded to this criticism at the NSC meeting of 5 August 1965. 'The military side of the war is not overstressed as some allege. Security must come before a satisfactory political solution can develop.'[41]

The decision to deploy significant additional troops to South Vietnam did not alter the priority given the air war over the North. Secretary McNamara responded to a Presidential request on 30 July 1965 with a lengthy memorandum concerning the efficacy of ROLLING THUNDER.[42] He described the major purposes of the effort as being to influence Hanoi to negotiate 'explicitly or otherwise' and to 'reduce the flow of men and supplies from North to South' so as 'to put a ceiling on the size of the war which the enemy could wage in the South.'[43] While granting that the first purpose had not been accomplished in the slightest, the Secretary believed that the second had produced some significant results.

(1) For regular North Vietnamese and Pathet Lao forces. The interdiction program has caused North Vietnam increasing difficulty in supplying their units in South Vietnam and Laos. How severe this difficulty is or how stretched North Vietnam's supply capabilities are, cannot be estimated precisely. Our interdiction efforts may have prevented or deterred the North from sending more troops than they already have. The interdiction programs in North Vietnam and Laos also may have influenced a Communist decision to forgo a 1965 offensive in Laos.

(2) For Viet Cong forces. Because the VC require significantly less infiltrated arms and ammunition and other supplies than do the North Vietnamese and Pathet Lao forces, the interdiction program probably has had less of an adverse effect on their operations. By raising VC fears concerning adequacy of supplies, however, the program may have caused the summer offensive to be less intense, aggressive and unrelenting than it would otherwise have been.[44]

Leaving aside the proof by negatives: the absence of the Laotian offensive and the perhaps less intense Viet Cong summer offensive and the paucity of intelligence information substantiating the Secretary's conclusions, the reality remained that the air war had been identified within the Office of the Chief of the Joint Chiefs of Staff as the most effective use of American force and the Secretary was reflecting this departmental consensus. The Secretary's support of the bombing campaign was assured even in the absence of information demonstrating its effectiveness because a consensus in favor of ROLLING THUNDER was present within the military high command as well as within his own Office. Objective support of a sort could be sought in the positive effect which the bombing campaign had produced on the morale of ARVN and the Saigon Government. McNamara concluded by recommending continuation of the effort with changes to make it more effective in the interdiction mission while reducing the collateral political damage to the US and the Administration.[45]

In a related memorandum John McNaughton assessed the effectiveness of the interdiction component of ROLLING THUNDER and came to the conclusion that it had not measurably affected the capability of the enemy forces in the South to fight or the ability of North Vietnam to meet its civilian and military needs.[46] He concluded that instead of splitting efforts between coercion and interdiction, the US should throw the entire weight of the attack behind the interdiction mission.[47]

There was an alternative to increasing the rate and weight of attack on the infiltration support target system. The ground combat forces in the South could operate to increase the logistics demands placed upon the lines of supply and supporting infrastructure by the PAVN and Viet Cong forces in the South.

This was the recommendation of a study and planning group within the Office of the Chairman, Joint Chiefs of Staff, which had been completed in mid-July 1965.[48] Anticipating the escalation of US forces in Southeast Asia, JCS Chairman Earle Wheeler on 2 July 1965 had requested a special assessment regarding the 'assurance the US can have of winning in SVN if we do "everything we can".'[49] The execution of this assessment and the conclusions reached by the Ad Hoc Study Group constitute an excellent view of shared intellectual heritage operating in a military context as well as the policy ramifications of the process.

Placing the conclusions and theory of victory recommendations of the Ad Hoc Study Group into perspective requires an examination of what the group members knew about the way in which the American ground combat forces would prosecute operations within South Vietnam. It is not necessary to look for specific directives given COMUSMACV regarding operational conduct to gain this understanding. It is necessary simply to recall the doctrinal focus of the Army, and to a lesser extent the Marine Corps, since it was doctrine which formed the operational concepts upon which all significant ground combat would be planned and executed. Doctrine, not orders or directives, established the universe in which General William Westmoreland and his subordinates could function.

One item of command guidance can suffice to demonstrate the correctness of this contention. Army Chief of Staff Harold K. Johnson sent a memorandum to his colleagues on the Joint Chiefs on 12 April 1965 concerning his view of the actions needed to be taken in South Vietnam now that the first US ground forces had arrived in the country.[50] General Johnson underscored the three 'basic requirements involved in providing security.'[51] They were: find the enemy; fix the enemy in place; fight and finish the enemy. Whether applied to ARVN or US ground combat elements the recipe remained the same. It represented with total fidelity the fundamentally Clausewitzian focus of Army doctrine.

Clausewitz stated:

> The *military power* [of an enemy] must be destroyed, that is, reduced to such a state as not to be able to prosecute the war. This is the sense in which we wish to be understood hereafter, whenever we use the expression 'destruction of the enemy's military power' [emphasis in original].[52]
>
> In this manner we see that the destruction of the enemy's military power, the overthrow of the enemy's power is only to be done through the effect of the battle, whether it actually takes place or that it is merely offered and not accepted.[53]

Through all editions of FM 100–5, *Field Service Regulations– Operations* published prior to the Vietnam war this focus was maintained. All US Army officers were developed in the cult of battle with its single-minded focus upon closing on the enemy and destroying his forces in the field through decisive combat. Not even the introduction of nuclear war and the concomitant cautionary notes against allowing limited (non-nuclear) war to cross the nuclear threshold served to diminish the Clausewitzian tone or modify the focus upon destroying the enemy's force in the field and thus his capability to conduct war.[54] The Clausewitzian approach was not limited to the higher operational levels, but extended to the conduct of tactics even at the company level.[55]

When considering guerrilla war, Army doctrine continued its basic concentration on destroying the enemy force in the field. Guerrillas might impose some modest changes in tactics or organization, but they were not immune to destruction through the application of superior mobility and firepower. Aggressiveness, mobility and firepower represented the solution to the problems presented by guerrillas.

> Operations to suppress and eliminate irregular forces are primarily offensive in nature. Thus, the conventional force must plan for and seize the initiative at the outset and retain it throughout the conduct of the operation.[56]

The 1965 edition of the Field Manual dealing with counterguerrilla operations emphasized offensive actions:

> Purely defensive measures only allow the guerrilla force to grow and become strong. They are justified only when the strength of the friendly forces available does not allow offensive action. Even limited offensive operations are preferable to a purely passive attitude.[57]

Aggressive patrolling, the maintenance of contact, the use of high-mobility ground and air tactical transport systems, the coordinated movement of air and ground mobile elements, the careful use of well-prepared artillery fire patterns as well as the use of artillery in long-range, unobserved harassment and interdiction missions are all stressed as appropriate operational modalities to find, fix and destroy the enemy guerrilla. Above all else the potential of the new Army airmobile forces was accentuated. Offensive-mindedness was a universal in the US Army. Counterguerrilla, particularly counterinsurgent, warfare was essentially defensive in nature at least at the strategic and operational levels. The limited historical experience with successful counterinsurgency had shown that the strategic defensive should be expressed in offensive small-unit operations in which the goal was not so much killing as demoralizing the enemy by depriving him of sanctuary. The Army did not understand this as it would run against the cult of the offensive.

> Superior mobility is essential in counterguerrilla operations to achieve surprise and to successfully counter the mobility of the enemy force. The extensive use of airmobile forces, if used with imagination will ensure the military commander superior mobility.[58]

> The imaginative, extensive and sustained use of airmobile forces offers the most effective challenge available today to this mobility differential of the enemy guerrilla force. It is imperative that, whenever possible, the concept of counterguerrilla operations be based on the maximum employment of this type force.[59]

It was certain that COMUSMACV and his field commanders would use mobility and firepower to take the battle to the guerrilla either out in the bush or within what the enemy considered to be safe havens using superior air and ground mobility to fix him in place. The application of superior firepower, both ground- and air-delivered, would destroy him whether he attempted to stand or to run. It would be equally certain that US forces would not attempt to hold the land they swept in offensive operations, for holding territory would be too demanding of scarce manpower resources and erosive of the offensive spirit held to be so important.[60]

The basic question confronting the Ad Hoc Study Group was simply that of making a strategic virtue out of an operational necessity. The solution arose from the Group's assessment of the logistic requirements of North Vietnamese regular forces and the Viet Cong and the role played by North Vietnam in meeting these needs. The Group accepted the argument that the Viet Cong were primarily indigenous Southerners, led primarily by native Southerners who 'procure most of their supplies in South Vietnam and are not solely dependent on an external supply system.'[61] In support of this insurgent interpretation, it was noted that only 20 per cent of the weapons recovered from the Viet Cong in 1964 were of PRC origin while 34 per cent were French and 31 per cent had been made in America.[62] It was concluded that the entire Viet Cong main force of 125 battalion equivalents required only ten tons of supplies per day from North Vietnam given the level of combat intensity which had prevailed through mid-1965.[63] This requirement was too small to allow for easy interdiction by either ground or air attack.

The Group was conservative in its assessment of the presence of PAVN units in South Vietnam. They accepted the 'accumulation of intelligence including two defectors and two prisoners' which indicated that one regiment, the 101st of the 325th Division had entered South Vietnam starting in January 1965, a date after the start of the US aerial interdiction and coercion effort.[64] Elements of two other regiments of the 325th might be present in the central highlands according to intelligence accepted by the Group. The purpose and role of the PAVN units was uncertain, and their troops had not been engaged in combat to a significant extent, which meant that the forces required no more than four tons of supplies per day per division.[65]

The small logistics requirements, not more than fourteen tons per day, coupled with the wide array of land and maritime infiltration routes explained why the aerial interdiction campaign had not impaired the ability of North Vietnam to supply its forces and assist the Viet Cong in the South.[66] The CIA agreed with the Group's conclusions.[67]

In an excellent application of 'if you can't raise the bridge, lower the water' logic, the Group concluded that the way to make the lines of supply and the North Vietnamese infrastructure more vulnerable to air attack was to increase the demands placed upon them by the consumers in the South. If the level of combat could be intensified even to that of 'a moderate combat situation as described in FM 101–10,' Viet Cong requirements would leap from 10 to 125 tons per day and PAVN demands would increase from 12 to 100 tons per day for each full-strength division.[68] At a sustained demand level of 225 tons per day, the logistic system would be far more susceptible to aerial interdiction and the North Vietnamese infrastructure far more vulnerable to ROLLING THUNDER.

Ground combat operations would serve to magnify the effect of the air operations against infrastructure and infiltration target systems by increasing the demands placed upon them by Viet Cong and PAVN forces.[69] The Group proposed that ground combat forces operate in support of the air forces as a matter of deliberate strategy. Not only was this a first in military history, it represented an inversion of the customary relationship which carried profound ramifications.

The Group defined winning in South Vietnam as

> achieving an outcome somewhere between, as a maximum, an end to the insurgency by DRV/VC decision and as an acceptable minimum, containment of the insurgency, except for minor areas and minor acts of violence, with an end to the need for the presence of substantial US forces. . . . Hopefully, the VC/DRV will become convinced that they cannot win in SVN, that continued efforts will be extremely costly and that time is on the side of the Free World.[70]

The Group developed a theory of victory which had three main components: ground combat operations against the Viet Cong main forces and any PAVN units which entered South Vietnam; interdiction of infiltration routes by air, sea and ground efforts; and air attacks upon infrastructure and economic target systems in North Vietnam. The theory of victory focused upon the use of US air power against infiltration routes and support facilities in North Vietnam with a secondary thrust on coercing Hanoi through air strikes. US ground combat operations were relegated to the status of force multiplier backing the air effort.

In considering ground combat operations, the Group made all the requisite genuflections before the Clausewitzian altar of 'the destruction as effective fighting forces of a large percentage of the main force battalions' and 'aggressive exploitation of superior military force to gain and keep the initiative' but, having done so, still saw the air war as the winning war.[71] Matters such as pacification, military civic action, regeneration of ARVN or how the pace and scope of the air war might be modulated to facilitate diplomatic exchange were not considered.

The Group was alone among military planners in accurately seeing the Viet Cong as an insurgent force with tenuous connections to the North. Having seen the situation in the South accurately, the Group did not develop a theory of victory directed at countering an insurgency, but produced a theory based on the standard view of guerrilla war as partisan conflict with North Vietnam in the role of external sponsoring power and, therefore, the main enemy. Instead of asking the correct question as to what history shows about the use of military force in the countering of insurgency, the Group simply accepted the embedded misconceptions and designed a theory of victory for partisan war.

There are several plausible explanations for this apparent lapse of intellectual courage on the part of the Group members. They were participants in the shared intellectual heritage which saw insurgency as an impossible phenomenon. As members of the military services they were aware of and conditioned by Air Force and Army doctrine which emphasized the physical destruction of the enemy's force in the field or his material capacity and political will to continue the war. As military officers of field rank they were also well aware of the utter impossibility of altering doctrine or organizations and tactics quickly. The United States had no alternative except to fight with the forces and doctrine which it had in 1965. As Americans, they undoubtedly had a very high opinion of the efficacy of US weapons systems and as a corollary they repeated the fundamental mistake of earlier generations of planners who relied on air power. In the Second World War, Germans, British, Americans had all assumed with a profound, but baseless conviction that the government and civilian population against which the planes were sent and on whom the bombs fell would suffer a collapse of structural integrity and political will. Finally, as officers well tied into the bureaucracy, they were aware of what was wanted and needed up the chain of command. They provided an assessment which comported itself well with the perspective of Earle Wheeler, John McNaughton and Robert McNamara.

It is important to understand the real function of the Ad Hoc Study Group in understanding the American theory of victory. It was not that their assessment and recommendation were precisely embodied into orders given by the JCS or Pacific Command (PACOM) to COMUSMACV. It was not that their assessment was debated in the Administration. Rather, it was their role as a nexus and explicator of the shared intellectual heritage which had served to make doctrine and policy alike.

In a capsule form, the Group's report reflected all that was going to be done anyway and all the assumptions that were to be made. General Westmoreland would have no alternative to massive search and destroy missions. The Air Force had no alternative to striking targets in North Vietnam. Given the shared intellectual heritage, the President and the senior policy makers like the military commanders had no option except to see the war as a partisan conflict in which the stakes were greater than a South Vietnam that was non-Communist. The Group reflected all the aspects of the heritage in a convenient package. There can be little doubt that General Wheeler and others read the report with a good degree of satisfaction for it contained the recipe for victory that they were quite well prepared to cook.

At the end of August 1965 the JCS sent a memorandum to Secretary McNamara in which the Chiefs laid out a general concept of operations for Vietnam.[72] Working from the statement of goals contained in NSAM 288, they identified the major 'problems to be dealt with in the conduct of the war' as being: 'The continued direction and support of the Viet Cong by the DRV' and 'The continued existence of a major Viet Cong infrastructure.'[73] They identified the basic tasks for the military as: forcing the North to cease its direction and support of the Viet Cong; defeating the Viet Cong so as 'to extend GVN control over all of the RVN' and deterring 'Communist China from direct intervention.'[74] Their theory of victory was taken virtually intact from the Ad Hoc Study Group report:

> intensify military pressure on the DRV by air and naval power; to destroy significant DRV military targets . . .; to interdict supporting LOCs in the DRV; to interdict the infiltration and supply routes into the RVN; . . . to defeat the Viet Cong. . . . By aggressive and sustained exploitation of superior military force, the United States/Government of Vietnam would seize and hold the initiative in both the DRV and RVN keeping the DRV, the Viet Cong and the PL/VM at a disadvantage, progressively destroying the DRV war-supporting power and defeating the Viet Cong.[75]

The emphasis was again on air power, on destroying the infrastructure, industrial base and political will of the North. The Chiefs agreed, at least implicitly, that the role of the American ground forces in the South was to act as a force multiplier in support of the air war over Laos and North Vietnam. The Secretary of Defense accepted the JCS position.

This made an advantage out of doctrinal necessity. All the troops had to do was increase the tempo and intensity of combat. The Army did not have to seize and hold ground. The troops did not even have to win battles, to kill the enemy or capture his supplies, although it was expected that they would do all these things. The only thing which the ground forces had to do when they went out to bash the bush in the big battalions was to make the enemy increase his logistics requirements. If this could be done successfully, then air power over the North and the trails of Laos would win the real war. It is probably a very good thing that the Eleven Bravos, the grunts, did not know why they were really in the bush.

3

EVERYTHING IS PERFECT AND GETTING BETTER

General William Westmoreland sent a letter and a nine-volume report to Army Chief of Staff Harold Johnson on 23 April 1966. The report was an extensive study of the combat operations in South Vietnam undertaken in the first three months of 1966 by the 173rd Independent Airborne Brigade, 1st Infantry Division, 1st Cavalry Division (Air Mobile) and the 1st Brigade of the 101st Airborne Division. The errata-riddled report, titled ARCOV for ARmy Combat Operations, Vietnam, came to no surprising or innovative conclusions.[1] The report contained two major recommendations: incorporate the lessons being learned in Vietnam within Army doctrine and training programs; improve the firepower and mobility of the maneuver battalions entering combat.[2] ARCOV's reassuring assessment and quite minor recommendations served as a predicate for MACV and Army operations for the balance of US ground combat. ARCOV validated the concepts of doctrine, organization and training provided to the South Vietnamese Army (ARVN) by US advisors. As a result, ARCOV's hand would rest heavily on South Vietnam until its defeat nine years later.

The sixty-one officers of the ARCOV team under the direction of Brigadier General George Mabry closely examined five combat operations taken to be representative of the overall operational profile of US forces. Two, WHITE WING, an airmobile search and destroy operation, and HAPPY VALLEY, an area-clearing and -securing operation, were conducted by the 1st Cavalry Division. The others were evenly distributed among the three other units studied and comprised two search and destroy and one area-securing mission. The sample emphasized the new and quite glamorous airmobile cavalry division as well as the search and destroy operations recommended by Army doctrine. Institutional imperatives operating within the chain of command legitimately may be assumed to have had a significant effect upon the assessments done by the ARCOV officers. The search and destroy operation was the fundamental doctrinal precept at work in Vietnam. The concept of air mobility had been expensively embodied in the highly publicized 1st Cavalry

Division. The Army would be quite embarrassed if its main operational concept and its most state-of-the-art division performed less well than predicted and advertised.

The ARCOV team accurately reflected the general understanding held by the US government and armed forces regarding the nature of the Viet Cong, the goals of the North Vietnamese and the partisan war nature of the conflict in South Vietnam. It was asserted that the military activities of the Viet Cong were directed by the North Vietnamese Ministry of Defense and the command structure of PAVN.[3] The National Liberation Front was held to be an exercise in strategic deception with the Central Office for South Vietnam (COSVN) being described as part of the North Vietnamese political–military command and control structure.[4] There was no possibility of the Southerners within the Viet Cong or National Liberation Front pursuing goals independent of Hanoi's policy directives.

The team accepted November 1964 as the month during which North Vietnamese Army units first infiltrated into South Vietnam. These regulars were credited as being superior to the Viet Cong main force guerrillas which were seen as clearly better personnel than those of the Viet Cong local forces and defensively oriented part-time militia.[5]

The individual Viet Cong was described as 'a good soldier' whose strengths were ideological motivation, personal toughness, endurance and offensive spirit. He was credited with having a good intelligence system, excellent foot mobility, a capacity for thorough planning and 'efficient' fieldcraft and minor tactics. Offsetting these strengths were several weaknesses: lack of skill with modern weapons, his 'peasant background,' the lack of sophistication in his 'war machine,' poor leadership in crises or 'when plans go awry.' His dependence upon the local population was seen as a liability and it was noted that he was vulnerable to crop destruction activities as well as the effects of artillery, air strikes, armor attacks, and his own logistics limitations.[6]

While no numbers were given about the combined strength of the several types of Viet Cong units and the PAVN formations in the South, ARCOV provided the following as the friendly force aggregate strength as of 28 February 1966: South Vietnamese armed forces, 581,000; free world military forces, 235,000, of which 213,000 were from the US.[7] The US Marine Corps had a total of thirteen maneuver battalions in the I Corps Tactical Zone (CTZ) in the northernmost quarter of the country, while the US Army disposed twenty-eight maneuver battalions in the II and III CTZs covering the center half of South Vietnam.[8]

Operational control of US forces in II and III CTZ was vested in the First and Second Field Force Headquarters which operated as corps level commands under COMUSMACV. Both of these Field Forces had established 'search and destroy operations against major Viet Cong forces and bases' as the primary task for their subordinate units.[9] Rules of engagement gave a priority to conducting military operations so as to minimize civilian casualties and damage to civilian property.[10] Units subordinate to the Field Forces or to the Marine Corps level command in the north, III MAF, divided their time between operations in their primary area of influence called a Tactical Area of Responsibility (TAOR) and those conducted at a greater or lesser distance from the TAOR in temporary Areas of Operation (AO). Even if a division or brigade was assigned to an AO, it still had the responsibility for its TAOR and thus its subordinate units would often be geographically divided.[11]

The policy of splitting divisions and brigades between a home TAOR and various temporary AOs assured that a fully effective use of the highly mobile American forces would be made. The policy also created deficiencies in unit integrity. More importantly, as the maneuver battalions moved around the country it insured that American troops were always strangers in a strange land, significantly alienated from the population as well as the intelligence support that locals could provide. It made problems of identifying the enemy or controlling the highly lethal American firepower all the greater. It might even have facilitated the American propensity to identify all Vietnamese as 'gooks' with all the implicit consequences such generalized dehumanization entailed.

The White House was informed of the first major American ground operation of 1966 by a Special Situation Report at 11:27 p.m. on 8 January.[12] Twenty-two hours earlier, the 173rd Airborne Brigade and the 3rd Brigade of the 1st Infantry Division had launched a search and destroy operation, dubbed CRIMP, in the Ho Bo Woods approximately 25 miles northwest of Saigon. The American movement was preceded by a massive air strike executed by B–52 strategic bombers. The target of the attack was a complex of bunkers and tunnels believed to house major Viet Cong command and logistics centers as well as two 800-man battalions of the 165th Viet Cong Regiment. The Administration was informed that in the first twenty-one hours of the operation the only friendly fatal casualties were four soldiers from the Australian battalion attached to the 173rd while Viet Cong losses were put at twenty-two killed and twelve captured.[13]

The after-action report filed by the 173rd enthusiastically spoke of the six-day operation as having been a complete success. The commander characterized CRIMP as having been 'one of the Brigade's most successful' considering the 'combined effects of Viet Cong killed or captured, weapons and materiel captured, installations destroyed and intelligence captured.'[14] The Brigade had fired over 7,000 rounds of artillery, received 171 sorties by US Air Force fighter-bombers, lost 15 Americans and 8 Australians killed in action.[15] In exchange it had a confirmed body count of 128 Viet Cong, captured 91 weapons ranging from a homemade shotgun to two AK–47 assault rifles, 100,000 pages of documents and 57 tons of rice.[16] More than one thousand civilians were reported as having been removed from the area of operations as 'refugees.'[17] The commander was pleased with the efficacy of the CS riot-control agent used to flush Viet Cong and civilians from the tunnel and bunker system.[18] He was even more satisfied with having successfully completed the major mission, 'to smash the politico-military headquarters of the Viet Cong Military Region Four.'[19]

Brigadier General Williamson wrote an extremely upbeat appraisal of Operation CRIMP which went to General Westmoreland, among others. In this report the 173rd Airborne Brigade's commander commented on the civilian population within the area of operations. He justified their removal on the basis of the long-term Viet Cong influence within the region which had resulted in the civilians having been thoroughly indoctrinated with Communist propaganda. After the evacuation of over 1,900 civilians, the lack of food and shelter prompted the Vietnamese provincial officials to stop the forced relocation.[20]

In a critique of CRIMP and the related Operation MARAUDER, Brigadier Williamson expressed concern regarding the confused nature of the refugee policy in place. In both operations the Brigade initially had forcibly relocated all civilians, but the shortages of food eventually compelled the Brigade to remove only males of military age.[21] As a combat expedient for future operations, the Brigadier recommended that civilians be detained within the area of operations until 'a decision is made as to their disposition.'[22] He added, 'They should be told that they are supervised for their own safety while combat operations continue in the area.'[23] He hoped that in the future ARVN would be in charge of the distasteful relocation effort.[24]

The evacuation provided an early demonstration of a conundrum never to be resolved satisfactorily: the effects upon the civilian population of search and destroy operations. Sound military reasons might require the removal and relocation of civilians but the relocation of peasants caused disaffection and impaired the pacification, re-volutionary development and nation-building programs recurrently urged by the United States. As the Herd's commander commented, it would take time to win over 'thoroughly indoctrinated' civilians, but it might be doubted that forced relocation aided the process.[25]

The commander of the relatively less experienced and less highly motivated 3rd Brigade, 1st Infantry Division, wrote 'Each action enhances the Brigade's ability to defeat the Viet Cong.'[26] He remarked that the B–52 strikes had effects which were difficult to evaluate and 'trench networks were found undamaged within twenty-five yards of craters.'[27] His Brigade had only indifferent success with CS and opposed the type of fast-moving sweep patrols favored by the 173rd.[28] In exchange for 2,650 rounds of artillery including those of the very large 8-inch howitzer, 226 USAF support sorties and six Americans killed in action, the Brigade claimed 22 confirmed Viet Cong killed, no weapons captured and 70 tons of rice destroyed.[29]

The 3rd Brigade had no sooner wrapped up CRIMP than it moved into another search and destroy operation, BUCKSKIN, in conjunction with the recently arrived 3rd Brigade of the 25th Infantry Division. In the course of the fourteen-day operation, the brigade saw no significant combat as it executed sweeps designed to secure the area into which the 25th Infantry Division was to move. Instead of conventional combat, the maneuver battalions of the 3rd Brigade came under repeated sniper fire and night-time perimeter probes by Viet Cong sappers.

Several guerrilla base camps and prepared ambush sites were located and destroyed, but on balance BUCKSKIN could not be rated as a success despite the 750 tons of rice captured or destroyed.[30] The exchange rate of 25 friendly killed with a further 209 wounded for a confirmed body count of 93 Viet Cong was poor.[31] Even though the operation took place in territory not previously entered by US or South Vietnamese forces, the commander's assessment of BUCKSKIN as 'a great success' was unwarranted.[32] A far more accurate conclusion was embodied in the intelligence evaluation, 'the VC did not present a lucrative target at any time.'[33] The Brigade did destroy some tunnels and bunkers in the Cu Chi area of operations, but other defensive works, even more extensive, were not discovered. The quantity of supplies destroyed or captured was minimal and the haul of weapons extremely small.[34]

The course of BUCKSKIN demonstrated some major points regarding battalion and larger search and destroy sweeps. The defender had the initiative. He could accept or reject battle essentially at will. He could refuse to become a 'lucrative target.' This reality was reflected in a routine briefing memorandum sent to the President from the White House Situation Room:

> The Viet Cong are continuing to avoid South Vietnamese and Allied troops participating in large-scale search and destroy missions. They are, however, persisting in their aggressive campaign of terrorism, sabotage and harassment of lightly defended and isolated outposts and villages.[35]

By employing snipers, night probes and passive mechanisms such as mines, booby traps and punji stakes, the Viet Cong could inflict casualties in sufficient numbers to adversely affect the morale of the US forces and, over time, the political will of the United States. Without accurate, timely intelligence and combat information, it was not possible to use effectively the superior American firepower in a way which would inflict either unacceptably heavy casualties or materiel damage upon the enemy. As a result, an operation such as BUCKSKIN did not further a strategy of attrition; neither did it make progress toward the goals of eroding the enemy's material capacity to wage war and exhausting his morale and will to continue the war.

The same points were demonstrated in a division-sized search and destroy operation, MASTIFF, undertaken by the 2nd and 3rd Brigades of the 1st Infantry Division between 21 and 27 February in an area of operation near the Michelin rubber plantation. The operational plan depended upon two brigades exploiting their superior air and ground mobility to pin the large, well-established Viet Cong force within the Michelin plantation against the Saigon river where it could be destroyed by firepower. The concept was taken directly from the counterguerrilla field manual.

The effort involved in executing MASTIFF was enormous. Over 1,000 helicopter sorties, nearly 100 Air Force C–123 sorties and 197 USAF fighter-bomber sorties, the entirety of the division's artillery and six battalions of combat troops were involved.[36] In return for this massive exertion and the loss of seventeen killed, ninety-four wounded and two M–16 rifles lost, the division could report sixty-one Viet Cong confirmed killed with six Viet Cong suspects, but no weapons captured and a large quantity of miscellaneous supplies destroyed. While the commander characterized the operation as successful, his assertion must be questioned.[37]

Significant contact and large-scale combat were absent. Snipers, mines and small probes were present. This pattern meant that the bulk of the Viet Cong main force had left the area of operations. The Viet Cong might have left the area prior to the start of the operation indicating either a failure of US intelligence or a failure of the American deception plan. As an alternative, the guerrillas might have escaped and evaded the US forces as they were inserted by air and ground, and then crossed the Saigon river with their movements remaining undiscovered by American reconnaissance aircraft. In either event, the guerrillas demonstrated that they had the initiative. It is doubtful that MASTIFF damaged either the material capacity or the moral ability and will of the Viet Cong to continue the war. It is doubtful that MASTIFF contributed in the slightest to the successful implementation of the Ad Hoc Study Group's concept of overstressing the enemy's lines of supply by increasing the tempo of combat.

From 3 to 6 March 1966, a battalion of the 3rd Brigade, 1st Infantry Division, conducted a search and destroy operation which worked exceptionally well.[38] This operation, COCA BEACH, was one of the five evaluated and used by the ARCOV team to support the assessment that US doctrine was proving itself correct for the war in South Vietnam.[39]

There can be no doubt that the operation constituted a complete success in that for a cost of ten friendly fatalities and twenty-nine wounded, there was a confirmed body count of 199 and impressive booty including four 50–calibre machine guns, twenty-four rifles and thirty hand grenades.[40]

The reason for the success was not properly underscored in the ARCOV study but was quite obvious in the Brigade's after action report. The local Viet Cong commander used his initiative incorrectly. When Viet Cong preparations for an assault against the perimeter of the 2/28th Infantry Battalion were discovered by an American patrol, the guerrilla commander imprudently proceeded with his planned dawn attack. His decision assured that the Viet Cong regiment became a 'lucrative target' for superior American firepower including the battalion's organic weapons, well-directed artillery fire and air strikes.[41] Despite the failure of a quickly inserted block force to finish the destruction of the rapidly withdrawing enemy, American firepower had done the job of finishing the enemy after he had found and fixed himself through an ill-considered attack.[42]

COCA BEACH was not so much an American victory as it was a self-inflicted Viet Cong defeat. As such it was quite misleading for the ARCOV team to have selected this operation instead of MASTIFF or BUCKSKIN which were far more accurate in their reflection of relative failure.

At the top of the chain of command, COCA BEACH was seen as a success, being reported to the President on 7 March along with the USMC–South Vietnamese Operation UTAH and the prolonged 1st Cavalry campaign in the central highlands, MASHER, as significant victories.[43] As the first week of March came to an end, the news reaching the Administration's senior members was quite encouraging. Viet Cong-initiated incidents were decreasing; ARVN morale was increasing.[44] The American forces were doing all that had been expected of them, and more.

Seen from close range, a picture which appeared pleasing from a distance could become ugly. So it was with the picture of unrelieved success presented by the US ground operations in early 1966. Fresh from the highly regarded, and publicized, success in operation MASHER/WHITE WING, General Harry Kinnard ordered his 1st Air Cavalry brigades to commence Operation JIM BOWIE on 8 March.[45] The new campaign was to last three weeks and involve two brigades as well as several artillery batteries attached to the division for the duration. The target of the search and destroy sweeps was a presumed Viet Cong base area in the Vinh Tranh and An Tuc districts of Binh Dinh province on the sea coast of II CTZ.

Weather problems caused the start of the operation to be postponed from 10 to 12 March. Citing a suspected Viet Cong captured on 13 March, the after action-report concluded that the reason for light initial contact was a timely dispersal order given to the local guerrilla units.[46] Whether this was coincidence or the result of a Viet Cong intelligence coup cannot be determined, but the result was an operation frustrating in its execution and disappointing in its results.

Over 30,000 helicopter sorties were flown. Nearly 20,000 rounds of artillery were fired. The Air Force provided 284 tactical sorties delivering 113 tons of general purpose bombs, 102 tons of napalm and 102 tons of fragmentation bombs. Over 95,000 gallons of fuel and 626 tons of supplies were expended. All of this and six battalions of infantry were employed to kill 27 Viet Cong, capture 17 more, recover 19 individual weapons and destroy 12 tons of rice and 4 'training camps.'[47] The commander concluded his assessment with a remark on the 'early and orderly withdrawal' by the Viet Cong without speculating as to its reason.[48] Much effort and materiel had been expended without useful result except perhaps to the morale of the enemy.

The 1st Infantry Division was no more successful during the sixteen days of Operation ABILENE between 30 March and 15 April.[49] The concept was one of a massive search and destroy sweep through territory in Long Khanh and Phuoc Tuy provinces extending in from the coast in III CTZ. The area of operations was believed to contain significant Viet Cong base camps and some combat units. Beliefs did not bring results as there was only one significant contact between troops of the Big Red One and main force Viet Cong. On 11 April Charley Company, 2/16th Infantry, found itself in a meeting engagement with the D800 Battalion.[50] Forty-one Viet Cong soldiers were killed, nearly one-half of the total confirmed body count for the entire operation.[51]

Other than this one major engagement Operation ABILENE was an exercise in tolerating heat, the effects of boredom and tension, snipers, mines and the occasional mortar round. Base camp facilities and supplies were found and destroyed. The divisional after-action report stated, 'the losses probably will not have any major adverse effects on future VC plans and operations.'[52] An unstated number of civilians were removed from the area of operation, which had the presumed effect of limiting the labor and local supplies available to the Viet Cong when the guerrillas returned to the region.[53]

A total of 25,000 rounds of artillery was fired including 1,200 rounds of 8-inch howitzer and 833 rounds of 175mm.[54] In addition 390 rounds of naval gunfire support were provided by two ships firing on a total of 17 targets.[55] The Air Force and Navy provided a total of 605 fighter-bomber sorties of which only four were close air support on 11 April on behalf of the hard-pressed Charley Company in its engagement against the D800 Battalion.[56] The effects of most strikes 'could not be adequately judged.'[57] This caveat did not prevent the results from being termed 'excellent.'[58] In addition to the tactical air strikes there were three B–52 ARC LIGHT missions executed in conjunction with ABILENE; the effects were unevaluated.[59] Forty-eight Americans were killed in action and 133 wounded.[60] A significant amount of equipment was lost including thirty M–16 rifles, ten M–79 grenade launchers, ten .45 calibre pistols and two M–60 general purpose machine guns.[61] One helicopter was lost and four more damaged as were two armored personnel carriers, two M–48 tanks and a 105mm howitzer.[62]

In return, 92 Viet Cong were reported killed and 20 more captured.[63] A superficially impressive amount of materiel was seized or destroyed including 36 small arms, 2 mortars, 3 tractors and 1,241 tons of rice.[64] To destroy 1,200 tons of rice, the 1st Infantry Division moved nearly 80,000 individual rations; to destroy 5,000 gallons of kerosene, the Division consumed 261,934 gallons of fuel.[65] Considering the Ad Hoc Study Group's theory of victory, the question as to which belligerent's supply infrastructure was being overstressed was relevant.

The commander concluded that the major Viet Cong units expected to be found in the area were absent, but the operation had dealt a major blow to the credibility of the Viet Cong as a military force.[66] It should be pointed out that the after-action report suffered from an internal inconsistency. The intelligence section disagreed completely with the commander's statement concerning the anticipated presence of major Viet Cong units stating instead, 'major VC forces were out of the province when the operation started.'[67] The removal of the civilian population was held to impair future Viet Cong operational capabilities as would the loss of the base facilities destroyed.[68] Unfortunately, neither the commander nor anyone else inquired as to the effect of forced removal to a refugee center upon the loyalty of the civilians to the Saigon government.

The National Security Council met to consider the course of the war on 10 May.[69] General Wheeler provided an optimistic briefing on American ground and air operations over the previous six months. The importance of US ground combat activities was underscored by the chronic political instability within South Vietnam.[70] Secretary McNamara summarized the situation: 'We hope that heavy pressure by US forces will carry us over the present period.'[71] Ambassador Lodge asserted that despite the current political turmoil in Saigon, 'military activity can go ahead and pacification proceed.'[72] The only real dissenter was Robert Komer who had recently been elevated to the rank of Special Assistant to the President with particular responsibilities for Vietnam and a distinctive interest in pacification and nation building. He expressed grave concerns about the effects of the US emphasis upon search and destroy missions upon the progress of rural development and pacification.

He believed the great and growing US presence was also having a profoundly negative effect upon the stability of the South Vietnamese economy by stimulating inflation. The overall effect of US operations was to increase anti-American attitudes with the concomitant potential of turning the political dynamic against the US.[73] No notice was taken of Komer's reservations.

There was a definite tension between efficient employment of US ground combat forces in South Vietnam and the need to develop more effective social, political and economic institutions within that country. The high lethality of American weaponry and the emphasis placed upon its employment in the doctrine governing the planning and execution of US operations served to disrupt traditional patterns of rural life, to place the lives of civilians caught in an area of operations in jeopardy and to force many to become rootless refugees or unwilling residents in the 'new life hamlets', as the refugee concentration centers were called.

The combination of extreme instability at the governmental center and social disruption under the pressure of rural war was recognized by the Johnson Administration as being a real barrier to the achievement of American policy goals. The deterioration of the economy under the twin pressures of war and rampant inflation, both of which were largely the result of US activities, was also a source of concern to some in the Administration. The central conundrum was: how to build a nation and win a war simultaneously without having the winning of the war destroy the nation under construction. A related difficulty of virtually insoluble nature, not recognized by the Administration, was that of gaining leverage on the South Vietnamese government. Any South Vietnamese regime, regardless of its composition, was immune to any unpleasant US advice on social, economic or political matters. This attitude was the expectable result of the pervasive belief that the Americans were going to fight the Viet Cong and the North Vietnamese for reasons of their own. As long as the United States had no credible capacity to withdraw, the Administration lacked effective leverage upon the South Vietnamese government.

A consistent focus upon the nature and relative priority of non-military actions in South Vietnam had been lacking since the March 1965 initiation of a major effort to implement a wide array of programs in the non-military sphere.[74] The same month, Carl Rowan, the Director of the US Information Agency, wrote to the President concerning efforts to address the major American shortcomings in the program of psychological operations designed to motivate the South Vietnamese people to greater support of their government and the war effort.[75] Despite the apparent full cooperation of the Embassy in Saigon, obvious Presidential interest and significant follow-up reports through

1965, the non-military program was lost in the increased pace of combat operations which followed the deployment of additional ground combat forces in the summer of 1965.[76] Political unrest in Saigon coupled with the combat in the bush and the bombing in the North to push pacification, psychological operations and nation-building activities into the shadows.

Ambassador Henry Cabot Lodge underscored this reality in his first telegram of 1966 when he accurately characterized the entrance of the North Vietnamese Army into the war as having 'transformed the nature of the war,' making it 'in effect a new war.'[77] To Lodge, the priority and the major opportunity for American success lay on the battlefield, where 'fundamental progress – decisive, perhaps,' might be expected in 1966.[78] Pacification must take a back seat to combat against the Viet Cong and PAVN, at least for the foreseeable future.

The obvious failure of the non-military program or, 'other war,' as President Johnson referred to it in his State of the Union address of January 1966, to accomplish any of the goals established for it was the reason behind the convening of an emergency meeting of senior US officials in Warrenton, Virginia earlier that month. Under the chairmanship of Leonard Ungar from the State Department and William Porter of the Embassy in Saigon, the thirty-five-man group including representatives from the Vietnam Coordinating Committee (VNCC), State Department, OSD/ISA, the Embassy, CIA, JCS, MACV and NSC met from 8 to 11 January 1966.[79] The major conclusions of the group were that 'under the current strategy several years more fighting on at least the present scale' seemed likely and that the relationship between continued, intense combat and the requirements of 'pacification/rural construction' remained unclear.[80] The group recommended the review of the 'current political-military strategy in Vietnam and related areas.'[81] The group also advised that there be 'provision for continuous coordination between civilian and military branches' to allow the effective reconstitution of social and governmental institutions following the conclusion of large-scale military actions.[82]

Problems of resource allocation and manpower shortages were considered as were the significant economic problems imposed by the US war effort. Figuring heavily in the discussions was the lack of South Vietnamese governmental cooperation. The various pressures which might be brought to bear upon the Saigon government to effect necessary political, economic and social reforms were considered without result. The conference report urged that pacification and revolutionary development be given an overall priority equal to that assigned to combat operations. To insure that this was a meaningful priority, the appointment of a Director of Civil Operations and Revolutionary Development to the Embassy staff with authority and rank equivalent to that of COMUSMACV was recommended.[83] Finally, the absence of 'any recent strategy paper' was noted with the recommendation that this deficiency be remedied.[84] Perhaps the participants hoped that a strategy review would resolve the tensions between large-scale military operations and pacification.

In part responding to the problems identified by the Warrenton meeting conferees and other Administration officials such as David Bell of the Agency for International Development, but to a larger extent responding to the political ramifications of the 31 January decision to resume bombing North Vietnam following an extended Christmas pause, President Johnson accepted the advice of domestic aide Jack Valenti to meet in Hawaii with the two leaders of the most recent, and most stable Saigon military government, Premier Nguyen Kao Ky and Chief of State Nguyen Van Thieu.[85] The decision was announced on 4 February 1966 and the meeting was held in Honolulu from 6 to 8 February with less than adequate preparation. It was announced that the President wanted to 'review our complete program' with the South Vietnamese leaders.[86]

The Honolulu Conference concentrated on the 'other war' of pacification, revolutionary development and nation building. The Vietnamese delegation took the lead with a presentation by Premier Ky which emphasized four points: defeating the Viet Cong, eradicating social injustice, establishing a viable economy and building a 'true democracy.'[87] These four points became the general framework of the joint communiqué, the Declaration of Honolulu. President Johnson, in private as well as in public, strongly supported nation building and psychological operations, even privately counseling Ky to spend more time in the countryside acting like a politician rather than staying in Saigon acting like a general.[88] Intentionally, military matters were downplayed and were not discussed by the principals until the closing minutes of the meeting. The President was quoted as having said:

> We have not gone into this [military effectiveness] because we did not want to overshadow this meeting here with bombs, with mortars, with hand grenades, with masher movements.
>
> But we haven't gone into the details . . . for two or three reasons. One, we want to be able to say honestly and truthfully that this has not been a military build up conference . . . . We have been talking about building a society following the outlines of the Prime Minister's speech yesterday. Second, this is not the place with a hundred people sitting around to build military effectiveness. . . . Third, I want to put off as long as I can, having to make these crucial decisions.[89]

The President, the Declaration of Honolulu and the Record of Conclusions and Decisions all accentuated non-military programs.[90] In a personal telegram to General Westmoreland, the President prompted,

> I know that you share my own views on the equal importance of the war on social misery and hope that what we did at Honolulu will help assure that we and the Vietnamese move forward with equal determination on that front.[91]

The word 'equal' had an ambiguous meaning as used in this telegram. Did it refer to a parity between Vietnamese effort and that of the US in the other war or did it, as the Warrenton Meeting participants had urged, mean equivalence between the other war and combat operations?

When General Westmoreland reported on the Honolulu Conference to his chief subordinates, he emphasized the Administration's backing: 'the President is 1000% in support of our efforts.'[92] The General discussed the problem of inflation in South Vietnam at some length, but gave little consideration to any of the other topics considered at the Honolulu Conference.[93] He was far more concerned with assuring that combat operations be sustained at a high tempo and that ARVN not be allowed simply to sit back and watch the Americans fight.[94] If the General accepted the President's position on combat operations and the non-military programs, it was not clear at the first council of war following the Honolulu meeting.

Only time and action on the ground would demonstrate whether the military and non-military programs enjoyed an equivalent priority. There were an impressive number of follow-up reports by the Vice President, Secretaries and assorted staffs.[95] In April, Robert Komer sounded a cautionary note in a lengthy and thoughtful analysis of the non-military programs to senior Administration personnel.[96] In Komer's view the military was sweeping faster than the civilian operations were pacifying. He recommended not a slowdown or redirection of the search and destroy operations but an enhancement of the pacification effort.[97] The long litany of difficulties on the civilian side of US policy in Vietnam which Komer recited suggested that the fundamental cause of problems including the relative slowness of pacification, the runaway inflation, port congestion, the absence of leverage on the Saigon government, the explosively growing refugee population and the increasing requirements for imported rice lay with US ground combat operations in the South.

The term 'other war' employed by the President and his Administration accurately connoted the nature of the relationship between ground combat operations and the non-military program. The real war, the central war, the war which would determine victory or defeat was that waged by the big battalion sweeps in support of the air operations against the Northern infrastructure, economy and political will. That was the war in which people were dying. That was the war in which the US was not dependent upon Southern cooperation and compliance. That was the war in which the results could be decisive and palpable. Non-military activities, pacification, nation building, all were relegated to subordinate status as the 'other war.' It probably didn't really matter to very many at the time if the US won or lost the other war.

Within six weeks of the Declaration of Honolulu, Lt. Colonel Kurtz Miller, the Assistant for Vietnam on John McNaughton's staff, wrote a memorandum to McGeorge Bundy outlining US military strategy and its progress in Vietnam.[98] Colonel Miller described the three missions of US ground combat forces as providing security for their own bases, disrupting enemy force concentrations and 'searching out and destroying Viet Cong and PAVN hard core and regular forces, based upon carefully evaluated intelligence as to their whereabouts.'[99] He argued that the American actions had been 'measured, limited and appropriate' and that all escalation had been driven by the North Vietnamese and their partisan ally, the Viet Cong.[100]

Key elements of US military strategy, in addition to the primary one of 'selective destruction of NVN war-supporting and war-making capability' were the 'liberation of selected areas dominated by the Viet Cong,' the destruction of enemy base areas, 'the defeat of the Viet Cong and PAVN forces in SVN' and the 'forced withdrawal of PAVN forces from SVN.'[101] The search and destroy operations conducted by US troops and ARVN units operating under American guidance and advice had 'sought out and defeated, time after time, Viet Cong and PAVN main force units.'[102] The Colonel's view, shared by the Defense Department, was that the US theory of victory was succeeding and should be continued even though it had been 'at times costly in lives and equipment' lest the initiative be lost to the enemy.[103]

A similar conclusion was reflected in a memorandum sent to John McNaughton and others by the co-chairman of the Warrenton Meeting and of the VNCC, Leonard Ungar, in April 1966. This memorandum contended that US military operations should 'continue in accordance with present concepts and at present levels aiming to destroy VC main force units and to clear and secure heavily populated areas in particular.'[104] Ungar was wrong in one salient respect. It should be recognized that US forces could not operate in heavily populated areas and the attempt to do so would have severely compromised their military strengths – firepower and air mobility. Further, American operations were aimed at searching and destroying, not clearing; even if the orientation were to be altered to one of clearing territory, the forces necessary to hold and defend the land cleared of major enemy units were not available.

George Carver, a senior CIA expert on Vietnam, viewed ground operations in a way quite similar to Ungar and Lt. Colonel Miller.[105] US forces must be 'aggressively and offensively employed' in order to harass the enemy and keep him from gaining the initiative.[106] While Carver and Ungar both argued for implementing options with a higher reliance upon non-military and diplomatic means of conflict termination, they both believed that the current American theory of victory on the ground was working.

Director of Central Intelligence Richard Helms, in a long memorandum written to Senator Edmund Muskie shortly after the Honolulu Conference, provided a summary of the apparent benefits of the increased US ground combat operations.[107] One major effect of American operations had been a decrease in large-scale Viet Cong attacks 'since the end of 1965' although this had been offset by 'some increase in the total number of armed attacks.'[108] This recently observed change in Viet Cong behavior might be attributed to either the demoralization resulting from US actions or a rationally calculated response meant to undercut the obvious American strengths in firepower and mobility, but Helms offered no analysis. A second positive effect of US air and ground operations was that of spoiling Viet Cong and PAVN attacks so that tactical initiative was swinging to the US/GVN forces. Helms commented for several pages about the perceived enervation of Viet Cong and PAVN morale by US ground attacks and the program of B–52 bombing in the South code-named ARC LIGHT.[109]

Helms' assessment of the effects upon Viet Cong morale, manpower and materiel stocks did not consider the effectiveness of PAVN or its ability to continue and even augment its effort. Having categorized the war in the South as a partisan conflict masquerading as an insurgency, it was not surprising that Helms chose to represent the increasing presence of PAVN units in the South as a sign of Viet Cong manpower problems.[110] Helms argued that the North had sent its regular forces south in a bid to avert imminent failure on the part of its partisan guerrillas. This interpretation comported itself well with the American view that all guerrilla wars were of the partisan form dependent on the external sponsoring power's conventional army to secure victory or not. The possibility that Hanoi was entering the war from any motive other than that of preserving its partisans was not considered.

Helms viewed the large number of refugees from the countryside as a clear indication that US and South Vietnamese actions were succeeding. The Director portrayed the 800,000 refugees as liberty-loving people who were voting with their feet to leave areas of the country which were 'insecure' and come under government control in 'temporary shelters' rather than face life under the Viet Cong.[111] In making this assessment Helms chose to overlook the contributory factor of US ground and air attacks or the policy of forced relocation of civilians, particularly males of military age, from Viet Cong-dominated areas. He also chose to ignore the effect of the many refugees upon the plans for nation building, rural development and pacification. It would have been more accurate for the Director to have argued that the massive American search and destroy operations along with air attacks transformed stable peasant communities into streams of refugees. From a military perspective this might have been desirable, but for the 'other war' it represented a major, perhaps insurmountable, obstacle.

Much of Helms' appreciation of the effectiveness of US ground and air operations in the South focused upon the decline in Viet Cong morale and faith in eventual victory. His appreciation paralleled closely a widely circulated study of Viet Cong morale during the period of June to December 1965 done by Leon Goure of the Rand Corporation in January 1966.[112] On the basis of 450 interviews with Viet Cong prisoners and defectors, of whom only 160 had come into government custody since the augmentation of US forces started in June 1965, Goure attempted to draw general conclusions concerning the effect of the American presence upon the guerrillas' will to fight and faith in victory as well as their psychological vulnerabilities.[113]

The report asserted that the increasing intensity and lethality of US ground operations had inflicted severe psychological as well as physical casualties upon the Viet Cong units, even those of the main forces. The air power and artillery of the Americans were particularly respected. US operations had prevented Viet Cong offensive successes during the rainy season in 1965 and the guerrillas' confidence in victory was fading along with their hope of surviving the war.[114]

Balancing these favorable effects was the Viet Cong belief that, while the American intervention might have created new and difficult problems, the US was incapable of fighting a prolonged and difficult war.[115] The Viet Cong informers observed that the US intervention provided justification for the entry of PAVN into the war, a development that was appreciated by the guerrillas.[116]

Serving to benefit the Viet Cong at a time when their increased exactions of manpower and resources were causing estrangement between guerrillas and rural villagers was the effect of US artillery and air power. Peasant resentment of the attacks, while not 'significantly' motivating the villagers to more active support of the guerrillas, did nothing to bind them to either Saigon or the Americans.[117] US combat operations motivated the villagers to become refugees 'regardless of their attitude toward the GVN.'[118] Helms' freedom-loving peasants voting with their feet were seen by Goure as people in fear of their lives, 'a fly caught between two fighting water buffaloes,' fleeing for any perceived safety.[119]

The Rand team interviewed thirty-nine captured North Vietnamese soldiers and found them to be 'well-indoctrinated and loyal' as well as imbued with a belief that it was 'their duty to liberate the South Vietnamese from American imperialism and capitalist oppression and to unify the country.'[120] While the captured troops reflected the grievances about food, medical problems, unappreciative civilians and dishonest superiors which are typical of any army at any time, there was no indication that the US ground operations in the South or the air war against the North had undercut the PAVN will to fight.

Goure's original study was expanded in a set of 'informal notes' sent by Walt Whitman Rostow and Maxwell Taylor to the President in early May 1966.[121] The refugee situation was considered at some extent and with insight. Goure saw refugee movement as incidental to US and South Vietnamese military operations rather than as a result of either Viet Cong or GVN policy. After critically evaluating the very negative attitude then held by the Saigon government concerning refugees, Goure proposed

> The available data suggest the desirability of giving serious consideration to a deliberate and systematic program of encouraging and manipulating rural population movements as a part of a broad, integrated and coordinated military, resource control and pacification strategy in South Vietnam [122]

Goure believed that refugees constituted an overlooked weapon in the US arsenal whose employment would do much to undercut the Viet Cong in manpower, resources, intelligence and morale. At the same time the extent of effective population control would provide a meaningful and easily understood measurement of success. Victory could be demonstrated by counting full refugee camps and empty villages. Goure discounted the possibility that the Viet Cong could exploit the refugee streams for its own purpose with the facile assertion that it should be easier to identify active Viet Cong agents and political cadre in a camp than out in a village which was 'undergoing pacification.'[123] While Goure might have been somewhat too exuberant in his enthusiasm for a policy of converting peasants into refugees, the idea did have the virtue of capitalizing upon the inevitable. The more the US engaged in large-unit sweeps, the more villagers would be placed in the crossfire. It gave a new meaning to the concept 'search and destroy.'

In a consideration of North Vietnamese morale and will to continue the war, the 'informal notes' echoed the conclusions reached in the earlier study. The PAVN soldier remained 'well disciplined and believing [he] had no option but to go on fighting.'[124] There was no indication that US operations were undercutting PAVN morale or faith in eventual victory.[125]

While these assessments gave no grounds for a belief that the ground combat operations would bring immediate success, the expectations of ultimate triumph on the ground remained strong for the American forces had been in the war less than a year and new divisions were arriving daily.

The 1st and 2nd Brigades of the 25th Infantry Division were among the recent arrivals with the last troops closing up in early April 1966. The relatively old hands of the 2nd Brigade who had arrived in South Vietnam in January went for a walk in the sun from 16 to 21 April in a search and destroy operation called KAHALA in honor of the Division's Hawaii home.[126] Two thousand infantrymen supported by tanks, armored personnel carriers and artillery conducted an airmobile sweep in search of a seventy-man Viet Cong local force company and a platoon of 'guerrillas.'[127] While the Trang Bong Local Force Company went unlocated, the troops did encounter Viet Cong, primarily self-defense militiamen from the Quyet Chien Platoon #5 as well as scattered base areas.

The sweep resulted in forty-seven Viet Cong killed, twenty-one as the result of artillery fire, while an additional six were credited to air strikes called in on a hostile mortar emplacement.[128] Viet Cong snipers and night raiders were constant problems as were mines and booby traps. These problems were overcome and the Brigade reported capturing twenty-two Viet Cong and detaining one hundred and five suspected guerrillas.[129]

In exchange for nine tanks damaged, one beyond repair, as well as damage to four armored personnel carriers and a helicopter, the sweep seized or destroyed over sixteen tons of rice, seven hundred pounds of peanuts and 125 buildings.[130] As part of what was described as a 'vigorous Civic Affairs program,' eighty-nine civilians were removed from 'VC controlled areas' and evacuated to the Bac Ha #2 New Life Hamlet.[131] The commander recommended that 'indiscriminate fire into villages must cease' and civilians should be evacuated at the earliest possible moment so as to free combat troops from the task of 'controlling civilians.'[132] It was a learning experience for the 2nd Brigade but probably not a demoralizing or destructive one for the Viet Cong.

A much larger operation was mounted between 24 April and 17 May by the 1st Infantry Division. Two Brigades reinforced with supporting artillery and armor were employed in Operation BIRMINGHAM.[133] The target of the operation was War Zone C to the west of Saigon along the Cambodian border. War Zone C had long been a center of Viet Cong activities containing numerous base camps and logistics facilities as well as the Central Office for South Vietnam (COSVN), the political headquarters of the National Liberation Front. At the time of the operation only two battalions of Viet Cong main forces were confirmed to be in the area of operations with the possibility that an additional two might be present.[134] Tay Ninh province was thoroughly penetrated by the Viet Cong and lay outside of South Vietnamese governmental control.

BIRMINGHAM was an important operation with the potential of severely crippling the Viet Cong in a politically and strategic significant area. The 1st Infantry Division was experienced and aggressively commanded. If any unit could effectively apply the American theory of victory in a potentially pivotal battle, it was the Big Red One. It was acknowledged that the Viet Cong could exercise any one of several options including a withdrawal across the Cambodian border or the waging of diversionary attacks by a regimental-sized force in any of four provinces, but there was always the chance that 'Mr Charles' would be forced to defend his positions, offering battle on American terms.[135]

In concept, BIRMINGHAM consisted of a series of interlocking battalion-sized sweeps from temporary base camps established during the initial phase of the operation. As planned, the operation was to have consisted of five distinct phases.[136] As executed, many changes in areas of operation and lines of advance were ordered to take advantage of the fluid tactical situation.

The operation terminated on D + 22 (16 May 1966) having had no major contact with the Viet Cong forces believed to be in the areas of operation.[137] There had been repeated light contact as well as the discovery and seizure or destruction of much materiel and many facilities and structures. There was disappointment in the failure to locate the COSVN headquarters complex even though a long-range reconnaissance patrol had penetrated close to this objective.[138]

Although hampered by deteriorating weather, which included prolonged, abnormally heavy rains, the Division's artillery provided continuous fire support including area interdiction, harassment and interdiction, directed fire and pre-planned missions.[139] During the operation 69,997 rounds were fired.[140] Air support was used heavily with a total of 1,046 sorties of which 115 were identified as close air support.[141] Altogether 384 tons of high explosive, 440 tons of napalm and 35 tons of fragmentation bombs were delivered along with 203 cluster-bomb canisters, 17 tons of white phosphorus and 48 Zuni rockets with the result that 9 Viet Cong were confirmed killed and 106 bunkers and structures were destroyed.[142]

The Air Force and Army aviation provided the logistic support without which the Division could not have undertaken the required rapid redeployments and sustained operations. The Air Force provided 716 sorties of C–123 and C–130 tactical airlifters delivering over 7,800 tons of supplies to the Division's forward airstrip.[143] Army helicopters flew 14,633 sorties, carried 29,496 passengers and over 3,900 tons of cargo during the operation.[144]

The 1st Division lost 56 killed and 324 wounded in exchange for 118 confirmed Viet Cong fatalities and the capture of 28 Viet Cong, 162 suspected Viet Cong and 130 weapons as well as the destruction of a wide variety of supplies including 2,103 tons of rice, 13,949 shirts, 175 bicycles, 3 typewriters and a printing press.[145] The materiel and facilities destroyed looked impressive when presented on an inventory list but did not impair the ability or will of the Viet Cong to continue to operate effectively in War Zone C or the nearby Michelin rubber plantation any more than the expenditure of 1,295,889 gallons of fuel and 318,643 individual rations impaired the capability and will of the US to continue operations.[146]

The Division commander declared BIRMINGHAM to have been 'another highly successful operation' and asserted 'possibly no other operation in Vietnam has accomplished such extensive damage to Viet Cong logistics and base systems.'[142] There can be no doubt that a significant number of bunkers, caches, buildings and trenches were destroyed, their replacement required only labor and time. The Viet Cong had both.

The most experienced Army unit in South Vietnam was the 173rd Airborne Brigade. When it undertook operation HOLLANDIA on 9 June 1966, it had been in-country just over a year. The Brigade's eight-day visit to the Long Hai peninsula in Phuoc Tuy province on the seacoast in III CTZ east of Saigon was officially described as being both a search and destroy and a clear and secure operation.[148] The area of operation was believed to contain elements of 860th Local Force Battalion.[149] Over the course of the operation the Brigade experienced seventy-six contacts with the Viet Cong of which forty-seven were initiated by the enemy.[150] The Brigade operated with its accustomed aggressiveness but without any positive results.

The Viet Cong used their terrain familiarity with skill, choosing to initiate contact under favorable conditions and fading into the bush when the advantage lay with the Americans.[151] A total of 2,267 helicopter sorties were flown; the Brigade artillery and heavy (4.2 inch) mortar units fired 3,244 rounds; 9 Americans were killed and 68 wounded.[152] The Viet Cong suffered four confirmed killed and four captured.[153] One US M–1 rifle, one US M–1 carbine, one US .45 pistol, one 'Chicom automatic rifle' and a small miscellany of munitions were seized.[154] By any standards the operation was completely unsuccessful. The Brigade's commander commented that in difficult terrain, local knowledge was the key to success. This commodity was possessed solely by the small, well led Viet Cong force on the peninsula. The stranger making a sweep would find his blows landing on air and his units becoming large, noisy targets.

The 1st Infantry Division went back to War Zone C on 2 June 1966. It would stay for three months in an interlocking series of search and destroy operations called EL PASO II/III.[155] The last time the Big Red One had fought in War Zone C in Operation BIRMINGHAM, the results had been unimpressive. Now, working with new intelligence, it was hoped that the Division and attached ARVN units would be able to verify the presence of several Viet Cong and PAVN formations and, in the process, find and destroy facilities, fortifications and materiel.

The initial sweep by the 1st and 3rd Brigades resulted in fourteen significant engagements between 8 June and 9 July. Of these, at least four were on Viet Cong initiative.[156] The most important of these, the Battle of Srok Dong on 30 June, resulted in a major defeat for the 271st Main Force Regiment.[157] The 3rd Battalion of that unit attempted to ambush an armored infantry task group at 9:30 on the morning of 30 June. All four tanks were disabled by recoilless rifle fire during the first thirty minutes of the battle, but the defenders responded with heavy 50–caliber and personal weapons fire while calling in air strikes and artillery support. When the Americans were able to establish a defensive perimeter, the Viet Cong commander made a fatal mistake by not breaking off the failed ambush attempt and executing a withdrawal through the heavy brush which lined both sides of the road.

The Division had reacted quickly during the early stages of the engagement, moving two companies by air and ground to reinforce the defensive perimeter and to conduct counterattacks. Additional forces were sent to establish blocking positions and ambush sites along the likely avenues of Viet Cong withdrawal. During the afternoon six full battalions as well as an artillery battery were prepared and moved to exploit the new opportunities. Over the next two days these forces attempted to find and destroy the withdrawing Viet Cong but without success.

The ambushed unit had been saved and the attacking Viet Cong defeated by overwhelming American firepower. Eighty-eight close air support sorties had been flown by the US and South Vietnamese air forces delivering forty-two tons of high explosive, forty-eight tons of napalm, twelve tons of cluster bomb units and one hundred and sixty rockets with great effect and accuracy.[158] Timeliness and accuracy of the air strikes had been assisted by luck: there was a preplanned strike in progress only a few kilometers away so strike and forward-control aircraft were immediately available. Artillery fire was controlled from the defensive perimeter and delivered 825 rounds of 155mm from the time of contact until dark fell at 7:00 p.m.[159] Helicopter gunships were active and delivered fire to within 25 meters of friendly positions. The Viet Cong had been defeated: 270 confirmed killed, 40 personal and 23 crew-served weapons recovered and 7 prisoners taken.[160] The number of weapons recovered was unusually large and serves to verify the always suspect body count.

The Viet Cong had used their initiative to attempt the classic guerrilla coup, the ambush. The location was well chosen and the original results good. The arrival of tactical aircraft and the success of the defenders in establishing a defensive perimeter should have cued the Viet Cong commander to execute a preplanned breaking of contact and withdrawal. His failure assured the defeat and virtual destruction of his unit.

There were four other significant engagements during the first several weeks of EL PASO II/III. On 8 June an armored cavalry unit of the Division spoiled an ambush planned by the 272nd Main Force Regiment when a forward air controller spotted the Viet Cong. In the course of a four-hour engagement, the armored unit reinforced by an infantry battalion and an ARVN mechanized unit inflicted either 93 or 105 confirmed kills on the enemy and captured weapons including a 57mm recoilless rifle.[161]

On 11 June a heliborne sweep of the Loc Ninh rubber plantation resulted in contact with a battalion of the 273rd Main Force Regiment emplaced in heavily fortified bunkers and trenches.[162] The encounter was developed in complete conformity with the tactical principles laid out in the Field Manual on counterguerrilla operations. Additional infantry and reconnaissance elements were quickly airlifted to the site of contact and deployed to fix the Viet Cong in their positions. Air strikes were used as a blocking method. After a thorough artillery preparation culminating in a 'sixteen volley bombardment,' an infantry assault completely overran the Viet Cong position.[163]

The action lasted a total of eight hours. The Americans lost thirty-three killed. There were ninety-eight confirmed Viet Cong dead.[164] A 60mm mortar, one Second World War German machine gun and a Russian SKS carbine were captured.[165]

The final significant action of EL PASO II/III occurred on 9 July when the 272nd Main Force Regiment which had been roughly handled in the abortive ambush on 8 June was lured into attacking an armored cavalry task group on the Minh Tranh road.[166] The 1st Brigade evolved a complex plan involving a simulated air assault and a B–52 ARC LIGHT strike to induce the target Viet Cong unit, considered to be the elite regiment of the 9th Viet Cong Division, to attack what appeared to be a road mobile unit operating in conjunction with the air assault.

The ambush site was compromised to the oncoming American tanks when Viet Cong troops were observed crossing the road. An incorrect reading of the Viet Cong positions resulted in inaccurately aimed artillery fire, but with the assistance of air strikes, the armored column was able to defend itself as reinforcements were airlifted to a nearby landing zone. Around 1:30 p.m., approximately ninety minutes after first contact, the Viet Cong attempted to disengage, but their lines of withdrawal were bracketed by the reinforcement infantry units. Additional units were airlifted to join the running engagement which continued until dark. The next day the American forces took up the chase with minimal results. Ambassador Henry Cabot Lodge enthusiastically informed the President of the success along the Minh Tranh road and concluded that the battle constituted 'a tremendously important development.'[167] Lodge overstated the case drastically.

The 272nd Regiment had suffered a second major defeat with 239 confirmed dead and the seizure by US forces of 13 crew-served and 41 individual weapons.[168] Almost overlooked in the American euphoria of victory was the unpleasant reality that the Regiment had apparently made good the casualties from its defeat a month earlier and that the unit's will to combat had not been sapped by that setback. While the American concept of operation had been well founded and carefully developed, it would not have worked if the Viet Cong were as demoralized by previous combat as might be assumed from the Goure reports.[169] It was unlikely that the second defeat served to destroy or demoralize the 272nd Regiment even if it did complicate problems of manpower and materiel replacement.

In addition to a good plan, the US victory was dependent upon artillery and air strikes which were credited with inflicting over half of the fatal casualties. In the engagement, the position of friendly forces was easily defined; the forward air controllers had no difficulty calling in 'massed 155mm and 8-inch fires,' and the pilots of the ninety-six fighter-bombers giving support had no questions about where to deliver their ordnance.[170] Provided the Viet Cong would accept battle on terms dictated by the Americans, the superiority of US firepower would assure a very high probability of an American victory.

The balance of the operational period was uneventful. EL PASO II/III constituted a major campaign not only in duration but in effort. A total of 3,955 close air support sorties were flown during the operation delivering 1,581 tons of high explosive, 827 tons of napalm, 171 tons of cluster-bomb units and 1,322 rockets.[171] Divisional heavy artillery batteries fired nearly 15,000 rounds of 155mm and 9,500 rounds of 8-inch during the operation.[172] The lighter guns organic to the individual brigades delivered a far greater, but unstated, number of rounds. The operation was a triumph of American logistics: nearly two million gallons of fuel, nearly four thousand tons of rations, nearly three thousand tons of ammunition and almost a thousand tons of other supplies were delivered to the troops or expended.[173]

American losses included 125 killed and 424 wounded, and the destruction of three armored personnel carriers, one tank and two helicopters.[174] The Viet Cong losses comprised 825 confirmed dead, 38 captured and 1 rallier as well as the loss of 154 individual and 44 crew-served weapons, 1,500 tons of rice, 1,000 gallons of kerosene, 275 tons of salt, 175 tons of fish and a wide variety of other supplies.[175]

One disappointment was evident within the usual inventory of damage done the Viet Cong. The division had employed what it considered to have been a major psychological warfare campaign during the operation. The effectiveness of the psychological warfare effort should have been enhanced by the several obvious American tactical victories. There should have been a sizable number of defectors as a result of defeat and propaganda. There was only one (or perhaps two) rallier(s) and he was a low-level member of a local force unit.[176] The Viet Cong troops were not noticeably demoralized and ready to surrender to the Americans or rally to the Government by the end of EL PASO. The Americans would have to return to War Zone C.

While the 1st Infantry Division was engaged in EL PASO II/III, the 2nd Brigade of the 25th Infantry Division went out between 13 June and 4 July on operation SANTE FE, a search and destroy mission in Hau Nghia province immediately west of Saigon.[177] The area of operation was believed to contain several small units of the local forces and the part-time militia. There were no main force units present, but the local force platoons had shown an aggressive predilection by planting mines, placing roadblocks, firing at ARVN units and attacking American ambush teams. The local force guerrillas demonstrated the same degree of aggressiveness during Operation SANTE FE.[178]

The American task force comprising a battalion of infantry and attached reconnaissance, supply and artillery units was defeated by the local force guerrillas. The Wolfhound Task Force killed four Viet Cong and captured eighty-six suspected guerrillas.[179] The Americans lost fourteen men killed, thirty wounded and fourteen weapons.[180] The commander asserted that the task force 'through a balanced combination of tactical opns [operations] and civic action programs was able to dominate the terrain and population.'[181] This was not supportable by either the results or the daily record of the task force. If the Viet Cong would not accept the American way of war, they could not be brought to battle and defeated by it. The simple fact that villagers expressed appreciation for medical care and gifts of toothpaste and soap did not justify the comfortable assumption that they had become born-again Saigon supporters or firm friends of the Americans.

The peripatetic 173rd Airborne Brigade was busy in the bush. On 9 July the Brigade terminated Operation YORKTOWN and immediately launched another search and destroy mission. This action, dubbed Operation AURORA I, would last eight days and would take the Brigade into Tuc Trung in northern Long Kanh province near the boundary between II and III CTZ.[182] The operation was foreseen to be a routine deployment against minimal opposition and with little likelihood of significant contact or results. There were twenty-seven contacts during AURORA I, seventeen of which were initiated by the Viet Cong; most of these were 'minor.'[183] During the operation Brigade helicopters flew 2,241 sorties while the Air Force supplied nineteen tactical sorties delivering fifteen tons of ordnance.[184] Brigade artillery fired 193 missions sending 2,415 rounds downrange.[185] The Brigade provided MEDCAP services in eleven villages for a total of 1,161 contacts. Medical outreach and twenty thousand leaflets constituted the Brigade's total civic action program during the operation.[186]

The commander viewed AURORA I in which no Americans and five Viet Cong were killed as a 'valuable training vehicle' for the 4th Battalion of the 503rd Regiment which had recently arrived in country.[187] No claims were made for success and this modesty was well warranted. AURORA I was neither a success nor a failure in the military sense; its effect upon the civilian population cannot be gauged. It is impossible to assess whether the cursory medical services were outweighed by the dislocative effects of artillery and air strikes. It is otiose to speculate how the peasants viewed the passage of 'The Herd,' a strange group of interlopers who blew into town unannounced one day and were gone just as fast.

Without a pause the 173rd went from AURORA I in Long Kanh province to AURORA II in Phuoc Long province to the north.[188] Once again the expectations were minimal, and these expectations were almost met by the twenty-seven contacts, eighteen of which were Viet Cong-initiated, over the seventeen days of the operation.[189] Two helicopters were lost on the 3,450 sorties flown during the exercise.[190] The firepower expended during the operation was moderate with only 20 tactical air sorties and 549 artillery fire missions.[191] The most significant use of air and artillery fire occurred on 23 July, six days into the operation, when twenty-five small sampans were observed, taken under fire and sunk.[192] Civic action again consisted of MEDCAP and leaflets. 897 medical contacts were made, leaflets were dropped on two occasions and an assortment of foodstuffs was distributed.[193]

The commander did not see AURORA II as having been useful even as a training vehicle. There were no American fatalities. The Viet Cong lost three killed and two captured; one M–1 carbine was recovered.[194] Eight tons of rice and a ton of coffee beans were destroyed along with the sampans. Once again 'The Herd' had crashed through with no apparent useful effect. No one stayed to ask the peasants their opinion of the American ritual of passage.

The 1st Brigade of the 101st Airborne Division undertook a major set of interlocking search and destroy operations dubbed JOHN PAUL JONES in Phu Yen province on the seacoast of II CTZ not far from Qui Nhon city between 21 July and 5 September.[195] In addition to search and destroy sweeps, the Brigade was to seize and hold vital terrain along National Route 1 near Vung Ro pass and to be prepared to exploit opportunities developed by three ARC LIGHT strikes by a total of forty-two B–52 strategic bombers. The terrain seizure and consequent search and destroy sweeps occurred without incident or major contact. The ARC LIGHT exploitation sweeps were likewise without major contact or result. Only after 16 August did Brigade sweeps yield any major contact with the Viet Cong forces believed to be in the area of operations.[196]

Between the B–52 bombings, tactical air strikes, helicopter gunships, artillery and infantry action, the Brigade reported a PAVN/VC body count of 209. There were eleven PAVN and twenty-nine Viet Cong troops captured along with a number of weapons including nineteen Mauser rifles, thirteen AK–47 assault rifles, six M–1 carbines, one M–16 and five RPD light machine guns.[197] American losses were 23 killed and 132 wounded.

In the area of civic action, the Brigade 'expedited the return of 1,354 refugees to GVN control.'[198] There was concern regarding the number of refugees generated by units operating in the field as this overloaded South Vietnamese refugee-handling capabilities. The refugee situation had not really changed since the 173rd Airborne Brigade had first expressed concern after Operation CRIMP. Large combat sweeps produced large numbers of refugees whether they were voluntary or forced evacuees. The refugee streams overwhelmed South Vietnamese facilities and became a permanent, semi-floating mass of exploitable discontent despite the Government's 'Back to the Village' campaign. Large-scale search and destroy sweeps and the requirements of successful pacification and nation building remained antipodal.

In this operation the 1st Brigade commander showed that he understood the tactical requirements for military success. He commented on the importance of moving units as large as company-size at night so as to clandestinely infiltrate a presumed enemy area of concentration. He argued against routine nocturnal harassment and interdiction artillery fire missions. He emphasized the utility of small 'stay behind' parties which could keep the swept enemy base areas under surveillance for several days after a search and destroy operation and call in either an air strike or a heliborne assault in the event the Viet Cong returned. He recommended that landing zones not be routinely prepared by air strikes and artillery fire as this obliterated surprise along with trees and bush.[199]

The intelligence catch during the operation was quite significant. Not only had the presence of two PAVN units been confirmed, which in itself was noteworthy, but the observations showed the Viet Cong and PAVN were both well-motivated and equipped for the type of war they intended to fight.[200] The enemy had deficiencies in medical supplies and were particularly vulnerable to malaria, but this did not materially cripple combat capability.

Of interest, although not commented upon in the after-action report, was the nature of many of the weapons captured: they were elderly. The Mauser rifles dated back to at least the Second World War while several of the others came from French forces of pre-1954. The implication that these weapons were captured in a cache or from second-line local forces is unavoidable as is the further ramification that the first-line PAVN and Viet Cong were well supplied with weapons of more recent vintage whether of Communist Bloc or American manufacture. It would have been legitimate to conclude that neither morale nor materiel had been impaired to any meaningful extent by either US ground or air operations after eighteen months of escalation.

'The Herd' was back on the search and destroy trail on 26 September where it would stay until 9 October. The area of operations was northwest of Xom Cat in III CTZ and the operation was SIOUX CITY, a component of a larger II FFORCESV sweep against PAVN and Viet Cong main force units and installations in the CTZ.[201] As was usual in 173rd Airborne Brigade operations, activities were conducted in an aggressive manner, well supported by heliborne mobility, organic firepower, armor and preplanned air strikes: 4,731 helicopter sorties, 8,611 artillery rounds, 17 tanks and 289 tactical air sorties.[202] A total of 2,300 pounds of CS tear gas was employed on three occasions, utilizing helicopters as the delivery system.[203] Results on the target were undetermined as no US ground troops followed up the chemical strikes although several fighter-bomber pilots reported ill effects when overflying the sites.[204]

The results of SIOUX CITY were unimpressive. Contact had been light and usually Viet Cong-initiated; American fatalities were greater than those suffered by the Viet Cong. The guerrillas had made very effective use of mines and booby traps while snipers had both slowed the tempo of American operations and caused the use of large volumes of fire on unimportant targets.[205] While the Brigade listed a superficially impressive inventory of destroyed enemy materiel, the commander accurately surmised that 'the VC will continue to use this area until it is saturated with permanent friendly military elements.'[206]

SIOUX CITY illustrates all the basic defects in the American theory of victory. The operational doctrine focused upon the destruction of materiel and the disruption of enemy organizational integrity. Neither of these could be accomplished in a way which would permanently diminish either the will or the capacity of the Viet Cong and PAVN to continue the war. American doctrine capitalized upon the inherent strengths of US forces, mobility and firepower, rather than seeking to identify and exploit intrinsic weaknesses of the enemy. Search and destroy was something that could be done; not something which should be done.

The Viet Cong or PAVN could neutralize the American proficiencies by proper use of their innate tactical initiative and by employing such simple expedients as snipers and mines. Snipers could slow sweeps to the proverbial snail's pace and, as the 173rd's commander observed, could threaten tanks to the point that he considered their use inappropriate.[207] The effect of the US operations upon the rural population was negative as search and destroy sweeps served to disrupt and dislocate the lives and social/economic structures of the inhabitants, and the liberally employed heavy firepower placed lives and property in jeopardy. It is doubtful that either effect did much to mobilize rural support for Saigon. The United States was being outthought rather than outfought: the operational doctrine of the Viet Cong and North Vietnamese was successfully attempting to identify and exploit the innate weaknesses of the American way of war.

Armored forces were employed in late 1966 on search and destroy missions despite their marginal utility in that role and their major irrelevance to an opponent whose tactical and operational doctrine made little use of roads and much use of trails impassable for tanks and armored personnel carriers. From 7 to 15 October the 3rd Squadron of the 11th Armored Cavalry Regiment conducted Operation HICKORY, a search and destroy sweep near Bien Hoa north of Saigon.[208] Some of the difficulties experienced by the Squadron such as problems in land navigation and poor judgement regarding the load-bearing capabilities of wet soil were not surprising as HICKORY was its first operational employment, but others such as the lack of a good road network were endemic to South Vietnam and served to limit severely the utility of tanks and armored personnel carriers.[209]

From 11 to 14 October the Squadron engaged in its major task during the operation, securing and retrieving a rice cache at Phu Hoi. The only major contact occurred on the 14th when a dismounted patrol was ambushed. In the ten-minute firefight which ensued, seven Viet Cong and one American were killed.[210] Two hundred tons of rice and several mines were captured and several tunnels and bunkers were destroyed.[211]

The entire operation was slow in tempo and dubious as to merit. Contact had been light except for the Viet Cong ambush of a dismounted patrol. The major reason for the slow pace of movement was the unsuitability of the terrain for armored employment. The commander noted that it had taken as long as three days to retrieve mired tanks. The employment of mines and sniper fire by the Viet Cong had contributed to the retarded rate of execution. The enemy had not opposed the Squadron's advance with ambushes or nocturnal attacks upon lagers, but this was scarcely surprising given the nature and size of the force.

The commander commented on the need for armored units to have attached infantry to conduct patrols in dense brush and other terrain not suitable for tanks and armored personnel carriers. He also expressed frustration at the problems of using the heavy firepower organic to the Squadron against the local force guerrillas he had faced as 'his tactics of using the local population for cover places a definite need for restraint on the part of the commander.'[212] The importance of that consideration moved the commander to recommend the evacuation to refugee centers of the entire population of two villages as they 'are VC controlled and serve as cover for the VC.'[213]

US ground forces returned to War Zone C in fits and starts during the ten-week course of Operation ATTLEBORO. This was an operation which grew as the illusion of opportunity presented itself between 14 September and the end of November. The major US units employed were the 196th Light Infantry Brigade which had arrived in South Vietnam the preceding month, the 2nd Brigade of the 25th Infantry Division and the 173rd Airborne Brigade; the major opponent was the 9th Viet Cong Division whose three regiments, the 271st, 272nd and 273rd had last seen combat in June and July against the US 1st Infantry Division during Operation EL PASO II/III.[214] Command of the operation started under the 196th Brigade, was transferred to the 1st Infantry Division on 5 November and one day later was assigned to II FFORCESV. As far as is known, the Viet Cong command structure did not change.

Air support for the operation was substantial. The 196th Infantry Brigade received 1,029 tactical sorties and, following initial contact with the 9th Viet Cong Division, eleven B–52 ARC LIGHT strikes.[215] The 2nd Brigade received an additional 233 tactical sorties and the 173rd during its twenty days with ATTLEBORO received thirty-nine tactical sorties.[216]

Artillery was employed liberally. The 196th reported 13,000 fire missions with a total expenditure of nearly 73,000 rounds.[217] The 2nd Brigade contributed an additional 4,100 missions and 24,000 rounds and the 173rd a further 719 missions and 4,600 rounds.[218] A more effective killer of Viet Cong than the air strikes, the artillery was attributed with seventy confirmed kills by the 196th, thirty-nine by the 2nd Brigade and none by the 173rd.

The operation developed slowly with September being a month of unproductive sweeps. In October the Brigade shifted its focus to a new area prompted by intelligence reports of lucrative Viet Cong logistics complexes. These reports were substantiated and a number of supply dumps were captured and destroyed. Contact with the Viet Cong remained light and sporadic, snipers and mines being the primary form taken.

On 3 November heavy contact finally occurred with the indications that the Viet Cong unit was of the main forces. This was substantiated the next day when three company-strength assaults were made on the Brigade's positions by the 271st and 273rd Main Force Regiments. These were repulsed with the Viet Cong leaving forty dead behind.[219] Shortly after midnight on 5 November, the 272nd Main Force Regiment which had been reported virtually destroyed as a result of twin defeats at the hands of the 1st Infantry Division during EL PASO II/III mounted a heavy and well-coordinated attack which was beaten back at high cost to the attackers.[220] Later that day elements of the 196th Infantry encountered portions of the 271st and 273rd Main Force regiments in fortified positions. The Viet Cong executed frontal assaults against the US units which allowed the majority of their forces to withdraw but with the heavy cost of 123 dead.[221]

The operational area was now expanded to include all of War Zone C and the 2nd Battalion and 173rd Airborne Brigade was assigned to ATTLEBORO to help exploit the opportunity presumed to exist now that the 9th Viet Cong Division had taken such heavy casualties in its attacks against the 196th Brigade. Possibly the long-festering sore of War Zone C could finally be cleansed. The American commanders undoubtedly hoped that the Viet Cong main and local forces would have no choice except to resist the penetration into their long-standing sanctuary.

The hopes were not to be realized. The 196th Brigade reported no reaction by main forces, which were presumed to have been so drained that they had gone to ground to recuperate. Local forces continued to harass the Americans with sniper fire and mines but did not attempt to prevent the seizure of further caches and dumps by the American force.[222] The experience of the 2nd Brigade was similar: minor sniper fire, probes and mines which cost time and blood but did not prevent the detection and destruction of several camps and many stockpiled supplies.[223] The battalion from the 173rd Airborne Brigade had an identical experience.[224] There was to be no final, decisive combat in War Zone C.

Heavy losses were reported for the 9th Viet Cong Division. The inventory of supplies and facilities captured or destroyed made for impressive reading, but the enemy had already demonstrated a skill at rapid recovery.[225] It could be hoped that replacing the supplies would add to the overstressing of the lines of supply from the North, place too many additional demands upon the North Vietnamese infrastructure and make the ongoing air war more effective. It might be supposed that the 9th Viet Cong Division had been demoralized by its unsuccessful attacks. It might be possible that the additional exactions placed upon the peasants for manpower and supplies would alienate them from the guerrillas. There were many possibilities, but the only reality was that somebody would have to go back to War Zone C again.

The 4th Battalion of the 503rd Infantry Regiment left the majority of the 173rd Airborne Brigade finishing Operation SIOUX CITY and executing Operation WACO and went north to Danang in I CTZ for a fifty-eight-day search and destroy operation, WINCHESTER, in cooperation with an armored element of the 1st Marine Division and a Combined Action Company to provide an additional intelligence capability.[226] For seven weeks the Battalion conducted aggressive patrols in an area believed to be used by at least one Viet Cong main force battalion of four hundred men plus two local force companies. In addition, a main force 'sapper' battalion was believed to be located just south of the area of operations.[227] There was ample justification for the expectation of significant contact and results.

The reality was seven weeks of heat and dust, much movement and little action; the boredom of endless tension which marked days and months in which the enemy refused to be found, fixed and destroyed. The Viet Cong initiated sixty-nine incidents, virtually 100 per cent of the contacts. The majority of the incidents were small arms and mortar sniping, followed by mines and booby traps.[228] There were five small-scale attacks or ambushes and one serious mortar attack. It was the lowest of low-intensity guerrilla wars.

Two Americans died and thirty were wounded; four Viet Cong were killed, and four were taken prisoner.[229] There were no important seizures of enemy materiel nor were there any significant facilities destroyed. The Battalion conducted some civic affairs projects among the 20,000 people living in the area of operations including MEDCAP, the provision of food, clothing and building materials and the distribution of 118,000 leaflets.[230] No finding, no fixing, no destroying, no seizing, no demoralization, at least among the Viet Cong, but the operation was declared a success by its commander.[231]

Operation WINCHESTER demonstrated once again what happened when the Viet Cong or PAVN correctly used their inherent tactical initiative to evade major contact. A contemporaneous search and destroy operation, ATLANTA, executed by the 11th Armored Cavalry Regiment confirmed the overwhelming superiority of US firepower when the enemy could be induced or forced to fight according to the American doctrine. The Regiment was directed to open lines of communication in Bien Hoa, Long Khanh and Phuoc Tuy provinces using both search and destroy and ROADRUNNER missions. Intelligence estimates indicated the presence of three Viet Cong main force regiments as well as an artillery battalion and the 5th Viet Cong Division headquarters for a total of just over five thousand men. Local force units with an additional one thousand troops had also been identified as being within the areas of operation.[232] The likelihood of significant contact was high, provided the enemy could be provoked or forced into battle.

Search and destroy missions had yielded little result and the first month of the operation passed without noteworthy incident. That changed on 21 November when a convoy escorted by nine Armored Cavalry Assault Vehicles was ambushed on National Highway 1 between Bien Hoa and Xuan Loc.

The convoy commander received warning of the ambush from Regimental Intelligence when his own vehicle was less than one thousand meters from the intended killing zone. When the convoy was roughly halfway through the zone Viet Cong recoilless rifle fire hit four trucks causing them to catch fire and stop so as to block the road. The front half of the convoy was escorted safely past the ambush and the escorting ACAVs turned back to assist the trapped portion. The 11th Cavalry's Aviation Platoon provided timely support to the trapped vehicles, delivering 42 rockets and 50,000 rounds of 7.62mm. The heavy volume of ground- and helicopter-delivered fire broke the ambush and the Viet Cong withdrew so rapidly that a 57mm recoilless rifle and AK–47 assault rifle were left behind with the bodies of thirty guerrillas.[233] Friendly losses included seven killed, two ACAVs and four 2.5-ton trucks destroyed.[234]

On 2 December another of the Viet Cong main force regiments tried to ambush a resupply convoy at 4:40 p.m. The convoy of 2.5-ton trucks was escorted by two tanks and three ACAVs. Personnel were alert to the potential of ambush because of the earlier incident as well as agent reports and infra-red detection reports from RED HAZE overflights. As a consequence, the reaction by the escorts to the burst of automatic weapons' fire was quick, correct and effective: the soft-skinned vehicles were taken from the killing zone and the escorts then returned and raked the guerrilla base of fire with 90mm canister and machine-gun fire. Within seven minutes additional tanks had left the base camp 5 kilometers away and were arriving at the scene. More tanks and ACAVs arrived over the next hour providing additional fire at the site as well as blocking avenues of withdrawal. The Viet Cong broke contact at 5:30 p.m. During the night air support in the form of fighter-bombers and an AC–47 gunship supplemented artillery in blocking and scouring the area. Ninety-nine Viet Cong dead were counted and a number of weapons including a 76mm recoilless rifle, two machine guns and a 60mm mortar were recovered. No Americans were lost.[235] Although the Regiment was incorrect in claiming that the counter ambush had destroyed the 275th Main Force Regiment as a fighting force, the action of 2 December demonstrated the awesome combat power of American doctrine and equipment under the proper conditions.

If the enemy cooperated, there was nothing wrong with the American theory of victory in ground warfare. The only real difficulty was that the enemy cooperated so infrequently in 1966.

'The Herd' faced that simple and unpleasant fact one last time that year as it went on Operation WACO, a week of search and destroy sweeps through a region believed to be used for clandestine traffic between War Zone D and the Mao Tao Secret Area.[236] The Brigade had used Long Range Reconnaissance Patrols (LRRP) prior to WACO and had established the presence of small parties of guerrillas thought to be members of local force units.[237] The execution of WACO proved a disappointment as no significant contact could be developed. There were a few small caches found and the usual snipers, small night probes and mines.[238] Five Viet Cong were killed, two captured and four weapons recovered.[239] There were no American fatalities.

The commander evaluated the operation as a good training exercise for new personnel. His characterization was accurate as was his major recommendation: the use of LRRPs as a means of harassing the guerrillas and preventing the massing of forces in an area of operation.[240] In a real sense Lieutenant Colonel Brownlee was reinventing the counterguerrilla wheel as the Marines had already been doing just what he was suggesting and the identical concept had been proven valid and valuable in Nicaragua, Malaya, the Philippines and Kenya. None the less, he should be congratulated for having stated the obvious ahead of most of his peers or superiors.

In Washington confusion over the purpose of the ground war was evident. The Ad Hoc Study Group had developed a theory of victory which used the ground operations as a force potentiator in support of the air war against North Vietnam's infrastructure and the lines of supply from North to South Vietnam. By mid-1966, the Administration was focusing upon the possibility that the Viet Cong, if not PAVN, was becoming demoralized as a result of the American search and destroy operations which were seen as inflicting large numbers of casualties upon the enemy.

Through August the demoralization effect was presented to the President as the most important benefit of the escalating US ground effort.[241] National Security Advisor Walt Whitman Rostow echoed this theme in a memorandum to the President at the end of the month. 'I'm fascinated by the weakening of the local VC in the South. Their morale is worse and their buildup seems to be leveling off (although our statistics on this are lousy).'[242]

In September it was becoming increasingly apparent that the presumed demoralization effects of ground combat had lost their appeal to the Administration. One major reason for the loss of interest was the obvious growth of a North Vietnamese military presence just north of the Demilitarized Zone and within I Corps.[243] Initially commented upon in March within MACV, the escalating PAVN presence in the uplands of northern I Corps was too large to contemplate with equanimity by late summer.[244] Coupled with this perception of increased military threat from the North was a growth in concern over the ability of the VC/PAVN to meet manpower and logistics requirements. A study completed in late August and sent to W. W. Rostow two weeks later argued that the interdiction effort had not paid off.[245]

The new primary concern was the number of Viet Cong and PAVN killed. If it was not possible to demoralize the Viet Cong and PAVN through ground combat success, and it now appeared that was the case, and if it was not yet possible to interdict supplies in a way which either meaningfully assisted the efforts in the South, it might be possible to kill our way to victory. If the Viet Cong and PAVN could be killed at a rate which exceeded their replenishment capacity, victory might be the result.

At the time of the Manila Conference in October 1966, General Westmoreland had become convinced that the North Vietnamese were pursuing a strategy of attrition. He wrote:

> The enemy has embarked on a war of attrition involving protracted guerrilla war supported by large formations of conventional troops operating from base areas and sanctuaries in difficult terrain and neutral countries. . . . He expects that he will be the victor in a war of attrition in which our interest will eventually wane. His weapons are not only military but political, psychological and economic.[246]

The General had all the components right, but he interpreted them incorrectly. The North Vietnamese were entering the war for their own goal and they intended to pursue a strategy of attrition against one of the other belligerents. That belligerent was the Viet Cong who would now be seen as both a useful tool and a potential rival. Against the United States and the South Vietnamese Government, the North Vietnamese intended to pursue the avenue to victory best called enervation, the progressive exhaustion of political will. While firepower gave the US a real advantage in a contest of attrition, all of the fundamental American understandings of war imbued the North Vietnamese with the advantage in a struggle of enervation. None the less, General Westmoreland came much closer to an accurate understanding of the emerging reality on the ground of Vietnam than did his superior at the Pentagon.

On 14 October 1966 Secretary McNamara wrote a memorandum to the President regarding his just completed trip to South Vietnam.[247] He conceded that pacification was going poorly and that enemy morale was unbroken and 'he [the Viet Cong] has apparently adjusted to our stopping his drive for military victory and has adopted a strategy of keeping us busy and waiting us out (a strategy of attriting our national will).'[248] The only bright spot was the number of enemy personnel which had been killed in the large-scale US operations.

McNamara reasoned that if the infiltration of men could be limited and if the US and allied forces could continue to kill Viet Cong and PAVN at the high rate which had been established in 1966, victory could be obtained. To this end the Secretary proposed levelling off the force strength at 470,000, constructing some type of physical barrier across South Vietnam to make interdiction more easily and completely achieved and stabilizing ROLLING THUNDER at the then current level of six thousand sorties per month.[249]

He recommended an increase in pacification efforts by dedicating at least one-half of ARVN and a portion of the US military forces to pacification, following a 'Clear and Hold' approach. It would be necessary to convince the South Vietnamese Government to undertake actions which were obviously in its own best interest but which it had resolutely resisted doing so far including ending corruption and delivering essential services to contested population areas.[250] He concluded by asserting that the US must find the solution to the Vietnam challenge by 'girding for a long war.'[251] Earl Wheeler writing for the Joint Chiefs of Staff concurred with Secretary McNamara in all respects.[252]

Robert Komer in a memorandum to Secretary McNamara, 'Vietnam Prognosis for 1967–68', written in late November 1966 viewed the nature, focus and success of the ground war in a similar fashion. 'I suspect that we have reached the point where we are killing, defecting or otherwise attriting more VC/NVA strength than the enemy can build up.'[253] Like McNamara and the Joint Chiefs, Komer engaged in musings about the statistical thaumaturgy of body counts, Viet Cong recruitment and infiltration rates. This constituted an exercise in pious hopes cloaked in the statistics of unprovable assumption which would increasingly captivate the Administration and COMUSMACV alike as all sought to measure the progress to victory and find a reliable route to that goal. Komer also considered the possibility that the US ground combat operations had caused 'the bulk of SVN's population (to) believe that we're winning the war.'[254]

After ruminating upon a number of possibilities and imponderables such as increased infiltration from the North, a reversion to guerrilla war by the Viet Cong, the political collapse of the South Vietnamese government and the effectiveness of the new pacification program, Komer looked ahead to 1967 with mixed feelings. He believed that there would be a continuation of positive trends from the ground combat operations. He was pessimistic concerning the results of the pacification and revolutionary development efforts, seeing no reason to expect a change in the flat performance of 1966. Komer asserted,

> If Westy can't clobber the large units with 470,000-odd Americans, plus ROKs, plus barriers, plus bombing, plus an even better logistics base, something unforeseeable will have happened [emphasis in original].[255]

Given that the CIA had estimated in August that there were real limits to the ability and will of the Viet Cong to continue the war even with increased Northern infiltration, Komer posited that as many as 30 per cent of the US forces could be dedicated to assisting a retrained and underemployed ARVN in the pacification program.[256] With the infusion of ARVN and American military assets, as well as the additional political stimulus given to pacification by the recently concluded multination Manila Conference, the revolutionary development and nation-building programs should be showing positive results by late 1967. To win in the South, Komer concluded, 'now that we are successfully countering NVA infiltration and the enemy's semi-conventional strategy', it would be necessary to achieve an 'increased erosion of southern VC strength.'[257]

Komer's primary interest in South Vietnam was pacification, the 'other war.' He had been appointed pacification 'czar' by President Johnson on 28 March 1966 with broad authority in directing, monitoring and supervising non-military programs.[258] He recognized the centrality of winning the war in the villages for the sympathies and loyalties of the peasant population to the achievement of American goals in South Vietnam. He should have recognized the negative effects which large-scale military operations had upon the task of pacification, but in late 1966 he had accepted completely the pervasive focus upon the killing of Viet Cong and PAVN personnel as the basic definition of victory. For Komer as for McNamara, the real war remained that of the big battalions seeking victory through attrition.

Secretary McNamara and Under Secretary of State Nicholas Katzenbach had lunch with the President on 13 December 1966. The third item on the agenda was a draft National Security Action Memorandum setting forth American strategy for the Vietnam war for 1967.[259] The American goal in the war was now expressed in terms of achieving 'a satisfactory outcome as soon as possible.'[260] The term 'satisfactory outcome' was undefined. The definition of victory was now given as three separate alternatives: forcing Hanoi to negotiate, 'weakening the VC/NVA to a point where Hanoi will opt to fade away,' and 'at a minimum, making it patently clear to all that the war is demonstrably being won.'[261] The theory of victory was to continue 'our anti-main force campaign and bombing offensive' and add increased efforts to 'pacify the countryside and increase the attractive power of the GVN.'[262] The importance of putting extra effort into pacification was underscored by Ambassador Lodge during the course of a meeting with the President in mid-December. 'The military do not think in terms of the police measures now required to achieve security in the countryside.'[263]

National Security Advisor Walt Rostow had made the same point to the President two weeks earlier in a memorandum which combined his thinking with that of Komer, Katzenbach and Cyrus Vance.[264] The familiar points of continuing the pressure on Hanoi, improving the efficiency of the interdiction effort and maintaining the pressure upon Viet Cong main force units in the South were all made. The necessity of significantly enhancing the pacification program was underscored. Rostow made another point, a point that was more salient than he perhaps recognized.

> The need to give our citizens a better sense of how to measure progress in a war of this kind. All our people have now is a bewildering statement of daily and weekly casualty figures plus accounts of occasional pitched battles on the ground and raids on the North.[265]

What Rostow wanted was a statement of the American definition of victory, a simple and unitary statement which would focus upon the goal of the war and allow meaningful measurement of progress toward or away from that goal. Not only did the public need such a statement, so also did the Administration, for it, no less than the man on the street, was barraged with a bewildering array of statistics and the sporadic, brief account of a battle or raid. The Administration needed a definition of victory so that it might put into a meaningful context the results of the theory of victory as it was implemented daily in the skies, bush and villages of Vietnam. Without a definition of victory which was relevant to and coherent with the goal of the United States in the war, it was impossible to assess progress and evaluate the need for change of policy or means of implementation.

In short, the US would continue what it had been doing. We would go on bashing the bush with the goal either of killing the enemy, of demoralizing him or, simply, of increasing the tempo of combat operations hoping to make the enemy's lines of supply more vulnerable to air attack. We would persist in bombing the North with any of a number of goals in mind. Perhaps we were bombing to induce Hanoi to negotiate, or to convince Hanoi to opt out. Maybe the bombs had as their purpose to show Hanoi the war was being won by us. Hopefully, the bombs were at least interdicting the lines of supply. In addition, the

US would again attempt to do something which had been tried often, but never with success: convince and assist the South Vietnamese government to engage in meaningful social, political and economic reforms which would build a nation and popular support alike.

The goal of the US remained diffuse. The American definition of victory in December 1966 was more ambiguous than it had been a year earlier. The theory of victory by which we proposed to achieve our goal was still predicated upon the questionable assumption that the North Vietnamese and Viet Cong were politically indistinguishable instead of representing two categorically different enemies. As a result the same operational concepts in the ground war to the South and the air war over the North that so far had yielded only defensive successes – the spoiling of the 1965 and 1966 VC/PAVN offensives – and had been counterproductive in terms of pacification would continue unchallenged. Everything was perfect and it was going to get better.

4

THE OPERATION WAS A SUCCESS BUT THE PATIENT DIED

The Ad Hoc Study Group had given priority to the use of American air power against North Vietnam and the lines of communication between North and South Vietnam, relegating ground combat to a support role. This inversion of the traditional relationship between ground and air elements of strategy was not the result of air power zealots dominating the Group. Neither was it a consequence of blind faith in the efficacy of aerial firepower. In its emphasis upon the air element, the Study Group reflected accurately an intellectual stream of depth, breadth and persistence within the Johnson Administration. Like the Administration, the Study Group focused upon air power, not because that was the instrument we should use, but because it was the instrument we could use.

The acceptance of the partisan model as applicable to the guerrilla war in South Vietnam meant that the highest priority effort was directed toward finding and interdicting the avenues by which the external sponsoring power, North Vietnam, provided men and materiel to the Viet Cong. Curtailing the flow should serve to reduce the guerrillas' morale and combat efficiency which in turn would make the tasks of creating stability and developing institutions more easily accomplished. If the partisan model did apply accurately to the Vietnam conflict in 1964, one major service the United States could provide to the Saigon government was the identification and interdiction of the lines of supply and communication.

The Taylor Report of November 1961 addressed the interlocking problems of infiltration and interdiction. The Taylor team defined the problem:

> To establish a force in Vietnam which will deny the northeast frontier bordering Laos to Communist infiltration and which will have the capability of penetrating Communist dominated areas outside South Vietnam to disrupt Communist lines of communication.[1]

Although it was known that North Vietnamese forces were present just north of the Demilitarized Zone [DMZ] and that Northern troops routinely operated in northern Laos, the precise strength, disposition and intentions of these forces were unknown.

It was assumed by the Taylor team that these forces had both the capability and intention of attacking the South and that prior to the actual conventional attack they would be used to support the infiltration of men and supplies into the South. It was also assumed that the infiltrated men and supplies had been and would continue to be central to the growing combat capacity of the Viet Cong. The team recommended the creation of a special South Vietnamese ground unit with American advisors which would seek to find and interdict infiltration routes on both sides of the South Vietnamese–Laotian border.[2] Brigadier General Edward Lansdale, who occupied an almost legendary position as an expert in counterguerrilla warfare, echoed the infiltration theme in his section of the Taylor Report, stating flatly: 'The border zone of Laos is now an area of Viet Cong infiltration into Vietnam from the Laotian panhandle.'[3]

The Taylor team did not inquire into the ability of the North Vietnamese to provide more than rhetorical assistance to the Southern guerrillas and was quite content to equate rhetoric with reality. There was no inquiry into the motivational schemata of the Viet Cong: were they seeking a unification under the dominion of Hanoi, or were they indigenous insurgents seeking revolutionary change in the South with no desire to lose Southern national identity to the Northern outsiders? Unasked questions bring no answers, so the assumption that the Viet Cong were Hanoi-controlled partisans dependent upon North Vietnam as the external sponsoring power stood as a major underpinning of US policy.

The US Military Assistance Advisory Group [MAAG] and its successor, MACV, reported upon infiltration from June 1961. For the twelve months concluding in mid-June 1962, it was estimated that between 5,100 and 8,800 personnel had infiltrated from North to South, primarily through the Laotian Corridor.[4] The argument contained in a widely circulated Rand Corporation report of August 1964 held that the quality of the men and materiel clandestinely sent to the South was far more important than the quantity.[5] The men were experienced, well-trained and highly motivated political–military leaders, while the supplies consisted of critical weapons, sabotage materials, communication gear and medical items. Without North Vietnam acting as a secure base of support and the source of trained and able leaders, the Rand analysts contended, the Southern guerrillas would have to fall back upon a smaller and less qualified leadership pool and would lack many of the necessities for war. The report asserted:

A fundamental reason for the strength, tenacity and military and political sophistication of the Viet Cong insurgents is the fact that their operations are planned, guided and supported from Hanoi. The DRV lends vital material support to the insurgency in the form of manpower, training, organization and supplies.

Thus, by providing material aid, spiritual leadership and moral justification to the insurgent cause, the DRV adds immeasurably to the insurgents' will to fight.[6]

This assessment was accepted by the Administration and military commanders without question because it reflected accurately the American belief that all guerrilla wars were of the partisan variety. Based upon a misappreciation of the post-Second World War insurgent guerrilla wars, the partisan model, as applied to the Vietnamese war, was impossible to refute. The perceived validity of the partisan model did not depend upon the quantity or even quality of infiltrated support, but upon the very existence of North Vietnam itself. At least implicitly, the only form of interdiction which would yield a truly useful result was one which removed Hanoi as a player in the Southern drama.

In spring 1964 there was evidence which indicated that North Vietnam, regardless of its rhetoric, was in no position to engage in Southern adventures. The intelligence community believed that Hanoi was in a period of retrenchment and felt no imperative to take action to extend its hegemony over Laos and South Vietnam. There had been a major agricultural crisis in the North that resulted from mismanagement, four years of bad weather and a growing population.[7] The North Vietnamese industrial base was rapidly developing but remained small and concentrated in only four centers which raised concerns among the Politburo regarding its strategic vulnerability. The North Vietnamese economy was heavily dependent upon aid and trade credits from the PRC, the Soviet Union and the Warsaw Pact nations which meant it was liable to outside pressures. There was a danger that these pressures might be exacerbated if the Sino-Soviet split worsened.[8] The North Vietnamese military was large with an army of 200,000 to 250,000 men and an 'experienced and loyal officer corps' and 'its disciplined and tightly controlled organization.'[9] What was known of PAVN deployments suggested 'a defensive posture.'[10] None of these significant structural features gave credence to the belief in significant North Vietnamese sponsorship of the Southern insurgency.

The CIA reported that North Vietnamese assistance to the Viet Cong was limited to technicians and political cadre.[11] While the North could increase its presence in the South to the extent of introducing entire PAVN units, this was thought unlikely as it would produce an American counterescalation. On balance, the CIA concluded, North

Vietnam would pursue a conservative strategy in both South Vietnam and Laos, holding on to its gains in the latter nation and depending upon the Viet Cong wearing down the will of the South Vietnamese government to continue the war so as to bring about a 'neutralist' regime. The Agency predicted that ultimately the 'neutralist' government would be operationally dominated by Hanoi.[12] The Southern insurgency benefitted from Northern rhetorical support and some material and manpower assistance. To some extent the presence of Northern political cadre polluted the insurgency, but the degree of Northern influence was not sufficient to change the character of the war from insurgent to partisan.

In summer 1964 the State Department was frankly skeptical of claims by the South Vietnamese government of General Khanh concerning the presence of PAVN formations in the South and of Peoples' Liberation Army troops in North Vietnam.[13] The MACV report of only thirty-seven Viet Cong infiltrators for the year to date was cited by the State Department as were preliminary reports that a further 180 had entered South Vietnam from Laos after May.

This State Department position was not generally accepted within the Administration. The reason for this was to be found in the continued deterioration of the political and military situation within South Vietnam.

In January and February 1964, all reports from Saigon had clearly demonstrated a continued and dramatic increase in Viet Cong-initiated actions which reached their highest level since before the coup against Diem.[14] The continued increase in the scope, frequency and competence of the Viet Cong actions had become very obvious. The reasons behind this unpleasant state of affairs were not so apparent. A strong case could be made that pervasive deficiencies within the South Vietnamese Army and Government had greased the ways upon which the Viet Cong were launching their successful efforts. In the alternative, it could be argued that while the Viet Cong were taking advantage of the precarious political situation in South Vietnam, it was Hanoi which was providing the directions and the necessities for the guerrillas to do just this.

Giving extra credence to the second interpretation was the North Vietnamese expansion of their forces and facilities in Laos. This slow, steady expansion in Laos caused concern in the Administration.[15] Also causing a degree of anxiety was the continued use of Cambodia as a sanctuary by the Viet Cong. CIA Director John McCone wrote to the President by way of Secretary McNamara:

> the GVN/US program can never be considered completely satisfactory so long as it permits the Viet Cong a sanctuary in Cambodia and a continuing uninterrupted and unmolested source of supply and reinforcement from NVN through Laos.[16]

On 14 March 1964, when the National Security Council made the decision to apply 'graduated overt military pressure,' it was generally accepted that the target of the pressure was to be North Vietnam.[17] Some anxiety existed that attacking the North directly would carry a risk of Communist Chinese intervention and this possibility exercised a distinctly inhibitory effect upon the Administration. As a result, the direct pressure option would be the last, rather than the first arrow in the American quiver. The US would attempt 'border control' activities including the use of American aircraft for interdiction efforts in Laos. In addition, 'tit-for-tat' retaliations would be executed against the North in the event of particularly egregious incidents against US installations or personnel.[18] American air efforts would be directed toward the goal of interdiction. Direct coercion of Hanoi had not yet become a policy aim.

The President signed National Security Action Memorandum 288 authorizing planning for actions against the infiltration routes in Laos and Cambodia as well as for the engagement of targets in North Vietnam. The planning efforts led to the development of CINCPAC OPLAN 37–64 which covered air and ground strikes against selected targets in Laos, 'hot pursuit' operations into Laotian border areas and 'tit-for-tat' retaliation efforts against North Vietnam by air strikes, the mining of ports and amphibious raids.

The basis was laid for a program of increasingly heavy air attacks as a sustained means of applying pressure on Hanoi. The US intended to use the sustained program of strikes against high-value North Vietnamese military, infrastructure and economic targets as the means of reducing the will and ability of Hanoi to support either the Pathet Lao or the Viet Cong and of inhibiting the North Vietnamese from taking direct military actions in either Laos or South Vietnam.[19] The initiation of this program would add coercion to interdiction as a policy goal.

The likelihood of this program accomplishing the coercion objective was dubious as the CIA reported in a Special National Intelligence Estimate in late May.[20] The only certainty was that the People's Republic of China would not become involved directly unless US troops penetrated deeply into North Vietnam.[21]

The first overt use of American aircraft outside of South Vietnam was in a reconnaissance role over the Laotian Corridor. The flights would be at relatively low altitude supplementing previously authorized U–2 flights. These flights went without incident until 5 June 1964 when a Navy RF–8 was shot down by ground fire near the town of Ban Bon in the Plaine des Jarres. The pilot was seen to safely eject and reach the ground where he was surrounded by Pathet Lao personnel.[22] The NSC agreed that it was important for the US to continue the reconnaissance flights which had detected 'a significant increase in night movement on the supply routes from North Vietnam into Laos.'[23] There was dissention over the question of attacking the antiaircraft positions in the area. Finally a compromise was achieved: future flights would be accompanied by armed escorts with instructions to return fire. The pilot, Navy Lieutenant Charles Klusmann, was returned to Saigon via Vientiane on 2 September following his escape from a Pathet Lao prison on 30 August with the aid of a Laotian purporting to be a disgruntled Pathet Lao soldier, but more likely an American agent, and contact with 'friendly guerrilla forces' on 1 September.[24]

The NSC met in July to review the continued deterioration within South Vietnam. Of particular concern was the great increase in the number of weapons reported lost to the Viet Cong by the various components of the South Vietnamese armed and security forces. The CIA reported during the first six months of 1964 the South Vietnamese had lost enough weapons, 4,700, to equip ten Viet Cong battalions.[25] The continued increase in guerrilla capabilities fueled by local recruiting and training as well as the involuntary quartermaster services provided by South Vietnamese government forces was reflected in the weekly intelligence summaries but was overshadowed by various North Vietnamese actions including the renovation of the north–south railroad below Hanoi and the improvement of all-weather roads into the Laotian Corridor which were seen by the Administration as potentially threatening.[26]

The Gulf of Tonkin Incident triggered the first application of the 'tit-for-tat' response option. The NSC held a twenty-five-minute meeting on 4 August 1964 for the sole purpose of authorizing a response to the attack by North Vietnamese patrol boats on two US destroyers operating under the DE SOTO program of electronic intelligence collection. Secretary of State Rusk asserted, 'An immediate and direct reaction by us is necessary,' for the attack had been 'an act of war for all practical purposes.'[27] Secretary McNamara informed the NSC that a total of four targets would be attacked but that a fifth had been deleted because of its proximity to China. The President asked if the North Vietnamese wanted war. Director of Central Intelligence McCone replied

> No. The North Vietnamese are reacting defensively to our attacks on their off-shore islands. They are responding out of pride and on the basis of defense considerations. The attack is a signal to us that the North Vietnamese have the will and determination to continue the war. They are raising the ante.[28]

McCone also assured the NSC that while the reprisal might cause a 'sharp North Vietnamese military reaction,' Hanoi would not 'deliberately decide to provoke or accept a major escalation of the war.'[29] McNamara's target recommendations were approved and the JCS execute order to 'conduct a one time maximum effort' was immediately dispatched.[30]

The retaliatory attack, code-named PIERCE ARROW, was delivered by fifty-nine US Navy fighter-bombers with the loss of two aircraft. Eight North Vietnamese patrol boats were reported destroyed while another nineteen were believed damaged. The Vinh petroleum depot was reported 90 per cent destroyed. There was no significant North Vietnamese response to the attack. The South Vietnamese government was reported to have been greatly encouraged by the US action. The nature of the responses was seen by some American officials as reason to believe that a resolute continuation of military pressure upon the North would redeem a situation in the South which appeared both bleak and deteriorating.[31]

Following PIERCE ARROW, the Administration decided to concentrate upon the use of Royal Laotian Air Force (RLAF), South Vietnamese and covert American aircraft under the FARMGATE and WHITE STAR operations in a carefully controlled program of interdiction-oriented attacks within the Laotian Corridor.[32] Authorization was given to US jet aircraft flying YANKEE TEAM reconnaissance missions over Laos to engage hostile aircraft and to engage in hot pursuit over South Vietnam and Thailand.[33]

In September 1964 YANKEE TEAM missions were flown at the rate of approximately one per day and provided coverage of lines of communication, supply dumps, way stations, troop movements and concentrations, military installations and infrastructure changes.[34] Despite repeated US diplomatic demarches, the Laotian government was reluctant to allow its small inventory of converted US training aircraft to be employed in attacking targets within the northern panhandle.[35] The Ambassador was authorized to inform the Laotian government:

> In summary, we would, in cooperation with the RLG, begin as soon as possible to hit the easy targets with RLAF T–28s and as operations progress, bring in [deleted] to strike more difficult targets or any extremely lucrative targets which are developed.[36]

The Ambassador was informed 'FYI' the 'overall objective of the operation would be to put increasing pressure on Hanoi and clearly indicate that we are serious.'[37] Even if the RLAF threw all its T–28s into the task, it might be doubted that Hanoi would get the message that the United States was serious.

It would take a heavier weight of attack than that which might be delivered by the RLAF or the quite modest American programs either to send signals of American resolve to Hanoi or to interfere with the complex of North Vietnamese facilities and activities within the Laotian Corridor. The North Vietnamese positions in Laos were viewed increasingly by American policy makers and military commanders as being essential to the constant improvement of the Viet Cong combat capabilities. If these facilities presented a major threat to American interests and policy goals in South Vietnam as so many in the Administration believed, then the US should attack them directly.

The Administration was caught between two perceived needs. South Vietnam needed assistance which would have a direct, immediate and visible effect upon the deteriorating military situation in the country. Political and diplomatic imperatives alike required that the US present the appearance of being reluctant to use its great military power against a small and relatively weak nation. A third factor which entered the calculus was uncertainty about the reactions of Hanoi, Peking and Moscow to an open employment of American military force on a sustained basis against North Vietnamese targets, even those located in Laos. The Administration attempted to balance these various imperatives through creative temporizing. The US would use only minimal, low-signature and plausibly deniable force within Laos.

There was a fundamental problem with the use of clandestine air power in the Laotian Corridor. If the force employed was small enough to remain clandestine, it was probably too small to be effective. This understanding probably lay behind the stance adopted by the JCS regarding the resumption of the DE SOTO program and other maritime operations directed against seaborne infiltration. During a meeting on 14 September 1964, as the President and the senior members of the Administration discussed a draft on proposed courses of action in Southeast Asia by Assistant Secretary of State William Bundy, the Chiefs indicated their disagreement with the clandestine approach being recommended for the resumption of maritime operations and air operations over Laos.[38]

In the same meeting, the Chiefs expressed skepticism concerning the Administration's 'tit-for-tat' concept as, to them, it placed too many limitations upon the nature and weight of any American response.[39] The Chiefs stated agreement with Ambassador Taylor:

> we should not purposely embark upon a program to create an incident immediately but that . . . we must respond appropriately against the DRV in the event of an attack on US units.[40]

The Administration saw that the only way to move beyond the militarily ineffective covert level of force was to await a major incident of Viet Cong or North Vietnamese creation. Then, as had been shown by the Gulf of Tonkin Incident, the US could respond openly and with a level of violence which might have significant military if not diplomatic effects upon the Viet Cong and their North Vietnamese sponsors.

On 31 October 1964, the Viet Cong attacked the air base at Bien Hoa with approximately thirty rounds of 81mm mortar fire killing four Americans, destroying five Air Force B–57 light bombers and damaging thirteen others as well as several South Vietnamese fighters.[41] The attack had been delivered against South Vietnamese aircraft which had been employed in tactical and close air support operations within South Vietnam and American aircraft which might be so employed. It had been executed by local Viet Cong forces using weapons readily available to them. It appeared to the Johnson Administration that the mortaring had been ordered by Hanoi, and an attempt was made to link the North Vietnamese directly to the attack. However, it was far more likely that the local Viet Cong commander had acted on his own volition to counter a threat which was very real and immediate to him and those under his command.[42]

The psychological effect of the attack was far greater than the material damage done. It had been comfortably assumed by General Westmoreland and his superiors that the enemy would respond in a conventional fashion, with an air attack by North Vietnamese planes upon the bases used by the US for its tactical efforts. American antiaircraft batteries with the latest surface-to-air missile, the Hawk, had been sent to protect against just that sort of threat. When the guerrillas instead attacked a base directly, it was simply not acceptable that the act had been conceived and executed as a matter of local initiative. The CIA, however, had detected no interest by the North in retaliating for PIERCE ARROW or for the use of jet aircraft in operations in the South.[43] Had the presidential election not been so close at hand and the Administration inhibited by that consideration, there can be little doubt that a retaliatory air strike would have been dispatched. The JCS recommended an extremely robust retaliation including a B–52 strike on the major military airfield near Hanoi along with fighter-bomber attacks on other North Vietnamese airfields and oil depots, followed by a sizable program of armed reconnaissance missions should be directed against the Laotian infiltration routes.[44] This package was not approved, but it was a clear indicator of the road ahead.

As has been noted, Assistant Secretary of State William Bundy and Assistant Secretary of Defense John McNaughton served as the principal architects of US policy in the fall of 1964. Their perspective on the state of play within South Vietnam and on the relationship between North Vietnam and the Viet Cong had a particularly large impact on the decisions made in the winter and spring of escalation. They commented in late November:

the basic elements of Communist strength in South Vietnam remain indigenous, the North Vietnamese (DRV) contribution is substantial and may now be growing. There appears to be a rising rate of infiltration.

We believe that any orders from Hanoi would in large measure be obeyed by Communist forces in South Vietnam. The US ability to compel the DRV to end or reduce the VC insurrection rests essentially upon the effect of US sanctions on the will of the DRV leadership and to a lesser extent on the effect of such sanctions on DRV capabilities. US-inflicted destruction in North Vietnam and Laos would reduce the elements of DRV support and damage DRV/VC morale.[45]

This assessment directed the Bundy–McNaughton, and subsequently, the Administration's theory of victory away from the seemingly intractable problems of South Vietnamese governmental and military competence to a debatably irrelevant, and dangerous, concentration upon coercing the North to end its presumed sponsorship of the Southern war, or through an interdiction effort to erode the material capacity of the North to provide effective assistance to the Viet Cong.

The force of the Northern assistance predicate of the Bundy–McNaughton thesis received support from an early-December CIA assessment of infiltration. Shortly thereafter it became the keystone of American policy. On 7 December 1964, President Johnson approved a position paper on Southeast Asia which would 'serve as guidance for our work in this field in the coming months, subject to such amendment and further development as I may approve from time to time.'[46] The first phase of implementation under the new guidelines covering actions to be taken over the next thirty days included

US air protection of Lao aircraft making strikes in the Corridor, US armed reconnaissance and air strikes against infiltration routes in Laos, and GVN and possibly US air strikes against DRV as reprisals against any major or spectacular Viet Cong action in the south, whether against US personnel and installations or not.[47]

The transition phase, to occur after the initial thirty days, included the option of low-level reconnaissance of infiltration targets in North Vietnam and the 'possible initiation of strikes a short distance across the border against infiltration routes from the DRV.'[48] After the transition phase,

if GVN improves its effectiveness to an acceptable degree and Hanoi does not yield on acceptable terms, the US is prepared – at a time to be determined – to enter into a *second phase* program, in support of the GVN and RLG, of graduated military pressures directed systematically against the DRV. Such a program would consist principally of progressively more serious air strikes, of weight and tempo adjusted to the situation as it develops (possibly running from two to six months) and of appropriate US deployments to handle any contingency. Targets in the DRV would start with infiltration targets south of the 19th parallel and work up to targets north of that point. This could eventually lead to such measures as air strikes on all major military-related targets, aerial mining of DRV ports and a US naval blockade of the DRV.[49]

The purpose of the proposed phased exercise was to provide to Hanoi (and all other interested observers) the impression of steady, deliberate resolve while maintaining a maximum degree of managerial control within Washington. Air power, unlike ground forces, was presumed to be susceptible to very precise control which would allow for fine gradations of weight, tempo and focus of attack, thus facilitating the use of force in support of policy. The US would maintain control of the options, to escalate or not, to provide pauses during which talks might be started, to closely monitor enemy actions and to modify the US effort appropriately. It was a policy of extreme rationality, and a theory of victory which played to American strengths very well. It also seemed to have the potential to protect the Administration's need to have and effectively exercise political, operational and even tactical control. Its relevance to the realities on the ground in Southeast Asia was doubtful.

As the position paper had made clear, the Laotian Corridor was to be the initial focus of increased American pressure. By early December, it had become obvious that the addition of RLAF T–28 converted trainers to the earlier FARMGATE and WHITE STAR covert attacks had resulted in no diminution of North Vietnamese or Pathet Lao activity in the area. It was time for the first openly American campaign of air attacks in Laos.

A new program, BARREL ROLL, was initiated. The first BARREL ROLL strike was delivered on 14 December 1964 by four USAF F–100 Supersabers on a bridge at Nape, Laos near the North Vietnamese border. The six 750-pound bombs dropped missed the bridge although a secondary target on Route 12 was hit with rockets and 20mm machine-cannon fire.[50] The inauspicious beginning was duplicated in the second strike by four Navy A1–H bombers on 17 December, the third strike by four Air Force F–100s on 21 December and in the fourth mission on 25 December.[51] The absence of military effect was equalled by the lack of political result. The CIA concluded that Hanoi had missed the fact that BARREL ROLL was 'the inauguration of a new and different policy.'[52] This tracked with what the Agency had estimated would be the effect of BARREL ROLL a month earlier.[53]

If the intention of the Bundy–McNaughton program was to send messages to a Vietnamese government, neither Saigon nor Hanoi had their receivers turned on during the phase one period. The BARREL ROLL sorties and other minor increases in the Laotian interdiction effort had not been noticed by Hanoi.[54] They had not exercised any positive effect upon the continual deterioration of political stability in Saigon. Through January, President Johnson was carefully briefed in a detailed manner upon political developments in South Vietnam and the baleful influence which these were having on the course of the war.[55] There was little doubt that as the center of the South Vietnamese government became less and less coherent, the success of the Viet Cong became more assured. Within the thirty days of phase one, the position of James C. Thompson, a major critic of the escalatory air war, seemed to have been proven correct.

> More fundamentally, I am struck by the basic phoniness of the escalatory options: . . . that high levels of action against the North are an act of desperation bearing little direct relationship to the problems we face in the South . . . our present Vietnam planning seems inordinately focused on how to punish the North, rather than on the intricate priority problem of how to improve our performance – and that of the GVN – in the South. I do not believe that the two problems are in any sense identical.

> This leads to a further and deeply rooted doubt, which I find shared by most of my friends who are familiar with the post war history of Vietnam: namely, a doubt that any degree of punishment which we care to inflict upon the DRV would induce them to give up their national revolutionary purpose and actions. . . . It is my impression that Hanoi will be able to bear the consequences of our northward push longer than will we.[56]

Thompson's criticisms were trenchant and salient as events through January 1965 had demonstrated. The central problem confronting the Administration was discriminating between what the United States *should* do and what it *could* do to influence the course of events in South Vietnam.

Early on 7 February 1965 (local time) the Viet Cong, after a week of 'virtual standdown' during Tet, attacked the US billeting compound and airstrip at Pleiku with mortars, killing eight Americans and destroying five aircraft.[57] A series of urgent NSC meetings were held on 6, 7 and 8 February to consider the implications of the Pleiku attack for American policy.

After the first of these McGeorge Bundy, in a memorandum to President Johnson, rehearsed all the reasons why the US must escalate the intensity of its operations over Laos and North Vietnam and provided a dismal, but realistic, appraisal of the governmental and military situation in South Vietnam. He urgently recommended both a direct 'tit-for-tat' reprisal for the Pleiku attack and its extension into a 'policy of sustained reprisal.'[58] Bundy was arguing for the immediate application of the phase two actions outlined in the position paper approved two months earlier.

When the final NSC meeting on Pleiku convened on 8 February at 10:30 a.m., Bundy's recommendations had been adopted and it was only necessary to formalize them and to gain the assent of the Congressional leadership which had been brought in for that purpose. The 'tit-for-tat' retaliatory raid had already occurred. The strike, code-named FLAMING DART I, had been executed by forty-nine US Navy aircraft, of which one was lost, against the North Vietnamese barracks complex at Dong Hoi.[59] The results were characterized at the meeting by Secretary McNamara as 'moderate to good.'[60] With this as the background, discussion on the formalization of the phase two actions, or to use McGeorge Bundy's term, 'sustained reprisal,' had come.

The President was reported to have summarized the present position:

1 Last December we had approved a program of further pressure against North Vietnam but did not initiate actions for the time being, in order to allow Ambassador Taylor a period of time in which we hoped he would be able to assist the Vietnamese in creating a stable government.

2 We are now ready to return to our program of pushing forward in an effort to defeat North Vietnamese aggression without escalating the war.

3 We were surprised by the attack on our personnel at Pleiku but we had to respond. If we had failed to respond we would have conveyed to Hanoi, Peking and Moscow our lack of interest in the fate of the South Vietnamese government. In addition, the South Vietnamese would have thought we had abandoned them.

4 There is a bad governmental situation in Saigon but it is our hope that current US action may pull together the various forces in Saigon and thus make possible the establishment of a stable government.[61]

There was an evident piece of illogic in a program which sought to defeat the North Vietnamese without escalating the war. There was an obvious irrelevance in the quest to win the war in the South by defeating the North. There was a sense of desperation in the desire that US actions against the North would serve as a stimulus to governmental effectiveness in the South. The President was less than candid in his assertion that the attack at Pleiku caught the US by surprise; if it had, there had been a breakdown not of intelligence but of command responsibility.[62] He was quite accurate about the poor political situation in Saigon.

JCS Chief Earle Wheeler described the difficulties of insuring security at Pleiku, and by implication all other bases in South Vietnam used by the US. Further details of the Viet Cong attack were provided by General Andrew Goodpaster, who along with McGeorge Bundy had just returned from South Vietnam. The President capped the presentation by adding 'we were up against highly skilled guerrilla fighters.'[63] Against this background McGeorge Bundy argued that the recent events had forced the US to act. He said that 'a rolling consensus as to the proper course of action' had emerged following his return to Washington.[64] When House minority leader Gerald Ford asked if the Administration intended merely to react to enemy provocations, the President replied that, while all Viet Cong actions called for a response, the Administration did not intend to limit its actions to those of a retaliatory nature. In this way, the President provided a nice backdoor definition of 'sustained reprisals.' It was clear what the US would be doing; none of the Congressional leaders dissented.

The formalization of the nascent air war continued on 10 February. Several salient points defining the 'rolling consensus' were obvious in the NSC meeting that day and the meeting of the principals which preceded it.[65] First, the Far East was vulnerable to Communist penetration, even domination, in the event of a perceived US defeat in South Vietnam. Second, the investment of US prestige and influence was of such a magnitude that an American pullout would have global consequences for the US. Third, with the possible exception of a ground force intervention, there was nothing the US could do in the short term which would directly and positively affect governmental stability and military effectiveness in the South. Fourth, the evil guiding genius behind the Viet Cong was Hanoi for the war was of the partisan sort. Fifth, the only actions the US could take which could have positive impact upon the situation in the South were those which had the potential of eroding the material capacity of North Vietnam to provide assistance to the Viet Cong or which might enervate the political will within Hanoi to continue the effort. From these points emerged the consensus that the best course of action was to proceed into 'Phase II' and implement a program of graduated increase in military pressure. This was the decision made during the 10 February NSC meeting.[66]

The extent to which the linkage of the war in the South to the actions and assistance of Hanoi was supported by the information available to the Administration is open to question. The intelligence reports circulated to the Departments of State and Defense and to the White

House provided ample reason to conclude that the war was running against the South Vietnamese government. There was repeated and convincing evidence of continued political deterioration within the Saigon government. Continued and increasing Viet Cong success on the battlefield was demonstrated in report after report. The intelligence record concerning the extent or the significance of infiltrated men and supplies to the improving fortunes of the Viet Cong was less clear, but tended to support the contention that the guerrilla movement was not dependent upon external sponsorship although it did benefit from outside assistance. The intelligence record was also unclear as to the nature and character of Hanoi's interest in the success of the Viet Cong: were they Hanoi's auxiliaries, or potential rivals of Hanoi for power in the South or were they simply a means of bringing about an intermediary stage of success, the neutralization of Saigon?[67]

There were close political harmonies between Hanoi and the National Liberation Front for South Vietnam (NLFSVN). Hanoi would have been gratified by an American withdrawal from the South. However, political commonality, even when coupled with geographical propinquity, did not imply automatically that Hanoi was providing significant military assistance let alone adopting the role of external sponsoring power. The NLFSVN contained within its leadership ranks an important number of genuine Southerners, and it had been developing an increasing amount of popular acceptance and support since its formation.[68] These were two factors which deserved close examination against the background of intense regional identification common in Vietnamese society. An early 1965 CIA study of the NLFSVN saw little influence from Hanoi in the growing competence of the NLF in propaganda which effectively exploited the domestic disaffection within South Vietnam. Hanoi was not seen as the reason that the NLF showed such skill in seizing the opportunities provided by the turmoil within the South Vietnamese government. Hanoi was given no credit for the competence which the NLF exhibited in effectively exercising the power and authority of a government in the areas dominated by the Viet Cong.[69] In short, the Agency saw the reasons for the political and military effectiveness of the guerrillas as arising more from Southern factors than from Northern sponsorship.

The NLFSVN and the Viet Cong were demonstrating the characteristics of an insurgent movement through early 1965. They were also demonstrating some of the attributes of a partisan group in that infiltration of men and supplies was a constant and constantly growing reality. Hard evidence of militarily significant infiltration was thin in 1964. Assessments generally agreed that the majority of guerrilla manpower and materiel came from Southern sources with the contribution from the North being limited to cadre, specialist personnel, and certain types of ordnance and equipment.[70] Both Cambodia and Laos, with their significant base camp and training areas, were larger contributors to Viet Cong military competence than North Vietnam.

The Viet Cong and NLFSVN had the capacity to operate independently of Hanoi's supplies and without regard to Hanoi's interests. At the same time the materiel and at least some of the manpower infiltrated from the North was welcomed by the Viet Cong. Depending upon how the politburo in Hanoi saw North Vietnamese goals and defined victory in achieving them, the Viet Cong could be a collaborator, competitor or disposable tool. The presence or absence of militarily significant infiltration was not a reliable cue to which role the Viet Cong were playing at any particular time.

By late 1964, evidence was accumulating that some PAVN units had infiltrated into the northernmost province of South Vietnam which would, if true and continued, change the character of the war. The initial indications came from the often self-serving and unreliable South Vietnamese intelligence services and were not given great credence. Movement of North Vietnamese troops as well as Viet Cong and Pathet Lao forces was more accurately and reliably reported from December 1964 with the introduction of US-controlled 'ROADWATCH' teams. The combination of ROADWATCH, YANKEE TEAM and BARREL ROLL provided far more reliable information on the looming first clouds of the infiltration storm yet to break.[71]

On the verge of the February NSC meetings at which the 'Phase II' programs of air attack upon North Vietnam and the infiltration routes were approved, a draft Special National Intelligence Estimate stated

> There has also been a steady improvement in the capabilities of the Viet Cong forces in South Vietnam. Some of the improvement results from stepped up North Vietnamese support, though detailed judgements are complicated by the spotty and frequently ambiguous evidence available.[72]

The same estimate noted improvements in the air defense capabilities of North Vietnam and in the PAVN and Pathet Lao forces in Laos since PIERCE ARROW and the start of BARREL ROLL. In general, the position of the Board of National Estimates was that the situation in South Vietnam was becoming increasingly tenuous, and that the reasons for this unpleasant reality were to be found in the South. This assessment was reinforced by a contemporaneous SNIE which considered the political turmoil in Saigon and the other major cities and its negative impact upon social cohesion throughout South Vietnam.[73] A strong cautionary note was introduced by the CIA on 11 February 1965, the day the US retaliated with an air strike on North Vietnam for a Viet Cong attack on an American billet in Qui Nhon the preceding day. The Agency concluded that the North Vietnamese would not be motivated 'to restrain the Viet Cong' by the initiation of the new policy.[74]

The pattern developed by all intelligence reporting through mid-February 1965 demonstrated an insurgent guerrilla conflict in which support from North Vietnam did not constitute the critical component in the successes enjoyed to date. The Viet Cong and NLF had been able to capitalize upon the pervasive weaknesses of the various governments in Saigon which had passed through with almost bewildering rapidity since the coup against Diem not quite eighteen months earlier. The chronic turmoil at the center coupled with the relative inefficiency of ARVN had given the insurgents all they needed; any assistance from Hanoi was a bonus. At the most the insurgency had been polluted by the Northern political cadre, but that pollution was not tantamount to control.

A strong argument might have been made for the proposition that the NLF/VC regardless of their original relationship with Hanoi had emerged as an independent Southern force by late 1964. As such the NLF/VC were, at the very least, immune to dictates from Hanoi and, in the view from the Politburo, might have become rivals for power in a unified Vietnam. The initiation of 'Phase II' actions against the North and the infiltration routes could have only a marginal effect, at best, on the battlefield capabilities of the Viet Cong, and carried no potential to facilitate a political solution to the war. The 'Phase II' actions held a great potential for counterproductive effects. The air attacks had the capacity to bring the North more directly and more vigorously into the war in pursuit, not of success by the Viet Cong, but of a North Vietnamese victory. The United States' policy interests would have been best served by ignoring the North Vietnamese pollution of the Southern insurgency, rather than by inviting Hanoi into the war in pursuit of its own goals. The American air war constituted an invitation best left unissued.

The intellectual myopia present within the Administration not only made the counterproductive nature of the 'Phase II' program invisible, it made the number of apparent policy alternatives seem quite limited. Through February all indications were that the situation continued to worsen.[75] The one bright spot reported from COMUSMACV was the improvement in ARVN command morale in the wake of FLAMING DART I/II.[76] The sinking of a coastal freighter laden with arms and other supplies in South Vietnamese territorial waters by a US Navy A1–H on 16 February sharply focused attention on the North Vietnamese–Viet Cong linkage.[77] The Administration also considered the possible effect upon North Vietnam of the introduction of US jet aircraft, such as the B–57s hit at Bien Hoa, into operations against the Viet Cong.[78]

On 19 February 1965 US jet aircraft were employed in ground attack missions within South Vietnam for the first time. This constituted a change in policy and might have been seen as an American escalation by the other parties in the war. The new authorization was used heavily: in Phuoc Tuy province between 19 and 28 February 146 B–57 sorties were flown delivering over 400 tons of high explosive and fragmentation bombs with mixed results.[79] The initial evaluation of US close air support and similar tactical employments in South Vietnam was generally favorable, a judgement that would remain largely accurate for the next several years.[80] Tactical successes notwithstanding, the new use of American jet fighter-bombers did nothing to alter the unfavorable overall trends in South Vietnam.

Inhibitory considerations, such as the possibility of Chinese intervention, were overridden by the apparent lack of other viable options and the long-delayed 'sustained reprisal' or 'Phase II' program was finally activated on 2 March 1965. One hundred US and South Vietnamese aircraft executed ROLLING THUNDER V against the North Vietnamese ammunition depot at Xom Bang and the naval base at Quang Khe. Five aircraft were lost in exchange for '78% damage to major structures' at Xom Bang and 'considerable damage to storage capacity' at the Quang Khe naval base.[81] This attack was followed by twelve more during the rest of March. Overall, 513 sorties were executed against seventeen targets with four restrikes against three targets. Damage ranged from none to heavy and a total of eleven more aircraft were lost.[82] The operational planning, execution and results were carefully monitored at the White House, a practice which would prevail over the next several months.[83]

Starting in the middle of March, the Administration attempted to assess the effectiveness of ROLLING THUNDER. First indications were mixed at best.[84] There was no immediate intelligence catch intimating that the program had affected either the will or the ability of the North Vietnamese to encourage or assist the Viet Cong. The US suffered some adverse diplomatic and public relations consequences. More ominously, in a memorandum to the President, DCI McCone raised a possibility which, if borne out by later developments, would severely undercut the entire basis of ROLLING THUNDER and BARREL ROLL. The Viet Cong might possess 'military strengths and capabilities greater than we have supposed as a review of the data now in process suggests.'[85]

At the NSC meeting of 26 March, McCone took an upbeat position on the effects of ROLLING THUNDER, suggesting that the bombing effort had 'greatly improved military morale and stabilized the government situation in Saigon.'[86] He acknowledged the consensus within the intelligence community that the bombing had not convinced either Hanoi or the Viet Cong that they could not win the war.[87] Secretary of Defense McNamara characterized the bombing as having been 'moderately effective from a military standpoint.'[88] He offered no proof of this assertion but did note that since the commencement of ROLLING THUNDER, Viet Cong-initiated incidents had decreased. No one challenged the validity of the correlation.

At the next NSC meeting on 5 April, John McCone modified his earlier position. He now agreed with CIA analysts who had concluded that the 'Communist position was hardening rather than the reverse as a result of the air strikes.'[89] McCone's position was reinforced three days later by a report of the United States Intelligence Board (USIB), the senior analytical component of the intelligence community. The USIB concluded that the bombing campaign had served to stimulate the Hanoi politbuJ not only to deliver diplomatic and rhetorical responses to the attacks, but to enhance the North Vietnamese military position on the DMZ, in the Laotian Corridor and in northern South Vietnam. The North had moved within weeks to match and raise the American escalation.

> This buildup in capabilities almost certainly indicates an intention
> to undertake offensive operations of greater scope and significance
> than hitherto attempted in this area. The security situation in this
> area has so deteriorated that an accelerated sustained effort by the
> VC or an attack on some key point could have grave consequences
> for the GVN.[90]

No longer inhibited by the fear of provoking an American response and with a popular political will stimulated by the lash of bombs, Hanoi could be expected to continue matching any further US escalations.[91] It could have been concluded in the first month of the new air campaign that the addition of ROLLING THUNDER to the ongoing programs of armed reconnaissance and strike in Laos had not impaired either the will or the ability of the Viet Cong to prepare for and engage in effective military action. There was no indication that Hanoi was willing, or even able, to leash the dogs of Southern war. There were many reasons to conclude that the Viet Cong and Hanoi, perhaps for quite disparate reasons, were each in the process of matching the US escalations in the air war by actions on the ground.

In response to the indications that ROLLING THUNDER was failing in its coercive thrust, the Administration adopted several proposals made by Army Chief of Staff Harold Johnson in mid-March. The General's recommendations included a reorientation of BARREL ROLL to increase the military effectiveness of the program and an increase in the tempo and scope of attacks under ROLLING THUNDER.[92] His proposals were supported by John McCone and the military command structure.[93] The BARREL ROLL program was expanded with the presumption that this would increase its effectiveness against infiltration. The decision was made to increase the tempo of ROLLING THUNDER slowly.[94] The JCS disagreed with this decision, preferring an approach they called the 'sharp knock,' implying a rapid and very violent, relatively short-duration campaign. Management of the bombing campaign would continue to rest with the Administration, and significant restrictions would continue to apply regarding munitions, targets and routing. Following a pause in the bombing program to allow damage assessment and target reconnaissance, May became the month of ROLLING THUNDER.[95]

With US troops on the ground of South Vietnam, interdiction of the flow of men and supplies had acquired a fresh urgency.[96] The increasing combat power of the Viet Cong was seen by the Administration and the commanders in the field as making the American interdiction effort the single highest priority. In April 1965 the Administration was informed by the CIA that while the introduction of US ground combat forces into the South presented a new problem for the Viet Cong and the increased use of American air power in the South had likewise challenged the flexibility of the guerrillas, 'there was no evidence that Viet Cong capability to increase military activity had been reduced.'[97]

Three weeks later, events had reinforced the initial assessment. In a memorandum that was sent to the President by McGeorge Bundy, the CIA reported in mid-May that Viet Cong-initiated incidents had surged to 542 in the first week of May, more than 100 higher than the spring 1965 average.[98] According to MACV, the Viet Cong had increased their main force strength from 39,000 to 47,000 and the presence of a battalion of the 325th PAVN Division had been confirmed in Kontum province. These data were taken by the CIA to mean that US intelligence on the ground had become more efficient in identifying the Viet Cong order of battle, that the Viet Cong were successful in their local recruiting and that the counterinfiltration operations had not yet succeeded although the attacks on the North had improved ARVN morale.[99]

With the strength and momentum available to them, it seemed likely that the Viet Cong would attempt to mount a major, perhaps decisive, offensive in the summer of 1965. This was the conclusion drawn by Dr Sherman Kent, the Chairman of the Board of National Estimates, at the end of April.

Their capabilities for enlarged military action are formidable: they have 38,000 to 46,000 hard core regulars and around 100,000 irregulars, MACV has recently confirmed the presence of a battalion of PAVN regulars with the Viet Cong and we believe that there are two more. Their concentration of forces in the northern part of South Vietnam gives them the capability of launching large scale attacks on one or more of a number of important centers or bases. In this part of Vietnam, the interior will be frequently under cloud cover during the summer rainy season. We believe, therefore that a major Viet Cong military effort is more likely to be launched against Kontum, Pleiku or some place in the interior.

If, during the next few months, the Viet Cong can pull off one or more spectacular military victories . . . the Communist effort in Vietnam would gain great momentum.[100]

US troops would be light on the ground through the early rainy season. The effectiveness of tactical air operations in the central highlands of South Vietnam would be reduced greatly by often poor weather conditions. Interdiction of men and materiel either in the Laotian Corridor or in North Vietnam was believed to have become top priority, if the possibility of spectacular Viet Cong military successes adumbrated by the Kent memorandum was to be forestalled.

Beginning with ROLLING THUNDER 12 on 28 April the weight of the attacks shifted increasingly to interdiction targets with the fixed-target strikes being directed against facilities and lines of communication associated with the perceived North Vietnamese support capacity. The targets were drawn from the JCS target list and included ammunition dumps, petroleum depots, logistics facilities and transportation-system choke points. The majority of sorties conducted from May onward emphasized armed reconnaissance over fixed-target raids. Armed reconnaissance missions were assigned a particular route or geographic area in which blanket authorization was given to engage all targets of opportunity, particularly those associated with transportation.

The White House monitored and controlled the ROLLING THUNDER program very carefully with the President receiving regular reports on the results of strikes upon both North Vietnam and Laos.[101] Occasionally, the White House modified orders as in ROLLING THUNDER 14 when the Song Chu Dam and Lock #3 were removed from the target list because the dam was used for agricultural irrigation and excluded Knon Nieu and Knon Matt Islands because it was not known what or who was on the islands.

The weight of the attacks under ROLLING THUNDER, BARREL ROLL and STEEL TIGER was heavy. For example, the Navy dispatched 154 strike aircraft on ROLLING THUNDER 13 during 29 and 30 April 1965.[102] Weather and the redirection of strikes from designated targets to armed reconnaissance often reduced the number of sorties from such a high daily level, but the effort could never be described as light or its prosecution as irresolute. The reported results of the strikes varied widely from none to the presence of secondary explosions and the destruction of buildings.

The increase in bombing efforts both in the North and through the

Laotian Corridor as well as the greater emphasis upon armed reconnaissance of infiltration routes or infiltration support activities did not
have any immediate or obvious effect upon the course of the war in
the South. In a monthly CIA situation report sent by Bromley Smith, the
Executive Secretary of the NSC, through McGeorge Bundy to the
President, it was observed that 'the violence of the Viet Cong actions
was greater in May than in any month this year.'[103] Despite the bombs,
'the Viet Cong sharply intensified their activities and dramatically
shifted their activities northward' during the last few days of May.[104]
Other than the morale boost given to ARVN by news of the campaigns,
ROLLING THUNDER, BARREL ROLL and STEEL TIGER were not showing any
benefits to the troops in the South or to the policy makers in
Washington.

Another air war option was placed before the administration in mid-
June 1965.[105] It was proposed that B–52 strategic bombers be used in
raids against targets in South Vietnam. The B–52 used in tight
formations could deliver devastating attacks against Viet Cong base
complexes, destroying their networks of deep tunnels and fortified
bunkers. The psychological effect of the unheralded arrival of hundreds
of tons of high explosives dropped by planes flying too high to be seen
or heard from the ground would be as intense as the physical
destruction. Eventually this idea would be put into operation as the ARC
LIGHT program in summer 1965.

The use of B–52 bombers was expected to erode severely the material
capacity of the Viet Cong by destroying major supply dumps and
hardened base camps deep in the bush. The B–52s would allow the US
to strike directly at these critical facilities which were still beyond the
reach of ground combat forces and whose massive caches of supplies,
arms and munitions, it was believed, served to mitigate the effectiveness
of the interdiction programs.[106] In order to assure that the strikes were
targeted appropriately and to facilitate press and diplomatic liaison
concerning a program which was potentially controversial, all ARC
LIGHT missions had to be cleared through and approved by the NSC
staff.[107]

To have a real material and morale effect, it would have been
necessary for the strikes to be nominated and approved on the basis of
sound, verifiable intelligence. In reality, as was reflected by the
obviously superficial and pro forma conduct of the review and approval
process, the intelligence base for most strikes was infirm or ambiguous.
In most cases, MACV described the target area as being under Viet
Cong control so that penetration by agents or reconnaissance patrols
has been 'infrequent and difficult.'[108] Electronic intelligence, specifically communications intelligence, and infrared emissions detected by
the RED HAZE program of airborne infrared sensors in conjunction with

the often questionable MACV order of battle intelligence constituted the basis for target nomination and approval. Occasionally, pilot reports of small-arms fire were used to reinforce the request. The expected results were often described in vague or ambiguous terms. As a rather typical example, the request for a strike in An Xuyen province on 1 September, expressed as the expected result:

> it is believed that the bombing of those targets could seriously disrupt VC operations throughout the general area in addition to contributing to VC demoralization.[109]

As there were no Viet Cong units with the possible exception of a headquarters element believed to be operating in the targeted area, the anticipated result seems to have been overstated. Demoralization was repeatedly expressed as an expected result. Whether expectations were consistently realized was a debatable proposition at the time as well as later.

ARC LIGHT operational effectiveness assessments, if commonly conducted as a part of the program, were not regularly reported to the White House except in the form of routine and often misleading bomb damage assessment photography. As a result the White House was reduced to approving batches of missions usually with a one-day turnaround time and without the necessary context of operational effectiveness assessment. Far from exercising careful management of a program involving the use of very expensive specialist assets of the Air Force, the NSC staff was reduced to the hurried application of a bureaucratic rubber stamp, sometimes by telephone, to a list of missions and targets nominated on a sketchy basis.[110] In early 1966, Bromley Smith sent a report on ARC LIGHT to the President.[111] Just over 6,100 sorties in 700 missions had been flown under ARC LIGHT with 132 having been directed against the suspected locations of COSVN in Tay Ninh province. There had been an additional 86 strikes in Laos and 11 in North Vietnam. Sixty-three per cent of the missions had harassment as their objective with 15 per cent having interdiction as their primary focus.[112] The effectiveness of the program had been difficult to assess because there had been only rare follow-up by ground units.[113] The conclusion reached on the very expensive ARC LIGHT program was:

> An overall evaluation of the effectiveness of B–52 strikes must be measured in a broad abstract sense, and – from this viewpoint – there is sufficient evidence to reach the conclusion that they are contributing significantly to the war effort.[114]

Fainter praise would be difficult to imagine.

By late summer 1965, while US ground combat forces arrived in South Vietnam in ever greater numbers and the Ad Hoc Study Group was in the process of redefining the purpose of ground combat to act as a force multiplier operating on behalf of the air war, the interdiction efforts, along with ARC LIGHT operations against Viet Cong supply dumps, troop concentration areas and command centers in South Vietnam, became all the more central to the American pursuit of victory. In a major report on infiltration and the effects of the interdiction programs, the CIA came to a set of disturbing conclusions. In the area of arms, new Soviet-Bloc and Chinese weapons which had first appeared in South Vietnam only in December 1964 were entering the country in ever larger numbers, apparently as part of a plan of weapons standardization which would increase the Viet Cong firepower but make more difficult future problems of ammunition supply.[115] Much of the new weapons and their ammunition was being infiltrated by sea, and the bombing campaigns were irrelevant to the problems of interdicting a coastline more than 1,000 miles in length and used by some 50,000 junks of various descriptions.[116] Even if the interdiction programs were suddenly and mystically to stop completely the flow of new Bloc and Chinese weapons, this development would not necessarily adversely effect the combat capabilities of the Viet Cong as the majority of their arms remained of American and French origin.[117]

Regarding Laos, the Agency concluded that despite the 'strenuous efforts' of the US to stem the traffic flow through Laos by flying more than four thousand BARREL ROLL and STEEL TIGER sorties against 'vulnerable portions of the Communist truck routes,' the traffic had continued to move, 'if at a somewhat reduced rate.'[118] The North Vietnamese had been able to adjust for the effects of the interdiction campaign as they had for seasonal weather problems which closed the road network in whole or in part every rainy season. The Agency conceded that measuring the effectiveness of BARREL ROLL and STEEL TIGER was difficult because it was impossible to determine what percentage of the supplies which crossed the border from North Vietnam into Laos was destined for South Vietnam rather than for use by the Pathet Lao in south Laos or by the PAVN forces in the Plaine des Jarres. The Agency had been unable to maintain ROADWATCH teams on two critical highways and problems of weather, darkness and foliage had limited the utility of aerial imagery.[119]

The gloomy picture of the Laotian interdiction effort meant that it was necessary to look to ROLLING THUNDER for any indications of success. The transportation system in southern North Vietnam had been systematically and continuously bombed since 3 April so that by June 'almost all' of the major bridges and many of the secondary ones had been 'destroyed or damaged.' Numerous trucks, barges, trains, supply dumps and petroleum depots had been attacked with unstated results. The overall effect was interpreted as the general constriction of the North Vietnamese transportation system throughout the southern part of the country. It was thought the need for constant repairs and improvisations to keep supplies flowing placed a 'considerable strain' upon North Vietnam. 'In short, support of the war in South Vietnam, while not impossible, has become more expensive for Hanoi.'[120] On balance, the interdiction effort had not worked except in terms of cost accountancy; the winning or losing of a war on the basis of cost–benefit ratios would be a first in military history. An important effect of ROLLING THUNDER overlooked by the Agency had been accurately reported by the State Department. The bombing had not had any significantly harmful effects on popular morale in the North and might have had just the opposite impact, improving the political will to continue the war by focusing hatred on the US.[121]

The CIA assessment was confirmed in a very long telegram from Ambassador Taylor which was forwarded to the President with a cover memorandum by McGeorge Bundy.[122] The Viet Cong had shown themselves 'quick to adapt' to new weapons and tactics introduced by the Americans. They had also shown the ability of their logistics system

> to provide adequate – or apparently adequate – support in the form of ammunition and weapons despite air strikes against land routes of supply and the efforts of the Seventh Fleet to blockade the coast of South Vietnam to prevent gunrunning. So far as can be determined, most, if not all, of the main force – and certainly some of the local force – battalions have been provided with the new family of weapons, a formidable accretation of firepower.[123]

The best news Taylor could offer was the opinion of the Rand team led by Leon Goure that American ground, and more particularly, air operations were having a significant, negative impact upon the morale of the Viet Cong.[124] Taylor concluded that everything the US was doing was correct in concept and implementation. Not enough of it was being done.

> The weight and duration of our air attacks in North Vietnam have been insufficient to produce tangible evidence of any willingness on the part of Hanoi to come to the conference table in a reasonable mood.[125]

The most noticeable result of ROLLING THUNDER had been the increase in North Vietnamese antiaircraft capabilities. The Soviet Union had furnished surface to air missile (SAM) batteries along with the necessary surveillance and target acquisition radars. Soviet technicians were in North Vietnam instructing the PAVN personnel in the operation of these systems as well as in the use of new antiaircraft artillery which was also arriving. US military commanders had correctly determined that the SAM–2 batteries constituted an unacceptable threat to ROLLING THUNDER missions and ordered strikes against the SAM sites.[126] The antiaircraft defenses including the SAM batteries would never be suppressed completely. They would represent a constant and growing threat in the months and years ahead. The North Vietnamese had made it quite clear how they intended to respond to the messages of ROLLING THUNDER.

Despite an increase in raids on the North the trends indicated in June had accelerated by October 1965.[127] While the 'largest quantity of manpower and supplies for the Viet Cong are obtained within South Vietnam,' the guerrillas were 'increasingly dependent upon outside sources for arms and ammunition, certain technical equipment, medical supplies, cadre personnel and trained technicians.'[128] The land routes through Laos from North Vietnam had been continuously improved and diversified so that their total traffic-handling capabilities had been improved despite the aerial interdiction efforts of the US although it was still not possible to estimate accurately what the volume of traffic moving along them might have been or might be.[129] Maritime infiltration had also expanded using small, inconspicuous junks. The amount of maritime infiltration was unknown.[130] Cambodia had also become more important as a base for infiltration because of the lax attitude of the Cambodian government, the maze of minor waterways that formed much of the border area and the number of Viet Cong base camps close to or even across the Cambodian border.[131]

There were at least three complementary infiltration systems that were individually difficult and collectively impossible to close or significantly constrict. Exacerbating the difficulty of meaningfully interdicting the flow of external supplies was the low demand which the Viet Cong placed upon the system. Even considering the continued influx of modern Bloc and Chinese weaponry, the guerrillas' requirement for external arms and ammunition was moderate. The CIA reported that the Viet Cong had an organic capability to reload cartridges and to manufacture grenades and mines from captured explosives.[132] While there was an ongoing need for medical supplies, the small bulk and weight of most pharmaceutical and medical equipment made their infiltration easy. In addition, medical supplies along with other categories of materiel were easily obtained from South Vietnamese sources by purchase, diversion or theft.

Overall, the assessment made by the USIB in fall 1965 must have made very depressing reading for any in the Administration who had placed great store on the counterinfiltration efforts. The Ad Hoc Study Group had assumed that as US ground combat units increased the tempo and intensity of operations, this would translate into an increased frangibility of the lines of supply. Secretary McNamara agreed with the Group's assumption as he had indicated in an optimistic memorandum to the President at the end of July.[133] This assumption had not yet been borne out in fact.

The best which might be said in support of the interdiction effort was that it *might* have slowed the rate of infiltration in mid-1965 as American troops were entering combat. Perhaps, in the absence of ROLLING THUNDER, BARREL ROLL and STEEL TIGER, the Viet Cong would have mounted a much more serious and extensive summer offensive. The overwhelming preponderance of evidence should have led policy makers to the conclusion that interdiction had not, and would not, become a war-winning concept no matter how much the US search and destroy operations might succeed in increasing the tempo and intensity of combat in the South. That being the case, the only purpose for ROLLING THUNDER was coercion directed at Hanoi.

By default, McNaughton's 'Progressive Squeeze and Talk' theory of victory was becoming central. By December the relationship of 'squeezing' and 'talking' was under active consideration by the Administration. The next round of 'squeeze' had already been established: General Westmoreland had proposed, with the support of the JCS and Secretary McNamara, a large augmentation in the number of US forces to be deployed to Vietnam during 1966 as well as an increase in the weight of the air attacks on North Vietnam. As McGeorge Bundy reminded the President in early December, the Vietnam augmentation already approved would average fifteen thousand men per month through 1966.[134]

There had been growing international and domestic concern over the 1965 escalation in both the ground and air wars which had led Bundy to favor a pause in ROLLING THUNDER to allow for 'talk' before the next round of 'squeeze.'[135] The pause, and a concomitant search for signals from Hanoi free of the background noise of exploding bombs had been suggested by Under Secretary of State George Ball, who had opposed the air campaign from the beginning. In a mid-November memorandum, Ball argued that a bombing pause would strengthen the American position in the eyes of the world community and would remove the largest impediment blocking the possibility of negotiations.[136] While there were a number of potential objections to the utility of a pause, Ball concluded that the advantages of garnering international and domestic support and in diplomatically conveying to Hanoi the US willingness to 'stay the course,' outweighed these. Ball reported that Secretary McNamara was in essential agreement: 'a pause with the associated obvious efforts to bring the DRV to a settlement, should be carried out.'[137] The Secretary of State, Dean Rusk, did not agree. By 3 December, McGeorge Bundy had become a supporter of the pause which he termed an 'open question' since the President did not yet favor one.[138]

McGeorge Bundy's support for the pause had been influenced strongly by George Ball's well-honed arguments and the support for these from McNamara; it might also have been influenced by a study of the effects of ROLLING THUNDER performed by the Deputy Director of Intelligence, Ray Cline, at the express request of Bundy in early November. Cline's assessment was that the strikes had been professionally executed and the ordnance delivered with great care which had assured maximum target damage with minimal civilian casualties, but the 'effects of the air strikes against North Vietnam do not clearly indicate how the Hanoi regime will react to various possible future trends.'[139] Stripped of its cautious ambiguity, Cline's conclusion was that ROLLING THUNDER had not coerced nor interdicted and might never do so.

On 4 December, McGeorge Bundy reported to the President that a consensus within the Administration had emerged for a pause. Rusk, McNamara, McNaughton, both Bundys, Cyrus Vance, Tommy Thompson and Ball all agreed that the pause was the 'best single way of making it clear that Johnson is for peace and Ho is for war.'[140] While there would be complications both international and domestic and there was uncertainty as to the time and duration of the pause, the senior policy makers all agreed that the benefits, including the preparation of opinion for the next round of 'squeeze,' far exceeded the problems.

Ten days later, McGeorge Bundy wrote to the President concerning the argument presented by Ball that the US should stop bombing the North altogether. While Bundy did not support this radical suggestion, he seemed somewhat in favor of a broader cease-fire coupled with a mission to Hanoi. This proposal was unanimously opposed by Westmoreland, Lodge and the JCS who thought a cease-fire would have a disheartening effect upon the Saigon government and surrender American initiative on the ground in South Vietnam.[141] Even with these unpleasant possibilities, Bundy concluded the potential rewards were meaningful, particularly the political and diplomatic advantages which would accrue if the North (or, it could be presumed, the NLF/VC) rejected the offer.

The cease-fire and bombing pause concepts were discussed in meetings of the Administration's foreign policy specialists on 17 and 18 December. The initial meeting showed elements of profound disagreement within the State Department, with Ball arguing that the bombing had hardened the will of Hanoi and, by implication, had driven the escalatory process and Rusk disagreeing completely with this assessment.[142] Ball had the weight of history on his side, as he knew from his work on the US Strategic Bombing Survey in Germany during 1945. The usual effect of bombing was to increase and solidify the target population's political will to oppose the perpetrator of the bombing.

McNamara seemed particularly confused and disheartened. At the beginning of the meeting he took the position, 'We will increase bombing. It is inevitable. We must step up our attacks.'[143] Later, with a perceivable tinge of anguish, he observed:

> We just don't know if we're hurting the North Vietnamese or the Chinese. We may be able to hurt them enough without 400,000 men to make them behave differently. If we don't, what should we do? We shouldn't be doing anything that has a one-in-three chance.[144]

His inclusion of the Chinese is mystifying.

When Ball argued that the US should stop the bombing and 'conduct the war in the South with redoubled vigor,' the President responded the idea had 'some appeal to him,' but the JCS 'go through the roof when we mention this pause.'[145] McNamara, now radiating decisiveness, said that he could take on the Chiefs. The President finally decided that he preferred a *de facto* pause. He would not define it as a pause, rather he would use weather and Christmas as factors causing a temporary cessation of raids. The proposed period was that of 22 December through 22 January 1966.[146]

The next day, the President again expressed reservations. 'The military say a month's pause will undo all we've done.'[147] Bundy and McNamara reassured him by pointing out that the US had the option to resume bombing at any time. There was much discussion over the duration of the pause particularly in view of the possibility that the North Vietnamese would exploit it to ship supplies and repair damage. Finally, the domestic political considerations, particularly those of proving to critics in Congress that the Administration really was in search of peace, convinced the President to accept the military risks.

After much speculation concerning the role of the Soviet Union in seeking a diplomatic end to the war, the discussion returned to the central point, the chance of a US military victory. McNamara was reported as having said. 'Military solution to the problem is not certain – one out of three or one in two. Ultimately we must find a diplomatic solution.' The President asked, 'Then, no matter what we do in [the] military field there is no sure victory?' The Secretary of Defense replied, 'That's right. We've been too optimistic. One in three or two in three is my estimate.'[148] Rusk was more optimistic but admitted, 'I can't prove it.'[149] McNamara either had lost or was in the process of losing faith in the theory of victory of which he had been a principal designer.

> I come to you for a huge increase in Vietnam – 400,000 men. But at the same time it may lead to escalation and undesirable results. I suggest we look now at other alternatives.[150]

The conversation lengthened and became somewhat desultory as the participants, including the President, considered the implications. If the pause brought either a North Vietnamese acceptance of negotiations on terms agreeable to the US or a tacit withdrawal from the war, the gambit would have worked. If Hanoi made neither move, the US would have no options except to escalate the application of the ground and air operations already under way. It would be necessary to do more of the so far unsuccessful same old thing.

The bombing pause started on Christmas Day 1965. The duration was an open question, depending upon the response of Hanoi and the effects of an American peace offensive. The American diplomatic efforts were intense as George Ball reported at the NSC meeting on 5 January 1966. The US had contacted all 113 countries with which it had relations; of these, 57 had responded favorably to the US peace initiatives. President Johnson had written personally to 33 heads of state; special emissaries had contacted 34 heads of state or government. It was a maximum diplomatic effort with little in the way of immediate result.[151] Ambassador Lodge threw another bucket of cold water on the diplomatic effort in a telegram on 4 January 1966. He had been asked by Secretary Rusk to consider the possibility of another Geneva Conference or the use of the International Control Commission to effect a negotiated settlement to the war. He argued that neither option would be appropriate as 'the Communists think they can win.'[152] He argued that negotiations would become a viable option when the US had accomplished three tasks: 'really punish them in the North, decisively defeat the North Vietnamese Army,' and 'root out the terrorists and rebuild the political structure in the countryside.'[153]

John McNaughton, who had been one of the two main architects of the bombing campaign nearly two years earlier, was having serious doubts about the American goal and theory of victory by mid-January 1966. Retreating from the expansive goal which he had espoused earlier, McNaughton now saw the goal of the United States as being 'to avoid humiliation.'[154] He believed that the war had become 'an escalating military stalemate.'[155] Diplomatic efforts had come to nothing because both the United States and North Vietnam were defining victory as being equivalent to 'unconditional surrender,' and neither side 'could give in' to the other without an unacceptable loss of international status and prestige.[156] What he did not recognize was the role which ROLLING THUNDER and 'Progressive Squeeze and Talk' had played in producing the situation which he described.

McNaughton now doubted the potential of ROLLING THUNDER to coerce North Vietnam and came to the conclusion that the program could not be expected 'directly or indirectly' to 'persuade Hanoi' that negotiations or withdrawal from the South might be in its best interests.[157] As a result he focused upon the potential utility of the air campaign in the slowing of infiltration. Following the lead of one of his staff, he had argued that with the proper selection of target systems, the US could hope to place a ceiling upon the number of troops the North could support within South Vietnam.[158] He understood the tension between attack profiles designed to coerce and those meant to interdict but saw no easy way to bridge the operational gap. Neither did he see any effective, politically acceptable way to end coercion and dedicate the bombing effort solely to interdiction efforts. Eventually he came to the rather weak conclusion that bombing probably would not interdict any better than it coerced, so the US should look for another means of interdiction and continue to bomb, not so much to coerce, as to provide a 'bargaining chip.'[159] The goal of the air campaign was again changing out of frustration rather than reflection.

On 24 January as the pause neared the one-month mark, President Johnson met with Rusk, McNamara, McGeorge Bundy and Taylor.[160] This meeting was the first of several on the pause and its effects. The concerns were the duration of the pause, which Westmoreland was urging be brought to an end within a few days, the domestic political consequences of ending the pause, the international effects of restarting ROLLING THUNDER and the nature and weight of the attacks upon resumption of bombing. The peace offensive had come to nought. There were members of Congress opposed to a resumption of bombing. There were friendly foreign governments including Great Britain and Australia which urged the United States to continue to show restraint while awaiting an acceptable reply from Hanoi. The US military commanders were increasingly concerned about the advantage being taken of the pause by the North Vietnamese. This fear had been confirmed by the CIA in mid January. In a review of Hanoi's reaction to the bombing pause the Agency determined that the North had 'moved quickly to take advantage of the cessation of the air attacks.'[161] Diplomatically, Hanoi had shown no willingness to offer concessions for a continuation of the pause.[162]

On the 25th the President, Secretaries Rusk and McNamara met with the Congressional leadership. There was resistance to resumption of the bombing from Senators Fulbright and Mansfield, but Republican Senator Dirksen set the tone for the majority of the participants when, after rejecting both withdrawal and a war of patient attrition, he concluded 'Or you can fight. You go in to win. If we are not winning now, let's do what is necessary to win. I don't believe you have any other choice. I believe the country will support you.'[163] This position was echoed by Gerald Ford, Carl Albert, Richard Russell and most of the rest of the Congressional leadership. With Fulbright and Mansfield isolated, the President felt sufficiently secure politically to authorize a resumption of the bombing.

Potential problems with the Laotian government were considered by the President and his senior advisors on the 26th.[164] The President did receive some good news in the midst of the inconclusive evaluation of Laotian assistance in the air war. John McCloy, Dean Acheson and Clark Clifford had all told McGeorge Bundy that the bombing pause had served its diplomatic and political purposes and should now be brought to an end.[165]

In a lengthy meeting the next day, the President along with Rusk, McNamara, McGeorge Bundy and Wheeler continued the process of developing a new 'rolling consensus' on resuming ROLLING THUNDER.[166] Rusk recommended proceeding with the bombing but under tight control because of the perceived danger of Chinese intervention. There was no dissent. The question of targeting brought some disagreement. McNamara wanted to strike 'perishable' targets such as trucks on the move while Wheeler wanted the weight of the attack to fall on infrastructure and industrial targets to assure that the North could not supply a larger force than that already in the South. McNamara questioned the supply figures upon which Wheeler was basing his argument.[167] McNamara also echoed Rusk's concern about the air effort inducing a Chinese intervention and insisted upon careful restrictions to militate against this eventuality. He was not certain if the bombing would do any good or even if the US would be able to measure its effectiveness, but he concluded, 'I'm sure we need to resume bombing.'[168] The bombing might not do any good. It had to be very carefully limited and controlled because of the Chinese threat which still existed in the collective mind of the Administration despite the CIA having long since concluded it was nonexistent. But the US had no apparent alternative to resuming the air raids on the North. This was the nature of the 'rolling consensus' on ROLLING THUNDER.

On the 28th the senior members of the administration and the 'wise men,' McCloy, Dulles, Dean and Clifford met for nearly two-and-a-half hours on the resumption of the bombing.[169] McNamara presented a rather pessimistic view of the bombing: 'We could eliminate some trucks – but they would probably use human backs.' and 'Don't think we can affect their will through bombing. The pressure on the VC in the South will affect their willingness to talk.'[170] General Wheeler was more optimistic than the Secretary of Defense. He agreed with McNamara that the US had to resume bombing so as not to encourage Hanoi and the PRC. Additionally, he believed that bombing reduced the flow of supplies, if the weight of attack was great enough.

By the end of the meeting all the 'wise men' expressed agreement with the resumption of bombing. Clark Clifford's view was summarized: 'Only way to get out of Vietnam is to persuade Hanoi we are too brave to be frightened and too strong to be defeated.'[171] The President concluded, 'I am not happy about Vietnam but we cannot run out – we have to resume bombing.'[172] Once again the decision was not made on the basis of assessing what *should* the United States do, but rather, what the United States *could* do. All that was left before ROLLING THUNDER could again fly was the ritualistic approval of the NSC.

The 556th meeting of the National Security Council commenced at high noon on 29 January. The actors knew their parts and the lines were easy to deliver. The new DCI, Admiral Raborn, presented a capsule briefing of North Vietnamese exploitation of the pause. UN Ambassador Arthur Goldberg commented on the failure of the peace offensive. Army Chief of Staff Harold Johnson talked about the major fighting in Operation MASHER and how much the US needed a new 'surge' of troops into South Vietnam.[173] The Air Chief of Staff, General McConnell, described the proposed air campaign:

> There is nothing unusual in the air effort recommended. It involves 330 sorties weekly [over the North], B–52 sorties at the rate of 300 a month [ARC LIGHT] and 1200 weekly sorties into Laos. When we resume the bombing, our losses will rise because North Vietnam now has a greater anti-aircraft capability.[174]

General Wheeler concluded by recommending the resumption of bombing as soon as was practical with an initial stress on targets associated with infiltration. General McConnell's parting shot was, 'Our bombing is ineffective because of the restrictions placed upon the Air Force. We should lift these restrictions and we would then get results.'[175] Restrictions still in place, ROLLING THUNDER resumed two days later.

The nature of target definition for the renewed ROLLING THUNDER was in large measure dependent upon the goal of the effort: interdiction or coercion. No consensus had been developed on that key issue during the January meeting marathon. As a result the primary focus of targeting was left unresolved when the campaign resumed. There were several alternative target systems that could be engaged by the bombers including the lines of communication south of the Hanoi–Haiphong line, the lines of communication north of Hanoi, petroleum storage and delivery facilities, military infrastructure, industry and key agricultural support facilities such as dikes and levees. The 1965 campaign had been characterized by a diffusion of effort with a percentage of the raids assigned to all target categories except the agricultural. In an effort to resolve the targeting issue, the CIA was asked to assess four different programs: one which followed the pattern of the pre-pause attacks, a second which focused upon lines of communication in southern North Vietnam, a third which included bulk petroleum storage with the line of communication focus and a fourth which included all target systems except urban population centers and agricultural facilities. The Agency was told that the bombing program should be measured in terms of securing two objectives within the near term (ten weeks): coercion and interdiction.

The response came on 11 February 1966. The first conclusion was that interdiction was an impossibility:

> We do not believe that even the most extensive of the programs of air attack would prevent the movement of men and supplies in quantities sufficient to sustain or even increase the scale of VC/PAVN activity. Our best judgement is that an average of about 12 tons daily has been required by the VC/PAVN from external sources over the past year. . . . The principal effect of different bombing levels probably should be measured in terms of slowing the supply effort . . . and setting a ceiling on future expansion of the supply rate. Critical to the significance of any ceiling . . . would be the rate of consumption of men and materiel which GVN/allied forces impose on the VC/PAVN forces.[176]

The Agency had come to the same conclusions as the Ad Hoc Study Group had concerning the crucial role of US ground combat forces in determining Viet Cong and PAVN supply and manpower requirements by dictating the tempo and intensity of combat, but the CIA had placed the air effort in its traditional role, supporting the ground forces by limiting the resources immediately available to the enemy on the battlefield. After an exhaustive examination of the several alternative programs, Dr Sherman Kent and the Office of National Estimates (ONE) concluded that the best option was the second, which focused upon the lines of communication south of the Hanoi–Haiphong line, although he conceded that this approach offered only a marginal chance of 'limiting and disrupting support to the VC/PAVN.'[177]

Concerns regarding adverse public reaction around the world and the dangers of escalation convinced the ONE to recommend against the program of virtually unrestricted bombing embodied in the fourth option. It was strongly implied that Hanoi and the North Vietnamese population had the political will to accept the wholesale destruction of option four and wait for international outrage to come to bear on the US with an effect which would narrow profoundly future options available to Washington.[178] The CIA assessment was sent to the President by McGeorge Bundy on the 25th to 'provide background for the continuing discussions you will be having with Bob McNamara on this.'[179]

Whatever those discussions might have been, the course of ROLLING

THUNDER did not show the focus recommended in the ONE assessment. In May General Wheeler assured the NSC

the air operations in the north have hurt the North Vietnamese. They are having transportation difficulties and are using at least 80,000 men to repair their LOCs [lines of communication]. They are calling for more trucks and have stepped up their imports of POL [petroleum, oil and lubricants].[180]

He also informed the NSC that the North Vietnamese had used the pause of 25 December through 31 January to repair the damage inflicted upon their lines of communication, expand their infiltration routes and improve their road networks. He did not remind the NSC that the CIA had demonstrated that the North Vietnamese had accomplished precisely the same undertakings while the bombs had been falling.[181] Sherman Kent had predicted in February the US had little chance of accomplishing the interdiction task successfully. In April the Agency reported that their pessimistic prediction had been proven correct. Infiltration of PAVN units was still on the increase, and the North had a considerable still-unused capacity to introduce even more troops into the South.[182] Although unstated, the report gave the clear impression that the Hanoi politburo had made the decision to pursue the goal of hegemony over the South regardless of the US, the South Vietnamese Government or the NLF/VC.

The US had started and the North had matched another escalatory round. In monthly assessments on the effectiveness of the air campaigns for May and June, the Agency determined that infiltration continued, perhaps at an increased rate and that the North Vietnamese had been repairing damage and extending their lines of communication as the attacks continued.[183] Despite the destruction inflicted by ROLLING THUNDER operations, 'the North Vietnamese have continued restoration and construction work on the LOCs at high levels and they retain the capability of meeting their logistics requirements for operations in Laos and South Vietnam.'[184] The obvious dichotomy between General Wheeler's optimism and the CIA assessment underscored the growing divergence between the military's view of the war and that of the Agency which would dog the Administration through the 1968 Tet Offensive. Events bore out the CIA position.

The next month, the Administration was in the process of shifting the focus of ROLLING THUNDER from North Vietnamese lines of communication to their petroleum storage facilities.[185] The President informed the NSC on 17 June that the decision to strike the POL target system was imminent:

In general we should seek, with minimum loss and minimum danger of escalating the war, to achieve the maximum effect on the

North Vietnamese. We know that the North Vietnamese are dispersing their POL stocks in an effort to anticipate our bombing. The effect of not disrupting POL shipments to the North Vietnamese forces in the field is to pay a higher price in US casualties. The choice is one of military lives vs. escalation.[186]

Secretary McNamara said that he had opposed POL strikes for months but that he had changed his mind because 'the military importance of their POL system is way up and will increase further.'[187] He gave three reasons for attacking the petroleum targets: 'our guess is that such attacks will limit infiltration,' PAVN troops in the South would worry about their source of supplies and 'pressure will be exerted on the political leaders in Hanoi.'[188] General Johnson stated that in spite of the line of communication thrust during the previous several months, the number of North Vietnamese trucks had increased from 6,900 to 10,000 and 'all need fuel to operate.'[189] The US had identified between seventy and eighty POL dispersal sites and was prepared to strike the main POL off-loading point in the port of Haiphong. By bombing Haiphong the US would be crossing a psychological Rubicon. The new National Security Advisor, Walt Whitman Rostow, strongly supported the POL strike concept, while Vice President Humphrey was far more cautious and worried aloud about the possibility of killing Soviet personnel on board a Russian ship in Haiphong harbor, an eventuality he termed 'a catastrophe.'[190] Walt Rostow had the final word:

> The decision is a rational one. Taking out the petroleum supplies sets a ceiling on the capacity of the North Vietnamese to infiltrate men into South Vietnam. A sustained POL offensive will seriously affect the infiltration rate.[191]

Reports from Ambassador Lodge which emphasized the continuing combat capabilities of the Viet Cong underscored the apparent necessity of effectively dealing with the matter of infiltration although the linkage between Viet Cong proficiency on the battlefield and POL supplies in the North was based more on assumptions and desperation than on intelligence.[192] Decision on the POL campaign was deferred.

A week later the matter was again discussed by the NSC. General Wheeler rehearsed the ceiling imposition argument in favor of the POL strikes noting that PAVN had another three divisions ready to go south.[193] It was his opinion that after the package of seven attacks North Vietnamese infiltration would be affected within sixty to ninety days. Wheeler also wanted to mine Haiphong harbor believing this would inhibit Bloc shipments of weapons and petroleum. Maxwell Taylor agreed.[194] Finally, all those present including George Ball, but with the single exception of UN Ambassador Goldberg, agreed to the POL campaign. Only Admiral Raborn supported Earle Wheeler and Maxwell Taylor on the question of mining Haiphong.[195] The POL strikes would be made, but the time had not yet arrived to mine Haiphong harbor.

Another facet of the air war was under discussion that summer. General Westmoreland was pleased that the ARC LIGHT program had achieved a 'quick reaction' capability on 1 July 1966. As of that date he had a force of six B–52 bombers at his disposal that was able to be over a target within ten hours of receiving information from MACV.[196] He was less pleased that 127 ARC LIGHT sorties had not been flown due to objections from the US Embassy in Vientiane leading to the disapproval of 25 targets in the Laotian Corridor.[197] He was hopeful that Admiral Sharp would support his request that the limitations be removed so that the heavy bombers might be more effectively used against the infiltration routes in the Corridor.[198] He also expressed a concern that the Administration had become so infatuated with strategic bombing in North Vietnam that the needs of tactical support and interdiction were being slighted.[199] There was cause for his anxiety. The absence of a fixed focus, a consistent purpose and goal for the bombing campaign in North Vietnam encouraged the Administration to look for a target system of the month, rather than rationally assess the utility of the air war and direct the bombers where they might have the greatest real effect.

In mid-October 1966, Secretary of Defense McNamara returned from his most recent trip to Vietnam. He presented the usual lengthy report to the President in which he made several recommendations regarding the air war.[200] He wanted to stabilize ROLLING THUNDER which had grown like a malignant weed from 4,000 sorties per month at the end of 1965 to 12,000 per month in October 1966. Some 84,000 attack sorties had been flown against North Vietnam. Of these 25 per cent had been against fixed targets with the balance falling under the rubric 'armed reconnaissance,' with 45 per cent of the total occurring in the seven months between March and October 1966. Despite this immense effort,

> it now appears that the North Vietnamese–Laotian road will remain adequate to meet the requirements of the Communist forces in South Vietnam – this even if its capacity could be reduced by one-third and if combat activities could be doubled.

> Furthermore, it is clear that, to bomb the North sufficiently to make a radical impact upon Hanoi's political, economic and social structure, would require an effort which we could make but which would not be stomached either by our own people or by world opinion, and would involve a serious risk of drawing us into open war with China.[201]

The intellectual predicates of the Ad Hoc Study Group and of the Administration fifteen months earlier had been proven incorrect while the CIA's relatively pessimistic assessment of February 1966 had been validated. McNamara wanted ROLLING THUNDER stabilized at some level well below 12,000 sorties per month. He could envision a search for negotiations which would involve discontinuing all bombing in the North or, at the least, bombing above the Hanoi–Haiphong line.[202]

The JCS did not agree with the Secretary of Defense and stated so in a separate memorandum presented at the October NSC meeting. In particular, the Chiefs disagreed with the stabilization or reduction of ROLLING THUNDER which they considered to be 'an integral and indispensable' portion of the overall war effort. The JCS believed: 'To be effective, the air campaign should be conducted with only those minimum constraints necessary to avoid indiscriminate killing of population.'[203] This position was echoed in a memorandum written by General Westmoreland to W. W. Rostow.[204] In a more specific proposal, the Chiefs recommended decreasing the Hanoi and Haiphong 'sanctuary zones' and authorizing attacks against the steel plant, cement plant, thermal power plants, rail yards, selected areas within Haiphong harbor and selected locks and dams associated with water LOCs and other currently prohibited targets.[205]

General Westmoreland was in complete agreement with the Chiefs. He offered a tightly argued justification of ROLLING THUNDER to Rostow in late October 1966 in which he maintained that, while not providing a leakproof barrier to infiltration, its cessation would 'adversely affect the war in the South to a serious degree' in that it would allow the movement of men and materiel with impunity.[206] Ending the effort would also significantly and adversely affect ARVN's morale and will to fight. The General characterized the ROLLING THUNDER campaign as having been one of 'creeping escalation,' which used air power inefficiently and expensively and he strongly urged a change in strategy to one which allowed for a greater shock effect or greater flexibility of targeting. Westmoreland finished with a plea that any change in the bombing program not restrict strikes within the 'extended battle area,' North Vietnam south of Vinh.[207]

McNamara had requested a special study of the effectiveness of ROLLING THUNDER from the CIA. The initial report was ready on 5 November 1966.[208] In the eighteen months since the inauguration of ROLLING THUNDER, US aircraft had flown a total of just under 84,000 sorties against North Vietnamese targets delivering approximately 125,000 tons of ordnance. While the loss rate had been low, 396 aircraft had been destroyed. An analysis of the damage inflicted as compared to US costs of inflicting the damage concluded it cost $8.70 to cause $1.00

worth of damage upon North Vietnam in 1966 alone.[209] The results had been disappointing.

> Despite the increased weight of air attack, North Vietnam continues to increase its support of the insurgency in South Vietnam. The ROLLING THUNDER program has not been able to prevent about a three fold increase in the level of personnel infiltration in 1966. The external logistic support needed to maintain the expanded VC/PAVN force in South Vietnam has been adequate. In particular, despite the neutralization of the major petroleum storage facilities in the North, petroleum supplies have continued to be imported in needed amounts.[210]
>
> Nor has ROLLING THUNDER served visibly to reduce the determination of Hanoi to continue the war. We see no signs that the air attack has shaken the confidence of the regime, and with increased Soviet and Chinese aid to bolster its capabilities, North Vietnam in the short term, at least will apparently take no positive step toward a negotiated settlement. . . . Analysis of popular attitudes in North Vietnam indicates a continued firmness in support of the regime's policies.[211]

The inventory of damage inflicted to fixed infrastructure, military and industrial targets convincingly demonstrated the destructiveness of modern air power.

The CIA revealed even more impressive evidence concerning the limits of air power and the inability of US policy makers to appreciate that history could repeat itself concerning civilian attitudes under the bomber's shadow.

> Evidence on the feelings of the North Vietnamese toward the war in the south prior to February was scanty. The available information suggested that the northerners were interested in seeing the insurgents win, but that they did not relish the prospect of having to risk their own standard of living, let alone their lives, on behalf of the southern struggle. Since the bombings of North Vietnam began, however, there appears to be more enthusiasm for supporting the war in the south.[212]

Due to material help from without, which had been predicted, and political will within, which should have been predictable, the massive and professionally executed ROLLING THUNDER program had failed to interdict or coerce alike. McNamara was right in his loss of faith.

To reinforce the points made in the November study, the CIA issued a second, longer and more detailed examination of ROLLING THUNDER in December 1966.[213] Considering the interdiction effort, the Agency recounted that over 98 per cent of 104,000 sorties flown over North

Vietnam and 57,000 of those sent to Laos had been allocated to the interdiction effort in the first nine months of 1966.[214] The cost of the interdiction effort to the North Vietnamese had not been excessive, let alone insupportable, although the manpower requirements to repair damage and to improvise solutions for road and rail cuts had been high. Despite the interdiction campaign and the heavy weight of the attacks delivered, the North Vietnamese had been able to expand the road net in the Laotian Corridor and to make improvements in their ability to move supplies during bad weather.[215] It was concluded:

> The historical experience of interdiction campaigns, particularly against a logistics target system such as that in North Vietnam, shows that they can yield only limited returns. Although the present campaign has created burdens and added to the cost of supporting the Communist forces in South Vietnam, these strains have been within acceptable limits.[216]

As early as September 1966, MACV had unwittingly confirmed the Agency's pessimistic assessment. In a memorandum to Ambassador Leonhart, MACV Chief of Staff, Major General W. B. Rosson stated that the enemy had the capability to infiltrate a daily average of 458 tons of supplies but the VC/PAVN forces required only thirty tons per day of infiltrated materiel.[217] It was hoped that this consumption could be forced to a much higher level during 1967 by greatly expanded ground combat.[218] It should be recalled that the CIA had concluded earlier that MACV was overestimating the current external supply requirements of the VC/PAVN which the agency believed was only twelve tons per day.[219]

The Agency concluded that the only possibility for success was the combination of intensive attacks against rail yards in Hanoi and Haiphong as well as port facilities with extensive twenty-four-hour armed reconnaissance and this would be difficult as well as expensive for the US to maintain for any duration. The effort would also be impaired by bad weather and improvements in North Vietnamese air defense systems, camouflage and concealment practices and repair techniques.[220]

The coercion objective of the US bombing campaign had been severely impaired by the reaction the bombing had engendered within the world community. The 'very strong popular opposition' in some neutral and allied countries had 'definitely limited official support for US policy in some countries.'[221] If the United States were to apply air power in a more vigorous manner to targets in North Vietnam in the hope of achieving the goal of coercing Hanoi to either the negotiating table or an implicit withdrawal from the South, the result would be a 'significant intensification of opposition to the bombing.'[222] Since the

US commitment in South Vietnam was part of a global policy matrix, it scarcely would make sense for the US to impair the matrix for the sake of the commitment. The bombing had affected not only attitudes and policy behavior in neutral and allied nations, it had done the same in the Soviet Union and PRC with the effect that both were providing great and growing military material, economic and diplomatic support to North Vietnam.[223] This would increase if the bombing effort were to escalate.

The political will of the North Vietnamese leadership had not been enervated by the bombing campaign. The public still firmly supported the policies of the leadership.[224] There was no reason to believe that this would change under any weight of attack which was acceptable to world and American domestic opinion. If history had been used as a guide, it would have been legitimate to assume that the longer the bombing lasted and the greater the damage and casualty lists became, the more the government and people would have been united in pursuit of an outcome to the war in which the rewards received would be commensurate with the sacrifices made.[225]

The CIA conclusions were echoed in December by a Rand study done for John McNaughton.[226] The internal political consequences of ROLLING THUNDER within North Vietnam were considered a major benefit offsetting some, if not most, of the physical damage inflicted by the campaign. The civilian casualties were seen as being sufficiently large and sufficiently well-distributed to assure that 'acute hostility to the attacker' existed and would serve as a motivator of behavior desired by the regime.[227] The morale factor coupled with the availability of external material aid from the Soviet Union and, to a lesser degree, from the PRC to assure that the bombing campaign had not achieved any useful result. As to the future, the Rand report concluded,

> it becomes increasingly doubtful that the advantages of continuation or intensification of the attacks outweigh the potential net gains from cessation or, at least, drastic and demonstrative de-escalation.[228]

These words were almost heretical coming from a longtime bastion of pro-Air Force thinking, but words which deserved a hearing.

The bombing would continue regardless of the assessments which called its effectiveness into question. The bombing would continue despite the doubts expressed by McNamara and probably felt by others. It would continue because it had been started, and to stop it without some concession from the North would appear perilously close to a partial American surrender. The dynamic had trapped the US and significantly limited its options. The bombers of ROLLING THUNDER were no longer implementing policy; they were dictating it. It is ironic that the air war had been conceived and implemented because it had appeared to be so manageable, so capable of assuring that Washington policy makers maintained control of options and means of implementation. Now, at the end of eighteen months, the policy makers had lost control and were running out of options.

Within the Administration there was a genuine and obvious dissatisfaction with the course of the war. There was an equal dissatisfaction with the continued emphasis upon bombing for the sterility of the action was well understood. There was a belief that new options must be found or that new vigor must be developed in old options. As the bombs fell and the search and destroy operations increased in 1967 according to the old, and so far quite unsuccessful definition and theory of victory, so also did the search for a new theory which might bring about an end to the war outside South Vietnam and an acceptable security condition within that country. A theory of victory must be found which would allow the war to be won without further damage to the global policy matrix on behalf of which the war was being waged.

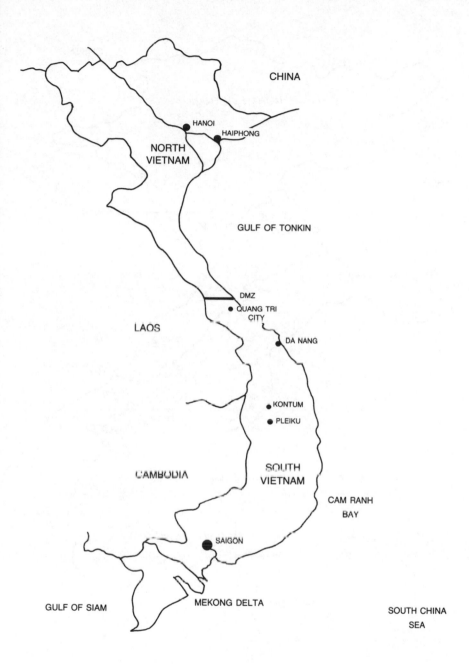

CHINA

HANOI
HAIPHONG

NORTH
VIETNAM

GULF OF TONKIN

DMZ
QUANG TRI
CITY

LAOS

DA NANG

KONTUM
PLEIKU

CAMBODIA

SOUTH
VIETNAM

CAM RANH
BAY

SAIGON

GULF OF SIAM

MEKONG DELTA

SOUTH CHINA
SEA

Map 1   Southeast Asia

119

CHINA

NORTH VIETNAM

DIEN BIEN PHU

HANOI

HAIPHONG

LAOS

20th PARALLEL

THANH HOA

BAN BAN

PLAINE DES JARRES

GULF OF TONKIN

VIENTIANE

VINH

DONG
HOI

THAILAND

DMZ

SENO

QUANG
TRI

MUONG
PHINE

ATOPEU

SOUTH
VIETNAM

CAMBODIA

VC / PAVN LOGISTICS AREA

Map 2 North Vietnam and Laos

120

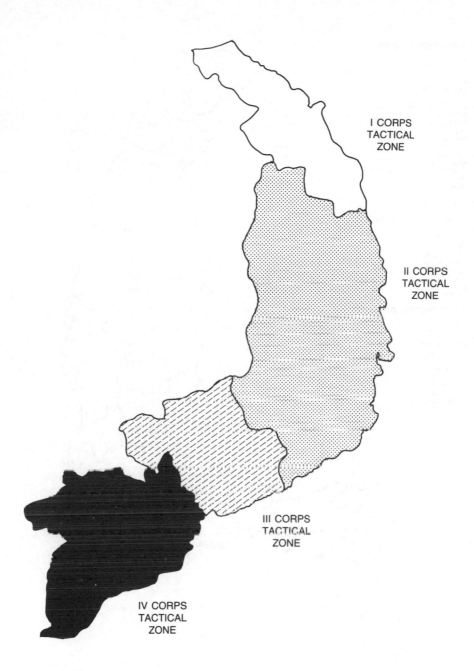

I CORPS
TACTICAL
ZONE

II CORPS
TACTICAL
ZONE

III CORPS
TACTICAL
ZONE

IV CORPS
TACTICAL
ZONE

Map 3   South Vietnam military regions

121

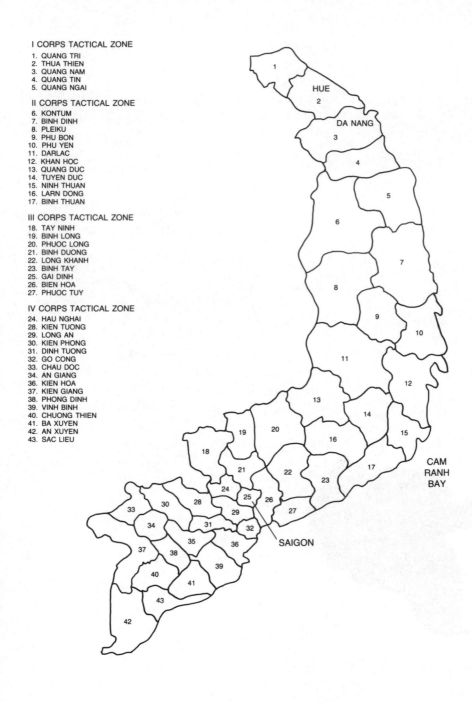

I CORPS TACTICAL ZONE

1. QUANG TRI
2. THUA THIEN
3. QUANG NAM
4. QUANG TIN
5. QUANG NGAI

II CORPS TACTICAL ZONE

6. KONTUM
7. BINH DINH
8. PLEIKU
9. PHU BON
10. PHU YEN
11. DARLAC
12. KHAN HOC
13. QUANG DUC
14. TUYEN DUC
15. NINH THUAN
16. LARN DONG
17. BINH THUAN

III CORPS TACTICAL ZONE

18. TAY NINH
19. BINH LONG
20. PHUOC LONG
21. BINH DUONG
22. LONG KHANH
23. BINH TAY
25. GAI DINH
26. BIEN HOA
27. PHUOC TUY

IV CORPS TACTICAL ZONE

24. HAU NGHAI
28. KIEN TUONG
29. LONG AN
30. KIEN PHONG
31. DINH TUONG
32. GO CONG
33. CHAU DOC
34. AN GIANG
36. KIEN HOA
37. KIEN GIANG
38. PHONG DINH
39. VINH BINH
40. CHUONG THIEN
41. BA XUYEN
42. AN XUYEN
43. SAC LIEU

Map 4 South Vietnam provinces

122

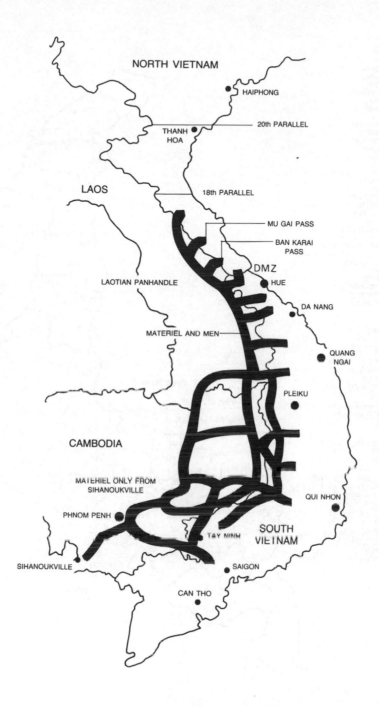

Map 5 Infiltration routes, 1967

123

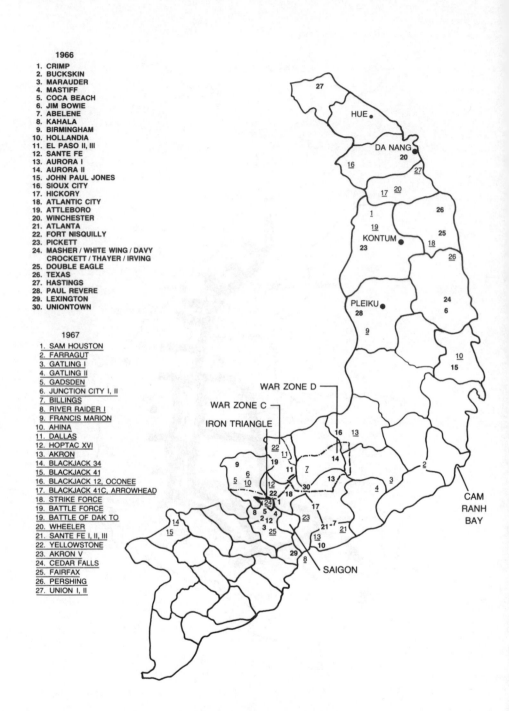

1966

1. CRIMP
2. BUCKSKIN
3. MARAUDER
4. MASTIFF
5. COCA BEACH
6. JIM BOWIE
7. ABELENE
8. KAHALA
9. BIRMINGHAM
10. HOLLANDIA
11. EL PASO II, III
12. SANTE FE
13. AURORA I
14. AURORA II
15. JOHN PAUL JONES
16. SIOUX CITY
17. HICKORY
18. ATLANTIC CITY
19. ATTLEBORO
20. WINCHESTER
21. ATLANTA
22. FORT NISQUILLY
23. PICKETT
24. MASHER / WHITE WING / DAVY
    CROCKETT / THAYER / IRVING
25. DOUBLE EAGLE
26. TEXAS
27. HASTINGS
28. PAUL REVERE
29. LEXINGTON
30. UNIONTOWN

1967

1. SAM HOUSTON
2. FARRAGUT
3. GATLING I
4. GATLING II
5. GADSDEN
6. JUNCTION CITY I, II
7. BILLINGS
8. RIVER RAIDER I
9. FRANCIS MARION
10. AHINA
11. DALLAS
12. HOPTAC XVI
13. AKRON
14. BLACKJACK 34
15. BLACKJACK 41
16. BLACKJACK 12, OCONEE
17. BLACKJACK 41C, ARROWHEAD
18. STRIKE FORCE
19. BATTLE FORCE
19. BATTLE OF DAK TO
20. WHEELER
21. SANTE FE I, II, III
22. YELLOWSTONE
23. AKRON V
24. CEDAR FALLS
25. FAIRFAX
26. PERSHING
27. UNION I, II

Map 6   Cited operations, 1966–7

124

5

THE BIG WAR AND THE OTHER WAR

When the decision to enlarge the American ground combat presence in South Vietnam and to increase the scope and weight of the air attacks on North Vietnam and Laos had been made in July 1965, there had been little consideration of any factors except the purely military.[1] None of the major participants in the decision-making process except Under Secretary of State George Ball argued that the governmental, social or economic conditions within South Vietnam should take primacy over military matters. There was little examination of the reasons why peasants might be supporting the Viet Cong guerrillas. As a result, little more than lip service was paid to the necessity or desirability of pre-emptive reforms calculated to demobilize popular support from the Viet Cong.

The narrow focus was understandable considering the perceptions which governed the decision makers. The emergency seen in South Vietnam was that of imminent military collapse. It was accepted that Hanoi's support was the sole reason for that dangerous situation. Military stability must be restored before any programs of pre-emptive reform might be initiated with any prospect of success. This perceptual set assured that non-military programs like matters of South Vietnamese political, economic and social dynamics would be placed to one side while the emergency was confronted. The underlying, but unrecognized, danger was that by the time the non-military programs were brought to the forefront it would be too late.

Initially, the role of diplomacy in securing the announced goals of removing the North Vietnamese presence from the South and ending the Southern insurgency was not a major concern except that the UN was explicitly and vigorously rejected as a forum for conflict resolution.[2] Secretary Rusk's position was summarized:

Very negative if we asked for meeting and didn't get it. International recognition of VC would undermine the Saigon government. We have to assume that a resolution that meets our approval would draw Soviet veto. [It] might make it difficult for Soviets to push quietly for talks. [It] might draw amendments that would be inimical to us. If we didn't get at least 7 votes, it would appear that the UN had repudiated us.[3]

The failure of the numerous diplomatic demarches attempted by the United States during the 1965 Christmas bombing pause had perhaps validated the initial decision to dismiss diplomacy as being less than attractive. However, after the pause there were members of the Administration who wished to refocus efforts on the diplomatic front. In the early spring of 1966, the VNCC carefully considered various alternative routes to negotiations as well as the likely course and outcome of negotiations.[4] John McNaughton went so far as to argue that the adoption of a physical barrier approach to the interdiction effort would provide a way of facilitating negotiations with Hanoi.[5] Despite all the planning and refining which continued throughout 1966, diplomatic efforts appeared no more likely to lead to a breakthrough at the end of the year than they had at the beginning. There seemed to be no way out of the impasse on the diplomatic front. The search for new solutions would have to be taken elsewhere, perhaps in the villages of South Vietnam.

The escalation of American ground and air combat efforts between late 1964 and mid-1965 had been met by a North Vietnamese response which was characterized by Ambassador Henry Cabot Lodge in his first dispatch of 1966 as having 'transformed the nature of the war,' making it, 'in effect a new war.'[6] As a result pacification and the rest of the 41–Point Nonmilitary Program had slipped to lower priority status, from which it was not immediately resurrected by either the Warrenton Meeting or the Honolulu Conference.

One fundamental flaw with the program of non-military operations had been identified by the Warrenton Meeting conferees. That was the absence of a central directorate both within the Mission in Saigon and the Washington bureaucracies. Until a central directorate might be created, it was believed that the non-military, pacification, revolutionary development and nation-building programs would be diffuse in application and unproductive in effect. That defect was not to be rectified during 1966, although the need to do so was becoming increasingly evident as the year progressed and the programs did not.

A comprehensive memorandum to President Johnson written by McGeorge Bundy in mid-February 1966 assessed the strengths and weaknesses of the senior US officials in Saigon with a specific reference to the needs of the non-military program.[7] Bundy provided an exceptionally detailed and perceptive assessment of Ambassador Lodge, General Westmoreland and Chief of Mission David Porter.

Porter had just been reassigned as the Chief of Staff for 'all aspects of pacification and rural construction,' and was described as 'the first indispensable man in this enterprise.'[8] The major deficiency identified by Bundy was the lack of an individual in Washington who could give Porter and the non-military program 'prompt executive support.'[9] Bundy recommended that such an individual be appointed so the other war might have the same degree of backing at the highest level as did the military and diplomatic programs. The President annotated Bundy's counsel, 'This is excellent – L.'[10] NSAM 343 designated a Special Assistant to the President as the specific focal point in Washington for the direction, coordination and supervision of all the non-military programs. Robert Komer was promoted to that post from his position on McGeorge Bundy's staff.[11]

Administrative reorganization was easily recommended and quickly accomplished. Effecting substantial change within South Vietnam could be realized only at a glacial pace. As Lodge reported, the political crises in Saigon and other major cities caused by antigovernment Buddhists led by Tri Quang had retarded both military and non-military programs.[12] Lodge also expressed strong doubts concerning the ability of American personnel to influence events in the provincial governments and among the politically potent sects. In the Ambassador's estimation one reason for the lack of success in swaying provincial officials and sectarian leaders was the generally mediocre ability of the individual American advisors and liaison personnel. He urged the upgrading of the US provincial representative effort so it would be 'considered a blue ribbon post,' to which the 'cream of the crop' might be attracted.[13]

Lodge's point was well taken, but incomplete as an analysis. To be successful the various non-military programs, particularly those which involved land reform and the creation of governmental and economic infrastructures, or which provided governmental services directly to the peasants, would succeed or fail in the provinces and would do so quite irrespective of turmoil at the Saigon center. Both the shooting and the 'other' wars had to be fought in the same geographic venue, the country-side. Unfortunately, Lodge did not recognize that fighting the first made success in prosecuting the second virtually impossible.

William Porter, the man in Saigon charged with waging the 'other war,' might not have completely understood the extent to which military operations rendered nugatory the attempts to implement the non-military programs, but he believed that it was 'national policy to give emphasis to civil reconstruction comparable to that given military operations.'[14] He argued that it was incumbent upon the United States to assure that the population within a cleared area was permanently defended. Porter also argued, as had Komer, that the rampant inflation within South Vietnam, largely caused by the American military escalation, served powerfully to assist the Viet Cong. He urged that all military and non-military programs be carried out in a way which lessened, rather than exacerbated, the fragile South Vietnamese economic state.

Porter, unlike Komer, saw a danger in the proliferation of non-military programs as this would breed a counterproductive competition for resources, enervate the main focus of revolutionary development, worsen inflation and overstress the weak institutions of the South Vietnamese government. 'In practical terms this means we must have a clear sense of priorities! Repeat, a clear sense of priorities!'[15] Unfortunately, this wise counsel was ignored by Komer and others in the Administration who did not realize that Porter had been correct when he concluded:

> Some programs, however desirable in the longer term must be postponed if necessary and fitted into a scheme of priorities whereby they will complement and build on the pacification programs rather than compete with them.[16]

Komer talked agreement, but the activities he proposed indicated otherwise.[17] Would the priority be given to inflation control or the Chieu Hoi (Viet Cong defector program), land reform, pacification and RD (revolutionary or rural, both words were used, development), or all of them? Each was an area of real concern and genuine merit; they were seen as equally important in Washington. Komer informed Porter, the 'highest authorities' were 'interested in stepping up defection programs.'[18] The same day, Komer excitedly informed Porter that McNamara, 'in presence of highest level,' had offered to attempt to assist in dealing with the inflation crisis, implying that managing inflation had now become the top priority. Within a very few days, Komer introduced yet another overarching priority, easing the port congestion and speeding the flow of non-military goods by temporarily taking over some military wharfs and warehouses. He warned, 'If we flub this opportunity levy on military will be harder uphill fight next time.'[19] The hard-pressed Porter responded the next day that it would be necessary to build a new civilian port 'on a crash basis as we did Cam Ranh,' if inflation was to be fought successfully and the crunch in food and other civilian requirements were to be met in a timely way.[20] Port construction had entered as a competitor in priorities. It had a good goal, reduction of inflation using McNamara's suggestion of 'flood[ing] the country with essential goods,' but would in the short term at least worsen inflation and overstress both the United States Operations Mission (USOM), a component of the Embassy, and the Saigon Government.[21]

The telegrams between Komer and Porter that summer seemed at times to be the bureaucratic equivalent of a firefight with automatic weapons. Komer had a petulant streak which he expressed quickly and later repented. He also demonstrated an unfortunate proclivity for confusing the appearance of dynamic activity with the reality of substantial action. He was too impatient for results and as a result, telegrams, ideas, demands and apologies flew like shell fragments. The reality rocketed ever more distant from Porter's rational ideal of priorities and careful building.

In one area the Porter–Komer directorship moved with a fair degree of harmony and effectiveness. That was the expansion of the number of revolutionary development teams operating in South Vietnam. Originally included in the program enhancement features considered at the Warrenton Meeting, the idea had languished until April 1966.[22] Finally, McNaughton communicated the grudging approval of the Defense Department and the Joint Chiefs of Staff for the expansion to Komer and Porter. The endorsement was made contingent upon Porter accepting a 'suggestion by General Westmoreland' that the proposed program be examined in detail by a 'working group with representation from all concerned agencies.'[23] From the perspective of the Pentagon and MACV alike, problems of resource allocation loomed large. There was genuine and realistic concern on Komer's part that Westmoreland's 'reservations' and the creation of a committee in Saigon to study the issue would put the revolutionary development program on hold.[24] Given the scale of the search and destroy operations and the ever growing air war, this concern was certainly understandable, even justifiable.

The non-military programs were considered at length during the NSC meeting of 10 May 1966. Ambassador Lodge was present along with all the key Administration officials. Komer argued for the creation of a general plan to coordinate military and non-military efforts. He presented a new plan to combat the fulminating inflation within South Vietnam which demonstrated his strong belief that the American military buildup had been in large measure responsible for the problem. He urged augmenting the pacification and revolutionary development efforts.[25] Secretary Rusk outlined American policy regarding South Vietnamese political reforms including the upcoming elections for the Constitutional Assembly and the formation of political parties.[26] The Administration properly understood the interrelationship of the direct non-military programs including pacification and the indirect process of encouraging and guiding the formation of a political culture culminating in the election of a legitimate and, it could be hoped, efficient government. It was equally clear that the participants did not understand the limits of leverage available to the US now that the shooting war had become an American rather than a South Vietnamese affair.

A month later Lodge took note of Porter's plans to field one hundred revolutionary development teams by 1 September in addition to the ninety already in the villages.[27] Taken in conjunction with the introduction of the first field police-force units and the increase in funding for various village self-help programs, Lodge considered the augmentation of the revolutionary development teams to be 'brand new and highly creative.[28]

If the potential of the Revolutionary Development Cadre was to be realized, and if their activities were to have any meaningful impact upon the course of the war, it would first be necessary to reduce the deleterious effects of the US military actions on the rural social, economic and political structures. The alleviation of social and political dislocations which were the inevitable result of military operations in populated areas was impossible. This reality would in time eviscerate pacification and revolutionary development and seriously impede the accomplishment of American goals in the areas of pacification, revolutionary development and nation building. Ultimately, the dichotomy between the big battalion war and the village war would present the United States with a very significant strategic impasse.

Two months later Lodge was expressing dissatisfaction with the pace of pacification.[29] He believed that the reason for this unfortunate state of affairs was the attitude and performance of the South Vietnamese Army (ARVN). ARVN was either unable or unwilling to support pacification because 'the present kind of war has become a way of life with the Army and that the American logistic support is making it even more so.'[30] While Lodge was unclear as to what he meant by the phrase, 'present kind of war,' the reference to American logistics support implied that he believed that ARVN was too eager to participate in search and destroy sweeps. It was clear that the Ambassador thought that these operations should be left to the US forces with ARVN units concentrating on pacification support.

Komer had developed a reputation as an extremely energetic individual with a capacity for prolonged, hard work. By fall 1966 his energy, dedication and bureaucratic infighting skills were put to the test as the number of problems laid before him grew. He had become increasingly involved in efforts to stabilize the South Vietnamese economy and reduce the inflation which sprang from the effects of war and the influx of American money.[31] The economy was battered by the dislocative effects of military operations, both friendly and hostile. American military infrastructure construction projects had placed inflationary pressures on the wage structure. The flow of refugees had created large pockets of unemployment. Manpower needs of the South Vietnamese military came into conflict with those of the civilian economy, particularly agriculture. Taken together, the economic aspects of the non-military program would have overloaded most men, but for Komer they were only a small part of the work load.

Komer saw the establishment of a sound and well-coordinated relationship between the big battalion war of MACV and the village war of pacification as the crux of his task. In a letter to Porter at the end of November 1966, Komer made several suggestions to enhance the slight initial momentum in the non-military program which he perceived to have developed over the previous few weeks.

The first of these suggestions was 'keep pressing and detailed pacification plan for 1967 [emphasis in original].'[32] He described this as 'our secret weapon for putting MACV and the JCS on the spot.'[33] Komer had no faith in the search and destroy concept, believing instead in the efficacy of a clear and hold approach. As he agreed with Porter that ARVN was not yet up to the task of pacification support, Komer sought a 'coherent, forceful way to tag the military' with the mission of providing effective security for the pacification and revolutionary development efforts.[34] The only way that the US military command might be forced to abandon the sterile approach of search and destroy for the potentially far more productive technique of clearing and holding an area in support of pacification was by establishing specific requirements which would be known to and approved by the President.

Beyond developing pacification plans calculated to force MACV cooperation, Komer emphasized to Porter the necessity of showing substantial progress in several key areas which would have a major impact on the quality of peasant life in the countryside as well as burnishing the image of the Saigon government at home and overseas. These included local elections, land reform, the anticorruption drive, economic stabilization and political reconciliation between the military rulers in Saigon and the Buddhist dissenters. He identified a significant problem in the effective pursuit of progress in these fields 'in all candor, the Mission has not been set up to give adequate, continuing attention in these problem areas.'[35] While this fact had been a major source of frustration, Komer concluded, 'we have nowhere to go but up.'[36]

The failures of nation building and pacification were the result of the profound and unresolvable tensions between the needs of the non-military programs and the effects of military operations upon society. Komer recognized the cruciality of non-military programs to any eventual American policy success in South Vietnam.

The military can win battles and prevent disaster, but (aside from major – and thereby highly risky – escalation) they can't win the war. Why? – because, they can't pacify the countryside. If Hanoi

131

gets smart, we also have to be ready for a period of negotiation, in which the question of who controls the countryside is critical.[37]

He was as correct in this assessment as he had been with the perception that the large and rapid US military buildup was responsible for the hyperinflation which was destroying the South Vietnamese economy. These were factors far more easily defined than changed, considering the nature of American military doctrine and the political potency of the military high command once troops were in combat.

Another significant contributor to the disappointing results of the pacification effort was the 'shocking lack of understanding among the Americans in the provinces as to what RD and/or pacification even mean.'[38] At this time, Komer regretted that US personnel, including provincial advisors, were oriented toward the building of refugee relocation facilities. Komer quite correctly construed this focus as indicating that the Americans were unaware of or indifferent to the intangible, but critical human factors of political and social cohesion. Between the heavy military actions of MACV and the inability of American personnel charged with implementing pacification programs to see beyond their role as general contractors erecting new buildings, the revolutionary development effort was structurally undercut before it had commenced.

The ultimate purpose of the pacification, revolutionary development and nation-building programs was to mobilize support among the peasants for the Saigon government. For this purpose to be realized, for the programs to have any chance of changing the peasants from their stance of indifference or cutting their support from the Viet Cong, it would be necessary for the military to diminish search and destroy operations and focus upon clearing territory and holding population. It would also be necessary for the American personnel working with the non-military programs to love the laying of concrete less and celebrate the creation of social cohesion more.

The non-military program had high-level advocates. As early as April 1966, Komer reported that Secretary McNamara was 'eager to provide more US military support of the civil effort.'[39] The President was vitally interested in the non-military programs and Komer believed that he had a Presidential mandate.[40] In his advocacy of the civil programs, Komer was working with one very significant disadvantage which he had recognized early in his tenure as pacification 'czar.' Unlike the military campaign which was largely self-contained, the pacification and other non-military programs had to work with and through the South Vietnamese government which Komer had characterized as 'weak and apathetic.'[41] He recognized that there was no alternative, the United States could not simply take over South Vietnam as 'this would miss the very purpose of the exercise.'[42] Even with the support of both the Secretary of Defense and the President, overcoming the institutional and intellectual inertia of the US military or offsetting the political strength of the Joint Chiefs of Staff during wartime eventually proved impossible for Komer.

The potential impossibility of changing the basic orientation or theory of victory of the military should have been obvious to Komer in July when General Wheeler sent a lengthy and detailed telegram to the other Chiefs and the senior Administration officials regarding the 'security aspects of the pacification program.'[43] Wheeler was clear that pacification was a secondary consideration. American forces would not be employed in support of it except 'to the degree which COMUSMACV believes desirable and feasible.'[44] Considering the zeal with which General Westmoreland applied the search and destroy doctrine, it should have seemed unlikely that much assistance would be forthcoming.

General Wheeler informed the Administration that MACV was in the process of forming fourteen ARVN mobile training teams each of which would receive a two-week course in the concepts and techniques of revolutionary development. The formation and training of these fourteen teams was expected to be completed by 15 December 1966 following which the teams would instruct ARVN battalions in 'all types of military operations in support of RD.'[45] Wheeler believed that all ARVN battalions would have completed the program by 31 July 1967. This timetable was quite optimistic considering General Wheeler's assertion that the training would necessitate 'a complete turnaround in the basic psychology of the Vietnamese soldier' which he thought would constitute 'a lengthy, evolutionary process.'[46] Apparently, General Wheeler was not bothered by the rather obvious inconsistency in his report, but any moderately perceptive reader must have concluded that ARVN support for revolutionary development was not likely to prove either extensive or effective. Apparently, Ambassador Lodge was not a perceptive reader since he fervently supported retailoring of ARVN into a pacification support force without questioning the time that would be required for the conversion or the effectiveness of the process.[47] His only concern was that the reorientation of ARVN would lead to the US forces undertaking more combat against PAVN and the Viet Cong Main Forces and receiving more casualties. This had the potential for negatively affecting American public opinion.[48] Wheeler maintained that the war in Vietnam was 'a single war and our existing plans and actions . . . support the accomplishment of RD goals and yet maintain the flexibility that will enable us to accomplish all our military tasks.'[49]

General Wheeler set the tone for the military commanders in the field. Rhetorical support of pacification and revolutionary development was plentiful. Unfortunately, civic action was defined as activities such as refugee removal and relocation which were incidental to combat. Regardless of the relevance to genuine pacification and revolutionary development, these activities on the margin of war were always represented in an appropriate statistical summary as having been successful.[50] In keeping with this tone, Major General Charles Timmes, the Director of Remote Area Conflict at the Defense Advanced Research Projects Agency reported to Komer in October that pacification projects were 'clearly more enthusiastically supported' by MACV and subordinate commands now than a year earlier.[51] Timmes' very favorable conclusions were supported by a report which focused upon the pacification efforts made by the 173rd Airborne Brigade and two Marine battalions. Taken as a whole, Timmes' report must have further confirmed Komer in his August 1966 judgement of Marine efforts as 'well-intentioned but shallow and naive.'[52]

This evaluation might have been applied with equal accuracy to the report on civic action incorporated in a comprehensive status report on all aspects of military operations provided by General Westmoreland to Admiral Sharp in July 1966. It is apparent that at this time military civic action in support of pacification and revolutionary development was limited to minor construction projects and the distribution of food, clothing and medical assistance to peasants.[53]

There were signs of change. At the end of August, Maxwell Taylor endorsed a major change in emphasis recommended by General Westmoreland.[54] As Taylor understood General Westmoreland's revised operational concepts, pacification and revolutionary development would receive a higher priority not only from ARVN forces but from those of the US as well.

> He endorses the expansion by US/Free World forces of control over terrain and population around base areas in application of the 'oil spot' concept as the Marines have been doing in the I Corps area (and other US forces elsewhere to a lesser degree).[55]

To Taylor the changed operational concept for 1967, if successfully inaugurated and carried forward,

> offers the hope of speeding up the termination of hostilities in South Vietnam and of advancing the important non-military programs directed at controlling the population and rebuilding the shattered society and economy.[56]

The implementation of this new operational concept would require a complete reorientation of American military doctrine, training and command structure imperatives. If American forces were to operate directly in support of pacification rather than to engage in high-firepower search and destroy operations, the command structure would have to abandon the focus upon finding, fixing and destroying the enemy's forces in the field. To expect such a radical reorientation in the midst of a shooting war whose outcome was still in doubt was to expect the impossible.

The American Army would have to lay aside its most cherished theory of victory and all the doctrine, tactics, organizations and equipment developed to implement the new operational concept in the field. Taylor might have recognized this underlying reality as his concluding recommendation was cautious. 'Perhaps it [the change in operational concept] should be approved,' he wrote, 'but only after a careful analysis and in full knowledge of its implications.'[57] Taylor, unlike General Timmes, provided an assessment that was short on exuberance but was long on honesty and accuracy.

The honesty and accuracy of Komer were open to question. It was necessary for him to applaud the accomplishments of the 'other war' seven months after the Honolulu Conference so that they might be heard among the noisy cries of success coming from the military if there was to be any hope of redirecting efforts to the task of pacification, but forty-two pages of numbers tortured to show smiling faces distorted the unpleasant realities of the non-military program which were so clear in the private correspondence of Komer and Porter.[58] He was quiet in his report on the dichotomy between the effects of large military sweeps and the needs of revolutionary development, muted on the inflationary effects of the US military buildup, silent on the need for and lack of progress on land reform, and remarkably quiet on the causes for and effects of the massive movement of refugees from the rural areas, the control of which was so central to both Komer's job and the accomplishment of American policy goals in the war.

Despite his earlier concern over the undue orientation of American provincial personnel to the building of civil relocation centers regardless of the effects upon social, political and economic cohesion, Komer now proudly reported on the number of refugees generated and relocated. He recounted that in the previous twelve months temporary shelter had been provided to more than 460,000 refugees. Of these 280,000 had been permanently resettled, 'either in new locations or by return to their native villages.' As the number of refugees continued to increase, the number of people in temporary shelters had increased from 320,000 a year earlier to over 500,000 by fall 1966.[59] No figures were provided as to the number of refugees who returned to their native villages as compared to the number resettled in the New Life Hamlet relocation centers. No insight was provided as to how it would be possible to redevelop and pacify a countryside in which a significant percentage of the population had been uprooted from ancestral lands, political traditions, social structures and economic patterns.

It could have been argued in a powerful fashion to the President that unless military operations which made homeless and desperate refugees out of the peasant majority of South Vietnam were halted, there could be no pacification, no revolutionary development, no mobilization of popular support for the Saigon government and against the Viet Cong and as a clear and immutable consequence, no US victory. Abandoning any previous beliefs to the contrary, Komer now did not view the flood of refugees as a sign of potential failure. Instead, he, with like exuberance, saw refugees as a 'systematic weapon in the war.'[60] Komer argued that the US should select specific target groups and by using 'a whole range of possible pressures, induce them to abandon their homes.'[61] After resettlement in accordance with the overall pacification scheme the refugees would be employed as 'GVN assets.'[62] Komer believed that it was unfortunate that the practice of using refugees as a weapon had fallen into disuse since the failed Agroville and Strategic Hamlet programs of the Diem era. Komer's astigmatic view of the role of the peasant in Vietnamese society and culture was unjustifiable. His ability to perceive a virtue in the unavoidable effects of military action was a mark of Komer's excellence as a bureaucrat. His failure to see and act upon the fatal inconsistency between the tasks of pacification or revolutionary development and the use of refugees as a weapon made Komer the wrong man to be field marshal in the 'other war.'

Komer demonstrated a remarkable lack of focus in his statement of goals for fiscal year 1967.[63] The goals were too diffuse to allow for either an effective allocation of resources or the proper concentration of effort on the most critical problems. Komer averred that the US should pursue expansive goals in the following areas: inflation control, import reforms, improvement of port facilities, the increase of rice supplies, resource controls and economic warfare, improvement of transportation security, police, improvement of governmental administrative services, pacification and revolutionary development, Chieu Hoi (the program of encouraging Viet Cong defectors), population control, health and medical services, education, agriculture, land reform, industrial development, refugee handling and resettlement, youth programs and improvement in the US Mission staff dealing with civil programs. While each of these areas might have had a degree of importance, the wholesale inclusion without any statement of priorities assured the expenditure of energy and money in a directionless fashion.

Had Komer desired to pursue matters in an intellectually honest fashion rather than in the thoughtless shotgun manner that gave the impression of energetic action without the reality of purpose, he would have narrowed the field and assigned priority to certain programs at the expense of others. Pacification and nation building were complex sets of interlocking tasks with some being predicates for others. Komer realized this as he demonstrated repeatedly in his private correspondence with Porter. Komer's failure to state clearly and categorically that some tasks, particularly pacification, revolutionary development, refugee return, land reform and inflation reduction must have priority so the others might be undertaken with a greater potential of success was not only unfortunate, it was a contributor to defeat.

The Seven Nation Conference in Manila, 23–25 October 1966, provided an additional impetus to the non-military side of the war. While the 'other war' was not the centerpiece at Manila that it had been at the Honolulu Conference, the non-military programs were repeatedly underscored by a President and an Administration attempting to convey a message of resolve to North Vietnam, hope to the South Vietnamese, encouragement to the other Asian nations and justification to an American public growing increasingly restive with the war. Secretary of Defense McNamara spent 10–13 October in Saigon in final preparation for the upcoming conference.

Upon returning from his eighth trip to South Vietnam, Robert McNamara as usual wrote a detailed memorandum to the President.[64] He urged that pacification be pursued vigorously. He recommended that ARVN be given the clear and hold mission as he did not believe that the US could do 'this pacification security job.'[65] His arguments for exempting US forces from the clear and hold mission were in large measure specious as shown by the assertion 'if our efforts worked at all, it would merely postpone the eventual confrontation of the VC and GVN infrastructure.'[66] McNamara embraced the concept that responsibility for pacification and revolutionary development be placed under MACV. This decision by the Secretary was important to the further evolution of the 'other war.'[67] Robert Komer supported the McNamara position on turning responsibility for pacification over to General Westmoreland as 'Westy is the only one who can move ARVN.'[68] Komer, like McNamara, exhibited a well-repressed but not completely suppressed fear of US troops being trapped in pacification support and security activities for years to come.

In the aftermath of the Manila Conference, President Johnson asked his National Security Advisor, Walt Whitman Rostow, to form an ad hoc committee including Komer, Nicholas Katzenbach, the recently confirmed Under Secretary of State, and Cyrus Vance the Under Secretary of Defense to consider a strategy for Vietnam. On 30 November Rostow sent the group's initial conclusions to the President.[69] There were three areas in which action was necessary: 'General Westmoreland must allocate more of his own military resources to pacification' while moving ARVN into this mission, the US must have a new ambassador in Saigon with managerial talent and the Washington end of the pacification program must be improved.[70]

The committee believed the massive US buildup had stabilized the military situation but the Viet Cong infrastructure, although damaged, continued to possess the capability to inflict heavy costs upon the South Vietnamese government and required the indefinite presence of the US forces to prevent a Viet Cong victory.[71] It was believed that as long as the Viet Cong infrastructure remained intact, Hanoi would continue to support the guerrillas regardless of the amount of punishment inflicted upon North Vietnam by American bombers. The committee assumed that the major factors holding Hanoi into its assigned role of external sponsoring power were the continued existence of the Viet Cong political infrastructure capable of waging guerrilla war, and the North Vietnamese ability to withstand the effects of the air war through its own efforts and assistance from the Soviet Union and Communist China.[72] Of these two factors, the United States could affect only the first.

The strategic solution was the effective neutralization of the Viet Cong infrastructure and the undercutting of its mass-support base. The ingredients for this comprised military pressure, psychological operations, accelerated pacification, and a land-reform program.[73] The enervation of the Viet Cong as a political–military force would serve to potentiate the effects of the air war by 'making Hanoi feel that it is paying a higher and higher price to preserve a probably diminishing asset.'[74] Additional pressures could be exerted on North Vietnam by erecting a physical barrier to infiltration, mounting a more effective attrition campaign against the land and sea routes of infiltration and mounting a campaign of increasingly heavy attacks upon high-value targets in Hanoi and Haiphong.[75] The mixture of higher costs with reduced benefits should provide Hanoi with the impetus to negotiate or tacitly end its support activities in the South.

Rostow and his associates continued to assume that Hanoi was playing the part of an external sponsoring power. They did not consider that the North Vietnamese might now be seeking the goal of forceful reunification in which case the Viet Cong might be as much the adversary as the Saigon government and the United States. If that were the case, the removal of the Viet Cong infrastructure would not constitute a diminishment of benefit but the converse. An increase in the weight of the US air war would not be seen as a price so much as a mechanism for the mobilization and consolidation of political will and support. The possibility that the eighteen months of escalating American ground and air actions had changed the nature and character of the war so that there were now two separate and distinct opponents, the Viet Cong and the North Vietnamese, was not considered although there was evidence to suggest this was the case.

Also unconsidered were the difficulties which the US ground forces would face in the attempt to shift their focus from the large search and destroy missions to an operational concept more suitable for pacification support. There were several separate factors that would directly influence the efficiency and thoroughness of the contemplated change in approach. It would be necessary for the US ground and air forces in South Vietnam to alter radically their fundamental doctrine, concepts, organizations and command imperatives. PAVN and the Viet Cong main forces would have to be willing to abandon their own relatively large-scale operations and allow the US to move from bashing the bush to securing the villages. ARVN, either alone or in conjunction with US and other Free World forces, would have to develop and to demonstrate the capacity for working the pacification security and support beat. Until large-unit sweeps and the concomitant dislocation of the civilian population were ended, pacification, revolutionary development and pre-emptive reforms would be substantially impossible. Unless the US could abandon search and destroy missions which would take the implicit connivance of PAVN and the main force Viet Cong, the Rostow group's emphasis upon destruction of the Viet Cong infrastructure would yield little in the way of useful result, except, perhaps, to Hanoi and its goals.

While the Rostow Group's assessments of the North Vietnamese imperatives were less than complete, and their evaluations of the South Vietnamese political situation tinged with a degree of unjustified optimism, the view taken of American domestic imperatives was both complete and free of undue optimism. The report quite accurately summarized the major domestic problem confronting the Administration in maintaining public support: 'The need to give our citizens a better sense of how to measure progress in a war of this kind.'[76] The Administration had not yet found a way to convey to the public in a clear and convincing way what progress the US and South Vietnam were making against the PAVN and the Viet Cong main force. Counts of bodies and accounts of battles in a war without fronts or lines had led to confusion and frustration. The Administration had not found a way to demonstrate 'what progress we may make in the countryside towards pacification and development.'[77] Had the Rostow committee been totally honest it would have admitted that the Administration as a whole had not yet found a way by which it could measure progress, and so it was scarcely a surprise that it had not been able to convey a positive and credible message about the 'other war' to the American public.

The report showed that Rostow and his three associates were attempting in a fundamental way to alter the American theory of victory. It is fair to argue that the approach they were advocating with

139

its emphasis upon pre-emptive reforms calculated to undercut the insurgents' mass-support base, psychological operations to magnify the effect of the reforms and to sap the will of the guerrilla rank and file to continue the fight and selective application of military pressures to remove the infrastructure was two years behind the actual character of the war in 1966. Arguably, the continued consideration of Hanoi as an external sponsoring power without considering alternatives eroded the applicability of the recommendations. None the less, the report had the advantage of proposing an alternative to the mere continuation of policies which had not yet worked.

The changing positions of other key participants in the Vietnam policy planning process served to reinforce the alternative operational concept espoused by the Rostow committee. General Westmoreland's newly discovered and less than complete commitment to pacification and the qualified endorsement given it by Maxwell Taylor indicated that the will to alter doctrine in the midst of war existed near the top of the chain of command, and this was an encouraging, if not particularly realistic, development. Ambassador Lodge had become another recent convert to pacification as William Leonhart reported to the President and Komer at the end of August.[78] Although Lodge was on the way out of Saigon by late 1966, his conversion to pacification assured that the Embassy staff moved effectively into the area with important results for 1967.[79] Rostow insured that the musings of General Edward Lansdale, a virtual counterinsurgency guru, were sent to the President in mid-November 1966 as they reinforced the basic thrust of the new strategy.[80]

The seriousness of Komer's commitment to bringing pacification and infrastructure neutralization to the top priority cannot be doubted. He sent a paper which he had written in early August to Secretary of Defense McNamara on 1 September.[81] In the cover letter he stated that the proposals had been shown to General Westmoreland who had agreed to take over pacification responsibilities.[82] In a very carefully worded conclusion filled with appropriate modesty and expressions of confidence in Westmoreland, he pitched himself to be the person responsible within MACV for pacification and revolutionary development.[83] The pitch was successful and Komer would have the job within six months. In a letter on the same subject to Maxwell Taylor later in the month, he claimed, with a degree of legitimacy, that his report had been responsible for securing McNamara's support for the shifting of pacification to MACV.[84]

A week later he sent a memorandum to McNamara in which several pacification issues were assessed. He approached the question of the number of ARVN and American troops that should be employed for pacification quite carefully.

To me the US forces are going to have to take on the difficult task of teaching ARVN how to pacify (paradoxical as this seems), and probably show them by example, by joining in combined operations. But my hunch is that, with at least 400,000 men in sight and main force targets hard to find, Westy could take this on as essentially a byproduct operation using those forces which are not otherwise engaged [emphasis in original].[85]

He asserted that 'offensive-minded' clear and hold pacification operations would take far fewer troops than many thought as the US now held the battlefield initiative. He was wrong in his assumption that the United States did hold the initiative in the shooting war, but neither he nor Taylor was aware of that. In other matters, he recommended a much larger psychological warfare effort if the 'hearts and minds' of the peasants were to be won over to the US/GVN cause. He undercut the potential of winning these organs a few sentences later when he again thumped the tub in favor of a systematic refugee generation program designed to deprive the Viet Cong of potential manpower.[86] Whether he recognized the unintentional irony is doubtful.

By the end of September Komer had defined the nature of the pacification program and the responsibilities of the proposed MACV Deputy for pacification.[87] His arguments for pacification receiving a high priority and for its centralization under MACV were later incorporated in the Rostow strategy proposal. In defining the responsibilities of the MACV Deputy, Komer showed an unusual sharpness of focus: 'only those field activities which primarily and directly contribute to winning the village war.'[88] These would include Chieu Hoi, refugees, resource control, and psychological warfare directed against the Viet Cong structure and the rural population. The deputy would have room to grow and MACV support to make growth possible, even probable. McNamara and Katzenbach concurred and recommended to the President in October that the pacification and revolutionary development program be placed under MACV.[89] Secretary Rusk agreed with the proposal, overriding the strong objections of Porter who had been in charge of pacification since spring and was familiar with Embassy and Saigon attitudes regarding the 'militarization of pacification.'[90] McNamara, Rusk, Rostow, the Under Secretaries of Defense and State and Komer all agreed, pacification and revolutionary development must be placed under COMUSMACV. It was only a matter of time before the President would authorize the assignment and select a director.

After Thanksgiving 1966, Komer was again at his typewriter. On the same day as Rostow sent the strategy memorandum to the President, Komer sent a memo with two enclosures to Cyrus Vance, Nicholas

Katzenbach and Walt Rostow.[91] His prognosis for 1967 was reasonably optimistic accentuating the success of the search and destroy missions in spoiling the potential offensives of the Viet Cong and PAVN and 'killing, defecting or otherwise attriting more VC/NVA strength than the enemy can build up.'[92] Komer believed that as a concomitant of these successes the population of South Vietnam had become more confident in its own government. In summary, he asserted, 'we're beginning to "win" the war in Vietnam.'[93] Because of a number of imponderables, he cautiously retreated from that roseate characterization slightly, but still expected that the trends for mid- and late 1967 would be favorable.

Komer posited that by the end of 1967 General Westmoreland's forces, assisted by the bombing campaigns, the construction of physical barriers to infiltration and the vastly improved logistics base, should have significantly hurt the enemy's large units. The General at that time should be able to dedicate roughly a quarter of his forces to pacification. The pacification program 'ought to show quite visible progress' with many key roads having been opened, and the Viet Cong's ability to recruit, tax and collect rice having been impaired significantly. As a result of the pacification successes and improvements in psychological warfare operations, the Chieu Hoi should have produced 45,000 'returnees' while new 'special operations should have turned up some high quality defectors.'[94]

The high figure predicted for the Chieu Hoi program was in part based upon the belief that the recommendations of Lucien Pye and the guidelines of Field Development Division of the Joint United States Public Affairs Office regarding psychological operations directed against the Viet Cong guerrillas and their families could be put into full effect by American combat units and ARVN.[95] Shortly after Komer's 'Prognosis' had been written and distributed, there was confirmation of his assumptions concerning palpable improvement in the operation of Chieu Hoi efforts. An all-time record high number of returnees was reported: 2,505 for the period 3–30 November 1966.[96]

Komer predicted that South Vietnamese political culture had a '50/50 chance' of reaching the level of representative elections with a reasonable system of checks and balances between the military and civilians. As a result of these favorable trends, 'Hanoi would start negotiating or withdrawing somewhere along this curve.'[97] Komer smoothly glissaded through a set of assumptions and hedged his assessments with subtlety, but asserted finally,

> the key to success in the South is an effective pacification program plus a stepped up defection program and successful evolution toward a more dynamic, representative and thus more attractive GVN [emphasis in original].[98]

These measures taken together could, he believed, lead to a 'band-wagon psychology' among the Southerners which, in turn, would lead to victory. Not surprisingly, Komer, who intended to take personal charge of the pacification program, had developed a theory of victory which emphasized the cruciality of pacification. Had he made the same argument in 1964 before the American air campaign had started to change the character of the war away from insurgency and toward a more conventional interstate conflict, he would have been correct beyond a doubt. In late 1966 with the North Vietnamese having entered the war with the expansive goal of total authority over all Vietnam, his theory of victory was less relevant to the realities on the ground.

Komer's strategy for 1967, which became a draft NSAM discussed with the President by McNamara and Katzenbach on 13 December, embodied a nine-part action program.[99] Komer sought to achieve three specific strategic aims: maximizing the chances for a satisfactory outcome by December 1967, making it clear to Hanoi and the VC/NLF that the war was being won by Saigon and the US and complementing 'our anti-main force campaign and bombing offensive' with pacification and nation building.[100] The nine elements of the action plan, presumably in order of priority, were:

- press a major pacification effort,
- increase the search and destroy operations against VC/PAVN,
- enhance the interdiction efforts and pressure against Hanoi,
- implement a major and ongoing National Reconciliation Program,
- press for a more democratic Saigon government,
- institute effective land reform and local governments,
- check inflation and maintain the civilian economy,
- devise negotiating strategies and pursue any diplomatic leads,
- mount a major public information campaign directed at American and world opinion including the development and use of believable ways to measure progress.

Not only was Komer's plan comprehensive, it played to all the propensities of the Administration including the continued focus on search and destroy, the seeming inevitability of the air war, McNamara's desire to erect a physical barrier against infiltration, fears of diminished public support and the need to demonstrate both the justice of the American cause and the success of American efforts. It is possible to fault Komer's action program on the basis of its relevance to the realities on the ground in Vietnam, but it is impossible to criticize it as a work of skillful bureaucratic manipulation.

Komer's analysis and recommendations received powerful support from Maxwell Taylor in January 1967. In a memorandum sent prior to General Taylor's departure on a ten-day fact-finding mission to

Southeast Asia including five days in South Vietnam, Komer stated that, as he saw it, 'the most important problem area needing a fresh look is that of *pacification* – especially the military aspects which are paramount.'[101] He helpfully supplied the general with a copy of his strategic plan for 1967. General Taylor must have found Komer's action program agreeable reading as the memorandum he sent the President upon his return reinforced its contentions.[102] Taylor was optimistic on the 'Big War (Search and Destroy)' and quite bullish on the air war if it were to be intensified, but considered 'RD is the weak sector of our efforts.'[103] He supported General Westmoreland's plans to continue and intensify the search and destroy operations while recognizing the 'necessity of supporting RD.'[104] He also approved of the centralization of the pacification and revolutionary development programs under a civilian deputy director, although not necessarily within MACV as he believed that revolutionary development was essentially a South Vietnamese task in which the American involvement and responsibility must be kept minimal or the likelihood of permanent progress in the area would be obviated. His conclusion was optimistic in expression but hedged in caution.

> We must do better in our ground operations in the south, raise the level of air operations in the north, inaugurate a constitutional president, hold the line against inflation and show significant progress in RD in the principal areas of population. If we can do these things in Viet-Nam while conducting ourselves at home in such a way as to show that, regardless of pressures, the U.S. will not change its course, I have the feeling that the Vietnamese situation may change drastically for the better by the end of 1967.[105]

In a critical, related matter, the search for a replacement to Ambassador Lodge, Taylor supported making William Westmoreland Ambassador as well as COMUSMACV.[106] Presumably, Komer would have supported this recommendation more enthusiastically than its companion, keeping the civil field activities of pacification and revolutionary development under the Embassy's Office of Civil Operations for the immediate future.

COMUSMACV would not become Ambassador but he would get the pacification mission and Komer as a deputy. McNamara, Rusk, Rostow and Komer were all in favor of that. The Secretary of Defense had adopted the idea as his own in September largely because it promised managerial efficiency and might serve to redirect some US military efforts into channels both more productive and more acceptable to domestic public opinion, points which Komer skillfully played upon.[107]

The strategic plans of Rostow, McNamara and Komer all converged in making effective pacification the centerpiece for success in 1967, although none addressed the tensions between continued large-scale search and destroy operations and the rural climate needed for effective pacification and development. Similarly, all had recognized the importance of inflation control and economic stability, but none questioned the difficulty of accomplishing this important task with the continuation of the big battalion sweeps. All emphasized the creation of a legitimate, viable democratic South Vietnamese government, but none asked how this might be accomplished in a society of refugees. All sought to remove North Vietnam as a supporter of the Viet Cong, but none considered the possibility that North Vietnam was not a sponsor but rather a competitor of the Southern guerrillas. The inconsistencies and intellectual dissonance within the strategic plans went unnoticed, apparently being obscured by the general background color of optimism. Whether the realities admitted of its accomplishment or not, pacification would be the theme of 1967, the new ingredient in the American theory of victory, and Komer would be in charge of the effort.

6

THE YEAR OF VICTORY?

Would 1967 be the year of American success in Vietnam or would it be the year of diminished American political will? The several assessments of the air war offered in November and December 1966 taken together with the blank indifference of Hanoi to all diplomatic demarches would have led many to conclude that 1967 would not be the year of American success. Continuing political turmoil within the South and doubts about the utility of ARVN or the viability of the pacification and revolutionary development programs would have strengthened further the hands of the pessimistic. The only bright spot was the apparent success of the US ground forces in blunting large-scale enemy offensives.

It was against this background that Secretary McNamara asked the CIA to perform an estimate of the state of play in Vietnam. The product was sent to the Secretary and Walt Whitman Rostow on 9 January 1967. The Agency saw only one clear trend as having emerged over the preceding eighteen months, 'the chances that the Communists would win South Vietnam by military victory have vanished.'[1] All other facets of the war effort were seen as inconclusive, except the air operations against North Vietnam and the lines of communication through Laos. The Board of National Estimates was conclusive in its tone when discussing this element of the American theory of victory. The bombing had not reduced either the will or ability of North Vietnam to continue the war. The bombing campaign had been successfully employed by Hanoi to 'discredit the whole US effort in Vietnam.'[2] The bombing had not resulted in materiel deficiencies among either PAVN or Viet Cong forces in the South. Perhaps most disturbing, neither the bombing nor the promise of ending it had induced a move by the North, nor presumably the NLF, to the negotiating table. Nor did there seem any likelihood that this would change in the near future.

The war on the ground had gone well for the US in the limited sense that the American intervention had prevented the chance of a conclusive and sudden victory by either the Viet Cong or PAVN on the battlefield. American firepower and mobility had assured that neither guerrillas nor PAVN troops could successfully invoke the Clausewitzian fetish of bloody and decisive combat. However, the US forces could not prevent the successful employment of protracted guerrilla conflict. The adoption of small-unit guerrilla and terrorist tactics would benefit the enemy as it could neutralize many of the American advantages in firepower and mobility while exploiting American weaknesses in political will. As the PAVN and Viet Cong main forces had been able to increase their total strength during 1966 from 83,000 men to 106,000, it was legitimate to assume that effective force levels could be maintained with greater ease if conventional operations were to be replaced at least in part by guerrilla tactics and terrorist actions.[3] It was still too early to declare an American military victory on the ground. It was still too soon to be certain that the US and South Vietnamese military forces had permanently gained the initiative or that the North Vietnamese could not successfully seek escalation dominance in one or more critical regions.

With the prospect of protracted conflict in mind, the Agency analysts focused upon the political struggle within the South and the question of the relative political will in North Vietnam, South Vietnam and the United States. In this context pacification and nation building loomed large. The capability to secure and pacify population and agricultural centers was crucial to the accomplishment of American goals. Unfortunately, most of this capacity had to reside with the South Vietnamese government and ARVN, and these were two weak reeds upon which to rest American hopes and the future of the South. ARVN was described as 'not in good shape,' with poor morale, and only four of its eleven divisions 'capable of reasonable performance in combat.'[4] ARVN would improve only slowly. The same was said of the South Vietnamese government. 'Progress in pacification and winning over the population is likely to come slowly and painfully.'[5]

If progress was made, it would affect the matter of political will. To the Agency, political will was seen as a crucial matter. 'Hanoi's determination probably is strengthened by hopes that the US will lose heart if the struggle is prolonged and by its belief that South Vietnam cannot create a viable political structure capable of winning mass support.'[6] The implication was inescapable: if these two factors could be addressed effectively and convincingly, Hanoi would abandon the struggle. The Administration might have entertained doubts about American will to persevere and its ability to focus this will. There are no doubts that the Administration had profound reservations concerning the ability and political will of the South Vietnamese government.

General Westmoreland's concept of operations for 1967 was based on what he called 'a two fisted strategy.'[7] One fist was to be directed

147

toward the task of pacification and the other against PAVN and the Viet Cong main force. He proposed seizing every opportunity to fight PAVN and the Viet Cong main forces through a systematic campaign of search and destroy sweeps which would require a large number of troops. The other fist was to be directed at the war in the villages. Westmoreland projected the use of reconnaissance and specialist formations to seek out and destroy the political and military infrastructure of the NLF/VC. He intended to mount operations directed at securing friendly lines of communication and harassing those of the enemy. Finally, he decided to expand the GOLDEN FLEECE program of securing rice harvests so as to deny food to the enemy.

As he had written the operational proposals for 1967, General Westmoreland viewed the increased PAVN presence in I Corps with calm confidence. He proposed maintaining 'the minimum number of battalions south of the Demilitarized Zone as deemed acceptable in consideration of intelligence on the enemy or weather and our ability to reinforce.'[8] Confident of having the initiative, the General initially had seen 1967 as the time to mount several offensive campaigns in Quang Ngai Province and the A Shau Valley with the intention of clearing areas long held by the Viet Cong and denying their future use.[9] He had been equally optimistic about the American potential to mount large offensive sweeps into the Viet Cong base areas of the Iron Triangle and War Zone C in III Corps Tactical Zone (CTZ).[10]

Altogether, his plan for 1967 was intensely optimistic and gave no sign of any impending difficulties. Within a short time his confidence wobbled, he altered his plans radically, finally gave credence to the CIA's early warnings of the previous November and cobbled together a special reserve maneuver force to counter the PAVN presence in and south of the DMZ. He would inflate discussions already under way to the level of debate with a request to the JCS and the Administration for an additional 250,000 troops.[11]

Both the air war and the 'other war' had been under examination almost from the first of the year. In January 1967, Komer wrote to Nicholas Katzenbach, who chaired the Under-Secretary-level committee which coordinated policy on Vietnam concerning his perception of the top priorities for 1967. At the top of Komer's list were completing the political development process in the South and bringing the pacification program up to an effective speed using 'the bulk of the revamped ARVN.'[12] Also on the list were holding local elections to undercut the NLF, keeping Saigon supportive of the National Reconciliation Program, and holding down inflation. A few days later Rostow wrote the President concerning means of evaluating the air war against the North and the desirability of developing new operational concepts in a way which showed that the President was troubled about ROLLING THUNDER and the reports of its inefficacy which had blossomed in late 1966.[13]

Concerns about the air war and pacification were equally in order. At the very least the lengthy reports of the CIA and the Rand Corporation in November and December 1966 had raised grave doubts about the effectiveness of the air war. Additionally, they should have raised significant warning flags regarding the nature of Hanoi's goals and its actual relationship to the Viet Cong, but such was not the case. William Leonhart had come back from this third visit to South Vietnam during 1966 and reported to the President that progress was being made in all the non-military programs except pacification.[14] He considered the lack of progress in pacification to be 'the crux of the Vietnam problem.'[15] He recommended a basic re-examination of intelligence concerning VC/PAVN force levels, infiltration and recruitment rates. He urged detailed planning to coordinate civilian and military programs for pacification and accelerating the rate at which ARVN could be fully retrained and redeployed on pacification missions.[16] The Administration faced substantial problems in facilitating and assessing the progress of pacification and revolutionary development.

The air campaign against the North took center stage at the NSC meeting in February. Earle Wheeler recited the accomplishments of air operations in all regions, mentioning that during 1966 US aircraft flew 81,000 attack and 48,000 combat support sorties against the North, 48,000 attack and 10,000 combat support sorties against targets in the Laotian panhandle, 130,000 attack and 31,000 combat sorties in South Vietnam and 5,000 B–52 sorties, most in South Vietnam.[17] These statistics were used to support his contention that the air campaigns had significantly and positively altered the course of the war in the South by effectively interdicting the flow of men and supplies while imposing a heavy drain upon North Vietnamese manpower by compelling Hanoi to establish elaborate air defense systems and to repair the extensive damage inflicted by the bombers. General Wheeler, following his trip to South Vietnam in mid-January 1967, had concluded that the air campaign against North Vietnam in conjunction with the 'vigorous and aggressive' ground combat actions in the South had assured that PAVN and the Viet Cong could no longer win the war. He reaffirmed the position of the Joint Chiefs that ROLLING THUNDER should not be halted without a 'substantial reciprocal action' on the part of Hanoi.[18] Obviously, the Chairman and the Chiefs as a body had not accepted the pessimistic appreciations of the CIA and Rand.

In all probability, the Chiefs were far more willing to accept the conclusions of a lengthy exercise in statistical thaumaturgy on enemy logistics and manpower requirements which had been executed in September 1966. Employing a mixture of smoke, mirrors and equations this JASON study performed by the Institute for Defense Analysis concluded that the aerial interdiction effort had been working, although it was admitted that some uncertainty existed regarding the effectiveness of the search and destroy sweeps in producing meaningful attrition.[19] The Administration faced a difficult task in assessing the significance and implications of the obvious dichotomy between the Chiefs and the CIA concerning the air war.

By 1967 the National Security Council was becoming an unimportant body. Decisions regarding the war in Vietnam were made by a much smaller group of senior Administration officials during meetings in more informal contexts such as lunch with the President. Secretaries Rusk and McNamara along with Walt Rostow held a working lunch with the President on 22 February 1967. These working lunches at which a wide variety of foreign policy issues were considered had been an almost weekly feature since the beginning of the year. The one that Wednesday stood out because of its importance in setting the course of the war in Vietnam for the balance of the year. The centerpiece of the discussion was an eighteen-page option package which proposed alternative military operations for use against North Vietnam and activities to be employed in the South. It established the boundary limits for American operations for the year. It demonstrated the tensions and contradictions which existed among the various components of the American theory of victory which were unseen at the time. It demonstrated as well the intellectual astigmatism of the Administration which prevented observing the tensions and contradictions which filled the portfolio of operational concepts.

One set of fundamental tensions existed between actions directed against the North and those employed in the South. The second set was between the American search and destroy sweeps directed at the PAVN and Viet Cong main forces and the clear and hold procedures required for the success of pacification and revolutionary development. A third locus of tension existed between the need to see the South Vietnamese government become more legitimate and more effective and the perceived requirement for military operations which hindered governmental efficiency and undercut legitimacy in the minds of the peasants caught in the crossfire. A final area of tension existed between the American need to see ARVN and the South Vietnamese government undertake more field operations and the desire of the Saigon regime to conserve resources and consolidate itself. The multipart American theory of victory which had emerged in all its contradictions by New Year's Day 1967 sought to find the appropriate balance between pressure on the North, interdiction, search and destroy sweeps, pacification, and nation building. It would be an extremely difficult search.

When Rostow, Rusk, McNamara and the President met for lunch on 22 February no progress had been made in resolving the difference between the assessment of the air war offered by the Chiefs and that argued by the CIA. No headway had been made in determining how to assess the achievements of the pacification and revolutionary development efforts. No breakthrough had been made in understanding or reconciling the inherently irreconcilable natures of the war in the villages and the war of the big battalions. There had been no improvement in the Administration's comprehension of potential changes in the goals held by Hanoi and the effect of the air war over North Vietnam upon those goals.

Four topics were discussed within an eighteen-page outline of potential actions against the North and within South Vietnam: air and naval attacks on North Vietnamese targets, interdiction efforts within Laos including increased use of small ground units and cloud seeding over the Ho Chi Minh Trail, expansion of the search and destroy operations, and improvements in pacification.[20] Of the eighteen pages fourteen dealt with the options for increased air and naval attacks. Among the choices were the eradication of modern industry, the destruction of the dams and levees used for agricultural purposes, the mining of ports and port approaches, the removal or reduction of restrictions on line of communication attacks, including eliminating the ten-mile Hanoi prohibited area and decreasing the prohibited area around Haiphong to four miles, and destruction of the six airfields in North Vietnam which could handle jet aircraft.[21] Rostow's manuscript annotations show that some of these options such as the reduction of the Haiphong prohibited area were specifically disapproved and others such as the gradual destruction of thermal power plants and selected rail facilities were approved while the majority continued under consideration.

The SHINING BRASS program under which platoon sized units of South Vietnamese and American personnel penetrated Laos to a depth of 20 kilometers (or 60 kilometers, according to General Westmoreland) to perform reconnaissance and attack targets of opportunity was to be expanded in frequency and to employ larger forces.[22] The employment of battalion-sized exploitation forces and the sponsoring of guerrillas within the Laotian panhandle were also approved, subject to the concurrence of General Wheeler.[23] Cloud seeding over the Corridor with the intent of causing rains of sufficient intensity and duration to hinder vehicular traffic was also approved.

The President and his advisors decided to accelerate the deployment of already authorized forces to South Vietnam so the level of 462,000 would be reached in September 1967 rather than December as originally scheduled.[24] Two additional squadrons of air force fighter-bombers would be sent, 'if Westy desires.'[25]

The final subject considered was pacification. This topic was characterized as 'the most important factor in convincing Hanoi to accept a political settlement of the war.'[26] The pacification picture was portrayed in bleak terms. Efforts to remake ARVN into a pacification force had not yet proven effective. US-sponsored attempts to improve local government in Saigon-controlled and -contested areas had been slow in producing results. There was no hard intelligence that the US search and destroy operations had produced a collapse of Viet Cong strength, and there were indications that the enemy was adapting to the US efforts by redirecting their forces to small-scale guerrilla and terrorist activities. None the less, it was concluded that there were no actions that either the US or South Vietnam could take 'which would markedly accelerate this program.'[27] Underlying this conclusion was the perceived deficiency of trained South Vietnamese civil administrators and local defense forces. There were other actions which the US could take, one of which was implied in the marginal annotation, 'improve pacification – especially campaign against hard-core cadres.'[28] Here might be seen the faint outlines of a component of the pacification effort which was to become quite controversial, Operation Phoenix.

There was no sign that any at the lunch meeting recognized the irony of their actions although it should have been apparent. The pacification program was seen as central to the favorable resolution of the war, but there was nothing immediate and significant which the US could do to improve the so far unsatisfying progress of the pacification and revolutionary development effort because of South Vietnamese deficiencies. There had been no persuasive indication substantiating the assertions of Earle Wheeler that the air war was paying any dividend and many indicators that ROLLING THUNDER had been completely counterproductive and instrumental in changing the character of the war. None the less, its continuation and enlargement were within the capacities of the United States. Again, the Administration authorized expansion of the air campaign, not because that was an action which *should* be done, but because it was one which *could* be done.

A week later, having just returned from his sixth trip to South Vietnam, Komer wrote a remarkably upbeat report to the President.[29] His general impression was that 'we are grinding down the enemy by sheer weight and mass.'[30] Komer argued that better management, better coordination between civil and military officials, particularly in the pacification program, and a more effective South Vietnamese government would allow the US and Saigon to develop and exploit the growing psychology of victory which he reported as emerging in the South. The Saigon government was in the process of transformation and, if the US worked quickly, the political situation could be manipulated to assure a more stable, responsive and legitimate regime.[31] This factor plus the upcoming six-round village and hamlet elections and the new interest in land reform exhibited by Ky and Thieu persuaded Komer to view the political dynamic for 1967 far more optimistically than had the senior Administration figures during their lunch with the President a week earlier.[32]

Komer was sanguine about the ground war while agreeing that Westmoreland's more sober appreciation was also correct. Komer believed that the enormous movement of the population, a total of 785,000 in 1966, from areas through which the US search and destroy sweeps were cutting their great swaths to the cities and towns 'can't help but constrict the VC's recruiting base.'[33] With this refugee flow and the concomitant urban population explosion, Komer saw only the potential for success. He saw no possibility that the refugees, the squalid urban shantytowns, the destruction of traditional economic, political, social and cultural patterns, might serve as a medium for further Viet Cong actions.

He was particularly buoyant about the progress in pacification. There was still a long way to go before there would be a fully effective pacification and revolutionary development effort in place because 'pacification is by its very nature the toughest job we face in Vietnam.'[34] In 1967, unlike earlier periods, pacification could proceed behind the shield of the massive American search and destroy sweeps and could bring adequate resources to the task including 'much of the ARVN,' more than 300,000 regional and popular militiamen, 400 RD Cadre teams and several thousand national police.[35] Komer observed, 'By sheer weight alone, this mass application cannot help but produce significant results in 1967 [emphasis in original].'[36]

Quite in opposition to the Administration's gloomy estimate of ARVN competence in pacification, Komer argued that the retraining of the South Vietnamese Army was progressing in a completely satisfactory way with 60 maneuver battalions of a total of 158 having been assigned to pacification support missions.[37] Organization, management and goals for the RD Cadre teams had been greatly improved in Komer's estimation. Their potential utility was endangered, Komer believed, by the South Vietnamese Ministry of Revolutionary Development having been too cautious in setting its goals for 1967. He argued that the result would be the creation of pacification vacuums in the wake of search and destroy sweeps.[38] Better intelligence, improved local command and control and improved coordination would still be necessary, but these were considerations which could be rapidly and effectively addressed by a dynamic MACV Deputy for Pacification.

While General Westmoreland may still have entertained doubts about taking over primary responsibility for pacification and revolutionary development support activities, he was enthusiastic about the use of ARVN in the pacification role. At a conference of senior American commanders in late January 1967, Westmoreland stated that the South Vietnamese government was 'very much behind' the use of ARVN in support of revolutionary development.[39] He requested all commanders to undertake measures which would encourage ARVN to support pacification and revolutionary development including taking an interest in the Mobile Training Teams which were giving two week courses in the basics of revolutionary development. General Walt, the Marine Corps commander in I Corps enthusiastically seconded Westmoreland concerning the importance of bringing ARVN into pacification and civic actions.[40]

The South Vietnamese government was accused by Komer of being unresponsive and uncooperative in economic matters. This unfortunate predilection was ascribed to the effects of ongoing election campaigns and an increasingly nationalistic climate attendant upon the elections. Perhaps Komer was oversimplifying the situation. The effects of the war including the vast military infrastructure being built by the US, the displacement of over 10 per cent of the peasant population, the 'war induced urbanization' mentioned favorably by Komer, and the exactions placed upon farmers by the Viet Cong had combined causing systemic inflation, reducing the rice crop and artificially raising the urban cost of living. While deficiencies in rice could be made good through US grants and subsidized sales of rice, other problems could not be so easily addressed without the full cooperation of the Saigon government.

As Komer informed the Administration, this collaboration was not forthcoming in key areas such as economic stabilization and land reform. It was fair to argue, as Komer did, that the election campaign of early 1967 and the nationalistic passions which it excited were in part responsible for South Vietnamese reluctance to accept and act upon American guidance. There was another, more fundamental, reason which was not mentioned by Komer or any senior member of the Embassy or MACV staff: the US had no influence. The Saigon government could afford to accept only the guidance which was agreeable to its own agenda. All other advice could be rejected with impunity.

The US had no credible threat to levy against the government. With several hundred thousand men in country and a full-fledged war underway, there were no costs which the US could impose for non cooperation in Saigon. The United States could not credibly threaten to withdraw, and the Saigon regime knew and understood this. The war had become an American war to be fought for an American policy goal and according to American theories of victory. To a significant extent the South Vietnamese had become participant-observers in the struggle around them rather than coparticipants in pursuit of a common goal.

Without effective leverage, without a means of influence, the US could only hope that the South Vietnamese leadership would see coinciding interests and act in harmony with American advice. The Saigon government and ARVN were not simply obdurate for the sheer fun of it. They selectively cooperated for reasons of their own while the US had neither the influence nor the credible threats necessary to induce a more expansive definition of cooperation. Komer did not recognize this nor the limits which it automatically placed upon the processes of revolutionary development and pacification.

The optimism of Komer's view must have been well received at the White House considering the mood of pessimism regarding pacification which had prevailed only a week earlier. There was probably no inclination to closely question Komer's assessments or his prognosis: 'we face plenty of problems in Vietnam, but these are increasingly the problems of gathering success – no longer those of forestalling disaster.'[41] There would be little tendency to doubt Komer as he was the primary in-house action-oriented expert on Vietnam. His knowledge of the country was considered extensive, and he capitalized upon this status, offering assessments and recommendations on any aspect of the non-military war. He had the most important trait of the successful bureaucrat, a capacity to tailor his recommendations and opinions to the proclivities of the audience. The President and his senior aides often heard from Komer the most pleasing of messages. There was no need to raise questions.

Pacification, pressure and politics continued as the dominant themes of Administration decision making through March 1967. When Mc-Namara, Rusk and Rostow had lunch with the President on 7 March to discuss Vietnam policy, personnel changes, and the upcoming strategy conference at Guam, more signs of progress in pacification were reported. The Chieu Hoi program was reported to have been notably cost-effective having produced 20,240 returnees during 1966 at a per capita cost of only $125.12.[42] Some improvements in the land reform were described, although the Saigon government was still reluctant to put forth a comprehensive program.[43] Komer saw this as an overstatement and advised the President on 6 March that Ky and Thieu had become more interested in land reform as the election campaign continued, but because of the President's concerns, Komer suggested, 'I revive my project, which Orville Freeman backs, for a dramatic but workable reform program.'[44] The President approved. Komer recognized that land reform and the upcoming presidential election in South Vietnam would be intertwined so he hoped to introduce both an organization and a plan before politics supervened.[45] The progress in revolutionary development was less obvious with at least one important consultant having questioned the paramilitary focus of the Revolutionary

Development Cadre teams believing that a more political orientation would yield more significant and rapid results.[46] Agricultural, fishery and forestry improvement programs undertaken by the US Department of Agriculture after the Honolulu Conference were reported as having made some progress, but staffing level deficiencies had impeded full effectiveness.[47] A similar report was made concerning the efforts by the Department of Health, Education and Welfare.[48]

The Guam Conference in mid-March would consider the non-military programs in considerable detail.[49] Many of the most important components of these were considered to have been disappointing in their performance during the preceding year. Revolutionary development, national reconciliation, land reform, inflation, and economic stabilization had been particularly frustrating. The progress toward developing a viable political culture and the prospect of a legitimately elected national government were the bright spots. Overall, the non-military side of American policy was a mixture of success and failure. As the areas of most pronounced failure were concentrated in the interlocking fields of pacification and revolutionary development, this gave greater impetus to the appointment of a dynamic personality to be the American director of the efforts. The appointment of a director would not be enough to guarantee success. However, the new US ambassador might be able to influence the newly elected South Vietnamese government after September so that the Saigon government might finally cooperate fully and effectively in the pacification and revolutionary development effort. There appeared to be reason for optimism.

Success in the air war against North Vietnam was still quite uncertain as was the effect of the air campaign on infiltration in Laos. The President had requested yet another CIA study on the matter, but it was not available for the March lunch review.[50] The ground war appeared to have been going quite well for the United States. Operation JUNCTION CITY I had concluded on 15 March. Featuring a combat jump by the 173rd Airborne Brigade, this sweep of the eastern portion of War Zone C had captured the attention of both public and Administration although a close examination of the operation would have indicated far more appearance than substance.[51]

Ambassador Lodge's reporting on the political situation within South Vietnam had become increasingly suspect giving extra impetus to the plan to replace him, 'soonist.'[52] The upcoming South Vietnamese elections were viewed by the Administration as both a matter of concern and an opportunity for change. A new ambassador would provide a better perspective on the emerging political dynamic and might represent the chance for greater influence. Personnel changes would be made. A new ambassador would be appointed and be at his post by May. Shortly thereafter, Komer would be sent to MACV as

Deputy for Civil Operations and Revolutionary Development Support (CORDS).

The quest for effective methods of pressuring the North would continue as would the search for the truth on infiltration and how to hinder it. The encouraging signs of progress reported to the Administration during the first two months of 1967 had erased some of the questions and doubts which had emerged during the winter of cold assessments. After all, the United States must be grinding them down, as Komer had written, by the sheer size and weight of the American effort.

Below the surface of success there were depths of continuing and emerging problems. Anxieties about the political dynamic continued and grew. The perception at the Embassy was that the pending change of ambassadors would provide an opportunity for adventurism on the part of some faction within the South Vietnamese military.[53] The potential for a military *coup* was real as was that of an open struggle for power within the military. There was also real doubt about the election having the appearance as well as the substance of legitimacy.

On the military side there were mixed signs. General Westmoreland was going ahead with plans for offensive operations in II and III Corps Tactical Zones. He intended to follow on the reportedly successful Operation JUNCTION CITY in War Zone C with a similar sweep through War Zone D.[54] At the same time a new concern was emerging over the situation in I Corps. Westmoreland expressed apprehension about the region in mid-April.[55] He believed that the forthcoming summer campaign in I CTZ 'could be a decisive period of the war.'[56] An American success would not only improve the security in the northern portion of South Vietnam, it could have 'a profound effect on the strategic thinking of the leadership in Hanoi.'[57] It was possible that General Westmoreland saw the Clausewitzian conditions for decisive combat as emerging in the northern provinces and relished the potentials this implied. He had already formed Task Force Oregon as an operational reserve which could assist III MAF in countering the threat posed by the PAVN buildup or, preferably, be used offensively to find, fix and destroy North Vietnamese units in northern I Corps in June.[58]

A month later the CIA reported on the new North Vietnamese offensive in northern I Corps.[59] The Agency concluded that the intention of Hanoi was to 'keep the area insecure and to subject allied forces to substantial and sustained attrition.'[60] The analysts argued that by so doing the Communists could block any demonstrable US/SVN progress toward winning and by so doing undercut the political will of the United States.[61] The concentrations of enemy units and supplies had taken place despite the air campaign and earlier defeats inflicted upon PAVN by American ground forces in I Corps during the first half of 1966. The new PAVN movements had provided both a north–south and an east–west axis of movement, thus enhancing North Vietnamese operational flexibility. The Agency noted that the twin lines allowed the enemy to mount 'a sustained threat around the Khe Sanh area necessitating a continued protective deployment by the limited allied reaction elements.'[62] The PAVN presence and the Khe Sanh locus could be interpreted by American command elements either as a threat or an opportunity. The offensive-minded doctrinal thrust of the military would have predisposed all US commanders in favor of the latter.

The PAVN buildup in northern I Corps and the Demilitarized Zone (DMZ) was not new, having attracted CIA comment the previous November.[63] At that time it was believed that the North Vietnamese intended to develop a stronghold in Quang Tri Province which would provide several military advantages including an enhanced ability to mount protracted conflict from relatively secure base camps conveniently close to both Laos and North Vietnam. To the Agency analysts, this suggested that a faction of the Hanoi Politburo led by Minister of Defense Vo Nguyen Giap had won out in a policy struggle.[64]

If this was true, the use of protracted conflict by guerrilla and regular forces having the goal of exhausting American and South Vietnamese political will should be expected. Additionally, the North Vietnamese force dispositions implied that PAVN might seek to fight a mini-Verdun campaign of attrition again directed toward the end of enervating American and South Vietnamese political will through the cumulative political and psychological effects of constant, purposeless bloodletting.[65] Left unsaid by the Agency analysts, but quite evident, the augmentation of PAVN strength just south of the DMZ indicated that Hanoi had entered the war in its own right for its own ends. In a protracted guerrilla conflict, the Viet Cong would become expendable bullet-catchers, abrading their strength and American political will simultaneously. An intact PAVN would then secure Hanoi's policy goal of forceful unification. Unfortunately, this possibility was not examined by the Administration at the time. A close examination of the new North Vietnamese dispositions would have alerted the American decision makers that another change in the character of the war was under way.

A final, subsurface problem was the continuing intellectual bankruptcy of much of the Administration's strategic thinking. In May, John McNaughton again mused on the course of the war.[66] His statement of goals was far less expansive than had been the case earlier. There was no mention of guaranteeing containment or upholding American credibility on a global scale. Now it was enough to leave behind a stable South Vietnam and a 'reasonably stable peace in Southeast Asia for several years.'[67] To accomplish these goals it would be necessary to convince the North Vietnamese to abandon their aggression and to neutralize the Viet Cong threat. He did not believe that these two tasks could be accomplished within the next eighteen months but he speculated that they might be realized in two or three years. John McNaughton, the once eager architect of expansive war, had turned dour pessimist.

The reasons for his pessimism were easy to discern. American ground and air operations had failed to break the morale of either PAVN or the Viet Cong. The enemy possessed both political will and military initiative, as shown by the North Vietnamese adoption of 'an intensive, grinding positional warfare campaign in the northern provinces' along with coordinated offensive thrusts with the object of inflicting 'maximum losses on the US/GVN in an effort to break our will.'[68] In short, the enemy had every prospect of successfully doing to the United States just what McNaughton had planned for the United States to do to him. Pacification was not yet working. McNaughton stated 'real progress' had been reported in only 14 per cent of the hamlets.[69] He believed the short-term prognosis was not good. The long-term outlook would become so only if ARVN was made more effective. He concluded that this was unlikely given the corruption, apathy and latent anti-Americanism and war-weariness of the population. Revolutionary development and the South Vietnamese political culture were relatively bright spots in McNaughton's grey-hued assessment, but these were simply slightly lighter shades of the same color.

The North Vietnamese were encouraged to continue the war by a number of factors, including the upcoming US presidential elections. McNaughton believed that American diplomatic rigidity and the bombing campaign had induced Hanoi to accept the incorrect idea that the United States sought 'total victory.'[70] All of these factors combined to make the possibility of meaningful negotiations occurring within the next eighteen months unlikely. 'Hanoi remains obdurate.'[71]

McNaughton considered several alternative strategies to see if any seemed to offer a greater hope of a more rapid and complete success than that already in place. He finally recommended only modest changes from the present mix. In the South, he suggested, 'emphasize the war of attrition,' keeping up the search and destroy operations in the hope of ultimately breaking enemy morale. He also thought that efforts to stimulate a greater refugee flow would be beneficial as would a more effective effort to attack the NLF/VC infrastructure. The South Vietnamese must become more effectively involved in the war with ARVN dedicated to the pacification mission. The US must use all the levers at its disposal to assure that the upcoming elections would be honest and to force the new government to open dialogue with the NLF and support a meaningful National Reconciliation Program.[72] In the North, McNaughton recommended that efforts be bent toward both interdiction and inducing Hanoi to negotiate. He specifically suggested air attacks on lines of communication be given priority and provided assistance by the erection of physical barriers to infiltration.[73] Mc-Naughton noted that there were many disagreements concerning portions of his assessment within the military, intelligence and policy communities. He did not acknowledge that he had offered nothing new; that he had proposed only tepid and denatured versions of his earlier, more robust judgements. Time and events had proven his earlier assessments and architecture to have been wrong. It was no wonder he had lost the courage of his convictions.

The JCS also examined alternatives in May 1967. The major task undertaken by this study was the examination of two alternative force levels in South Vietnam. One, prompted by General Westmoreland's request, would require the addition of 250,000 personnel to the forces in Southeast Asia. The other, prompted by the Administration, would call for an augmentation of only 70,000 men.[74] The first option would provide an additional four-and-two-thirds divisions and constituted an optimum force.[75] It would require the mobilization of the Reserves. The second option did not bear that heavy political freight, but would add only one-and-one-third Army divisions to the ground combat force, much less than the optimum. The forces of the first option would allow a significant increase of troops in the threatened portion of I CTZ as part of Task Force Oregon while providing for a two-division exploitation reserve to be used in major operations such as JUNCTION CITY. The smaller second option would allow for the reinforcement of Task Force Oregon but not provide for a mobile strategic reserve.

The Chiefs believed that one result of selecting the second, smaller option would be the inability of American forces to participate in revolutionary development support activities without introducing a significant dilemma: endanger revolutionary development by reducing the level of military security provided to a pacified area or limit new large-scale offensives meant to open new areas to pacification.[76] A second result of restricting augmentation of ground combat forces to those available under the second option was adumbrated.

> The present situation wherein all forces in SVN are fully committed in their respective areas denies COMUSMACV the means to influence effectively the course of one operation without disengaging from another. If the enemy should threaten other areas, such as along the Laotian and Cambodian borders, a diversion of forces, similar to that in I CTZ, would be required at the expense of other high priority missions in SVN.[77]

In short, without a politically risky major escalation in the forces committed to South Vietnam, PAVN and the Viet Cong would continue to enjoy the initiative: the enemy had obtained escalation dominance. The Chiefs were attempting to whipsaw the Administration by holding revolutionary development hostage and hinting darkly at the consequences of allowing the enemy to maintain the initiative. Lost in the mists of time were the roseate reports of a few weeks earlier that assured the National Command Authority that the enemy had lost the initiative and with it the chance for a military victory.

The Chiefs wished to continue and increase the air campaign against North Vietnam. They recommended that ROLLING THUNDER be oriented toward isolating the 'Hanoi–Haiphong logistics base' by an integrated air interdiction effort against all means of transportation including the importation of 'war-supporting materials.'[78] Attacks would be permitted against 'all worthwhile military targets' except the Chinese Buffer Zone.[79] In addition, the Chiefs urged the expansion of BARREL ROLL and STEEL TIGER and the initiation of similar programs directed at Cambodia.[80] These actions, plus expansion of SHINING BRASS and PRAIRIE FIRE ground reconnaissance and ambush operations in Laos would enhance the effect of American interdiction efforts. Finally, the Chiefs advised doubling the B–52 strikes in North Vietnam and Laos from 800 sorties per month to 1,600.[81] The Chiefs had not been impressed by the lack of positive results so far demonstrated by any of the air interdiction campaigns.[82] They were opposed to any restriction or cessation of ROLLING THUNDER.[83]

The Chiefs also advocated that ground combat operations be undertaken on a regular basis into the Cambodian and Laotian sanctuaries. These could be of battalion, brigade or even division size and would be search and destroy in their orientation. Raids or transient invasions of Cambodia and Laos were not seen by the JCS as constituting horizontal escalation. Neither did the Chiefs see incursions as posing any domestic, political or diplomatic complications to the Administration.[84]

The substance of the 'Alternatives' study was distilled in a Draft Memorandum to the President on 19 May 1967.[85] It was argued that the United States could no longer lose the war militarily despite the Vietnamese escalation dominance in I Corps. The lack of success in the 'other war' had prompted the enemy to believe that the United States would be unable to translate its success in the big battalion war to success in the overall conflict. General Westmoreland was quoted with approval, 'In the final analysis we are in a war of attrition.'[86] This assessment was justifiable if the North Vietnamese were permitted to set the tone and character of the war. The military commanders were willing to grant this permission. As a result the additional troops would be necessary if the United States was to meet the mincing-machine challenge in I Corps and still be able to handle the requirements of pacification support.

The Chiefs and General Westmoreland understood attrition as one of the classic avenues to victory, the gradual destruction of the enemy's forces in the field until he was no longer militarily capable of continuing the war. Using this understanding as a basis it is easy to appreciate how the US military high command welcomed the apparent blunder by Hanoi. In a contest of attrition against the United States, North Vietnam was at a significant disadvantage. Superiority in firepower and mobility together with the absolute air dominance enjoyed by the US and its allies should assure a bloody North Vietnamese failure. If the North Vietnamese did not share this classic, Clausewitzian understanding, but rather saw the correct avenue to victory as being enervation, the gradual exhaustion of the enemy's political will to continue the war, then the ability to inflict casualties was less important than the capacity to accept casualties. Further, if the North Vietnamese saw the NLF/VC not as allies but as rivals for power in a unified Vietnam, then losses inflicted on the Viet Cong by the US and ARVN would be a matter of sublime indifference to Hanoi.

The possibility that the North Vietnamese were in the process of trapping the US in an unsolvable dilemma was not considered by the American military high command. The nature of the dilemma was easy to see and is even implied within the JCS draft presidential memorandum. By inveigling the US into a continuation of the 'big war' of search and destroy operations against PAVN and Viet Cong main force units, the North could assure continued social, political and economic chaos within South Vietnam. This would impair efforts at pacification and nation building and a continuation of American losses without apparent useful result. Thus political will within South Vietnam and the United States would be undercut. The use of sanctuaries along the DMZ and Cambodian borders allowed PAVN and the Viet Cong main forces to tie down a significant percentage of American ground combat strength. By using the Viet Cong main forces as the primary offensive instrument, Hanoi could use Southern blood to further ablate American will. If the US diverted its ground resources to deal with pacification, the PAVN force in being could threaten a spectacularly successful operation against a population center such as Quang Tri City, Hue or Pleiku, again undercutting American and South Vietnamese political will. Hanoi could rely upon the ongoing air war against the North to maintain and consolidate the popular support of its citizens for the war, particularly for the expansive goal of unification under Northern control.

Whatever the United States forces did against the PAVN defensive locations would allow greater freedom of operation to the guerrillas;

whatever the US did against the guerrillas would invite a PAVN spectacular. Whatever the US did to expand the scope of the big war hurt efforts at pacification and nation building. Whatever the US did from the sky over the North would further consolidate political will in the North. More fundamentally, the JCS and General Westmoreland sought victory through the attrition of enemy forces in the field and the erosion of the enemy's material capacity to continue the war. Arguably, Hanoi sought victory through the exhaustion of American and South Vietnamese political will. As a result, whatever we did to further our course helped them further theirs.

Although the interlocking quandaries were implicit in both the draft presidential memorandum and the 'Alternatives' study upon which it was based, there is no indication that the Chiefs directly considered their ramifications.[87] Rather, the solution was sought as it had been sought earlier, by an increase in the number of US troops and aircraft brought into action. The Chiefs recommended the request of General Westmoreland, endorsed by Admiral Sharp, to increase the number of maneuver battalions from 87 to 129. The addition of 200,000 men would bring the total number of forces approved for Vietnam from 470,000 to 670,000 by mid-1968.[88] An augmentation of this magnitude would necessitate calling up the Reserves and 'an eventual increase of approximately 500,000 in military strength from 3,600,000 to 4,100,000.'[89] If this course were to be adopted along with an increase in ROLLING THUNDER and the other measures recommended in the 'Alternatives' study, General Westmoreland and the Chiefs estimated that the war would continue for another two years.[90]

The second, smaller option would, in the estimate of General Westmoreland and the Chiefs, prevent defeat, but would not assure victory in less than five years.[91] The Chiefs saw the second option as being a sort of uncertain trumpet as it focused on maintaining a military status quo while making improvements on the pacification and nation building fronts. The hope was that this mixture would convince the North Vietnamese that continuing the war was futile and Hanoi would be better served by negotiations.[92] The second option more clearly recognized the nature of the war as a contest of political wills, but did not address the underlying dilemmas posed by the North Vietnamese strategy. Arguably, this option was more relevant to the realities on the ground as well as more consistent with the less expansive goals and definition of victory expressed by McNaughton and Komer.

The Chiefs preferred the first option (Course A) but did acknowledge that the second (Course B) had merits as their comparative assessment of the options demonstrated.[93] The Chiefs expressed their criticism of Course B as a question: How long could Course B be followed if progress was slow and the North Vietnamese unmoved toward a settlement?[94] Course A had risks, but it also had the best chance of success in a reasonable length of time. As a result the Chiefs clearly preferred Course A, although, as General Wheeler wrote on 29 May, they had 'not recommended the deployment of COMUSMACV's optimum force or adoption of Course A.'[95] The JCS later reaffirmed that they were not proponents of Course A. That might have been correct in some narrow sense, but the tone and thrust of both the 'Alternatives' study and the draft presidential memorandum showed a marked predilection for that option including both the force level augmentation and air war escalation.[96]

Cyrus Vance, the successor of John McNaughton, was not so inclined. He recommended against the large augmentation. Instead, he proposed a seven-stage operational concept to the VNCC which would start the process of American disengagement. He based the process on a redefinition of goal and victory. For Vance the goal was 'to permit the people of South Vietnam to determine their own future.'[97] Victory could be declared at any time after the September 1967 South Vietnamese elections, provided that the US had not further escalated by that time. Vance believed that the process of politically co-opting the Viet Cong could be commenced under a policy of national reconciliation after September. He was quite optimistic about the possibility of disengagement. He was quite in the dark concerning the North Vietnamese goals and how the character of the war had changed. He stood at the antipodes from the Chiefs regarding the course of the war. He stood with them in his lack of understanding of its nature and character.

Secretary McNamara was closer to Cyrus Vance than to the JCS in his view of the future. His initial reaction to the Chiefs' recommendation and the proposal of Vance was to order another reevaluation of the air war and to take a close look at the situation in I Corps. As McNamara and the CIA went about the process of assessment, the new ambassador, Ellsworth Bunker, arrived in Saigon to take up his post amongst the ongoing political turmoil. Bunker's first report emphasized the ongoing village elections which had been long seen by the United States as a critical component of nation building and the continued rivalry at the center between Ky and Thieu.[98] Bunker commented on the military situation in northern I CTZ where the PAVN buildup continued. He expressed a belief that enemy intentions were unclear but cited a number of reports which held 'the enemy may calculate that a spectacular victory of some sort in the First Corps area is needed either to bolster enemy morale or as the prelude to negotiations.'[99] Bunker stressed the unspoken reality that the initiative lay with PAVN when he reported that the attack may come in the western highlands rather than in I Corps.

Intentionally or not, the Ambassador was repeating the implicit assessment of the JCS. The American ground and air operations had not prevented the North Vietnamese from gaining escalation dominance and the freedom of action which went with it. The US was not a military actor but rather a military reactor since the augmentation of PAVN in I CTZ.

Saigon politics and the military situation in I Corps continued to dominate Bunker's reporting throughout his first month in South Vietnam although the arrival of Komer to take up the position of MACV Deputy for CORDS introduced pacification and revolutionary development as a subsidiary theme.[100] Bunker commented on progress he had made in integrating MACV and Embassy planning as well as the advances made by Westmoreland and Komer on the new Revolutionary Development organization.[101] He was moderately optimistic concerning the Ky–Thieu political rivalry, but he observed that the Vietnamese seemed constitutionally incapable of frank, candid talk on political and personal matters.[102] The Ambassador was most impressed with his trip to I Corps and concluded that the military and pacification situations alike were well in hand.[103] His earlier anxieties had been assuaged by the briefings and demonstrations arranged for his benefit.

General Westmoreland's priorities paralleled those of the Ambassador. His close personal relations with Ky, Thieu and other senior South Vietnamese military commanders allowed him a unique insight, which he conveyed regularly to Admiral Sharp and General Wheeler.[104] While he may have entertained a degree of optimism regarding the opportunities presented by the PAVN concentrations in I CTZ which was similar to those now held by the Ambassador, his thinking regarding future force levels and operational concepts in Vietnam were identical to those contained in the May JCS study and a successor review in early June which focused upon the air war over North Vietnam.

In the June air war examination the Chiefs were responding to a request from the Secretary of Defense made on 20 May [105] The Chiefs considered four approaches to the air war: the unrestricted campaign recommended in the previous study, and three alternatives, I, in which bombing north of the 20th parallel would be ended; II, which focused on the lines of communication with two variations, ports open and ports closed, and III, a new suggestion by the Chiefs under which the prohibited areas around Hanoi and Haiphong would be constricted and selected port facilities would be attacked. The Chiefs concluded that their original recommendation remained the best of the four alternatives.[106] The Chiefs might have shown the slightest degree of hesitation in their recommendation regarding General Westmoreland's request for more troops, but they were resolute on the air war. They still saw the air war as the key to American success, echoing and expanding on the position taken by the Ad Hoc Study Group nearly two years earlier.

> The campaign against the North, in addition to reducing the flow of men and materiel to the South, must bring about a deterioration in the enemy's total environment so as to curtail his over-all efforts to support the war. This can be achieved by causing increasing expenditures of time and effort manifested by drains on the enemy's materiel resources, management skills, human energy and morale. When this curtailment is achieved, the turbulence in the South can be reduced more rapidly by military forces to a level where internal political action can effectively maintain stability.[107]

The correctness and relevance of the predicates upon which the assessment was based were left unexamined.

Secretary McNamara on 20 May 1967 had requested the CIA to evaluate two alternatives to the expansive JCS bombing proposal. The Agency replied on 1 June.[108] In estimating the effects of an interdiction program limiting bombing to the area south of the 20th parallel, the Agency concluded that even if the air effort could double the historical maximum reduction of the road system's carrying capacity from 25 to 50 per cent, 'the capacity remaining on the two major routes into Laos would still be at least five times greater than that required to move supplies at the 1966–1967 dry season rates.'[109] The reserve capacity of the road network coupled with the demonstrated ability of the North Vietnamese to repair installations quickly assured that the geographically limited interdiction program would not reduce the flow of supplies and men. The second alternative examined was that of a line of communication attack throughout the country with the exception of the eight-mile prohibited zones around the centers of Hanoi and Haiphong. Two variants of this alternative were assessed: one including and one excluding attacks on port facilities. The Agency concluded that both variants would be equally ineffective in reducing the flow of military materiel and war-supporting supplies into North Vietnam. It was also determined that the broader effort would reduce pressure on the road system which would assist the North in moving supplies into Laos and South Vietnam.[110] The second alternative, if applied with resolution and completeness against ports and land lines of communication with China, would reduce the North Vietnamese economy to a subsistence level, but this would not impair war-related activities.[111] The Agency believed that efforts directed against the ports would produce international complications particularly with the Soviet Union. It would also promote Chinese influence in Hanoi as all remaining lines of international supply would be under their control.[112] It would be otiose for the US to follow either of the two alternatives examined by the

Agency. If the Agency's assessments were to be accepted, ROLLING THUNDER would have to be either canceled or greatly expanded as the Chiefs recommended. Rarely were choices presented in such a stark manner.

The Secretary of the Air Force, Harold Brown, entered the assessment arena in June. He equivocated in a memorandum to John McNaughton, recommending 'from a purely military point of view' an all-out attack on the northeast and northwest land lines of communication and closure of the ports, but concluding that diplomatic and other risks militated against this course.[113] As an alternative, he advised a continuation of the harassing attacks on the railroads coupled with an effort to cut off Haiphong from the internal communication system. In a memorandum to Secretary McNamara, he engaged in an exercise in cost accounting, demonstrating statistical crossover points between American expenditures and losses in interdiction air strikes and the manpower requirements and losses in ground combat operations. He concluded that if 'we have reduced allied deaths by one' for every 881 attack sorties in Laos, or 557 attack sorties in southern North Vietnam or 123 attack sorties in northern North Vietnam, then the air campaign had paid for its aircrew losses.[114] In terms of dollar cost, Brown concluded that if the requirement for US ground troops was reduced by 300 men for every 1000 attack sorties in Laos and North Vietnam assuming that each 1000 sorties killed 37 infiltrators, the air war had paid its way.[115] In defense of the air war, Brown had offered an involuted exercise in assumptions disguised as facts by the questionable use of statistics which was of little relevance to the requirements of policy definition or the realities of war.

The Air Force Secretary again offered advice in early July. This time he almost refrained from equivocation and undue statistical prestidigitation alike, recommending that ROLLING THUNDER be concentrated on lines of communication south of the 20th parallel, but that 20 per cent of all attack sorties be reserved for targets north of that line.[116] He did not argue that this plan would have any major effect upon the war in the South, simply that it was the most cost-effective and diplomatically least risky alternative.

General Westmoreland supported the Chiefs' recommendation for the expansion of ROLLING THUNDER. He argued that the bombing had two purposes: the curbing of infiltration and logistical support for the Viet Cong, and acting 'as an instrument for concession in return for negotiations.'[117] The General asserted that the latter purpose was the more important, now agreeing with the much earlier thinking of John McNaughton. As a military instrument, bombing could not, in Westmoreland's evaluation, halt all infiltration, destroy the morale of the North Vietnamese population, endanger the regime, or crucially affect the ability of the Viet Cong to continue the war in the South. Westmoreland believed that bombing could erode the North Vietnamese economy to a dangerously low point, particularly if the dikes and levees were to be attacked, raising the costs of supporting a large expeditionary force in the South to an unacceptable level. Westmoreland concluded that this had already happened, noting that a 'plateau of about 110,000 main force Viet Cong and North Vietnamese Army units in SVN has been maintained since September 1966.'[118] As a result the air war was placing intense political pressure upon the North, which raised its attractiveness as the bargaining chip which could best be played to bring Hanoi to the negotiating table. Interestingly, Westmoreland had used the threat of an open-ended escalation by the North in I CTZ as an argument in favor of the large troop augmentation request and now he used the apparent plateau of PAVN and Viet Cong as an argument in favor of ROLLING THUNDER.

During the first week of July 1967 Secretary McNamara and Under Secretary Katzenbach visited South Vietnam. The President hoped that they might be able to get a feel for developments and provide guidance on the vexing choices regarding the augmentation request and changes in the air war strategy which were still pending. It was also hoped that a better sense of South Vietnamese political dynamics might be achieved.

In his briefing, Ambassador Bunker stated that the military situation had improved greatly, noting that the North Vietnamese had not won a 'single major victory' while suffering large losses on the battlefield.[119] Infiltration continued to run at a rate estimated as 6,500 men per month.[120] Within South Vietnam there had been significant changes, most of a positive sort: pacification was gaining some momentum, the government had been stable for almost two years, ARVN was showing some real improvement as a fighting force and inflation had been kept under a reasonable degree of control. There were still real problems: the Ky–Thieu split had exacerbated tensions within the military, ARVN participation in pacification remained disappointing, and the South Vietnamese civil administration and military alike demonstrated a pervasive apathy, corruption and indifference.

Bunker found these political and social matters to be particularly worrisome and difficult to overcome.[121] In comparison, he was most sanguine about the conduct of the war during the last six months. He characterized the operations undertaken since April including JUNCTION CITY as 'splendidly executed' and noted that they had inflicted a total of more than 12,000 fatalities upon the enemy.[122] He also commented on the improved performance of ARVN in the search and destroy sweeps. The sense of improvement carried him forward through a brief recitation of military challenges remaining such as the two or three PAVN divisions in northern I CTZ and the increased infiltration through Laos and into the Cambodian sanctuary which he described as 'unwarranted.'[123] To Bunker the crux of the remaining military problems was the need to choke the infiltration routes from the North although he proposed no specific solution.

He also considered pacification to be the key to solving the military challenges presented by PAVN and the North Vietnamese government. If the pacification and revolutionary development program were to be successful, there would be no political or insurgent movement left in the South for Hanoi to support.[124] This assessment overlooked the possibility that the North Vietnamese were no longer supporting any organization in the South, if, indeed, they ever had been.

Bunker announced the finalization of the long-pending effort to merge all responsibility for pacification under MACV with Komer as the Deputy for Civil Operations and Revolutionary Development Support. This would simplify management and streamline procedures. When and if these administrative improvements would show themselves by increased effectiveness in the villages remained to be seen. The Ambassador properly noted that the US could not and did not take responsibility for the success of pacification and revolutionary development as the South Vietnamese were the primary players in these programs. Bunker was optimistic because of the comprehensive plans developed by General Westmoreland for the 'reorientation, motivation and improvement in quality and performance' of ARVN so that it might properly perform pacification and security functions.[125] Many programs had been initiated with the intent of improving ARVN and the Regional Force/Popular Force militia (RF/PF or 'Ruff Puffs'). The Ambassador observed that many improvements had been made as indicated in the new aggressiveness and energy of many ARVN and RF/PF units as well as such dry statistics as the number of weapons lost by friendly forces.

Considering the Ambassador's view of the military and pacification programs, which was generally upbeat, and his favorable impression of the developing political culture and improving economic base, the listener or reader must have felt greatly encouraged about the trends in the war. The only flat note on the Ambassador's score was the continued unwillingness of Hanoi to recognize the great progress made by the US and South Vietnam and come to the bargaining table.

The briefing given by Westmoreland was not so sunny.[126] His goal was to convince Secretary McNamara that JCS Course A should be adopted so that he would receive an augmentation of more than 200,000 men. To do this he emphasized, correctly, that the war had become increasingly a North Vietnamese affair. Noting that infiltration by sea had been reduced to an insignificant level, Westmoreland stressed the PAVN buildup south of the DMZ and his increased use of land lines of communication. The capabilities offered by Course A would allow the US to increase disruption of these lines, and to conduct operations against border sanctuaries in Laos, Cambodia and North Vietnam. In the South it would be possible to 'increase the tempo of air and ground operations,' and provide the security and support necessary to invigorate revolutionary development.[127] He concluded that the cumulative effect of Course A efforts would be to 'shorten the war and reduce overall US costs.'[128]

Course B would provide the enemy easy sanctuary in Laos, Cambodia and the North Vietnamese heartland. It would facilitate North Vietnamese ground and air defense force concentrations. MACV would be forced to divert troops to duty as 'containment forces' primarily in I Corps and, rather illogically, would compel the installation of improved air defenses in the same region.[129] Course B would adversely affect the United States by requiring a reduction in the number of combat troops available for offensive ground operations and revolutionary development support. The aggregate effect of Course B in Westmoreland's estimate would be 'a shift in favor of the enemy's strategy with decreased US options and flexibility and increased enemy options.'[130] Course B was a defensive package which would prolong the war.

A MACCOC briefing on current operations did not support the pessimistic picture.[131] A wide variety of operations was presented in précis including those of a containment orientation, CROCKETT, BUFFALO, GREELY and FRANCIS MARION; two directed against local guerrillas, FAIRFAX and ENTERPRISE; and several directed against PAVN and Viet Cong main forces including DIAMOND HEAD, JUNCTION CITY, PERSHING, BYRD and MALHEUR. Task Force OREGON, which had been implemented under emergency conditions on 7 April 1967, was depicted as having successfully blunted the enemy threat in I CTZ.[132] Operations PERSHING and FRANCIS MARION in II CTZ were portrayed as having effectively turned back the 1st and 3rd PAVN Divisions, leaving the only locus of concern Kontum Province near Dak To and Kontum city where the 173rd Airborne Brigade executing Operation GREELEY had required reinforcement by two ARVN battalions and a brigade of the 1st Cavalry.[133] In III CTZ Operation JUNCTION CITY I had seen the destruction of the 9th Viet Cong Division for the third time in eighteen months. The conclusion was that American forces after major and rapid redeployment and heavy fighting had hurt the enemy and arrested his plans for a summer offensive in both I and II CTZ while JUNCTION CITY in III CTZ had been so successful that the enemy was evading contact.[134] Threats remained in Quang Tri and Kontum provinces, but the briefing gave no cause for anxiety and no support for the adoption of Course A.

There must have been some confusion within the minds of McNamara and Katzenbach as they returned to Washington. The Ambassador had been reasonably confident about the current situation and the prospects for the future. The MACCOC briefing on current operations had indicated success for the US and ARVN forces overall. The briefing had confirmed that the threatened areas were well identified and easily reinforced. Only General Westmoreland and the JCS seemed doubtful about the future unless there was a major infusion of forces.

In the 'other war,' Komer's war, there were several encouraging developments. CORDS had started operations in early June with an integrated organizational chain which extended down to the district level providing for the first time an integrated civil–military structure for pacification and revolutionary development.[135] Komer and his liaison in the White House, William Leonhart, had established a firm fix on the requirements for land reform.[136] Within a week of its official inauguration CORDS had taken the first step on a campaign which was believed to be central to the success of pacification and revolutionary development, the neutralization of the NLF/VC command structure.

Komer, working with John Hart and MACV, had laid out a plan and organization for attacking the infrastructure. This would be incorporated in the overall revolutionary development program, Operation TAKEOFF. The organization responsible for detailed planning and implementation was to be called Intelligence Coordination and Exploitation (ICEX). Komer informed Ambassador Bunker that General Westmoreland had approved the recommendations and that unless the Ambassador had objections, he proposed to commence implementation.[137] It was Komer's intention to develop fully and at least partially staff the ICEX Committee and its subordinates and obtain the cooperation of the South Vietnamese government by mid-July.[138] ICEX would require twelve military, three CORDS and seven CIA officers as well as 123 enlisted men and nineteen clerks or secretaries. One hundred fourteen of the enlisted men would be counterintelligence specialists to staff the seventy district operational intelligence coordinating centers and forty-four provincial coordination offices.[139] Komer realized his goal, and ICEX and its collection, analysis, and field operation components were ready to go by the end of July.[140] It is reasonable to assume that McNamara and his party were briefed on the progress of this high priority project while they were in Saigon.

Still the question must have persisted: where was the US on the course toward victory? Major policy decisions hung upon the answer and the answer seemed very elusive. So many indicators appeared to be pointing toward success at some time in the not too distant future, but General Westmoreland, so long described as the indispensable man, was less hopeful. He and the Joint Chiefs were concerned about

171

achieving a favourable outcome in any reasonable period without major troop increases and an escalation of the air war. The CIA had concluded that the air effort had been and continued to be unsuccessful and counterproductive. Escalation and augmentation would unleash a host of political and diplomatic complications, yet they might be necessary. Confusion must have hung thickly on the flight home. How can we know if we are winning?

7

HOW DO WE KNOW IF WE'RE WINNING?

The war in Vietnam did not lend itself to tidy and convenient ways of measuring progress toward seemingly elusive victory. From the very beginning of the American involvement, determining who was winning and to what extent on the battlefields and in the villages alike had been a constant concern of Administration officials, military commanders and intelligence analysts. An interlocking and more fundamental problem, determining the proper basis upon which to assess the degree and rate of progress, received only sporadic attention. This was a mistake of major proportions.

In a conventional war, possession of real estate has generally been the measure of success, but progress in the Vietnam war was not to be assessed in this straightforward manner. In part, this was the consequence of the war having started as an insurgent guerrilla conflict and in part it was result of the American theory of victory. Had the US military and Administration opted for a clear and hold strategy, it would have been easier to accurately differentiate areas controlled by the government from those controlled by the enemy. However, the reliance upon search and destroy missions assured that the military presence would be both transitory and disruptive, making difficult or impossible the task of assessing where and with what effect the government's authority extended.

Problems of assessing progress to victory had been a recurrent but sporadic focus of the Administration's attention during 1965 and 1966. Within MACV there had been much attention paid to the question of progress toward victory. The measurements had been statistical in nature and the conclusions they supported generally quite favorable. Initially, the Administration's decision makers had simply accepted the MACV and Embassy reports of success without question. However, the increasing disparities between these reports and other studies such as those done by the CIA had caused doubts to emerge. In 1967, the question of progress toward final success arose as a major consideration as a consequence of the Administration's need to convince Congress and public of real progress in South Vietnam and the real conflicts which existed between CIA and JCS, between MACV and Embassy regarding the success of US activities to date.

If US policy had been working as hoped, there would have been no need to reconcile the confusing perspectives on the air war, the ground war and the non-military programs which had become so evident between November 1966 and spring 1967. If American programs had been performing as well as had been expected, it would have been easy to demonstrate success to all onlookers. It was an implicit warning sign that the Administration had to embark upon a search for measurements of victory.

William Corson, in a bitter book with a bitter title, accused Robert Komer of manipulating statistics and reports to provide the appearance of success at the cost of programmatic failure.[1] Without examining the specifics, the basic charge levelled by Corson was accurate. All institutions, as well as the individuals constituting the chain of command within each, are driven to a substantial degree by a high regard for the appearance of success. Careers, budgets, influence and status depend upon this. In addition, institutions and the individuals who comprise them possess expectations of perception: certain results are expected from certain actions. Consequently the results are both seen and reported although their existence may be quite invisible to another observer. The contentious, time-consuming and ultimately quite irrelevant debate over the enemy order of battle and the number of casualties inflicted by ground and air action on the enemy which was waged between the military and the CIA in 1967 constituted an excellent example of this phenomenon as well as its results on the confidence of decision makers.

General Westmoreland and the Joint Chiefs, having defined the war in Vietnam as a struggle of attrition, would have been expected to focus upon the number of enemy killed and the ability of the North Vietnamese and Viet Cong to replace casualties as an excellent measure of the American progress toward victory. In the absence of any other dramatic and easily comprehended standard of success, it was not surprising that the body count should grab the attention of policy makers, media and public alike. Although only one of many statistical measures of results reported by military commands and intelligence agencies throughout the war, the body count and the exchange rates rose to the forefront as a result of the ever lengthening list of American dead through 1966.

To a military intelligence organization, the number of enemy troops, the disposition of enemy units and the ability of the enemy to make good his losses are central considerations. In a conventional war where lines of contact, axes of advance and the targets of operation are clear, an accurate understanding of the enemy's order of battle is not only critical to the discernment of his intentions and the formulation of operational plans, it is relatively easy to accomplish. Military intelligence units such as those within the US Army have developed effective procedures for estimating enemy strength, disposition and related matters in an accurate and timely way. The estimation of guerrilla force strengths, dispositions and replacement capacity was more difficult for a number of reasons rooted in the nature of guerrilla forces. When confronted with a mixture of regular forces, guerrillas acting as regular forces and pure guerrillas, the task of order of battle estimation becomes more complex and laden with broad uncertainties.

Military operations were expected to produce enemy dead. Virtually every American military sweep or other combat operation reported having counted enemy dead. But a corpse was only evidence that someone had been killed. Unless the body was found in association with a weapon, military equipment or appropriate identification, it was impossible to be certain that he had been an enemy and not merely a civilian unfortunate enough to have been in the wrong place at the wrong time. Without very specific identification it was difficult or impossible to tell if the dead person had been a PAVN regular or a Viet Cong main force guerrilla or a member of one of the various grades and types of local force and support units. Further complicating the task of ascertaining how many members of the various enemy units had been killed was the practice of reporting not only the physically counted dead but estimating how many might have been killed. The reliance upon estimates coupled with the operating practices of both friendly and hostile forces to pollute the reliability of the body count as an indicator of combat success. Despite this, the counting of corpses exercised a real compulsion at all levels of the chain of command from platoon to White House.

In Malaya the British had addressed the uncertainties concerning the number and nature of the presumed enemy dead by requiring that all corpses be either retrieved or photographed so that comparisons with extensive police records might be made and positive identification made. This option was not open to the Americans in South Vietnam. In view of the uncertainties automatically surrounding the body count as well as the dilemmas surrounding the appraisal of infiltrator numbers and estimation of Viet Cong recruitment capabilities, it was not surprising that differences arose between the MACV and the CIA over the subjects of order of battle statistics and infiltration trends.

While one CIA analyst, Sam Adams, achieved notoriety as the major precipitator of the flap over enemy order of battle statistics, and while it was certainly true that Adams was a zealous and active advocate of

175

much higher estimates of enemy strength than those generally accepted by MACV and the higher military command, by late 1966 there was a pervasive sense of contradiction between various estimates. The credibility of the statistics was at stake at the same time as the statistics on numbers of enemy killed, infiltrated and recruited locally were increasingly important in assessing which side was winning in a war which was now described as a battle of attrition. The Chairman of the Joint Chiefs sought to restore confidence in the enemy order of battle, casualty and infiltration statistics by ordering an interagency conference on these matters in mid-January 1967.

The conference was held at Honolulu from 6 to 11 February 1967 with its results being communicated to the Joint Chiefs through the Director of the Defense Intelligence Agency (DIA) on 21 February.[2] Convened by CINCPAC, Admiral U. S. G. Sharp, the conference brought together representatives of CINCPAC, MACV, CIA, DIA, and the National Security Agency (NSA) with representatives of the Defense Department's Comptroller and Systems Analysis Office as observers.[3] The conferees had an ambitious agenda including the establishment of definitions, criteria and methodologies for calculating the statistics on order of battle, infiltration and related matters; the development of a standard reporting system, the formation of guidelines for interpreting and disseminating order of battle and related data; and the setting of a procedure for informing consumers on methodology and 'limitations on the use of this information.'[4] The three working committees established to accomplish the agenda were successful in papering over the major, glaring differences which existed between the competing assessments.

At a more fundamental level there was nothing the conference participants could do which would make the statistics more exact and, as a result, more reliable as a measurement of American success. The nature of the Viet Cong local forces and infrastructure limited the precision with which their numbers could be gauged.[5] Using MACV as the sole source of infiltration data made verification or accuracy assessment impossible.[6] Lack of knowledge regarding the Viet Cong capacity to recruit or conscript caused such confusion that the conference conclusions in this area were eventually deleted.[7] The question of enemy killed in action figures was clouded with the ambiguity of assertion. As North Vietnamese regulars served in Viet Cong main and local force units and did not always wear national uniforms, there was no meaningful way of differentiating between Viet Cong and PAVN.[8] Statistically justifiable, but arbitrary, mathematical relations between the number of bodies counted and the assumed number of wounded personnel, men who died of wounds and those considered permanently disabled were established.[9] The effects of illness and exfiltration, the

176

first believed to be a major factor in enemy strength and the second a relatively minor one, were impossible to determine.[10]

The failure to establish agreement on the methods by which Viet Cong recruitment or conscription capabilities could be calculated constituted a major flaw. This failure was compounded by the inability to reliably distinguish between PAVN losses, those suffered by the Viet Cong main forces and those of the Viet Cong local forces. Without a sound grasp of the Viet Cong capacity at personnel replacement, it was impossible to develop reliable and consistent attrition figures. The lack of a dependable way to assess the impact of disease and exfiltration on the enemy strength constituted another serious omission. The employment of statistical correctives to determine the actual number of enemy killed, injured and permanently disabled from the number of bodies counted might have been justifiable statistical practice but automatically introduced a measure of softness in the final data which could be used to impeach the entire process.

Determination of infiltration rates was considered at length and some important areas of confusion were addressed. It was agreed that all agencies would use the same categories to describe infiltration and that all agencies would employ the same time frames for determining and reporting infiltration averages and rates.[11] It was admitted that the data base constantly changed so that statistical trends did not become stable for a period of 'three to six months' after the fact.[12] As an example, a monthly infiltration figure of 500 men might be revised upwards by as much as a factor of ten six months later. This experience-based conclusion implied that infiltration figures must be considered quite soft in the short term and by the time the figures were reliable, they might be of little consequence in the planning and evaluation of policy options. The changing character of the data base, and the variable length of time during which data must be considered suspect combined to 'make statistical analysis of infiltration trends a misleading proposition.'[13]

The most critical question considered at the conference was the projection of net gains or losses for the enemy forces. It was agreed that there were several statistical methods of equal validity for establishing projections. It was also agreed that there were many reasons why mere methodological correctness did not assure accuracy of projection. Several were mentioned: undetected infiltrators, undetermined numbers of PAVN within Viet Cong units, unknown total PAVN losses, and uncertain Viet Cong replacement rates.[14] Unmentioned but still quite relevant were other factors including the essential unreliability of the body-count figures upon which so much was predicated and questions about the precision and credibility of South Vietnamese intelligence reporting. In summary, a wide variety of considerations existed which,

177

taken as a whole, rendered all estimates of enemy strength, losses and order of battle unreliable as measures of American and South Vietnamese progress toward victory.

The unreliability of appraisals had been made abundantly clear in February 1967 with the publication of a MACV Order of Battle Reference Manual which provided in its preface a chart purporting to demonstrate the factors determining overall enemy strength and its changes between 1 October 1965 and 31 December 1966. A total of forty-one data cells were marked as unknown including the numbers of PAVN, Viet Cong main force, Viet Cong guerrillas and Viet Cong political infrastructure killed, captured, wounded or returned under the Chieu Hoi program.[15] Considering how little was accurately known about key elements of the baseline data, it did not matter how sophisticated and theoretically correct the statistical methodologies might have been. It was inappropriate to rely upon a series of admitted assumptions and torturous number crunching to determine what enemy strengths might become through 1967.[16] It was even less appropriate to compare the presumed effectiveness of US and South Vietnamese ground and air combat actions against the assumption-based projections of North Vietnamese and Viet Cong strength to measure progress toward victory.

The attempts to retrospectively adjust the accuracy of data and the correctness of past attempts at projection did little to improve the inherent reliability of the process.[17] All that could be certain was that North Vietnamese infiltration had been increasing steadily since March 1965. The actual numbers and rates of change were quite flexible and could be used by a prudent policy planner only as the roughest guide to just how bad the bad news from the infiltration front had been.[18] To push the past experience into the future as a projection of probable success was to engage in a dangerous act of self-delusion.

Some in the Administration recognized that the focus on body counts and the attempt to see success through the assessment of net gains or losses in enemy strength was too narrow a gauge of achievement. Military operations should be expected to produce more measurements of accomplishment than the body count. In addition to personnel losses, military operations should have positive results in the number of captured weapons and in the decrease of enemy-initiated actions. These latter indicators were more reflective of progress in the ground war. The loss of weapons represented both a loss of immediate combat power and an increase in the drain on supply lines. A decrease in enemy-initiated actions revealed a forfeiture of initiative. Unfortunately, statistical appreciations of these factors were scarcely less riddled with uncertainties than were the enemy casualty estimates.

The CIA explicitly acknowledged this in an exhaustive report on the war's progress performed at the request of Walt W. Rostow in May 1967. The Agency employed the technique of moving averages with several indicators to establish trends and turning points in the war between late 1963 and early 1967.[19] At the outset, the Agency's analysts stated a reservation often ignored by others.

> Obviously, statistical manipulation cannot overcome the basic limitations of the data. Statistics on the war in South Vietnam contain even more than the usual number of problems associated with the interpretation of numbers.[20]

In addition to these problems, the Agency mentioned another difficulty which cast great doubt on the use of statistical techniques to assess progress over the short term.

> Even more important to the interpretation of developments is the fact that a major change in the trend of numbers reported may be more related to a changed political situation or a military command decision than to a change in enemy capabilities.[21]

Not only did this comment undercut the general utility of any statistically based assessment system to measure progress to victory, it also recognized a very unpleasant reality all too often ignored. The enemy, particularly the North Vietnamese, had been enjoying the strategic and operational initiative. The North Vietnamese and, to a lesser extent, the Viet Cong were not being forced into a purely reactive posture. This constituted a real, albeit implicit, judgment on the degree of US success to date.

The assessment of the war through 1966 was based upon casualty exchange rates, weapons recovered and enemy-initiated actions, both large and small. Using these factors alone, the introduction and augmentation of US and other third party ground forces into the war had been successful in the short term.[22] The use of the past experience to predict the future course of the war was not apposite. The enemy was in the process of adjusting his doctrine and operational concepts to cope creatively with the tactics employed by the US forces through late 1966. The Agency analysts correctly concluded that this 'has a significant impact on the trend of statistical indicators and their use to project the progress of the war.'[23]

In early 1967 it was obvious that the enemy had the option of launching large attacks under favorable conditions which 'could suddenly change the course of the statistical trends that presently reflect Allied successes.'[24] It was equally evident that the enemy could re-emphasize guerrilla tactics, and this would affect statistical measurements in a potentially misleading manner. On the surface, the statistical trends all seemed to be favoring the American cause. There was no guarantee that these appearances represented the reality. There was no promise that these trends, if true, would continue into the future.

In the first quarter of 1967, there were statistical indications that the North Vietnamese and the Viet Cong were suffering major personnel and weapons losses and that the initiative had been lost to the US/GVN forces.[25] In all categories of Viet Cong actions except anti-aircraft fire, the number had been slipping rapidly since the third quarter of 1966.[26] With mounting losses of men and weapons and a decrease even in the standard components of guerrilla war, terrorism and harassment, it would seem legitimate to conclude that the US was winning on the ground.

There was an equally likely, but unpleasant, explanation of the trends: the enemy was in a period of retrenchment, a period of change and a period of preparation. Nothing in the trends reported by the Agency, even if optimistically interpreted, could substantiate the conclusion that the US efforts and those of South Vietnam had undercut significantly the enemy's will and ability to continue the war. When the PAVN dispositions in I Corps are considered, there was no legitimate ground upon which to transmogrify pleasing trends into a future of certain victory. Political will, material capacity and initiative could not be measured and treated by statistical legerdemain; neither had they been enervated by the American actions to date.

As 1967 continued so did the Administration's interest in statistical measurements of American success. Numbers were generated, repeated and recycled. Projections continued to be based upon the extrapolation of current general trends, despite the strong cautionary note introduced by the CIA. In a staff study performed for Walt W. Rostow at the end of October, forecasts of the military situation for the upcoming year were explicitly based upon a continuation of general trends without regard for either friendly ground force improvements or changes in enemy operational concepts and strategy.[27] The forecast, combining the projection of general trends with assumptions concerning the improvement of the infiltration interdiction efforts, concluded that pacification, defined as the progressive reduction of the potential manpower pool available to the Viet Cong, was the critical area of operations. Although cloaked in the costume of statistics, the optimistic projection was simply a restatement of the position taken a month earlier by William Leonhart, Komer's successor in Washington, who had argued pacification was the crux and, with its success, the North Vietnamese would have no option except to terminate the war.[28] Statistics and assumptions had been bent to give a reinforcing shot to a preferred option.

In an effort to end the confusion over the use of enemy casualties as an index of success, the CIA reported on a six-month-long attempt to compile the data for a new National Intelligence Estimate on the capabilities of the Viet Cong to continue the war. The new estimate was a gratifying demonstration that the statistical trends continued to be borne out and that American efforts at attrition were continuing to be effective.

The summary estimate sent by DCI Richard Helms to the President in mid-November 1967 contained the usual cautionary notes, but concluded in a very positive vein. While much of the past data had been wrong, and the estimates based upon them incorrect, an exhaustive reassessment had confirmed that Viet Cong were being killed or captured in satisfyingly large numbers.[29] If the 'assumption that there is no radical change in the scale and nature of the war' proved to be correct, the Agency concluded that Viet Cong manpower was scarce and would grow scarcer with the result that the capacity for protracted guerrilla war would fade in the next year.[30] Without a single dissent the United States Intelligence Board had put its imprimatur upon an optimistic response to the question: are we winning?

Walt Whitman Rostow presented a summary of the NIE to the President in a memorandum in mid-November.[31] Rostow underscored the most favorable conclusions of the intelligence community, in particular those which emphasized the success with which the United States was fighting the war of attrition imposed by Hanoi's strategy. The only darkish spot commented upon by Rostow was the inability or unwillingness of the CIA to confirm an important estimate regarding the number of 'combat effective' enemy battalions made by MACV and the Joint Chiefs of Staff. Citing JCS Chief Wheeler, Rostow stated that in October 1965 the enemy had possessed 123 maneuver battalions all of which were combat-effective, and in October 1967 the enemy was believed to field a total of 162 maneuver battalions of which only 87 were rated as being combat-effective.[32] The CIA was unable to verify this assertion thus casting doubt on the military's capacity to estimate enemy force strength.

A week later DCI Helms provided the President with further assurance that the US strategy of attrition was working and that the reliance upon the body count of enemy dead was 'a useful indicator of the level of combat and a conservative, general estimate of the damage inflicted on the enemy.'[33] Helms stated that he believed the enemy casualty counts to be reliable, conservative and verified.

In making these assurances he depended upon a MACV study completed earlier in November which had verified the accuracy of the reported count of enemy casualties.[34] The report concluded that there were no significant or substantial inaccuracies within the current system of counting and reporting the enemy dead. Where there were ambiguities or inaccurate counts they tended to favor undercounting rather than the opposite.[35] An examination of seven survey report discrepancies demonstrated an undercount of seventy.[36] The overall impression conveyed by the report was that the enemy dead had been properly counted. If anything, the US ground and air units and ARVN forces were killing more Viet Cong and PAVN than they were reporting. Problems such as that of properly differentiating between civilian and Viet Cong corpses were considered minor vexations rather than major sources of error.[37] Other problems, such as distinguishing between Viet Cong and PAVN personnel serving in Viet Cong units were simply not discussed, despite their relevance to the question of attrition.

In late November the Embassy adopted the position that attrition was working to the advantage of the US and South Vietnam. After acknowledging that the entire assessment might shortly be rendered irrelevant by 'possible changes in enemy political and military strategies [which] could portend a radical alteration in the situation in the near future,' the Embassy emphasized that the combat power of the enemy forces had been significantly reduced by attrition.[38] From the Embassy's perspective, the US and South Vietnamese had been killing or otherwise removing enemy personnel at a rate faster than that of replacement for approximately a year. The net loss to the Viet Cong and PAVN had been at least 50,000 men over the preceding twelve months.[39] Additionally, the US combat operations had caused 'a very serious deterioration of morale among the Viet Cong,' and, to a lesser extent, among PAVN troops.[40] Attrition, including the virtual attrition of demoralization, was an accurate and effective demonstration of the progress toward victory made by the United States and South Vietnam.

Attrition was working. This was the message of Leonhart in September, the NSC staff in October, and of the CIA and the Embassy in November. Body counts were reliable and could be used as a measure of success. This was the message of MACV and of the CIA in November.

The mood music which was reaching a swelling crescendo of victory had been increasing since summer. In the first of a regular series of monthly assessments of the situation in Vietnam, General Westmoreland had set the theme in August. Looking back over the month of July, the General pronounced himself satisfied with the manner in which he and his forces had used economy of force measures and superiority of mobility and firepower to contain the enemy main forces and progressively weaken his military forces.[41]

In a special assessment sent to the JCS at their request near the end of August 1967, Westmoreland reinforced the upbeat tone of his earlier monthly report.[42] In I Corps, General Westmoreland saw 'steady progress' in the 'destruction of enemy forces' and reported nearly 30,500 confirmed enemy killed with another 31,000 dead being considered probably killed for an exchange rate of no less than nine to one.[43] As a result of the heavy attrition, the enemy had not been able to mount any major offensives despite his secure geographic location along the DMZ. Unfortunately, the heavy tempo of military operations had slowed pacification, but that was seen as constituting a temporary setback. The III CTZ was depicted as having been transformed in two years from a stronghold of the Viet Cong to a killing field for them. Almost twenty thousand enemy had been killed in the preceding two years so that he was now 'on the run, fighting only defensively with twenty-five per cent of his base areas being 'considered neutralized.'[44] The General considered the military successes to be mirrored in improvements in pacification and revolutionary development as noted by 'the peasant's growing disenchantment with the VC cause.'[45] In IV Corps the ARVN units were showing marked success having inflicted a series of 'stunning defeats' upon the Viet Cong which had forced them to revert to guerrilla tactics.[46] He concluded by asserting 'the VC are losing the battle of attrition in IV CTZ.'[47]

General Westmoreland's monthly assessment for August 1967 was sanguine.[48] He summarized the progress of the month by noting that the expected I CTZ offensive had not occurred, 'primarily as a result of our successful application of intensive artillery, tactical air and B–52 strikes.'[49] He adumbrated the effects of aerial interdiction in the area just north of the DMZ, holding them to have been particularly effective, and noted that Seventh Air Force tactical efforts within South Vietnam had been reported as a 'major factor in deteriorating morale' among the enemy.[50] As he reviewed events in each of the Corps Tactical Zones, Westmoreland presented an agreeable picture of continued and growing military success. Only in pacification and revolutionary development was progress not as rapid as hoped and planned, but this was presented as a manageable problem. In all other respects, including the continued improvement of ARVN as an organization capable of conducting American-style big battalion sweeps, the prospect conveyed by COMUSMACV was of slow, but steady and measurable progress toward victory.

In a telegram which was not transcribed and forwarded to the White House, General Westmoreland expressed a tone of anxiety which had been absent in his monthly reports.[51] He was 'concerned over' the I CTZ situation for two reasons: high friendly casualties as a result of enemy mortar, rocket and artillery fire which was not being suppressed effectively by American actions, and 'the grave possibility' that the unpleasantness along the DMZ would be viewed 'out of perspective' by the American public.[52] He had taken a number of actions which he trusted would limit American casualties and make American firepower more effective, but desired others be approved by Pacific Command

(PACOM) and the JCS including an increase in B–52 sorties with a goal of 1200 sorties per month in the DMZ and coterminous areas and the employment of 2,000-pound and larger bombs in the B–52 strikes.[53]

In his next monthly assessment, which went to the White House, General Westmoreland played down his concerns about the situation in northern I Corps.[54] An upsurge of enemy activity was mentioned, but in a way which minimized any threat and maximized the successful determination of the defenders.[55] The importance and large size of the tactical air operations within South Vietnam was accented in a way which alleviated any anxiety felt in Washington about the sudden recrudescence of enemy artillery, rocket, infantry and terrorist attacks.[56] The III and IV Corps Tactical Zones were portrayed as having been relatively quiet during the month. The II CTZ was marked by enemy attacks which the General characterized as failed attempts to terrorize the civilian population during the national election period.[57]

In I Corps the fighting had been more serious, but General Westmoreland remarked on the successful defense offered by ARVN units giving the clear impression that the PAVN and Viet Cong attacks were not noticeably threatening.[58] In a monthly report on US Marine Corps actions in I Corps during September 1967 which went to the White House, the pleasant appearance of success was underscored.[59] In a summary highlighted for the President, the body counts of several major operations against the PAVN 2nd Division were presented. Without a careful reading of the operational summaries and the Marines' cautious conclusion that the victories were tactical only and the enemy maintained the capacity for future offensive operations, it would have been quite simple to conclude that affairs were progressing satisfactorily even in the most threatened section of South Vietnam.

No concerns about friendly casualties and no indications that the enemy might be holding the initiative were presented which might obscure the impression of continued progress on the road to success. General Westmoreland's upbeat reporting was reinforced by other summaries which asserted that Viet Cong manpower in I Corps was collapsing and that the introduction of PAVN personnel into Viet Cong units had been counterproductive as it hurt Viet Cong morale.[60]

During November the assessments offered by the Embassy seconded the optimistic view presented by General Westmoreland and the recent National Intelligence Estimate. The flat assertion was made in a Joint State-Defense Message at the beginning of the month that the US and South Vietnam now possessed and were utilizing the capacity for coordinated offensive planning aimed at ejecting the enemy from vital populated areas and returning them to Saigon's control.[61] The enemy was described as no longer feeling safe in any part of South Vietnam and as avoiding large engagements with the US and allied forces.[62] The change in tactics and operational concepts displayed by the Viet Cong and PAVN was interpreted by the Embassy, and presumably MACV, as 'reflective of the change for the worse in the enemy's capabilities.'[63] The possibility that the North Vietnamese and their junior partners, the Viet Cong, were following a choice of their own option which sought to exploit identifiable weaknesses within the US and South Vietnam was explicitly and definitely rejected.

Statistical analyses were employed to demonstrate not only the effectiveness of ARVN in both pacification and search sweep missions, but the overall progress of the war through the third quarter of 1967.[64] The only acknowledged hole in the statistical web of unmitigated success was the impossibility of providing a breakdown of enemy killed among the various forces.[65] The air war over the North was seen as being successful. 'Based on all available sources of intelligence and specifically photo reconnaissance of LOC facilities in NVN, the enemy is having considerable difficulty repairing bomb damage to highway and railroad bridges.'[66] The Embassy almost presented a picture of a victory parade.

There was a tendentious basis to the Embassy's evaluation. The reason was evident in a memorandum to the President from Walt W. Rostow on 10 November 1967.[67] The Embassy was deeply concerned by a rising perception within both South Vietnam and the United States that the war had entered a period of prolonged stalemate eroding the political will of both nations, and playing into the hands of Hanoi. To counter this unpleasant phenomenon, the Embassy proposed mounting an aggressive program of public relations designed 'to demonstrate to the press and public that we are making solid progress and are not in a stalemate.'[68] It was clear that the imperative existed to demonstrate progress toward victory by all methods and tools at the disposal of the Embassy and MACV. There was concern that the indicators used to demonstrate American success be able to withstand the scrutiny of an increasingly distrustful press corps. There was no interest in questioning the validity of the indicators of success or examining just what the various indices actually measured and their relevance to the course of the war. As a result, emphasis was given to force ratios, exchange ratios, net changes in enemy force strength, the effectiveness of the air war over the North, demonstration of enemy demoralization, improvements in ARVN performance, expansion of government control and successes in pacification and revolutionary development.[69] The indicators which were favorable were accepted uncritically; any which were not favorable, simply were ignored.

The Administration undoubtedly welcomed the Embassy's relentlessly positive stance. A major topic discussed at a lengthy meeting on 2 November 1967 between Administration officials, including President

Johnson, and senior foreign policy advisors such as Dean Acheson, McGeorge Bundy, Maxwell Taylor, George Ball, Omar Bradley and Clark Clifford was the erosion of public and editorial support for the war in Vietnam.[70] One element of consensus which emerged in the large and vastly experienced group was the need to adequately convey the impression of success to the American people. There was an imperative at the top to accept positive indicators without deep inquiry into their meaning, significance or relevance and to ignore any facts which cut across the relentlessly happy talk of progress.

By the end of the month some doubts were entering Embassy reporting, but close inspection was needed to see these against the bright appearance of success.[71] The major leitmotif was that US ground and air operations were still killing enemy personnel faster than they could be replaced.[72] Subsidiary themes described the enemy as demoralized, lacking combat effectiveness and afflicted with serious logistics problems.

Despite this array of serious problems, the enemy had launched an offensive campaign in late October with 'a series of well coordinated attacks in Kien Hoa and Dinh Tuong Provinces' as well as rocket and mortar attacks on Pleiku City.[73] After several attempts to deprecate the logic of an offensive, the Embassy concluded that the most likely course of enemy action in the short term was a continuation and possible expansion of the offensive in the central highlands of II Corps as well as in northern I Corps.[74] The commencement, let alone the continuation and possible enlargement of an offensive campaign was scarcely congruent with the depiction of the PAVN/Viet Cong as a depleted, demoralized and all but defeated force which could only hope to continue hanging on in a protracted guerrilla conflict. Yet, it is dubious that the still small voice of warning could be heard through the loud horns trumpeting a victory almost at hand.

General Westmoreland's report to the Administration, Congress and American public in November 1967 was optimistic in tone. He presented a view of the war which emphasized the accomplishments of American troops and civilians in South Vietnam over the preceding two or three years. He depicted an enemy whose only hope for an approximation of victory was 'the delusion that political pressure here combined with the tactical defeat of a major unit, might force the United States to throw in the towel.'[75] He summarized the thrust of his reports to the Administration, Congress and public in a telegram to his deputy, General Creighton Abrams.

We are grinding down the Communist enemy in South Vietnam and there is evidence that manpower problems are emerging in North Vietnam, our forces are growing stronger and becoming more proficient in the environment. The Vietnamese forces are getting stronger and more effective on the battlefield. The Vietnamese armed forces are being provided with modern equipment. These trends should continue with the enemy becoming weaker and the GVN becoming stronger to the point where conceivably in two years or less the Vietnamese can shoulder a larger share of the war and thereby permit the US to begin phasing down the level of its commitment. This phasedown will probably be token at first.[76]

This was an accurate reflection of the General's message to America. Unfortunately for him and his command, people heard what they wished to hear from his presentation. As a result the emphasis in the mind of Administration and public alike was placed upon the most optimistic aspects such as the promise of imminent success. To most, the General was heard to say, 'We are winning and winning rapidly.'

The General was not alone as a source of this favorable impression. All the reporting coming into the Administration had indicated that the US was on the verge of success. There were a few problems around the military edges, such as the annoying North Vietnamese concentrations in northern I Corps and along the margins of the central highlands in II Corps. For an enemy repeatedly viewed as defeated, defensive and increasingly desperate, the North Vietnamese and Viet Cong continued to exhibit an irritating degree of initiative and offensive spirit. There were also hints that the enemy was following his own theory of victory and his own operational concepts. There were insinuations that he had not read the American script. There were some disturbing dark cracks in the sunny prognosis of success.

Had the Administration been able to view closely the progress of ground operations through 1967 some of these cracks would have been evident. It should be recalled that the senior decision makers of the Johnson Administration did not follow the course of ground combat in any except the most cursory manner, unless a particular engagement was unusually bloody or had captured a high degree of media attention. It should be noted also that the after-action reports filed several weeks or months after an operation by the units involved were not circulated to the policy level either civilian or military. They were not available or used as sources of information concerning the rate of advance toward victory. As the conclusions of the reports were unrelentingly positive, it is doubtful that their availability would have altered in any significant way the perceptions of the Administration and senior military commanders. Only close examination would have caused the raising of cautionary flags regarding the success of American doctrine and policy on the battlefield or the relevance of apparent combat success to the accomplishment of policy goals.

In War Zone C of III CTZ, Operation GADSDEN conducted in four phases between 2 and 21 February 1967 by two Brigades of the 25th Infantry Division, the 3rd Brigade of the 4th Infantry Division and the 196th Light Infantry Brigade demonstrated the persistence of the search and destroy focus and the still inconclusive nature of this type of operation.[77] This multibrigade sweep against an old adversary, the 9th Viet Cong Main Force Division resulted in an impressive list of facilities, material and food destroyed, a less imposing body count and a commander's conclusion that the enemy had been 'forced to abandon a major base area and exfiltrate to another safe area' thus making him resort to a lengthy period of reorganization.[78] The question of initiative was never discussed. The assumption that the operation had forced the Viet Cong to withdraw for a prolonged period of reorganization was never examined.

It was, however, immediately shown to have been wrong by one of the largest and best-reported search and destroy operations of early 1967, JUNCTION CITY I/II. More a campaign than an operation, JUNCTION CITY was a multidivision sweep in War Zone C conducted between 22 February and 15 April.[79] The two-phase operational concept sought to block routes of withdrawal from War Zone C into Cambodia through the insertion of major forces by ground and air, including the first battalion-sized parachute assault since the Korean War, following which pressure would be applied from three sides upon the 9th Viet Cong Main Force Division. The concept and plan had been drawn directly from the Army's basic doctrine. Its execution demonstrated American competence at mobility, logistics, engineering and communications. The Air Force again exhibited its ability to deliver support to the troops in the field with a total of 2,483 tactical sorties which expended 3,235 tons of ordnance.[80] In addition, twenty-two B-52 strikes were executed in support of the operation.[81] What the operation did not reveal was significant results.

The goal of the operation was to force the 9th Viet Cong Division to fight and by so doing face destruction by superior American firepower. The presence of the blocking forces was planned to prevent easy exfiltration to the Cambodian sanctuaries or adjacent areas of South Vietnam. The concept succeeded to a limited extent. On three occasions, 1 March, 10 March and 20 April, the Viet Cong attacked American defensive positions only to be thrown back with heavy losses. In the first event, the 273rd Viet Cong Regiment which had been reported destroyed or demoralized in previous operations attacked the perimeter of Fire Support Base 14 which was held by Alfa Company of the 3–5th Cavalry. The combination of artillery fire, air strikes and the arrival of reinforcements enabled the position to be held during the over-six-hour enemy night assault.[82] In the second failed Viet Cong attack, the always overly aggressive 271st Regiment which had been reported destroyed at least three times in the preceding year assaulted the perimeter of the 2/16th Infantry with losses too heavy to be credible during the night of 1 April.[83] In the third, the 272nd Regiment struck the 2/2nd Infantry position with 200 mortar rounds and a two-battalion assault with severe losses and no success.[84]

Beyond the three failed Viet Cong attacks and one meeting engagement there was no notable contact during the course of what the commander of the Big Red One called 'the largest operation of the Vietnam War to date.'[85] The 9th Division had not been destroyed; COSVN had not been eliminated. While there had been the usual impressive body count and the typical lengthy roster of captured or destroyed enemy material and facilities, there was no indication that the enemy had been cleared from War Zone C or that he was incapable of further offensive operations.

In terms of assessing American success in the war generally, Operation JUNCTION CITY might have been taken either as a very positive sign or a dark indicator. A focus upon the body count or an unquestioning acceptance of the statement made in the 1st Infantry Division's after-action report that all four regiments of the 9th Viet Cong Division, which now included the 101st PAVN regiment, had been defeated would support the positive interpretation. There was no doubt that when the enemy incorrectly used his initiative to attack American defensive positions he was routed. The overwhelming quantity of US firepower, the weight of the half million artillery rounds fired during the operation and the volume of air strikes insured his tactical defeat.

An appraisal based upon less dramatic and attention-riveting factors than body counts and failed night assaults did not allow such an optimistic perspective. When the enemy used his initiative correctly, when he exploited his strengths and American weaknesses rather than playing to the strengths of US forces, he could evade contact and employ a growing array of countersweep tactics to vex, frustrate, exhaust and inflict casualties. The mere fact that the components of the 9th Viet Cong Division remained so active, aggressive and well-equipped despite previous setbacks at the hands of American search and destroy sweeps in War Zone C should have been seen as reason to doubt the apparent success of the American theory of victory.

Even the distinction between the US and North Vietnamese theories of victory might have been inferred from a close examination of JUNCTION CITY. The US focused upon attrition of combat strength and erosion of material capacity to continue the war. This was evident in the attention paid in the assessment process to the destruction of enemy formations and facilities. The North Vietnamese sought victory through the exhaustion of political will and this was visible in the ability of Hanoi and PAVN to accept the appearance of defeat while supporting the substance of prolonging the war.

The nature of the enemy theory of victory and the fundamental irrelevance of the American suppositions were evident in a number of search and destroy operations occurring in the first half of 1967. The six-month-long series of sweeps in Binh Duong Province northwest of Saigon conducted by the 3rd Brigade of the 4th Infantry Division between November 1966 and May 1967 had minimal results. This was attributed to Viet Cong operational concepts which emphasized the avoidance of decisive engagement except under unusually favorable conditions.[86] The Viet Cong had also developed techniques which allowed them to evade American attempts to cordon and search villages while still maintaining effective contact with the civilian population. The casualties on both sides were light, nineteen Americans and twenty-six Viet Cong were reported killed.[87] The Viet Cong had destroyed one tank, seven armored personnel carriers and two trucks which was a fair exchange for the twenty-three individual and two crew-served weapons captured from them.[88]

The after-action report made quite clear that the enemy had resumed guerrilla war. This was usually interpreted by American commanders as a sign of American success. A more skeptical observer would have seen the resumption of guerrilla tactics as an indication that the target of enemy operations was the political will and integrity of the South Vietnamese and American governments and people, not the military forces. The skeptic would have noticed that the Brigade did not do much in the pacification and revolutionary development sphere and that its civic action program was quite limited.[89] This reinforced the effectiveness of the guerrilla tactics employed to counter the US attempt to project influence and presence into an area long used by the Viet Cong.

The 1st Brigade of the 101st Airborne Division encountered the same enemy operational concepts while executing a search and destroy sweep in Kontum Province during December 1966 and January 1967. The enemy forces, which included both Viet Cong main forces and PAVN, evaded engagement using an elaborate system of trail watchers.[90] As a result, the enemy personnel losses were light as were US casualties. The capture of 109 weapons by the US forces was seen along with the evasive tactics of the enemy as signifying a loss of morale and the will to fight by the Viet Cong and PAVN.[91] If the list of captured weapons had been closely studied, it would have been noticed that more than half were elderly and had been long superseded in the inventory of both PAVN and Viet Cong main forces by modern assault weapons.[92]

Arguably, there had been no real loss and the conclusion that the enemy was demoralized and eager to evade contact was not justified. It was justifiable to see the enemy's operational concept as appropriate to a war prolongation strategy with the emphasis upon the exhaustion of political will.

The 4th Infantry Division encountered a different enemy operational concept directed toward the same goal during the last five weeks of Operation SAM HOUSTON during March and April 1967. The enemy forces encountered during this search and destroy sweep in Kontum Province were primarily newly infiltrated PAVN units.[93] When the PAVN-held areas were finally penetrated after a period of desultory contact with Viet Cong local forces, combat became heavy. North Vietnamese tactics were well designed and were applied with proficiency and even panache. As a result casualties were heavy on both sides with 725 PAVN personnel being reported as the confirmed body count and 155 Americans killed in action.[94] The capture of 181 individual and 11 crew-served weapons verified the enemy losses as having been very heavy, perhaps heavier than the confirmed body count.[95]

Skillful exploitation of the terrain and the judicious use of snipers, surveillance units and ambushes marked the PAVN tactical doctrine. It was difficult to find the enemy units and even more difficult to employ supporting firepower with full effectiveness. The North Vietnamese had obviously learned much regarding American strengths and weaknesses and were now operating to limit the former and to exploit the latter. To the cautious observer not mesmerized by the appearance of success contained in the five to one exchange rate, the PAVN doctrinal alterations demonstrated an impressive flexibility, a tightly integrated command and control system, well-trained and highly disciplined soldiers and considerable morale.[96] The commander of the 4th Infantry Division stressed the physical and psychological effects of PAVN's new operational and tactical doctrine upon his troops. The demands of terrain, the claustrophobic nature of the bush, the enemy's use of mines, snipers and mortars, the sudden, unexpected and violent nature of the fire fights all combined to create 'a certain degree of tension with individuals and units.'[97] Exhaustion and demoralization constituted a double-headed ax. It could cut American forces at least as deeply as it cut the enemy.

The three-month, four-phase search and destroy operation carried out by the 101st Airborne Division's 1st Brigade in Binh Thuan, Ninh Thuan and Lam Dong provinces on the southern coast of II CTZ during January, February and March 1967 further verified the Viet Cong's readoption of guerrilla tactics.[98] There were no major engagements but light contact occurred on a daily basis. As a result casualties were relatively light although 115 enemy were claimed killed.[99]

On the basis of statistics, the operation was a complete success, but the consideration of other factors would have undercut this interpretation. The Viet Cong forces were almost exclusively local force units. None the less they were characterized as well trained and organized and their use of escape and evasion techniques was favorably regarded by the Americans.[100] Morale, the integrity of the command and control system, the competence of the commanders were all of a high order. This did not allow for the conclusion that the Viet Cong were losing either the will or the ability to fight. The reported presence of PAVN advisors indicated the further extension of North Vietnamese control over the guerrillas. This is consistent with the interpretation that the North Vietnamese were now using the Viet Cong as expendable partisans as part of a new overall theory of victory.

A ten-day excursion by a portion of the 1st Brigade during FARRAGUT served to underscore the actual lessons of the larger operation.[101] The purpose of the operation was exploitation of ARC LIGHT strikes. The technical proficiency demonstrated by the heliborne raids was substantial; the results were minimal. The reason for the insignificant results was simple and should have been alarming. There had been no PAVN or Viet Cong units present to be bombed and raided.[102] The intelligence upon which the ARC LIGHT missions and the GATLING raids had been based was flatly wrong. The important question was not asked: was this the rule or the exception?

The importance of the unasked question was supported by a multibrigade operation of the 25th Infantry Division undertaken in War Zone C during mid-May 1967.[103] The purpose of the five-day sweep was to exploit ARC LIGHT strikes.[104] One brigade established blocking positions and a second constituted the maneuver element. The execution was thorough and professional, again demonstrating American competence in engineering, logistics, helicopter mobility and overall administration. The results were unimpressive with fourteen Americans and nine Viet Cong reported killed.[105] A number of structures were destroyed and a minor amount of weapons and equipment seized.[106] While the commander characterized the operation as a success due to the 'vast quantities of enemy material and equipment captured and destroyed,' the absence of contact and the long-deserted state of many of the enemy camps entered by American troops indicated that the intelligence upon which the ARC LIGHT strikes and AHINA were based was wrong.

The mobility, tactical initiative and war-prolonging tactics of the Viet Cong and PAVN forces were demonstrated in a 1st Infantry Division search and destroy operation conducted during late May between Saigon and War Zone D.[107] Also illustrated in this operation were structural deficiencies of American combat information collection, particularly in the technical programs such as RED HAZE and the use of Side-looking Airborne Radar (SLAR).[108] If the 273rd Viet Cong Regiment was present during the operation, it evaded contact, allowing the destruction of old bunkers and buildings and the capture of unimportant material including nine individual weapons, twenty pounds of peanuts and a flag in exchange for destroying one tank, one truck, one helicopter and two armored personnel carriers.[109] The operation was a success as the American commander asserted, but only for the enemy, if the goal was exhaustion of political will through protracted conflict.

Some American search and destroy operations were quite successful, as shown by Operation HOPTAC XVI, a single-day strike by 2nd Brigade, 9th Infantry Division in Dinh Tuong Province.[110] This search and destroy operation, one of the first in IV Corps, was completely successful. The Viet Cong were forced to fight as a result of proper and prompt exploitation of intelligence, an appropriate use of helicopter and riverine mobility and the superiority of firepower. As the commander summarized, the operation was an excellent example of the American doctrine at its best.[111] It should be noted that the Viet Cong of IV CTZ had not fought the US forces to a significant extent before and had not learned the lessons necessary to exploit weaknesses and negate strengths to the extent of their colleagues in the other areas.

While search and destroy operations continued to manifest little success beyond the specious one of fatality exchange ratios and the meaningless one of empty structures destroyed and replaceable material captured and substantial, albeit less obvious, indications of failure, small-unit and irregular force operations exhibited a capacity to injure the enemy, at least on the margins.[112] This dichotomy, if it had been apparent up the chain of command, would have served to call into question the comfortable assumption that the American theory of victory was working. The small and irregular force operations cost little in lives and less in the disruption of village life. Arguably, they served to produce more intelligence and proportionately more defectors from the Viet Cong. The focus upon attrition and the increasing acceptance of the enemy body count as a reliable measure of American progress toward victory assured that the accomplishments of small and irregular forces would be unnoticed. As a result a valuable comparative tool for the assessment of the validity and relevance of the big battalion sweep was overlooked.

The differences between operations against the North Vietnamese and the Viet Cong established in early 1967 held true through the year. In September 1967 the 1st Brigade of the 101st Airborne Division started a ten-week search and destroy campaign in Quang Tin Province at the southern edge of I Corps.[113] The target of the operation was the 2nd

PAVN Division, which was believed to be in the western portion of the area of operations. Contact with the PAVN force was made after a preliminary period of skirmishing with local force Viet Cong. The PAVN division was characterized as well trained and very well equipped with the latest Soviet Bloc weaponry.[114] The North Vietnamese were aggressive and operated not only at night but by day. Combat was heavy as were losses. The Brigade commander stated, 'Operation WHEELER produced the largest number of enemy killed (by body count) of any single operation conducted by the Brigade since its arrival in Vietnam twenty-eight months ago.'[115] Interestingly, even though the major combat was against the 2nd PAVN Division, more than twice as many Viet Cong, 793, than North Vietnamese regulars, 312, were included in the confirmed killed category.[116]

If the Hanoi leadership was pursuing victory against the United States by seeking the exhaustion of political will and was seeking victory against the Viet Cong through attrition, if Hanoi sought to ablate American will with Southern blood, Operation WHEELER was a success from the Northern perspective. In that it did little to reduce PAVN's capacity to continue domination of western Quang Tin Province, the operation did little, if anything, to advance American hopes of victory. Fundamentally, WHEELER constituted a misleading indicator of success if viewed through the myopic lens used to count bodies.

Further south, in the May Tao Secret Zone, the 9th Infantry Division undertook a two-month, three-phase search and destroy offensive against the 5th Viet Cong Division.[117] The commander declared the operation to have been 'an overall success although it failed to locate, fix and destroy' the targeted division.[118] The absence of contact, the lack of material captured or destroyed, the apparent age of bunkers and other structures along with the lack of signs indicating recent use, combined to furnish convincing proof that the intelligence upon which the operation had been planned and executed was wrong.

In operations against the Viet Cong throughout 1967, there had been a pattern of intelligence failure. Even when the intelligence had been accurate, the Viet Cong had often been able to evade engagement while using guerrilla tactics to vex and inflict casualties upon the Americans. The absence of significant contact and the willingness of the Viet Cong to evade combat should not have been taken automatically to be a sign of American success without any consideration of alternative explanations for the enemy's behavior. The CIA, as previously noted, had raised the cautionary flag against the simple assumption that evasion meant a lack of will and capability for combat, but the warning had been too low-key. As a result it was lost in the noise of bodies falling to be counted.

The overall pattern of operations had never been made available to policy-level personnel in the Administration. The small hints of pattern which might have impinged on the policy consciousness were obliterated by the din of big battle, particularly the biggest battle of the year, the 'Battle for Dak To.'[119] The series of engagements that stretched through November 1967 that collectively constitute the Battle for Dak To occurred within the context of a major search and destroy operation directed against PAVN forces in the highlands of Pleiku Province. The 4th Infantry Division was responding to an upsurge in North Vietnamese-initiated incidents near the junction of the Laotian, Cambodian and South Vietnamese borders which started in early October following three months of relative quiescence.

The interlocking series of sweeps and engagements was too complex to fully anatomatize, but the essential features can be outlined. Accurate information regarding the PAVN plans and dispositions concerning forthcoming attacks was provided to the Division by a North Vietnamese sergeant who defected on 2 November. Rapid movement by US forces pre-empted the attacks and the PAVN regiments withdrew to prepared positions apparently in the hope of provoking the Americans into costly assaults against ready defenses. Elements of the 4th Infantry Division and the 173rd Airborne Brigade accepted the challenge. Over the next three weeks numerous battles occurred around each of the fortified PAVN bases in which casualties ranged from moderate to heavy. Despite the superior American firepower and repeated air strikes, the PAVN formations held their positions. As an example, the 174th PAVN Regiment slugged it out with the 173rd Airborne Brigade at Hill 875 from 12 to 23 November when the position finally fell to the 'Herd.'

In addition to effective and tenacious positional warfare, the North Vietnamese employed diversionary attacks delivered by Viet Cong main force units. Heavy fire from 122mm rockets and 120mm mortars was employed directly against US forces and against diversionary targets such as Kontum City. The lack of coordination which had delayed the originally contemplated attack until it was fatally compromised by the defection of Sergeant Vu Hong was not apparent when the North Vietnamese went on the tactical defensive. Their effective change of plans and dispositions in the face of the US pre-emption was a mark of high professionalism and unusual command flexibility. Their willingness to use the tactical defensive to further a strategic offensive demonstrated that the overall Northern theory of victory was not dependent upon spectacular successes in either the capture of territory or the destruction of forces.

The territory selected by PAVN was well suited for defense as it was mountainous, heavily covered with dense vegetation and well provided with caves. The PAVN engineers had improved on the terrain, so it constituted an even more formidable obstacle for the American and

ARVN troops who attacked. American and ARVN forces used artillery liberally with nearly 152,000 rounds of 105mm and larger caliber being fired during the course of the Dak To campaign.[120] Air strikes were employed heavily, with over 2,000 tactical and 305 B–52 sorties flown.[121] In all, the aircraft delivered over six thousand tons of ordnance.[122] Maximum use of helicopter mobility enabled the Americans to move artillery, large masses of supplies and quantities of men quickly around the rugged terrain.[123] The reported figure of 1,644 PAVN dead was believed to be low due to the enemy's policy of emphasizing the recovery of dead and wounded personnel from the battlefield which was facilitated by the nature of the terrain.[124] American forces lost either 283 or 290 killed in action with the ARVN units losing either 56 or 73 more.[125]

The commander of the 4th Infantry Division, General William R. Peers, thought 'the Battle for Dak To might well become the turning point of the war in the Central Highlands.'[126] He was too optimistic, but his view was echoed up the chain of command. The competent and courageous performance of the US forces and the large number of PAVN bodies counted obscured the less pleasant realities. The battle developed as it did in large measure because of one defector's information and good luck of this magnitude was not an expectable commodity. The North Vietnamese had broken contact on their own initiative and withdrawn in good order, probably to sanctuaries across the Laotian or Cambodian borders. The performance of PAVN on the defense had been excellent, the leadership quite professional and troop morale high as indicated by the small number of North Vietnamese defectors, five in addition to the talkative Sergeant Vu.[127] The 314 individual and 96 crew-served weapons captured did not seriously affect the capability of the PAVN 1st Division to fight on.[128]

The commander of the 173rd Airborne Brigade, the unit which had suffered the most fatalities at Dak To, was more sober in his assessment, commenting on the enemy's determination, fighting qualities and material strengths.[129] Dak To looked like a real victory to the Administration and to the public alike, having been reported as such by the legion of journalists who landed in the combat zone.[130] Dak To was interpreted as a milestone on the road to overall success in South Vietnam. This was an interpretation which was not justifiable. The will, capability, integrity and initiative of PAVN had not been eroded or seriously affected by the Battle for Dak To or the larger Operation MCARTHUR. There had been no turning point in the central highlands.

If the Administration had been able to closely examine the after-action reports during 1967 and if it had been possible to abandon the body count fixation, the picture of US success which was being painted so ardently in November could not have been so easily accepted. It was true that the American operations were killing an impressive number of people, capturing an imposing quantity of supplies, equipment and weapons, destroying a very large number of structures and facilities. But, was it true that these were relevant indicators of progress on the battlefield?

The debate over enemy order of battle and rates of replacement had resulted in sterile statistical scholasticism of dubious relevance. The enemy had shown no difficulty in replacing losses. The CIA had confirmed in August that the war was 'becoming an increasingly North Vietnamese show.'[131] This would reduce Viet Cong manpower requirements and difficulties of maintaining morale within the guerrilla forces. The operational and tactical concepts employed by the Viet Cong during 1967 were assisting in the process of conserving manpower while buying time during which remedial actions could be taken to improve morale. In any event, despite losses and an increase in the number of low-level, local force defections, 'VC troops continue to fight well and there have been no mass or unit defections.'[132] American ground and air actions had not broken the morale or will to fight of either the Viet Cong or PAVN troops.

American forces had killed a lot of enemy soldiers, but it did not seem possible to kill our way to victory. The losses so eagerly counted by field commanders and Washington decision makers alike had not translated into a denial of initiative or political will to the enemy. In short, below the appearance of success, the military situation was at best battlefield stalemate in which neither side could hope to obtain a quick or decisive advantage. Rather, the military balance resembled the almost motionless embrace of two equally matched sumo wrestlers, a dynamic stasis awaiting some small slip or hesitation.

If the ground war was not providing a meaningful measure of progress toward victory, then some sense of success or failure could have been sought in assessing either the air war or the 'other war' of pacification and revolutionary development. The assessment of progress in both was of great importance to the Johnson Administration. Appraisal of success or failure in each, but particularly the second, was subject to distortion through ambiguities and deceptive indications.

The programs subsumed in pacification, revolutionary development and nation building were numerous, interlocking and complex. As was the case in the ground war, the programs were liable to statistical manipulation such as to provide numerical factoids masquerading as substantive facts. As was the case in the ground war, the programs' actual success or failure could be hidden from view by the screen of numbers which seemed to guarantee stately progress toward victory.

Professor Sam Huntington, a social scientist, wrote in a report on the progress of the pacification and revolutionary development program,

'The crucial test of pacification is that a locality develop the will and means to defend itself against VC subversion or attack once the US or GVN troops are withdrawn.'[133] While there were other measurements of pacification program success, Huntington was correct in his identification of the most important one. Without the ability and will for self-defense, a village would be subject to repeated Viet Cong exactions, attacks or attempts at propagandization. Without the will and ability for local self-defense, the control of a village by Saigon would be dependent upon the capacity of ARVN or the US forces to provide a constant presence.

No official in either the US or South Vietnamese government believed that their armed forces had the manpower to provide a constant security presence in each of the thousands of villages open for contest between the Government of Vietnam and the VC/NLF. The control of village populations was considered central to the denial of resources, manpower and intelligence to the Viet Cong and PAVN. As a result it was critical to the appraisal process for the Administration to have an accurate understanding of the success of the pacification programs and their companions: revolutionary development, Viet Cong infrastructure neutralization, the development of the regional and popular forces and the augmentation of a national police force.

Most evaluations of progress in pacification and related programs were so circumscribed with caveats that their utility as measurements of progress toward victory were severely restricted. It was held that pacification was an activity 'which must be accomplished by the GVN' with the American role being limited to support, advice and supplementary functions.[134] It was argued that pacification could only occur in an environment of military success free of interference by PAVN or main force Viet Cong units. Notwithstanding the relevance and accuracy of these two caveats, their very existence went far to assure that except in the broadest terms no meaningful sense of progress could be derived by the Administration from reports and other assessments of pacification and revolutionary development.

Project TAKEOFF, the integrated CORDS pacification effort, was established by Robert Komer shortly after his arrival in Saigon as COMUSMACV Deputy for Civil Operations and Revolutionary Development Support on 9 May. A multivolume report setting forth programmatic goals and evaluating the course of pacification through the end of May 1967 was issued in mid-June. This constituted the first effort to assess the direction and progress of pacification. As such it served as the baseline for further measurement attempts through the balance of the year.[135]

The Komer-directed assessment effort noted that all pacification efforts prior to his appointment had lacked central direction of planning and execution which marred their effectiveness.[136] Now that the centralization had been effected and that 'the military situation is in our favor,' it was believed that significant progress would be seen in the pacification and revolutionary development programs.[137] There were significant problems that needed to be addressed including the regrettable reality that the programs had exercised little effect upon the perceptions and loyalties of the villagers at whom they were directed and that the Viet Cong organization and infrastructure were tight, well-knit and virtually impossible to penetrate. Compounding the challenge confronting the pacification and revolutionary development efforts was 'the failure of the Vietnamese leadership to cope with the enormous demands placed on it' as well as pervasive corruption, inefficiency and inertia.[138] The pacification effort would require an ever increasing amount of military support if it was to accomplish the task of extending security and South Vietnamese governmental authority to a greater area of territory.[139] Consequently, any setbacks in the big battalion war would impair pacification progress. With these handicaps, it was clear that any progress, no matter how slight, would be seen in Washington as an indication of real American movement toward victory.[140]

A major independent evaluation of pacification and revolutionary development programs was completed contemporaneously with the Project TAKEOFF study.[141] Project PACKARD had been initiated by the Pentagon in September 1966 with field research into pacification issues continuing through April 1967. As a result the June draft report served as an alternative baseline to that presented by the Komer-inspired TAKEOFF assessment. The authors of the report, Doctor Menkes and Colonel Jones, drew conclusions that in some ways were identical to those of TAKEOFF, but in several key matters were substantially at variance. While agreeing that pacification could not be successfully undertaken in areas under domination by PAVN or Viet Cong main forces, the PACKARD study argued that pacification could not be deemed a success merely because of the ability to provide local security. Pacification could only be considered a success when the guerrillas had been deprived of popular support and thereby rendered obsolete.[142] When revolutionary development efforts had succeeded in demobilizing support from the guerrillas, then pacification and the provision of local security against any re-emergence of the Viet Cong would be automatic.

Unlike TAKEOFF, the PACKARD report tended to de-emphasize the role of the US and South Vietnamese military in support of pacification, arguing instead that the regional/popular forces and police would provide longer-term, less expensive and higher-quality security.[143] This position tended to decouple progress in the villages from success in the bush. Importantly, the PACKARD report explicitly defined refugee migration to urban areas as an indication of failure, which was the antithesis of Komer's position.[144]

On the matter of assessing progress, Menkes and Jones recommended that reliance on short-term indicators be avoided as they could be highly misleading. Decision makers were reminded that real progress in pacification and revolutionary development would take years, not months, and proper measurements of success would recognize this.[145] The Menke–Jones approach had much to recommend it, but their notion of progress measured against the yardstick of years and the implication that realistic milestones were not of a sort which would allow facile statistical manipulation and glib expression assured that no Johnson Administration official or military commander could or would accept it. Project TAKEOFF would be the baseline.

As in the Project TAKEOFF assessment, the pacification progress reports through the balance of 1967 were exercises in statistical manipulation in which the appearance of success was well maintained regardless of the underlying reality.[146] Two statistical systems for measuring progress in pacification were established: the Pacification Evaluation System (PACES) and the Hamlet Evaluation System (HES). As was explained by Brigadier General Knowlton to the Senate Armed Services Preparedness Investigation Committee in October 1967, both were considered valid means of establishing success in pacification and revolutionary development programs as well as reliable instruments for predicting trends.[147] The same focus upon statistical appearance rather than substantial reality could be seen in such important component parts of pacification and revolutionary development as the regional and popular forces and the Chieu Hoi Program.[148]

The Marines, having always been quite proud of their orientation toward pacification and revolutionary development support, were eager to demonstrate success in these areas up the chain of command. In October and November, the reports from III MAF which went to the White House presented, with appropriate numerical justification, the strides which were being made in I Corps despite the large-scale combat against PAVN.[149]

Soft data collected by the Joint United States Public Affairs Office (JUSPAO) in Saigon were employed to demonstrate that the villagers who were the target population for pacification and revolutionary development activities had a positive orientation toward American military forces and operations. In one interim study of attitudes in II CTZ, JUSPAO concluded that villagers attributed only 3 per cent of the attacks on hamlets to US combat forces despite the high number of search and destroy sweeps conducted in the region.[150] In I Corps, the same sort of soft data, interviews with civilians on a limited and haphazard basis usually conducted through an ARVN interpreter, were used to support the contention that only 11 per cent of the population perceived their villages to have been attacked by American forces and that only 1 per cent of the attacks were seen as having been unjustified mistakes.[151] In both I and II Corps, 71 per cent of the respondents were reported as welcoming the American presence.[152] Similarly positive attitudes regarding American-supported civic action and revolutionary development programs were described. It was stated that the vast majority of the respondents saw the Viet Cong in the most negative terms. If the numbers were accepted without questioning the methodology of their collection, the honesty of the responses or the accuracy with which the respondents reflected generally pervasive attitudes, the JUSPAO reports underscored the progress toward success. Uncritical acceptance of collector-friendly numbers seems to have required a dangerous, willing suspension of disbelief which is scarcely apposite in the policy evaluation process.

The persuasiveness of the smiling numbers regarding pacification was reinforced within the White House with the arrival of a MACV study of Viet Cong perceptions of revolutionary development and pacification.[153] Using captured documents and debriefings from defectors and captured Viet Cong, the study reflected back to the period from mid-1965 to late 1966 and concluded that the Viet Cong had seen the American-backed pacification and revolutionary development programs as a particularly menacing threat and that the Viet Cong had lost control of one million South Vietnamese.[154] The implication was clear. If the programs had been so successful in their first, chaotic year of operation, it was logical and justifiable to assume that they had become even more effective during 1967.

The almost pornographic pandering to the American lust for numbers pretending to be facts assured that only the shortest of short-term criteria would be employed and that highly subjective data would be used to generate final numbers with the appearance of objectivity.[155] Both of these factors as well as the ability to explain all inconcealable failures as the result of the want of effective South Vietnamese governmental action or the lack of sufficient military manpower assured that no substantial assessment of progress toward the goal of victory could be found in the pacification reports.

The Embassy employed the same statistical approach to evaluating progress in pacification and related matters. In a telegram which was transcribed for the President, the Embassy in early October outlined a new plan to 'demonstrate to press and public that we are making solid progress.'[156] The tool to be used in this exercise in opinion molding was the same as that used within the Embassy and Administration: statistics. Whether infiltration, the morale of the enemy, the Chieu Hoi program, pacification, elections or revolutionary development, happy numbers told the happy tale of progress toward victory. The same tack was taken a month later in a joint State/Defense telegram from the Embassy.[157] Numbers that illustrated success were given emphasis while those that did not, such as the decrease of defectors under the Chieu Hoi program, were explained away.[158] Only in the matter of the pervasive and highly damaging matter of continued inflation were neither statistical magic nor facile explanations employed to conceal failure in November 1967.[159]

The plethora of statistics served not only to guide the Administration as well as the Embassy and MACV away from examining the type of substantial benchmarks implied in the Project PACKARD study but into a set of expectations which were transmitted to the Congress, press and public. The Administration expected to see victory within the pacification and revolutionary development programs and they did see it, thanks to the miraculous ability of statistics to obfuscate fundamental realities in a pleasant cosmetic of appearance. The cosmetic became so thick that the reality could not be determined.

It should have been easier to assess progress toward victory with the air war than with pacification, but this was not the case. The air campaigns against North Vietnam had acquired significant political and emotional freight by the time of the 1966 pause. By the end of that year it had become clear that many in the Administration including John McNaughton, Robert McNamara and, at least to some extent, the President had lost faith in ROLLING THUNDER as an instrument either of coercion or interdiction. It was equally clear that the senior military commanders continued to believe that the air war had imposed significant restrictions on the ability of Hanoi to support larger forces in the South and still carried the potential of effective coercion. The bombing had continued through 1967 as a result of two major considerations. The first reason was a belief that to stop it without any concession from Hanoi would look suspiciously like a partial American surrender. It was generally accepted within the Administration and its circle of advisors that an appearance of surrender would have serious, albeit unknown, repercussions around the world. The second reason was the political strength of the JCS. The Chiefs had authority in the eyes of public and Congress as well as independent access to the media and Congress. As a result they were in a position to execute a political end run in support of the air war which would damage the Administration and the President.

The air war continued to be a locus of debate in the fall of 1967. The central question concerning the air campaign against North Vietnam was that of effectiveness. There had been no doubt expressed concerning the way in which ROLLING THUNDER had been executed. It had been generally agreed by all observers that the implementation of the air campaign had been marked with skill, professionalism and courage by the pilots and aircrew involved. The qualms expressed within the Administration had been caused by the actual effectiveness or even the relevance of the effort. These reservations had gained saliency with the growing domestic and foreign reaction against the American bombers.

In early fall 1967, there had been a general underlying assumption that the air campaign would continue. In an outline of programs and proposals for the future, a fundamental postulate was the continuation of ROLLING THUNDER which was described as 'having become increasingly effective.'[160] The air operations were credited with having produced a great reduction in the transportation capabilities of the North, a reduction in the PAVN order of battle, and destruction of a major portion of the North Vietnamese infrastructure, particularly that connected with energy production. The execution of the air campaign was presented as having improved. This was indicated by the reduction in the bomb jettison rate and the refinement of flak and antiaircraft missile suppression actions. All of these observations were correct, as was the key comment: 'In spite of such airstrikes a substantial amount of equipment and large numbers of men are still moved into South Vietnam from the North.'[161] Instead of examining this dichotomy and assessing options for policy change, the authors of the 'Blueprint for Vietnam' recommended 'intensification of our bombing efforts and destruction of all targets that can be hit without unacceptable risk or extending the war to Soviet Russia or Communist China.'[162] Unaddressed by the 'Blueprint for Vietnam' was the central conundrum: in spite of the heavy weight and high tempo of the bombing campaign, the North had been able to enter the war in South Vietnam in an increasingly effective manner. The military situation in I and II Corps had made abundantly clear the unpleasant reality that the war had become increasingly a contest between North Vietnam and the United States, even as the bombs had fallen in an ever greater rate and weight.

The Bureau of Intelligence and Research came very close to identifying the reason for the existence of the conundrum. The Bureau concluded that Hanoi viewed its losses as not being disproportionate to the goals it sought.[163] Invert this. The losses suffered by North Vietnam, primarily to the bombers of ROLLING THUNDER, demanded a commensurate reward. Against this, an assumption, the falsity of which could not be proven, was offered: without the bombing, the military situation in South Vietnam would be much worse.

At the end of August, Director of Central Intelligence Richard Helms provided a personal assessment of the air war in the North to the President.[164] Helms commented on the increased effectiveness of the air war and the damage which had been inflicted by ROLLING THUNDER upon Northern facilities, factories and infrastructure. Despite this, he stated, 'Hanoi continues to meet the needs of the Communists in South Vietnam and essential military and economic traffic continues to flow.'[165] The intensified air war which averaged ten thousand sorties per month had inflicted between March and July 1967 an amount of damage almost equal to that accomplished in all of 1966.[166] Even with that level of punishment and the consequent effects upon the civilian economy and morale, Hanoi had not been coerced into reducing its efforts in the South.[167]

Diplomatic activities in late summer 1967 provided mixed signals regarding the air war against the North. Henry Kissinger had been engaged in highly secret preliminary conversations through inter-mediaries with North Vietnamese representatives.[168] In late September, Kissinger's interlocutor reported that the North Vietnamese Prime Minister had 'made it clear that there could be no formal discussions between North Vietnam and the United States as long as any level of bombing continued in the North [emphasis in original].'[169] There was some debate over whether this implied that the bombing campaign was working in its coercive intent or not. The final decision was that the North was not yet serious concerning negotiations other than time-consuming preliminary, informal and secret conversations. ROLLING THUNDER was not yet coercing, although it might have served Hanoi to convey that impression in order to halt the bombing. There was no reason to believe that ROLLING THUNDER was hurting the North so much that they were willing to accept a reduction of their efforts in the South as the price for halting the bombs.[170]

Not surprisingly, the JCS dissented vigorously from the position of the CIA and the State Department that the bombing had continued to fail in its objectives of coercion and interdiction. In early October 1967, the JCS staff stated:

> The fact is that there is not sufficient evidence in CIA, DIA or any other US agency upon which to base any reasonable conclusions on the military effectiveness of the bombing campaign upon NVN [emphasis in original].[171]

The memorandum then went on to assess the military effectiveness of ROLLING THUNDER, concluding that the CIA's evaluation was based on false premises and was without probative value. The JCS staff argued that the interdiction effort had been directed at the attrition of trucks, locomotives and other vehicles. As a large number of these items had been destroyed, the campaign had been working well.[172] Without going into the details of the convoluted reasoning and the blind rejection, not only of the Agency's assessment methods, but also of previous JCS staff statements concerning the thrust of the ROLLING THUNDER interdiction attacks, suffice it to state that the protest was wrongheaded, unjustifiable and tendentious. The Agency's response two weeks later was a restatement of the already painfully obvious. The interdiction effort had not placed a meaningful ceiling on North Vietnamese supply capabilities and the North pursued its strategy in the South 'with little reference to the air war in the North.'[173]

The monthly assessment of ROLLING THUNDER performed by the DIA and CIA for the thirty days ending 16 October 1967 demonstrated the continuing obscurity of the air campaign's effects.[174] Although bad weather had limited air operations to some 7,000 sorties, which was considerably below the 10,700 average of the preceding three months, effects on the major military and infrastructure target systems were reasonably good. North Vietnamese efforts offset much of the damage. Improvisations such as shuttle systems and cable bridges mitigated the destruction inflicted by the strikes. On the material level, the best which could be said of the air effort was that the cumulative effects of the air strikes had reduced North Vietnamese capacity for 'sustained large-scale military operations against South Vietnam,' although the capacity to continue activities in the South or Laos at the present or increased combat levels and force strengths was unimpeded.[175] The political will of the North Vietnamese leadership was untouched as demonstrated by declaratory policy through the month. There were 'no significant signs of a decline in popular morale nor any indication that the conditions of the people will force the regime to alter its war policy,' despite the effects of the bombing on the quality of civilian life.[176] Overall the report did not present an imposing picture of American success.

It was against this background that Secretary McNamara on 1 November 1967 wrote a lengthy memorandum regarding military operations over the next fifteen months.[177] In considering the air campaign, McNamara observed that any intensification of the air campaign, including the removal of all restrictions, would not be likely to prove effective; 'expansion could not produce results which would offset the loss of support for our effort.'[178] He recommended that ROLLING THUNDER be halted, arguing that this would serve to 'clear the atmosphere,' improve American standing in the world and Administration standing at home and place great pressure on Hanoi to end overt efforts in the South thus facilitating negotiations.[179] While his optimistic expectation concerning a favorable reaction from Hanoi to the end of the bombing might not have been realistic, his conclusion that the bombing program, even if extended, would not be likely to have positive effects was well founded. There had been no objective indications of success.

McNamara was virtually alone in his appreciation and recommendation. McGeorge Bundy opposed both an intensification and any unconditional pause or cessation of the air campaign. He believed that the bombing had real military advantages and recommended that the US look for a way of maintaining these advantages while giving the appearance of reducing the attacks.

> I think we should have a careful staff study of the possibilities for continuous bombing of the North which avoids startling targets and has the public effect of deescalation without seriously lightening the burden on the North Vietnamese.[180]

Walt Whitman Rostow was against McNamara's proposition primarily on the basis of its presumed domestic political effects although he did believe that the bombing had exercised coercion to some degree and that it was helping the ground war in the South.[181]

Clark Clifford wrote in violent opposition to the McNamara position, arguing that the end of the bombing, or for that matter any reduction or stabilizing of the military effort, would be tantamount to signalling to Hanoi that the US was losing its political will which would be to play into Hanoi's hands.[182] Clifford had adopted the position that the effectiveness of the bombing was irrelevant. It had to be continued or Hanoi's strategy of winning through the weakening of American political will would succeed. At least he understood that Hanoi intended to win through enervation, even if he did not understand the implication of the bombing for North Vietnamese political will.

At the 2 November 1967 meeting between the President and his foreign policy advisors consisting of Clark Clifford, George Ball, McGeorge Bundy, Bill Bundy, Maxwell Taylor, Omar Bradley, Robert Murphy, Henry Cabot Lodge, Dean Rusk, Nicholas Katzenbach, Averell Harriman, Dean Acheson, Abe Fortas, Arthur Dean, Douglas Dillon, Walt Whitman Rostow, Richard Helms and Robert McNamara, opinion on the efficacy and necessity of ROLLING THUNDER ran against the position taken by the Secretary of Defense.[183] Dean Acheson commented that the importance of the bombing was not its military effect, but its value as a signal to Hanoi.[184] In his interpretation Acheson was reflecting a prevalent view. The bombing was a sign of American political will and its cessation would be an encouragement to Hanoi.

What this view failed to address was the simple reality that the capacity to bomb was not so much a reflection of political will as the ability to tolerate being bombed. A review of the record of ROLLING THUNDER to date should have demonstrated persuasively that bombing assisted the consolidation of political will in North Vietnam. This implied that even at the late date of December 1967, a bombing halt with the threat of renewal could have exercised a corrosive effect upon Northern cohesiveness.

Omar Bradley summarized the other strain of support for continuing the bombing. He maintained that it had a positive military effect.[185]

George Ball remained consistent with his previous opposition to the bombing. He argued that bombing 'won't limit the flow of supplies into the South significantly.'[186] Further, the bombing made it harder for the North to seek conflict resolution since the view from Hanoi was that the war had become one between North Vietnam and the United States. The Hanoi Politburo could not afford to be seen as having lost. In effect, Ball was the strongest supporter of the McNamara recommendation to end ROLLING THUNDER.

In a memorandum to the President the next day, Maxwell Taylor strongly opposed an end to the bombing, stating that the effect would be to demoralize the South Vietnamese. He contended, 'our own forces would regard this action as a deliberate decrease in the protection which, they feel, is afforded them by the bombing.'[187] The perception, rather than the reality, of effectiveness governed Taylor's position.

Taylor amplified his position in a memorandum sent to the President on 6 November 1967.[188] General Taylor assessed three alternative strategies for the United States and three for North Vietnam. His conclusion was that the United States would be best advised to continue doing what it had been doing rather than escalate or commence disengagement. The Administration should make 'every effort to stiffen the home front,' and should be prepared to escalate 'as a means of pulling together the U.S. home front if it seems in danger of collapse.'[189] Taylor recommended to Ho Chi Minh that the North Vietnamese keep on doing what they had been doing until Hanoi could 'understand better the situation on the United States home front.'[190] Taylor understood that the war was a contest of political will more than it was one of military force. He did not realize that Hanoi already had a very good feel for the American political dynamic and their use of military force showed this quite well. His advice for Ho Chi Minh was gratuitous; his recommendations for the United States were wrong.

Justice Abe Fortas, whose expertise at assessing such matters was in no way manifest, advised the President 'Our strategy should be to exert increasing and continuing pressure on the North Vietnamese [emphasis in original].'[191]

Walt Whitman Rostow buttressed the case made by Taylor, Fortas and the other supporters of continuing the present course in mid-month. In a memorandum addressing 'seven key difficult questions' Rostow attempted to demonstrate that the US efforts were resulting in genuine progress.[192] Rostow employed statistical indicators to address questions on the number of South Vietnamese under government control, enemy losses of strength, Viet Cong loss of morale and improvements in the South Vietnamese government and armed forces.

Rostow stated one very important sign of the progress toward victory made by the United States. 'The enemy has been unable to mount a major offensive although intelligence indicated he planned to do so last May and June.'[193] This was true up to a point, but misleading to the point of danger.

By the end of the month Bunker and Westmoreland weighed in against any cessation of the bombing campaign.[194] They were joined in part by Secretary of State Rusk who strongly supported 'intensive bombardment of infiltration routes' but rejected 'the political judgement that a continuous escalation of the bombing will break the political will of Hanoi.'[195] Rusk was apparently arguing for a continuation of the present course. His reasons for believing in the efficacy of prolonging an effort whose success had been questionable at best were unstated.

Only Under Secretary of State Nicholas Katzenbach swam against the stream. He joined his predecessor, George Ball, in recommending that ROLLING THUNDER be reconsidered. 'Nobody really believes that the war can be won with bombs in the North. We may lose it with bombs – here in the United States.'[196]

The President, in mid-December, decided to continue ROLLING THUNDER with some slight modifications hoping to make the program less ineffective and less visible or controversial in the public mind.[197] He was wrong. President Johnson had been trapped by a classic Goldilocks gambit offered by his foreign policy advisors. He had been presented with one option that was too hot, the virtually unrestricted air campaign favored by the JCS, General Westmoreland, Clifford and Rostow. He had been handed another option which was too cold, the unconditional pause or cessation favored by McNamara, Ball and Katzenbach. He had chosen the option that was 'just right,' the continuation of ROLLING THUNDER with changes at the margin which might make it less high-profile and less unsuccessful. In the one area of American strategy where happy numbers could not conceal unhappy reality, in the one area where there should have been no ambiguity on the question of progress toward an American victory, the President chose to ignore fact and opt for hope, no matter how forlorn, or desperation.

The intelligence assessments continued to show that the air war was not succeeding. The monthly appraisal for the period ending 16 November concluded that even with good weather over central and northern North Vietnam, even with a heavy weight and tempo of attacks, there had been no productive result beyond the routine destruction of vehicles, facilities, factories and infrastructure.[198] This report was another small tack in the coffin of ROLLING THUNDER.

Heavy spikes were hammered in during December 1967. On 13 December 1967, Walt Whitman Rostow forwarded to the President two 'major CIA studies,' published five days earlier that had been recommended by Secretary McNamara.[199] The first of these constituted a complete evaluation of the progress of American policy in Vietnam to date. Concerning the air war, the conclusion was quite straightforward and unambiguous.

> Despite the achievements of the bombing program, however, no significant deterioration in North Vietnam's military capabilities or its determination to persist in the war can be detected. The flow of men and supplies to the South has been maintained; and the cost of damage has been more than compensated by deliveries of foreign aid.[200]

The outlook was equally stark.

> There is no reason to believe that additional pressure which might result from a more extensive or intensive bombing – barring attacks against cities or the dikes – would be sufficient to induce Hanoi to alter its goals in the war. Moreover, it is difficult to conceive of any interdiction campaign that would pinch off the flow of essential military supplies to forces in the South as long as combat requirements remain at anything like current levels.[201]

While the Agency analysts might have been wrong about the strategic avenue being pursued by Hanoi, believing it to be one of protracted attrition rather than enervation, they were right about the progress toward victory which had been made by ROLLING THUNDER.[202] At best, there had been none; more likely, the bombing campaign had been an impetus to Northern success.

In the second study, the Agency reinforced the conclusions offered in the first. The analysts concluded that the bombing had killed not more than 2 per cent of the personnel infiltrating into the South during 1966 and that it had not impaired the ability of the North to meet the supply requirements of PAVN and Viet Cong forces which were estimated to be approximately fifty-five tons per day by late 1967.[203] The figure of 55 tons represented about 25 per cent of the daily requirements, so roughly 165 tons per day were acquired within South Vietnam.[204] There was no evidence that the bombing had weakened the will of the North Vietnamese leadership, and no reason to believe that the bombing was causing significant dissent within the North Vietnamese population.[205] There were some observers, 'including some in Hanoi,' who were convinced that the bombing had strengthened the political will of the Northern leadership and population, although the CIA was 'inclined to take at face value' the statements from the leadership that the bombing was an inconclusive factor in determining the outcome of the war.[206] The North Vietnamese economy, manpower reserves and foreign assistance levels were sufficient to continue the war effort even in the face of increased air attack.[207] Any way the question was examined, the Agency concluded that the air war against the North had been a failure.

Onetime architect of the air war, John McNaughton, had authorized the Institute for Defense Analysis (IDA) to conduct a far-ranging review of ROLLING THUNDER and the several aerial interdiction campaigns including BARREL ROLL and STEEL TIGER in Laos. The four-volume report was issued on 16 December 1967.[208] While there were detail differences between the JASON Study and the assessments performed by the CIA, the general conclusions were identical. 'As of October 1967, the US bombing of North Vietnam has had no measurable effect on Hanoi's ability to mount and support military operations in the South [emphasis in original].'[209] Regarding the political will of the Hanoi leadership, the JASON study paralleled the CIA's conclusion that the bombing had 'not discernibly weakened' their determination to persevere.[210] The IDA analysts agreed with the CIA, 'no bombing campaign can be designed that can either reduce the flow from North to South significantly or raise the cost of maintaining the flow to some unbearable level.'[211]

The analysts who prepared the JASON study came closer than those of the CIA to understanding that the strategy being pursued by Hanoi was not one of simple attrition but rather one of enervating American and South Vietnamese political will.[212] They also properly noted that the North Vietnamese were 'still able to demonstrate military initiative' and that the North possessed the potential for continued escalation dominance.[213] This was a significant indication of the failed nature of the air war, particularly ROLLING THUNDER. The report was not at all sanguine concerning the potential for successful aerial interdiction. Even an increase in the effort south of 20 degrees which prevented all use of trucks would result in a dislocation of supply efforts lasting only a few months. There were probably 'enough supplies stored in Laos to maintain the flow south to South Vietnam.'[214] In short, the interdiction campaigns within North Vietnam and Laos had failed to a substantial extent.

There was criticism of the JASON study. Robert Ginsburgh, an assistant of Walt Whitman Rostow, wrote a five-page critique in mid-January 1968 which he sent to Rostow.[215] He characterized the effort as 'intellectually dishonest,' and then proceeded to twist the conclusions and much of the analysis out of all recognizable form.[216] While there were some questionable uses of statistical analysis within the JASON study, these in no way obviated the essential thrust of the argumentation and conclusions. Further, Ginsburgh was wrong in his assertion that the JASON study misrepresented the American air effort as an attempt to seek victory through air power. While the IDA team never made such an assumption, both the Administration and the Ad Hoc Study Group had, more than two years earlier when ROLLING THUNDER was initiated. The air war had been the focus of effort and the air war over the North had driven policy to a large extent. Now the air war had failed. JASON and the CIA had both brought that message unmistakably to the Administration. It was too late to cry foul. It was too late to expect the air war to succeed.

In another of the high points of irony within an irony-ridden war, the air war was the only major component of the American effort about which there was no ambiguity. There was no way in which smiling numbers could bemuse and distract from the unpleasant reality of failure. In the context of ROLLING THUNDER, and to a lesser extent, BARREL ROLL and STEEL TIGER, the answer to the question, 'are we winning?', was clear, obvious and unavoidable. We were losing. Yet it was the only portion of the war for which the President gave a clear authorization to continue.

In two of the three critical areas of American endeavor, the ground war and the war in the villages, the Administration simply did not know how to know if we were winning. The goals and definitions of victory employed by the Administration were fuzzy, incongruent with one another and irrelevant to the way in which the war was developing on the ground.

The change in the character of the war which occurred in 1967 with the entrance of the PAVN in force was not recognized. Also unacknowledged was the change in the relationship between Hanoi and the NLF/VC. The North Vietnamese ended their brief period as an external sponsor of the Southern guerrillas which had obtained from late 1965 through late 1966 and were now seeking the goal of unification under Hanoi's domination. The NLF/VC had become potential rivals for power and thus were now expendable tools. The presence of the North Vietnamese regulars in I Corps and the central highlands of II Corps complemented the Viet Cong forces to present the United States and South Vietnam with an operational dilemma. Actions against the PAVN forces facilitated the guerrilla activities of the Viet Cong; concentrations of force against the Viet Cong whether in big battalion sweeps or pacification support missions laid I and II Corps open to a PAVN spectacular. In any case the prolongation of the war, the infliction of casualties and the increase of chaos in the South had the strong potential of enervating the political will of the US and the Government of Vietnam to continue the war.

The American planners assumed that Hanoi not only was continuing as an external sponsoring power but was pursuing a strategy of attrition. As the US was following a strategy which mixed attrition with

211

the erosion of the North's material capacity to continue the war, this constituted an exercise in mirror-imaging. It also constituted an exercise in wishful thinking, for American advantages in ground- and air-delivered firepower would prove decisive in a contest of attrition. The assumptions were not correct. Despite the rhetoric issuing from Hanoi regarding the role of the NLF as the sole legitimate representative of the South Vietnamese people, there was strong reason to assess the role of Hanoi as rival rather than patron of the NLF/VC. There was no reason to see the strategic avenue of attrition as the one pursued by Hanoi. On many occasions individual policy makers made reference to a perception that Hanoi hoped to triumph by exhausting the political will of the United States. Had this interpretation prevailed as a coherent under-standing and predicate for policy, the goal and definition of victory employed by the US might have been more relevant.

As it was, the misunderstandings and confusions regarding the changing character of the war as well as American goals and definitions of victory were so pervasive and pernicious that it was impossible to establish realistic and meaningful measurements of the progress toward victory. By default, the focus upon statistics emerged. Numbers pretended to be facts and statistics were seen as realities. The real accomplishments of 1967 such as the village and national elections and the improvements of ARVN floated in an amorphous mass of irrelevant or dangerously misleading statistics like bits of fruit in a Swedish pancake, real progress overwhelmed by the misleading appearance of success. Below the smiling faces of the happy numbers, there were ample dark signs that all was not well. The enemy maintained the initiative and escalation dominance. Real pacification and revolutionary development progress was difficult to establish. The 'other war' was undercut by the destabilizing effects of the big battalion sweeps and free fire zones. The generation of refugees, an approach urged by Komer, was incompatible with the establishment of a secure rural economy, polity and society.

The crosscurrents and cross-purposes which lurked beneath the pleasant statistics of success could have been seen had the Administration the wit and intellectual courage to look for them. The numbers that promised progress toward victory were belied by the events on the ground. That dichotomy should have attracted the attention of the Administration and adjustment of policy goals and means. That it did not stands as an indictment of the Administration at its middle and upper levels.

The Administration, in particular the President, is open to a more damning indictment with regard to the air war. Here the Administration knew how to know if the United States was winning. It was clear from all the intelligence assessments that the air war over the North was a counterproductive failure which should be terminated. There were good pragmatic reasons for its ending and a real possibility that benefits would accrue from stopping the bombing. The President chose to reject or ignore excellent counsel and intelligence and authorize a continuation of an aerial campaign which had all too obviously failed. He may have had political reasons for doing this, but that constitutes no justification. At root, the President demonstrated a lack of intellectual, moral and political courage when he chose to continue the air war.

As the new year dawned, uncertainty and ambiguity surrounded the issue of measuring American success. There was still doubt within the Administration on the nature and rate of progress toward a favorable end to the war. There were a number of mixed intelligence signals regarding enemy intentions for the new year. Outside of the Administration there was doubt and uncertainty as well, although many had accepted the optimistic projections of General Westmoreland and other spokesmen. Within a month optimism would die a sudden and very violent death.

8

SHOCK AND REASSESSMENT

The Administration was given no cause for alarm as 1968 began. The flow of information to the White House continued to give reason for optimism and no particular grounds for pessimism. The sense of stasis was enhanced by an extract from the MACV J–2 November Intelligence Report forwarded to Rostow early in the new year. Brigadier Philip Davidson provided an unremarkable and not particularly insightful appreciation of the probable course of enemy action in the near term.

> He is expected to continue his present peripheral strategy while reinforcing with units from his strategic reserve to maintain combat effectiveness. He will also infiltrate replacements from the North and recruit as many men and women in the South as possible.
>
> The enemy will initiate major offensive action when he sees a high probability of success, or when he deems it militarily, psychologically or politically necessary to do so. He retains the objective of winning at least one, significant, exploitable victory for propaganda purposes, and to gain the appearance of strength from which he might choose to seek negotiations.[1]

In essence, Davidson was saying that the enemy had the initiative and escalation dominance. The PAVN/Viet Cong combination could strike when and where they chose. The United States and South Vietnam could only react. Neither General Davidson nor any of his superiors saw this as cause for alarm. They should have.

The CINCPAC year-end review provided reinforcement for the positive view.

> The combination of military operations in South Vietnam, North Vietnam and Laos during 1967 produced a definite shift in the military situation favorable to the US. As a result the enemy is no longer capable of a military victory in the South.[2]

From the perspective of Pacific Command, 'the enemy did not win a single battle in Vietnam in 1967,' while the anti-transportation efforts of ROLLING THUNDER were credited with destroying or damaging over 56 per cent of all North Vietnamese trucks and railroad rolling stock.[3] A number of other measurements of success were trotted out to support the overall appearance of definite American progress toward victory. The only deficiencies noted were in the areas of revolutionary development and Viet Cong infrastructure neutralization, but it was confidently predicted that 1968 would see a turnaround in both areas.[4] ROLLING THUNDER received the most positive report being characterized as 'the one element of our strategy where we truly have the initiative.'[5] A resolute push from the sky could bring about a Northern collapse in the forthcoming year.

Almost lost in the signals of success was one unsettling message. 'Recent large unit deployments from North Vietnam indicate that the enemy may be seeking a spectacular win in South Vietnam in the near future.'[6] That fact plus the equally unpleasant realities of the enemy's use of his initiative 'to draw allied forces into remote areas of his choosing,' and that 'the VC infrastructure persists as a significant influence over portions of the population,' combined to portray an active enemy still confident of his ability to use the battlefield to secure a political victory.[7]

A flurry of State Department assessments covering December 1967 arrived in the White House in mid-January which carried the same positive signals as had the PACOM and MACV reviews.[8] The only sour note in the period was played by the CIA. As relayed by Rostow to the President on 11 January 1968, the Agency perceived an emerging threat directed against the American position at Khe Sanh in northern I Corps.[9] The Agency analysts had first warned of the implicit threat directed against Khe Sanh in November 1966. Now the movement of PAVN formations into the Laotian Panhandle west of the DMZ had given additional saliency to the threat. A recent increase of PAVN reconnaissance probes near the Marine Corps firebase persuaded the Agency to conclude that there would be an offensive directed against Khe Sahn after Tet to which the North Vietnamese could dedicate more than twenty thousand troops from four PAVN divisions. The Agency believed that the mini-Verdun which had been long anticipated would shortly be begun.

Khe Sanh was the focus of a debate over the nature and extent of any Tet truce. Because of the obvious preparations for an offensive directed at the Marine firebase, General Westmoreland and ARVN General Vien went to President Thieu and persuaded him to cut the scheduled truce from forty-eight to thirty-six hours. This started a debate within the Administration with Secretaries Rusk and McNamara opposing the

215

unilateral change in the duration of the standdown.[10] Both the DIA and the JCS focused on the situation at Khe Sanh to support the proposed reduction of the Tet truce. The estimate of General Westmoreland was underscored. 'The attack could begin before or immediately after Tet.'[11] The additional twelve hours of cease-fire would allow the enemy to receive an additional 11,100 tons of supplies before launching the attack at Khe Sanh.[12] In his summary, Rostow stated to the President that he believed any Tet truce to be an error considering the evidence that the North Vietnamese were on the verge of a massive attack at Khe Sanh.[13] Five days later, the matter was still under consideration when both Ambassador Bunker and General Westmoreland urged canceling the truce in Quang Tri Province and continuing the bombing of North Vietnam during Tet.[14] From the perspective of Saigon, the Marine firebase at Khe Sanh was under attack already and any observation of a truce would be a one-way charade.

General Westmoreland had certainly sounded the alarm two days earlier. In a dispatch which went to the President, Westmoreland not only reported on the start of what would be known as the 'Siege of Khe Sanh,' but warned that 'the enemy will attempt a countrywide show of strength just prior to Tet, with Khe Sanh being the main event.'[15] Less than two hours later, Rostow relayed a longer appreciation of the situation from General Westmoreland to the President.[16] The major question considered by the General was the offensive's probable duration. His conclusion, which was underscored for the President's benefit by Rostow, was:

> In summary, the current winter–spring campaign is unusual in its urgency and intensity. The bulk of our evidence suggests that the enemy is conducting a short-term surge effort, possibly designed to improve his chances of gaining his ends through political means, perhaps through negotiations leading to some form of coalition government.[17]

Westmoreland believed that North Vietnamese and Viet Cong manpower deficiencies assured that the present level of effort could not be maintained for any length of time. The inference which would be drawn from his assessment, particularly against the background of repeated statistical demonstration of the success of the American war of attrition was that the enemy had made a desperate roll of the battlefield dice in the hopes of a quick political payoff. By exposing himself to the overwhelming American firepower, his casualties would be very heavy. It takes no unjustifiable leap of imagination to see Westmoreland and his superior grinning wolfishly over the great opportunity to show just how well firepower kills which had been handed them by a desperate enemy.

A week later the situation had not changed in its essentials as reflected in a COMUSMACV situation report forwarded to the White House by Earle Wheeler.[18] Importantly, General Westmoreland stated that the enemy was 'well into his announced Tet standdown period with no discernable decrease in significant activity.'[19] On the morning of 30 January 1968, the President was informed that the enemy had launched a series of coordinated mortar, rocket and ground attacks in several areas of I Corps and heavy fighting continued in several cities in II Corps.[20] Within hours additional details of the coordinated attacks within I and II Corps came into the White House.[21] General Westmoreland in an early report on 30 January summarized the attacks as 'desperation tactics, using NVA troops to terrorize populated areas.'[22] The general believed that the situation was well in hand because the 'enemy has exposed himself, he has suffered many casualties.'[23] A true assessment, as far as it went. It was too early to be implying success or even reading the enemy's intentions.

The big shock came in a short message from the CIA Station in Saigon. 'Flash Director. Embassy compound now under rocket or mortar attack. Also small arms fire outside Embassy compound. Will advise by FLASH precedence when more info avail.'[24] The word was passed to the White House and all other agencies of cognizance by a CRITIC message.[25] Within an hour a second CRITIC stated that small arms fire continued in the Embassy compound as of 3:31 p.m. Eastern Standard Time.[26] Rostow responded on behalf of the White House:

> We shall be meeting at 8:30am breakfast with the President. If, at the end of the first day of these fun and games, you and Westy have any recommendations for Washington statements or actions, we'd be glad to have them. Good Hunting![27]

The notably hawkish Walt Whitman Rostow might have believed that the Viet Cong and PAVN offensive was a heaven-sent opportunity to use superior American firepower for a decisive result, but the attack on the Embassy was seen as something far different by many Americans. Sun Tzu had recommended a millennium ago that the correct target of military actions was the mind of the opposing commander. That recommendation was at work on 30 January 1968.

The mood at the White House was not immediately one of out-of-control crisis. The information flow into the message center was dense and comprehensive. Summaries of the traffic showed a complete and not overly alarming picture of events in South Vietnam. Even the dramatic Viet Cong sapper attack on the Embassy, after the lapse of a few hours, did not present any indication that there was a need to reassess or to question the implicit assumption that the North Vietnamese and Viet Cong were in the process of inflicting a major defeat upon themselves.[28] Early on the morning of the 31st, Wheeler was able to relay a very comprehensive review of the situation in Saigon and other regions of South Vietnam.[29] Admiral Sharp, reflecting General Westmoreland's perspective believed the attacks in Saigon and other urban areas were 'diversionary efforts while the enemy prepares for his major attack in Northern I Corps.'[30] Already declaring a victory, and again reflecting the views of Westmoreland, with whom the Admiral had a long conversation over a secure telephone, Admiral Sharp stated, 'The enemy attempts have thus far produced no significant military results and have cost the enemy heavily.'[31] This interpretation imputed an operational concept to the North Vietnamese based upon the American theory of victory. It failed to acknowledge the possibility, even the probability, that the series of coordinated attacks during Tet were directed toward securing psychological and political, not military results. Neither was there any assessment of whose units were suffering the heavy losses referred to, PAVN or the Viet Cong. These were not academic questions. Their answers would have pointed directly toward the enemy's theory of victory in the Tet offensives.

General Westmoreland provided a reinforcement to the Sharp telegram in his answers to a series of questions from the President. The General emphasized the better than ten-to-one exchange ratio which typified the first two days of the urban offensives. He considered the urban attacks to have constituted the second of a three-stage enemy offensive strategy which would culminate in 'massive attacks in Quang Tri and Quang Nam provinces.'[32] The incorrectness of this under-standing equalled that embodied in his linkage of the urban offensives and the North Korean seizure of the electronic intelligence collection ship, *Pueblo*.[33] Finally, the General considered that the urban offensive had turned the initiative in favor of the South Vietnamese government and its allies. General Westmoreland could often invoke the idea that the North Vietnamese were seeking a political victory through a military spectacular, but when presented with just that species of event, he could see it only in the narrowest military terms.

Not surprisingly, the CIA Station in Saigon provided an instant assessment that was quite different from the MACV view. After showing a high degree of honesty by bluntly admitting that there had been no intelligence catch which would have allowed warning of the urban attacks of Tet, the Chief of Station proceeded to consider a series of questions concerning the effects of the offensives.[34] The immediate evaluation of the effects of the urban offensives was candid.

> Regardless of what happens tonight or during the next few days,
> the degree of success already achieved in Saigon and around the

country will adversely affect the image of GVN (and its powerful American allies as well) in the eyes of the people.[35]

The Station predicted that the politically articulate portion of the South Vietnamese population would be polarized between those who would now demand a tough and efficient military government and those who could not accept such a government and who would call for negotiations instead. Clearly, the Agency analysts in South Vietnam correctly understood the non-military goals of the urban offensives. There must have been some satisfaction in the Saigon station as the preceding December the Station analysts had differed markedly from their colleagues in Langley over the question of the forthcoming winter–spring offensive. In Saigon, the Station personnel concluded that the offensive would in all likelihood determine the future direction of the war, while the Headquarters' analysts had argued that any offensive would be indecisive.[36] The Station staff was right, even though the reasoning was wrong in detail.

The political and psychological effects of the Tet urban offensives were demonstrated within a series of Agency situation reports which came to the White House at roughly twelve-hour intervals.[37] While the military situation was recovering rapidly and American, ARVN and other allied forces were successfully recovering urban centers lost in the opening hours of the Tet period, Hanoi, the Soviets and the French were all taking the public position that the offensives demonstrated that the US could not accomplish its objectives by military force and that the war was in a stalemate. The continued existence of a military stalemate in the city of Hue would seem to underscore this theme in the days and weeks to come.

Within the South Vietnamese population itself, the effects of the Tet urban offensives were all that the North Vietnamese might have hoped for and certainly were not what the NLF/VC would have liked to see. In so far as the NLF/VC had still been independent actors at the start of the Tet offensives, it is quite likely that their leadership had hoped that the attacks would have stimulated the long-desired general uprising.[38] There had been no indication that any significant portion of the population had joined with the Viet Cong attackers. The North would have hoped that the population would have been demoralized to a significant extent and would have lost faith in the new Southern government, ARVN and the Americans. There was evidence that this had occurred. The CIA reported on 1 February that significant blocks of the Southern population had been 'dismayed and intimidated by Communist strength.'[39] This was reinforced by several of Ambassador Bunker's messages of 1 and 2 February.[40] For Hanoi, war-weariness and loss of political will in the South was sufficient. The North Vietnamese

Politburo would have seen no need for, nor would it have desired, the general uprising so dear to the NLF/VC. Indeed, it could be argued that any phenomena which served to strengthen the Viet Cong redounded against Hanoi in pursuit of its goal of a unified Vietnam under Northern domination.

The first American attempt to synthesize an appreciation of the enemy strategy and goal came from the US Embassy in Saigon on 7 February 1968.[41] Ambassador Bunker saw the fundamental question as being the nature of the Tet urban offensives. Was the campaign an act of Viet Cong desperation or an exhibition of strength meant to offset the appearance of progress presented by US and ARVN military operations? A subsidiary question involved the relationship between the PAVN offensives in I Corps and the Viet Cong urban offensive. The second question could not yet be answered. Without answering that question and without establishing the actual nature of the relationship between North Vietnam and the NLF/VC, it was impossible to answer the primary question with any pretense of accuracy. The Ambassador hazarded no conclusions regarding the relationship of Hanoi and the NLF/VC and so beggared the very question which he had considered central. He finally concluded that the objective of the urban offensive was to show the strength of the Viet Cong in an American election year. He then characterized the Viet Cong attempt as having been successful as

> this offensive revealed more clearly than ever before the nature and extent of Viet Cong organization, discipline and power. It confirmed what has been said many times, that the solution of the Vietnam problem must be political, not simply military.[42]

In the eyes of the Ambassador, the largest American failure demonstrated by the urban offensive was that of not insisting the South Vietnamese make genuine efforts to thwart the type of infiltration that made the offensive possible. A subsidiary American mistake was overconfidence, believing that the Viet Cong would not run the risks and accept the casualties that were a necessary concomitant of coming into the open sights of American firepower.

Ignored in the Embassy's analysis, which correctly fixed on the political ramifications of the urban offensives, was the possibility that Hanoi had urged the Viet Cong to undertake the risky campaign. The role of the North, again as correctly seen by the Embassy, was to preoccupy the US with the PAVN offensive in I Corps at Khe Sanh. Had the Embassy taken the analysis one step further, they could have determined that the goal of the North under this interpretation would have been the use of the Viet Cong to enervate the political will and integrity of the United States and South Vietnam while employing

220

American firepower to eliminate the Viet Cong as a viable fighting force and political rival to Hanoi in the post-war period.

The National Security Council met on 7 February 1968 to consider what was already being called the 'Tet Offensive.'[43] General Wheeler drew three conclusions concerning the urban offensives. They had caused fear and confusion in South Vietnam. Because the North Vietnamese and Viet Cong 'have no regard for life and property,' and because the attacks had violated the Tet holiday, the offensives 'have aroused anger among the South Vietnamese people.' Finally, the offensives had caused 'some loss of confidence' in the Saigon government and the United States.[44] The good news was the body count. According to General Wheeler the enemy had suffered some twenty-five thousand fatalities of which six thousand were PAVN personnel and the balance 'a mixed variety of South Vietnamese enemy.'[45] Turning to the besieged outpost of Khe Sanh, General Wheeler stated:

> Mr. President, this is not a situation to take lightly. This is of great military concern to us. I do think Khe Sanh is an important position which can and should be defended. It is important to us tactically and it is very important to us psychologically. But the fighting will be very heavy and the losses may be high.[46]

The President was concerned about the PAVN campaign in the Khe Sanh area. The situation had taken an alarming turn for the worse when elements of the 66th PAVN Regiment supported by light armor overran the Special Forces Camp at Lang Vei.[47] The US might have to send more troops to South Vietnam. Between the Tet Offensive and the North Korean seizure of the *Pueblo*, the Administration was feeling real pressure. As a preliminary to relieving the pressure on both issues, the President authorized the Secretary of Defense and the JCS to undertake 'whatever emergency actions that will be necessary.'[48] There was no evaluation of enemy goals, strategies or effectiveness.

Confusion was introduced on a central and critical topic, enemy intentions. General Westmoreland took the position that the combined I Corps and urban offensives signalled a change in enemy strategy from protracted conflict to 'one of quick military/political victory during the American election year.'[49] In making this assessment, General Westmoreland was departing completely and radically from the position held by the Embassy and the CIA and from his own previous analyses of enemy intentions. No longer was the war one of protracted conflict fought with limited means. To the General the war had suddenly become 'a new ball game, where we face a determined, highly disciplined enemy fully mobilized to achieve a quick victory.'[50] This being the case, General Westmoreland concluded, the United States must send additional combat units without delay. More American troops would inflict more casualties upon the enemy. The General did not see 'how the enemy can long sustain the heavy losses which his new strategy is allowing us to inflict upon him.'[51] General Westmoreland, having concluded that the enemy had embarked upon a 'go for broke' operational concept, decided that the US should do the same.

General Westmoreland supported his contention with a long consideration of enemy losses during the present interlocking offensives.[52] He also buttressed his case with a complete revision of the enemy order of battle showing that the Viet Cong actually had more main force personnel than previously indicated but fewer overall forces.[53] His implication was clear. The initial success of the Viet Cong was due to their greater strength in main forces but the effort could not be maintained because of the shallowness of the overall personnel base. The General also informed the Administration that ARVN was weaker than had been originally reported and that the Marines in I Corps were overstretched and could be placed in serious difficulty if PAVN undertook an inclusive offensive along the forty-mile front from Khe Sanh to the coast.[54]

Only a few months, even weeks earlier, the music from COMUSMACV had been of reassurance and victory. The enemy was being weakened by the successful American strategy of attrition. There was no chance that the enemy would attempt to do more than hang on waging protracted conflict in the hopes of American loss of political will. Now, the trumpet of alarm had the first chair. Unless more troops were sent at once, the US would not be able to secure the cities and guard against military defeat in I Corps. Perhaps the bugle of opportunity was being blown. Without more troops the US would not be able to fully exploit the great opportunity for military victory that the misguided enemy strategy had provided to it. Westmoreland's changing estimates and interpretive strains were introducing significant confusion into the Administration's attempt to get ahead of events on the ground in South Vietnam.

In essence, General Westmoreland had called for a continuation of the American strategy of attrition with the addition of more men. His thinking paralleled that of the Army Chief of Staff, General Harold K. Johnson. The Army Chief had written a memorandum to the President on 1 February 1968 evaluating the validity of American strategic and operational concepts.[55] Not surprisingly, he had concluded that there were no flaws in the American theory of victory. The use of large and small search and destroy operations was leading to an erosion of Viet Cong and PAVN strength and the erection of barriers between the enemy personnel and the civilian population. He saw no reason to change as a result of the unfolding Tet urban offensives. Indeed he saw the urban attacks as a sign that the American theory of victory had been working.[56]

Maxwell Taylor must have been experiencing some doubts about the success of the American theory of victory when he wrote the President on 10 February 1968.[57] While he endorsed General Westmoreland's request for additional reinforcements, the endorsement was not unqualified, nor was it enthusiastic. He urged that the bombing campaign against the North be continued 'at maximum levels of effectiveness.'[58] When considering the deployment of an additional fifteen maneuver battalions, he was concerned that once ashore they would stay long past the end of the current emergency and this would be an undesirable state. Instead of an unconditional escalatory commitment, Taylor recommended that reinforcements be sent, but that the Administration 'concurrently review and clarify our military and political objectives for the remainder of the year.'[59]

General Wheeler saw no need to review and clarify goals and means of achieving them as he developed three alternatives for deploying additional forces to South Vietnam.[60] Wheeler noted that nearly all Viet Cong main and local forces had been committed 'down to platoon level' with the exception of some six or eight battalions in the Saigon region. In comparison, only 20–25 per cent of PAVN's units had been committed so far.[61] General Wheeler did not inquire into the all-too-evident implications of these numbers. Instead, he, like General Westmoreland, simply stated that it was unclear when or if the enemy would be able to resume the second phase of his offensive operations, scheduled to commence around the middle of the month, but, in any event, there were insufficient US forces in South Vietnam either to defend effectively or to allow full exploitation of opportunities which had been presented. Real shortages in the number of combat-effective units within the United States and the need to have troops on hand to deal with 'widespread civil disorders,' rather than any fundamental disagreement with Generals Westmoreland and Johnson, compelled JCS Chairman Wheeler to recommend that any decision on actual deployment of additional forces to South Vietnam be deferred while legislation to allow for a wider call-up of reserves and other measures be sought from Congress.[62]

In a White House meeting on 12 February 1968, discussion centered on reinforcements and upon the desirability for a change in American strategy. General Westmoreland had expressed an urgent desire for additional troops, at the least a Brigade of the 82nd Airborne Division and a Marine Regiment in order to capitalize upon opportunities, but he did not fear 'defeat' without the requested units.[63] Because COMUSMACV did not state that the US might experience real military defeat without the additional troops, they would not be sent immediately. There was a perceived need for additional examination of the course of the war and the possible need for a change in the

American theory of victory.[64] One person who saw this need was Maxwell Taylor. He had become convinced that the utility of Khe Sanh was minimal and the costs of defending and relieving it were maximal. He urged that the position be abandoned, despite General Westmoreland's strongly held opinion to the contrary.[65]

General Wheeler, with his obvious and long-standing desire for a mobilization of the Reserve forces, might have played into the mood of re-examination. Given the JCS recommendation that the decision on additional deployments be deferred pending legislation on the Reserve call-up and active duty extension, there is a strong possibility that General Wheeler made no strong pitch on behalf of Westmoreland's request.

While the temporizing, reassessing and general dithering continued in Washington, so did the fighting in South Vietnam. Khe Sanh was the center of Presidential attention as indicated by the daily written briefing he received from General Wheeler on the status of the besieged firebase.[66] Also of concern to the President and the Administration alike was the possibility of a second-phase urban offensive. There were indications by mid-February that the enemy might have the capacity and the will to carry one off.[67]

Shock had bred temporizing. As the ripples and waves of the urban offensives and siege at Khe Sanh spread through American society, and as the doubts and uncertainties spread through the Administration, the first reaction had been to temporize. By late February, it was becoming obvious that the Administration could get ahead of public and Congressional opinion and move beyond the uncertainties within only by a reassessment of the means by which policy had been implemented in Vietnam. To answer critics and quell skeptics, it would be necessary to determine what the events of Tet had meant and what the United States should and could do in their aftermath.

The process of assessment began with a lengthy report from Earle Wheeler late in February. The Chairman of the Joint Chiefs had spent three days on the ground in South Vietnam. The impressions which he and his party gathered during their visit were summarized for the Administration along with recommendations regarding the MACV force requirements.[68] General Wheeler painted a dismal picture in his summary. The enemy had failed in the objective of stimulating a general uprising and causing the collapse of the South Vietnamese government and had taken heavy losses. However, the Viet Cong and PAVN were 'operating with relative freedom in the countryside, probably recruiting heavily and infiltrating NVA units and personnel.'[69] The enemy quite plainly had the will and ability to continue operations.

Wheeler stated that the South Vietnamese government had been badly shaken and greatly reduced in its efficiency of operation. He commented that ARVN was now on a defensive posture and would take as long as six months to make good its losses. It was obvious that the revolutionary development programs had been set back severely. South Vietnamese civilian confidence was reported as having been badly shaken, particularly in the cities. On the bright side, General Wheeler reported that American forces had lost none of their pre-Tet capacity. He underscored the importance of US forces by noting that the enemy attack had nearly succeeded in a dozen places only to be thwarted by the timely and effective reaction of American troops.

MACV was faced by several interlocking problems in Wheeler's estimation. The PAVN threat in I Corps had forced General Westmoreland to deploy a full 50 per cent of all American maneuver battalions to the region which meant there were inadequate reserves in the rest of the country. The reversion of ARVN to a passive defensive posture was allowing the Viet Cong to make advances throughout the countryside. As a consequence of American commitment to I Corps and ARVN's lack of combat capacity, the enemy had the initiative. Wheeler was finally admitting what should have been obvious for over a year. If the enemy employed mounted synchronized attacks in I Corps, the central highlands and around Saigon, MACV would be 'hard pressed to meet adequately all threats.'[70] Recognizing this reality, General Westmoreland was reviving his request of a year earlier, a three division and fifteen tactical fighter squadron increase in his authorized forces. This augmentation would provide MACV with a general reserve and an offensive capacity which was lacking.

It was estimated that 22,000 PAVN and 45,000 Viet Cong personnel were committed to the Tet urban offensives supplemented by 17,000 or so conscripted peasants serving in support roles.[71] The majority of the estimated 40,000 enemy fatal casualties and 3,000 prisoners were Viet Cong, not PAVN, although North Vietnamese losses in I Corps were believed to be heavy. The PAVN losses would be made good quickly. While the Viet Cong might have some difficulty replacing losses, this did not matter, as the North Vietnamese forces would 'take on an increasing role in any future combat activity.'[72] Morale among the PAVN units remained good, although it had fallen off among the Viet Cong units, as the Southerners had undertaken the majority of the combat during the urban offensives and suffered the most casualties. The heavy expenditure of ammunition by both Viet Cong and PAVN units during the offensives as well as the introduction of new and heavier weapons indicated that the American interdiction efforts had not adversely affected the enemy's logistics capability.[73]

The pessimistic assessments of the CIA concerning the effectiveness of the air war had been proven correct. The optimistic reports of Embassy and MACV had been demonstrated to have been wrong.

Despite all the apparently favorable indicators so eagerly reported and avidly read during 1966 and 1967, and despite all the search and destroy operations and all the interdiction programs, PAVN and the Viet Cong had not lacked the materiel, manpower or morale necessary to have mounted the Tet offensives. There was no indication that the heavy losses taken by the Viet Cong during the offensives had changed the situation in any respect, except that the North Vietnamese role in the South had been strengthened and its potential for ultimate success reinforced.

The enemy was believed to have both the capacity and desire for future offensives. The intelligence assessment provided by Wheeler's report was both convoluted and complicated in its appreciation of the enemy's future strategy. In pursuit of the intricate, Wheeler's intelligence staff did not see the simple. Hanoi was going to pursue the same theory of victory which had served so well over the previous year, use Viet Cong blood to enervate American and South Vietnamese political will to continue the war. This would eliminate all three rivals to Northern domination. A tidy solution to a complex problem which required only time and a cynical capacity to exploit the Southern guerrillas. Hanoi possessed both in abundance.

To Generals Wheeler and Westmoreland, the strategy on both sides remained one of attrition.[74] If the new enemy threats were to be countered, the US forces would need an increased capacity to inflict attrition. MACV requested 206,756 men above the present ceiling of 525,000 for a total force strength of 731,756.[75] The report was silent on two important points. The JCS had previously stated that an augmentation of this magnitude would require mobilization of the Reserves. Considering the capacities, resources and external support available to North Vietnam, there was no reason to believe that the enemy would not retain escalation dominance.

A factor considered numerically and financially but not strategically was that of refugees. The Tet offensives had produced, or, in Wheeler's term, 'generated,' 471,455 refugees, a third of which were from the Saigon area.[76] These were over and above the 793,944 refugees already in temporary camps on 1 January 1968.[77] To the JCS Chairman, as to most American officials including the President, the refugees represented simply another management task.[78] To Hanoi, they represented an additional and important component in the disintegration of the South Vietnamese society and polity. Over two and a half million people had become refugees over the past several years, some more than once. The cumulative effect was the loosening of social, political and economic ties, the loss of coherence within South Vietnam. Chaos and political will are mutually exclusive. By failing to understand the true strategic significance of the refugee population and by failing to realize how ground and air operations of the American military contributed to the 'generation' of refugees, the United States was assisting Hanoi's theory of victory. Overall, the Wheeler report demonstrated a complete absence of comprehension regarding either the nature of Hanoi's doctrine or the inapposite nature of American doctrine.

Hanoi did not simply have the initiative on the ground in South Vietnam. As the CIA reported in late February, the North had the political initiative as well.[79] If the South Vietnamese government fell into disarray, Hanoi could seek negotiations under very favorable conditions. If the US and South Vietnam were able to regain their poise in the wake of the Tet offensives, Hanoi could retrench militarily and seek negotiations as part of an overall protracted conflict strategy. The overall weakening of the South Vietnamese government which had occurred as a consequence of the Tet offensives reinforced the initiative of Hanoi. The same might be said of American public and Congressional opinion. Regardless of the details of battlefield victories and defeats, the Tet offensives had powerfully underwritten and advanced Hanoi in the search for control of the course and tempo of both political and military activities in the Vietnam war. It would be difficult or impossible for the US and South Vietnam to regain even a measure of authority.

Secretaries Rusk and McNamara, Secretary of Defense Designate Clark Clifford with Rostow, Katzenbach, William Bundy and Joseph Califano met on 27 February 1968 to consider Wheeler's report and Westmoreland's request for additional forces. There was deep division and deep pessimism demonstrated at the meeting.[80] Walt W. Rostow and Dean Rusk were the most optimistic and determined to stay the course. McNamara, reflecting the pervasive loss of faith which had propelled his memorandum of 1 November 1967 and had caused the President to seek his resignation, cautioned, 'We are dropping ordnance at a higher rate than the last year of WW II in Europe. It has not stopped him.'[81] Under Secretary Katzenbach reported on his conversation with Phil Habib who was returning from Saigon. There was serious disagreement within American circles in Saigon over the Westmoreland request. Katzenbach was also quoted as mentioning the simple fact that world and domestic opinion alike believed that the US had suffered a serious setback with the Tet offensives. He went on to identify the core of the problem confronting the Administration:

> The problem is, how do we gain support for a major program, defense and economic, if we have told people things are going well? How do we avoid creating feeling that we are pouring troops down a rathole? What is our purpose? What is achievable? Before any decision is made, we must re-evaluate our entire posture in SVN.[82]

McNamara quickly agreed. He had profound doubts about the military, economic, political, diplomatic and moral consequences of another escalation. 'Q is whether these profound doubts will be presented to the President.'[83] That would be up to his successor.

Robert McNamara's successor as Secretary of Defense, Clark Clifford, had been a consistent and robust supporter of American policy and its means of implementation during the preceding months. It had been Clifford's resolute rejection of the McNamara memorandum of 1 November 1967 which led to his designation as Secretary of Defense.[84] President Johnson saw Clifford as a loyal supporter of Administration policy and efforts in South Vietnam, an appropriate replacement for the architect who had lost faith in his own vision and creation. The outgoing Secretary might well have wondered if Clifford would have the intellectual and moral courage to reverse his opinions.

Clifford was sworn in as Secretary of Defense on the morning of 1 March. That afternoon he started work with his task force which included experienced men such as Nicholas Katzenbach, William Bundy and Maxwell Taylor. The President had given Clifford's committee a narrow brief, determining the means by which the request for additional men and material might be met.[85] Initially there was no discussion of whether the request should be met, only of how it might be accommodated. The very process of determining the 'how' led inexorably to the larger question: why and to what avail?

Maxwell Taylor set forth the policy parameters and alternative force structures.[86] The goal he adopted as the predicate for his presentation of alternatives was of a minimalist nature. He used the statement of President Johnson in the Johns Hopkins University Speech of April 1965, 'Our objective is the independence of South Vietnam and its freedom from attack.'[87] Taylor recognized that several different definitions of victory might be employed ranging from the unconditional surrender of North Vietnam to a unilateral American declaration of victory as a prelude to a total pullout. He argued that there should be no change in goal without the most compelling of reasons but that the United States could define victory in any one of several ways. Depending upon the definition of victory employed, the theory of victory and force structure needed to implement it might be selected. Taylor believed that there was no reason to redefine victory to replace the definition which he believed to be in force at the time, Hanoi's acceptance of the San Antonio formula. The so-called San Antonio formula was American declaratory policy announced by President Johnson in a speech in San Antonio, Texas on 29 September 1967. In essence it was a promise by the United States to stop the bombing of North Vietnam in exchange for an undertaking by the North to enter into negotiations and to refrain from infiltrating men or supplies into

South Vietnam. As a result the US had a limited number of options. One was granting all or part of the augmentation requested by General Westmoreland. The second was the converse, not granting any of the requested reinforcements. The third was not granting any reinforcements but giving new strategic guidance which would allow for the relinquishment of rural areas in I Corps and the central highlands. On the air war, Taylor was firm. There must be no reduction in the air effort directed at the North without Hanoi's acceptance of the San Antonio formula.

William Bundy saw matters in a larger context. He almost reinvoked the credibility of the United States as an international guarantor, the expansive purpose previously used by McNaughton as the American goal in South Vietnam, but backed off. He asserted that the United States had two goals in South Vietnam. The first was to avert a 'forcible takeover' by Hanoi and the second was the maintenance of a non-Communist Southeast Asia.[88]

In a related memorandum, Under Secretary Katzenbach assessed the state of American public opinion.[89] He concluded that there was little support for an American withdrawal and equally little for an increase in troop strength on the ground in South Vietnam without an expansion of the air war against North Vietnam. He predicted that without indication of genuine progress within a few months, public opinion would coalesce into a 'win or get out' mentality.[90] Tangible progress would assure popular support; its absence would assure that opinion would turn decisively against both the war and the Administration. American public opinion placed severe constraints upon the options available to the Administration.

Western European opinion likewise placed limits upon the options which might be selected. Of particular importance was the high probability of adverse reaction to an increase in the air war.[91] An enlargement of the US ground war would not bring about so negative a reaction, but would do nothing to dispel the prevalent mood of pessimism with which Europeans viewed the American effort in South Vietnam.[92] To the foreign policy professionals, if not to the military commanders, it was obvious that the public and governmental opinions within the western European community required consideration, lest the United States, in attempting to win a war in support of policy, destroy the policy matrix.

The staff officers of the JCS Organization weighed in on 1 March 1968 with an elaborate analysis of several alternative courses of action.[93] The summary was attention-grabbing in its pessimism. The JCS Plans and Policy Directorate found it impossible to predict whether the enemy offensive could be broken by the forces available in South Vietnam, but it was possible to predict that 'our objectives in South Vietnam and the tasks associated with them will be unobtainable' unless the enemy offensive could be broken.[94] The only way an American defeat could be prevented and victory yet achieved would be the provision of significant reinforcements to MACV. Specifically, the recommendation was the provision of the 206,500 men requested by COMUSMACV. This would provide 133 maneuver battalions, an increase of 25 over the number available on 1 March 1968.[95] In addition, restrictions on operations into Laos, Cambodia and North Vietnam should be relaxed so as to allow effective air and ground actions against PAVN and Viet Cong sanctuaries and supplies throughout the region. If that option was too hot to be acceptable, the JCS Staff recommended, as its second choice, the provision of the additional troops without the changes in the rules of engagement.[96] Either option would require mobilization of at least 160,000 Reserve personnel and partial industrial mobilization.[97] A third option provided only 10,000 troops over the 525,000 already authorized. This alternative might not even stave off defeat, as the North was conceded to have escalation dominance.[98] The fourth and fifth options provided for augmentation levels between the minimum supplied by the third option and 206,500 under the first. The fourth option was portrayed as providing a minimal capacity to prevent an American defeat by adopting an enclave strategy.[99] The fifth option which provided an augmentation of 100,000 men was seen as the minimum necessary for military stalemate.[100] The JCS wanted one of the first two options, regardless of foreign or domestic implications.

An alternative to the escalatory recommendations of the JCS Staff came from the OSD on 1 March. The heart of this proposal was a change in the political guidance given to General Westmoreland.

> MACV should be provided with a political directive stating that his mission is to provide security to populated areas and to deny the enemy access to the major population centers. The directive should indicate that MACV should not sacrifice population security or incur heavy casualties in an attempt to attrit the enemy or to drive him completely out of the country.[101]

Search and destroy would be replaced by an enclave strategy. It would be an American style of protracted conflict, denying the North any sort of conclusive victory while limiting American casualties. It was a viable alternative to the JCS full mobilization concept.

In the same document consideration was given to the problem of negotiations. The difficulty seen was that of North Vietnam suddenly accepting the San Antonio formula while the Government and armed forces of South Vietnam were in disarray or after a spectacular North Vietnamese military success. As Hanoi had the political initiative, this possibility was real and alarming. A second difficulty foreseen was that of 'managing' the South Vietnamese government during negotiations. It was feared that some South Vietnamese officials would panic and others attempt to sabotage the negotiating process. However, the draft presidential memorandum noted, 'Since the overthrow of Diem, it has been possible to find Vietnamese of about equal ability willing to go along with virtually any policy firmly supported by the US.'[102]

The CIA in an assessment published on 1 March 1968 concluded that Hanoi would be able to adjust its tactics and operational concepts to any increase in US combat forces.[103] The resources, manpower and external support would not be reduced by the American troop increase. At the same time, an American escalation would result in a worsening international climate for the United States.[104] The Agency also concluded that the 'Communist position is much enhanced, for the time being at least, by their possession of the strategic initiative.'[105] The combination of initiative, internal resources and external support from both the USSR and PRC immunized the North against any American escalation of air or ground combat operations and forces. Taking the Agency's conclusions in conjunction with the difficulties connected with building and maintaining a domestic political consensus in favor of an escalation, there was little immediate willingness on the part of Clifford and his colleagues to accept the JCS recommendations.[106]

On 4 March the Clifford Committee presented its first recommendations to the President. They were of the temporizing sort as the Committee had not yet come to a conclusion on the Westmoreland request and JCS Staff recommendation. For the moment, MACV would receive a small increment of reinforcements up to the previously authorized ceiling. As a precautionary move, the reconstitution of the Strategic Reserve was recommended. Other matters would have to await further evaluation.[107] General Wheeler had a 'most interesting and informative conversation' with Clifford on 8 March in which the Secretary made quite clear the effects which the Tet offensives had engendered in American public opinion.[108] The guidance given General Westmoreland was to downplay predictions of victory, forecasts of enemy plans and the toughness of the fighting.[109]

Slightly over a year later, Clifford recalled his sense of frustration with the military which had grown rapidly during the review period.[110] The Joint Chiefs were unable to estimate how long it would take for the United States to bring the war to a successful conclusion on a military basis. Exasperated, Clifford quoted himself as saying, 'The fact is that we do not have a plan for military victory.'[111] More correctly, the American military high command had no new theory of victory and could not admit that the old one had failed. As a result the JCS would only assure Secretary Clifford that if the United States continued to pour men, munitions and materiel into the war, at some unknown and unpredictable future date, attrition would force the enemy to sue for some sort of peace.

By mid-March, the debate over alternatives was on within the Clifford task force and the Secretary was conveying his doubts to the President. The CIA presented an assessment of several operational alternatives encompassing two levels of force structure augmentation and an expanded bombing campaign directed at the North including mining of Haiphong harbor.[112] The Agency concluded that only mining of Haiphong had any possibility of directly affecting the situation in the South. An escalation in the air war was quite unlikely to have any positive effect. The same was true of any ground force augmentation. The Agency also presented a pessimistic assessment of the pacification and revolutionary development efforts, concluding that the Tet urban offensives had negated much of the progress made since 1965.[113]

The Agency's assessment might have reinforced the conclusions which were emerging in Secretary Clifford's mind. Increasingly, he was becoming convinced that the United States was on 'the wrong road' and that the time had come to get off that one and on to another.[119] On 18 March 1968, the second version of the Draft Presidential Memorandum on Vietnam was floated.[115] A full analysis of different force structures and bombing campaign designs was conducted in order to determine which of two alternative American goals was more achievable and which of several operational concepts was most relevant to securing the more achievable goal. The recommendations were: hold US force levels to the 525,000 already authorized, emphasize population security, work on improving ARVN, concentrate bombing on the southern portions of North Vietnam and seek early negotiations after consultations with the government of South Vietnam. The recommendations constituted a major shift in the American theory of victory, rejecting a continuation of the search for victory through attrition and erosion and substituting an American version of protracted conflict in which enervation of political will was the way to success.

There was full recognition finally of the nature of Hanoi's theory of victory, but not of the relationship between North Vietnam and the expendable Viet Cong.[116] The population security orientation coupled with an emphasis upon improving ARVN would present the North with a clear demonstration of American political will. It would also lower US casualties, reduce domestic expectations for a quick victory and place pressures upon the Northern political will by removing the bomber as a reinforcement of cohesion. Not only was the American theory of victory altered, so also was the goal. It was now stated as 'a settlement we would consider honorable.'[117] It was still too early to say that the North was winning, but it was not too soon to say that Hanoi could not now lose.

The outlines of the Clifford strategy would percolate through meetings on 19 and 22 March 1968.[118] The Clifford recommendations were not accepted immediately nor completely, but they formed the basis for a third 'rolling consensus' within the Administration.

The final support for the emerging consensus came from the 'wise men,' the senior foreign policy advisors who had as recently as November 1967 resolutely supported both policy and its means of implementation in South Vietnam. Brought together in the last week of March 1968, the group was briefed on the situation and prospects by the CIA's expert on Vietnam, George Carver, Philip Habib and William Bundy from the State Department and General Depuy from the Pentagon.[119] Cyrus Vance recalled that the briefing was not unduly pessimistic, but seemed to be 'an accurate evaluation of the same kind that I'd heard before.'[120] Vance believed that most of the men who met with the President on the night of 25 March had already made a decision on the course of action to pursue in Vietnam so that the briefings had nothing to do with the final advice given to the President.[121]

The advice was for disengagement. Ball recalled that the theme of the majority was, 'you've got to lower your sights. We can't achieve these objectives.'[122] As had been the case before, Dean Acheson spoke for the majority. McGeorge Bundy reported that Acheson had 'summed up the majority feeling when he said that we can no longer do the job we went out to do in the time we have left and we must begin to take steps to disengage.'[123] This position was shared by George Ball, Arthur Dean, Cyrus Vance, Douglas Dillon, Henry Cabot Lodge, Omar Bradley and McGeorge Bundy. Ball thought that the President 'was greatly shaken' by the consensus and particularly by Acheson's participation.[124]

George Ball, the longtime opponent of bombing, now saw his position become the majority view. A more cold comfort is difficult to imagine. Ball urged that the air war against North Vietnam be stopped at once. Omar Bradley agreed. 'We do need to stop the bombing, if we can get the suggestion to come from the Pope or [United Nations General Secretary] U Thant, but let's not show them that we are weakening.'[125] Cyrus Vance echoed the call to end ROLLING THUNDER. Henry Cabot Lodge urged shifting from search and destroy to a tactic which used the American military as a shield for South Vietnamese nation building. Douglas Dillon concurred. Taken as a whole, the position of the majority of senior foreign policy advisors was virtually identical to the Clifford proposal embodied in the 18 March Draft Presidential Memorandum. Maxwell Taylor dissented. 'I am dismayed. Let's not concede the home front; let's do something about it.'[126] He was joined by Robert Murphy. 'This is a give-away policy.'[127]

The distinguished professional diplomat was wrong. The changes in the American theory of victory recommended by the Clifford Committee and subscribed to by the majority of the 'wise men' were a realistic, even creative response to the realities which had developed on the ground. The lonely prophet, George Ball, had been right all along, now the Administration had caught up with him. It was a painful process. There was no one for whom it was more painful than the President. For him and him alone among the Administration some sympathy was and is due.

The pain of the President was obvious in the speech to the nation which he delivered on the last day of March 1968. Stripped to its essentials, the speech was one of disengagement and disenchantment alike. The disengagement was evident in the new American policy which would limit the air war and future troop deployments. The disenchantment was apparent in the President's announcement that he would not seek another term. Lyndon Johnson was not a man who would seek disengagement nor accept disenchantment easily. Neither was he a man who acknowledged defeat readily. Both had been forced upon him. It was not that the President had ill served the nation and its interests in Asia with his withdrawal from reelection an acknowledgement of that. Rather, it was that the President had been ill served in his pursuit of the nation's interests by military commanders and civilian advisors alike. The American war in Vietnam had been irrelevant to the Vietnamese wars. The intellectual failures that had created this situation were not apparent, but the result was unmistakable following Tet. The 31 March speech was a only a punctuation mark of this realization and its companion, frustration. Let a new man take over the watch.

OUTBRIEF

By April Fools' Day 1968 American policy in Vietnam had not yet failed, but it was in the process of doing so. Incontrovertibly, the means of implementing that policy had failed. These are hard words. Yet there was no intellectually honest way of assessing the situation which existed after the Tet urban offensives that did not use these hard terms. There was no way of softening the reality which had been recognized by Clark Clifford, the Clifford Committee and, finally, the 'wise men.' Walt Whitman Rostow tried to buck up Presidential resistance to the disengagement recommendation by alleging that the briefing officers had provided an unduly negative treatment of the offensives and the enemy's capabilities; that they had not properly emphasized the American and South Vietnamese military victories in the post-Tet counteroffensives. The President's National Security Advisor was wrong.

Many factors had conspired to bring the President, the Administration and the nation to the dark crossroads of March. The most important of those were intellectual in nature. Intellectual insolvency undercut the riches of technology, materiel and manpower dedicated by the United States to the Vietnam War over the previous three years. Exacerbating the cerebral destitution was a pervasive lack of intellectual and moral courage. If intellectual and moral courage had been as prevalent in the corridors of power and chain of command as physical courage was in the bush of the South and the sky of the North, failed concepts and theories could have been recognized as such and their consequences mitigated in a timely fashion.

The record of the period between the escalation decision of July 1965 and the post-Tet reassessment of March 1968 is one of the repeated failure of Administration and military command to see and recognize the obvious, or, having seen and recognized, to act upon that understanding. As a result the fundamental misconceptions concerning the nature and character of the war which had been made during 1964 and early 1965 were reinforced and their effects magnified.

To reiterate, the basic error had been that of seeing the emerging war in South Vietnam as being of the partisan sort. By not viewing the Viet Cong as an insurgent force, by not granting the possibility that the guerrillas constituted the armed expression of organic political disaffection, the Administration looked beyond the venue of conflict in search of an enemy. Given the pervasive influence of the bipolar world view and the misunderstanding of previous guerrilla wars such as those in Malaya and the Philippines, this expansive focus was expectable but cannot be justified. There is no doubt that the Viet Cong during 1964 and early 1965 were polluted by North Vietnamese-trained cadre or that the guerrillas received a very modest amount of materiel support from Hanoi, but as the intelligence reports of the day showed, the guerrillas were Southerners in pursuit of a Southern agenda. There is no doubt that Hanoi would have been gratified to see a neutralist regime emerge in the South, but as the intelligence showed, there was little motivation in Hanoi to take any risks or invest any resources beyond the rhetorical into the Southern struggle. The degree of Northern pollution was not great enough to justify a characterization of the Viet Cong as partisans operating under the direction and sponsorship of North Vietnam.

Rather than focusing upon the legion of seemingly intractable problems in South Vietnam which had powerfully assisted the Viet Cong through 1964, the Administration without a sound basis in fact determined that the source of the guerrillas' success was North Vietnam. This decision might not have been justifiable by the realities on the ground of South Vietnam, but it did provide an opportunity for direct American involvement in the conflict. The Administration was not in search of enemies, neither was it eager for war.

The guerrilla conflict in South Vietnam and its apparent Northern sponsorship were seen as significant challenges to the core American foreign policy of containment and to the role of the United States as a guarantor of national sovereignty threatened by Communist-directed or -inspired threat. American attempts to ward against the threat to South Vietnam through military and economic aid and advice had brought no joy. From an American perspective, the situation in South Vietnam appeared to have steadily deteriorated despite the efforts of years. The Administration concluded that were containment to be breached in South Vietnam, the consequences globally would be as potentially great as they would be unpleasant. A goal as expansive as the maintenance of containment seemed to many in the Administration to be worthy of the commitment of American military force.

The discussions within the Administration did not focus so much on what the United States should do as they did upon what the United States could do in support of the threatened containment policy. To his credit President Johnson did not immediately accept the advice of McNaughton, McNamara and McGeorge Bundy, but eventually persuaded by the continued Viet Cong battlefield successes and the belief that South Vietnam represented a major challenge to containment, the President authorized the use of air power against the North and the presumed lines of communication. From February 1965 American air operations against North Vietnam would be the prime determinate of policy implementation in the war. Air power seemed to promise so much. It was easily and precisely managed. American casualties would be low. The damage it could inflict was expected to be insupportable by North Vietnam.

The 'tit-for-tat' and graduated escalation of military pressure programs were not only massively irrelevant to the real war in South Vietnam, they were completely counterproductive in effect. Far from coercing Hanoi, the bombers issued an invitation to the North to enter the war in pursuit of its own goals. Within weeks the irrelevance of the air campaign to the course of the war in the South had been demonstrated by the Viet Cong attacks against US installations in the South which necessitated the introduction of ground combat forces. The counter-productive effects of the bombing campaign took longer to become obvious, but by late 1965 it had become evident that North Vietnamese armed forces were entering South Vietnam. ROLLING THUNDER had changed the character of the conflict from an insurgency to a partisan war.

From the Christmas bombing pause of 1965 on, one intelligence report after another demonstrated that the air war had failed in its objectives of interdiction and coercion. It was concluded in several major assessments that the American bombers had served Hanoi well by reinforcing North Vietnamese political will and allowing Hanoi to seek its own goals in the South. Despite the intelligence picture, the Administration was powerless to end the bombing. There were two reasons for this unpleasant state of affairs. The first was a lack of moral courage. The Administration and President simply could not act upon their knowledge for fear that by ending the bombing without a concession from the North, the United States would give the appearance of political irresolution. The second was fear of the political power of the Joint Chiefs of Staff. Civilian control of the military had run against a real limit. The Chiefs had independent access to Congress and press. As a result, the Administration could be attacked for placing the lives of American servicemen in South Vietnam at risk by halting the bombing of the North.

The senior military command structure had a limitless faith in the efficacy of the air war. A monolithic resistance to re-evaluating ROLLING THUNDER existed throughout the senior commanders. If the bombing had not accomplished its objectives of coercion and interdiction, it was because the United States had not bombed with sufficient intensity and duration. The JCS called continually for a removal of the restrictions placed upon bombing by the Administration. The Chiefs discounted completely the effects of the air war upon North Vietnamese political will. They discounted completely the impact of the American air war on public opinion in the United States and around the world. Indeed, the chiefs demonstrated repeatedly that they could not understand that the war in Vietnam was a war in support of policy and that as such it made no sense to destroy the policy matrix in order to win the war.

The war on the ground in South Vietnam was in large measure subordinate to the war in the air over North Vietnam. This was not so much the result of policy decisions as it was the inevitable consequence of the American military theory of victory. The ground combat forces, in particular the Army, had developed a doctrine, a theory of victory, appropriate to combatting the presumed major threat, a Warsaw Pact invasion of western Europe. The assumption that the same theory of victory with its emphasis upon finding, fixing and destroying the enemy through high-lethality firepower would work in the bush of South Vietnam was wrongheaded. It flew against the experience of earlier guerrilla wars. Worse, it capitalized on American strengths instead of exploiting enemy weaknesses. Worst of all, it assumed that it was possible for an army to kill itself to victory.

The JCS Ad Hoc Study Group had attempted to integrate the inevitable American ground combat operations with the air war. While giving priority to air power as the decisive instrument of victory was at best questionable, the Study Group's proposal had the single advantage of accepting the fact that the US ground forces would not be seeking to take, clear and hold ground and the population which lived there, but rather would be searching for the enemy so that he might be destroyed in the Clausewitzian cycle of bloody and decisive combat. The search and destroy operations which characterized the years from June 1965 through the Tet offensives would perhaps be bloody, but they would not be decisive. Search and destroy certainly did not bring about an American victory.

American forces won a number of engagements. American forces killed a large number of people. American forces did not win on the ground in the months between July 1965 and January 1968. Without a definition of victory which allowed for an accurate measurement of progress and with a theory of victory which did not accentuate the holding of ground or the provision of palpable security for the population, the United States was reduced to statistical measurements of success. The happy numbers told a tale which was pleasing to the Administration's ears, but did not properly reflect either the changes in the character of the war or the actual effect of American ground operations.

By late 1966 the North Vietnamese had changed their relationship to the Southern guerrillas. After acting as an external sponsoring power for some twelve to eighteen months, North Vietnam was in pursuit of its own goals by fall 1966. This meant that the Viet Cong had become completely expendable. The North Vietnamese theory of victory sought success through the enervation of the American and South Vietnamese political will. To the extent that the Americans killed Viet Cong, Hanoi was winning. To the extent that the war was protracted and made inconclusive, Hanoi was winning. The combination of PAVN divisions acting as forces in being throughout northern I Corps and the central highlands with Viet Cong guerrillas operating elsewhere in the country assured that Viet Cong casualties would mount as would those of the United States. As intelligence reports demonstrated from November 1966 and General Westmoreland acknowledged early in 1967, the North Vietnamese had the initiative and the capacity for continued escalation dominance. It has generally been accepted that in war the belligerent which enjoys the initiative is the belligerent which is winning. In South Vietnam, it was Hanoi, not Washington or Saigon, which had the initiative from late 1966. It is only fair to conclude that North Vietnam was winning the ground war.

The American ground force's theory of victory had failed. The North Vietnamese had the initiative and, despite the air war, the capacity for escalation dominance. Because of the air war, the North Vietnamese had the political will to employ that capacity. The American ground operations had been responsible for failures in two other significant areas: pacification and the will of the South Vietnamese government and Army.

The big battalion sweeps had impaired the American-sponsored efforts in the 'other war.' Much of the peasant population had been turned into rootless refugees. The traditional structures of society, polity and economy had been destroyed or seriously disrupted by American ground combat operations. Komer had recognized these and other negative effects of the ground war in his backchannel correspondence prior to becoming Director of CORDS. He had developed a theory of victory which emphasized pacification, revolutionary development, Viet Cong infrastructure neutralization and a diminishment of large-scale combat operations. Had this approach been implemented in 1965, it might have proven effective, but by 1967 the character of the war had been changed and it was no longer relevant. The failures of the air war and ground war had made success in the 'other war' both problematic and largely irrelevant.

The obvious entry of the United States into the Vietnamese war with air and later ground forces had an effect which had been dimly foreseen by some such as Maxwell Taylor but not accepted as a possibility by the

Administration. The war became an American war and as a result influence over the policies and behaviors of the South Vietnamese government and military forces decreased. As an interventionary power, the United States was ultimately acting in support of the host government. If that government and its armed forces would not undertake measures necessary to gain legitimacy and demonstrate competence, the interventionary power could not succeed on its own. This was recognized by the Administration. What was not recognized was the unfortunate reality that the United States had lost the credible capacity to withdraw from the war and as a result had lost the capability to coerce Saigon into taking necessary but unpleasant reforms. The South Vietnamese could assume with a degree of legitimacy that the United States was fighting the war for reasons of its own and would not withdraw without having accomplished its goals. As a result Saigon and ARVN could cooperate or not at their sole discretion.

Komer and others from the Embassy had often complained of South Vietnamese foot-dragging on essential programs in the 'other war,' but they had never argued that the reason for this was the very presence of US ground combat forces. Overall, the ground and air operations within South Vietnam through their effect on the civilian population had exercised a malign effect which had been disguised by smiling numbers and facile excuses. Disrupted society and rootless refugees might or might not have directly assisted the Viet Cong. These factors did contribute to the growing international and domestic disenchantment with the American effort in South Vietnam and so played into Hanoi's theory of victory.

The genius of the North Vietnamese theory of victory, seeking enervation of the political will of the United States and South Vietnam through protracted conflict, was that it identified and exploited weaknesses inherent in the target nations. An additional astuteness was seen in the way that the Northern theory turned American strengths against the United States. American air power consolidated Northern political will. American ground forces in the South disrupted the society, killed primarily the eminently expendable Viet Cong and alienated domestic opinion. American materiel and money helped undercut the efforts to build a nation in South Vietnam.

The fuzziness of the American war goals, the absence of a realistic and relevant definition of victory toward which progress might be charted, the theories of victory employed by American commanders and decision makers, all contributed to the climate of public questioning which so concerned Administration and Embassy alike by fall 1967. The statistical thaumaturgy and reassuring message of General Westmoreland in November 1967 were intended to quiet the questions and mobilize support for another year or two of war. Instead they served as the background music for the shocks of the siege at Khe Sanh and the urban offensives of Tet.

These shocks should have come as no surprise to the Administration, MACV and the American public. If the information long in the possession of the intelligence community had been properly understood and used by the Administration and MACV, the offensives might not have been prevented, but their shock value would have been significantly mitigated. Of course, the acceptance of and acting upon this information which demonstrated the enemy's degree of initiative and capacity would have required not only the rejection of all the happy numbers and smiling reports of 1967, but a sweeping reconsideration of the American theories of victory. The Administration did not have the collective intellectual and moral courage for this.

Neither did the Joint Chiefs of Staff whose Chairman, General Earle Wheeler, was playing a malevolent and manipulative game. Wheeler, and perhaps the Chiefs as a body, had wanted to force the Administration into agreeing to something more closely approximating total war. The Chairman of the JCS and quite possibly the Chiefs as a body did not understand, or did not want to understand, the nature of a limited war in support of policy. Repeatedly, their reports showed a jejune and puerile comprehension of the global policy matrix of which the Vietnam war represented only one portion. Invariably, the Chiefs demonstrated a complete willingness to sacrifice the policy matrix and the domestic consensus in order to win a military victory in Vietnam. They were eager to redefine Pyrrhic victory.

The urban offensives of Tet made manifest the failure of the American theory of victory. Clark Clifford demonstrated both intellectual and moral courage when he reversed his earlier and strongly held convictions regarding the war. Dean Acheson and his colleagues among the 'wise men' displayed the same qualities on 25 and 26 March 1968. It was rather late in the game to see the state of play. It is a pity that education always takes so long.

It had taken years for Robert McNamara and John McNaughton to learn the limits of rationality. It had taken years for McGeorge Bundy to learn that George Ball had been right all along. Others, such as Earle Wheeler and his fellow Chiefs, Walt Whitman Rostow and Maxwell Taylor never did learn. Lyndon Johnson finally learned the truth. His instincts as demonstrated by his repeated reluctance to authorize the air war and his continued return to the 'other war' as the priority had been correct. He had been misled by the calculus of rational reward and punishment advocated by McNamara and McNaughton. He had been misdirected by the theories of victory employed by the military commanders. He had been seduced by the shared intellectual heritage. He had not read the lessons of history.

241

The ultimate tragedy of the American intervention and its failures is that there had been no need to learn on the job. The correct and incorrect lessons of counterinsurgency and interventionary warfare were all to be read in the pages of history. The Americans had written the earliest pages in their own success in the first insurgent war of national liberation, the War of Independence. The Americans had written additional pages in their success against the Filipino insurrectionists at the turn of the twentieth century. More recent chapters had been written by the British in Malaya, the Americans during the Huk Insurrection and the French in Indochina. Thucydides had written the first work of history for the instruction of generations of statesmen and generals yet unborn. What he did not realize was the futility of pursuing history for that end when the generals and statesmen lack the wit and will to read.

BIBLIOGRAPHIC NOTE

The overwhelming majority of the sources used or cited in this book are from the Lyndon Baines Johnson Presidential Library in Austin, Texas. The following collections were used:

White House Central Files (WHCF)
White House Central Files, Confidential Files (CF)
Meeting Notes Files
National Security Files (NSF)
  Agency Files
  Aides Files
  Country Files, Laos
  Country Files, Vietnam (CF/VN)
  International Meetings and Travel (IMT)
  Memos to the President
  Name Files
Files of Walt W. Rostow
Komer–Leonhart Files
Papers of McGeorge Bundy
Papers of Clark Clifford
Papers of Paul Warnke–John McNaughton Files
Papers of William C. Westmoreland
Oral History Collection
  Sam Adams
  George Ball
  William Bundy
  Clark Clifford
  Ray Cline
  William Colby
  Chester Cooper
  Richard Helms
  Roger Hilsman
  Douglas Pike

Maxwell Taylor
Cyrus Vance
Earle Wheeler

The Combat After-Action Reports used and cited are in the author's · personal collection, but many are available in various microfilm compendia. The ARCOV document and its companion, *Mechanized and Armored Combat Operations in Vietnam* (MACOV), are in the author's personal collection but are available at the Pentagon Library and the Center for Military History.

NOTES

INBRIEF

1 Larry Cable, New York, 1986.

1 THE VAST VOID

The note format for Lyndon Baines Johnson Library documents (identified with the prefix, LBJ) is collection/series/box number/folder/document.

1 LBJ/NSF/NSC Meetings1, 2/27 JULY 1965/1.
2 Ibid./2.
3 LBJ/NSF/NSC Meetings/1/27 JULY 1965/1.
4 Ibid.
5 WHCF/Meeting Notes File/1/Meetings on Vietnam/21–27 JULY 1965/p. 41.
6 Ibid., p. 43.
7 Ibid.
8 Ibid., p. 5.
9 Ibid., p. 6.
10 Ibid.
11 LBJ/Papers of Paul Warnke–John McNaughton Files/1/McNaughton Drafts 1965 (1)/60a, 60b.
12 Ibid., pp. 4 6.
13 WHCF/Meeting Notes File/1/Meetings on Vietnam, p. 8.
14 Ibid., p. 10.
15 Ibid.
16 Ibid., p. 12.
17 Ibid. In his recent political memoir, Paul Nitze significantly dilutes the strength of his position at this meeting and states that as Navy Secretary he had little to do with policy or operational matters. See Paul Nitze, *From Hiroshima to Glasnost: At the Center of Decision – A Memoir*, New York: Weidenfeld, 1989, pp. 257–60.
18 Ibid., p. 14.
19 Ibid., p. 17.
20 Ibid., p. 23.
21 Ibid., p. 37.
22 On the bipolar imperative see Douglas Blaufarb, *The Counterinsurgency Era*, New York: Free Press, 1977.

23 For a full discussion of the relationship between incorrectly understood historical experience and the decisions regarding South Vietnam through April 1965 see Larry Cable, *Conflict of Myths: The Development of US Counterinsurgency Doctrine and the Vietnam War*, New York: New York University Press, 1986.
24 See as examples of the numerous studies which reached this conclusion: Special Operations Research Office (SORO), *Case Studies in Insurgency and Revolutionary Warfare*, 2 vols, Washington, DC: American University, 1963; Andrew Molner *et al.*, *Undergrounds, Resistance and Revolutions*, Washington, DC: American University SORO, 1963; Paul Jureidini, *Case Book on Insurgency and Revolutionary Warfare*, Washington, DC: American University SORO, 1963; Otto Heilbrunn, *Partisan Warfare*, New York: Praeger, 1962; Otto Heilbrunn and C.D. Dixon, *Communist Guerrilla Warfare*, New York: Praeger, 1955; Fred Barton, *Salient Operational Aspects of Paramilitary Warfare in Three Asian Areas*, Chevy Chase, MD: Johns Hopkins University Operational Research Office, 1963; Edgar Howell, *Soviet Partisan Movement 1941–1944*, Washington, DC: Department of the Army, 1950; A.H. Peterson *et al.*, *Symposium on the Role of Airpower in Counterinsurgency and Unconventional Warfare*, Santa Monica, CA: Rand, 1963.
25 On ground doctrine see US Army Field Manual (FM) 100–5, *Field Service Regulations: Operations*, 1954, 1962; FM 31–15, *Operations Against Irregular Forces*, 1961; FM 31–16, *Counterguerrilla Operations*, 1962, 1963; FM 31–21, *Guerilla Warfare and Special Forces Operations*, 1958, 1961. On air doctrine see United States Strategic Bombing Survey, *Overall Report (European War)*, Washington, DC: USGPO, 1945; USAF, *United States Air Force Operations in the Korean Conflict*, Historical Studies numbers 70, 71, 72 and 127, Washington, DC: USGPO, 1955; Air Force Manual 1–2, 1959.
26 LBJ/NSF/Agency/30/JCS Wargames/V. 1(1) and V. 2(1, 2) (declassified June 1986).
27 LBJ/NSF/Agency/30/JCS Wargames/V. I(1)/D. 5.
28 Ibid., G 5–26.
29 LBJ/NSF/Agency/30/JCS Wargames/V. II/D. 1–26.
30 Ibid., G 3–21.
31 LBJ/NSF/National Intelligence Estimates/7/Southeast Asia/1, NIE 50–61, 'Outlook in Mainland Southeast Asia,' dated 28 March 1961, p. 14 (declassified March 1990).
32 LBJ/NSF/CF/VN/54 SEA 3/96A/p. 6 (declassified December 1986).
33 Ibid., p. 2.
34 Ibid.
35 LBJ/NSF/CF/VN/180/DIA Report/1 (declassified November 1989).
36 Ibid., A(3).
37 Ibid., D(1); D(11).
38 LBJ/NSF/CF/VN/210/1 (declassified March 1987).
39 Ibid., p. 2.
40 Ibid., A.6.
41 LBJ/NSF/CF/VN/199/3 (declassified December 1985).
42 LBJ/NSF/CF/VN/260/Taylor Report/29b.
43 LBJ/NSF/IMT/3/12–16.
44 LBJ/NSF/National Intelligence Estimates/7/Southeast Asia/2a, SNIE 50–64, 'Short Term Prospects in Southeast Asia,' dated 12 February 1964 (declassified March 1990).
45 LBJ/NSF/NSC/1/5/2;   LBJ/NSF/CF/VN/2/M4/94;   LBJ/NSF/CF/VN/2/C5/69b;

LBJ/NSF/CF/VN/2/M5/73a; LBJ/NSF/NSC/1/5/9; LBJ/NSF/CF/VN/52, 53/SEA/1/2a; LBJ/NSF/CF/VN/2/C5/57, 57a) LBJ/NSF/CF/VN/3/M7/182; LBJ/NSF/CF/VN/52, 53/SEA/M IIB/12b; LBJ/NSF/201, 202/Special Meetings/1a; LBJ/NSF/CF/VN/6/M13/55a.

46 LBJ/NSF/CF/VN/10/C21/90; VN/8/M17/103; VN/9/M18/249a; VN/10/C21/32, 46, 61, 54, 69, 70, 89, 173, 178; VN/10/M21/201a, 201b; VN/11/M23/116; VN/13/C28/20; LBJ/AF/MP/2/7/53, 53b; VN/12/M25/111b, 111c, 131, 141; VN/12/C26/24: VN/13/C27/3, C28/6, 104; NSF/NSC/1/3/3; LBJ/AF/MP/2/8/54; NSF/RP/I/168–71; VN/14/C29/37, 38, 41, 49, 97; VN/14/C30/22; VN/15/M30/134, 144; M31/181a, 188b, 194.

47 LBJ/NSF/CF/VN/15/M31/248; 16/M32/253, 254, 255; 16/M33/137, 138; 18/M35/324, 325, 325a, 383.

48 LBJ/NSF/CF/VN/49/SEA VI, Special Intelligence Materials/2a/pp. 1, 10, 11. On the increasing capabilities of the Viet Cong since the start of ROLLING THUNDER see LBJ/NSF/CF/VN/50, 51/SEA VI (b) Special Intelligence Materials/13 dated 9 June 1965.

49 Ibid., p. 11.

50 Ibid., p. 15.

51 LBJ/NSF/CF/VN/13/M27/104, p. 6 (dated 1 February 1965). See also the summary of Special National Intelligence Estimates (SNIEs) contained within LBJ/NSF/NSCH/42/Deployment of Forces/12b, in particular Part II.

52 LBJ/NSF/NSCH/42/IV/43a.

53 Ibid., section 3, p. 2.

54 LBJ/NSF/CF/VN/16/M33/16a, p. 3.

55 LBJ/NSF/NSCH/42/IV/60a.

56 Ibid., p. 2.

57 LBJ/NSF/NSCH/42/IV/59a, p. 5.

58 LBJ/NSF/CF/VN/20/M37/338a.

59 A similar position had been taken on 12 May in a memo sent by the new Director of Central Intelligence, W. F. Raborn, to the President, LBJ/NSF/CF/VN/50, 51/SEA VI (b) Special Intelligence Materials/20, 20a, 20b.

60 For the background on this as well as an extended discussion of the role of North Vietnam in the Sino–Soviet dispute see LBJ/NSF/National Intelligence Estimates/5/14.3 North Vietnam/1, SNIE 14.3–63, 'The Impact of the Sino–Soviet Dispute on North Vietnam and its Policies,' dated 26 June 1963 (declassified March 1990).

61 LBJ/NSF/NSCH/42/V/11a, p. 2.

62 LBJ/NSF/NSCH/42/V/16a, p. 6.

63 LBJ/NSF/NSCH/42/V/46a.

64 LBJ/NSF/NSCH/42/VI/77a.

65 LBJ/NSF/NSCH/42/VI/38b.

66 LBJ/NSF/NSCH/42/VI/56a, pp. 5–6.

67 LBJ/NSF/CF/VN/190, 191/NODIS-MAYFLOWER/2, 2a.

68 Ibid., p. 21.

2 PLOTTING THE QUEST

1 LBJ/NSF/CF/VN/180/DIA Report/1, p. A(3) (declassified November 1989). See also LBJ/NSF/CF/VN/210/Taylor Report (3 November 1961)/1 (declassified March 1987) and State Department drafts 'Communist Aggression in

Southeast Asia, Targets: South Vietnam and Laos' dated 22 August 1964 and 'A Dangerous Game: North Vietnam's continuing Aggression Against South Vietnam' dated 15 February 1965; LBJ/NSF/CF/VN/199/Briefing material/31, 32.

2 LBJ/NSF/CF/VN/2/M5/73a, p. 1.
3 LBJ/NSF/NSCH/42/VII/T436/36a.
4 LBJ/NSF/CF/VN/54/SEA III/89L, pp. 11–13, 29–32 (declassified June 1986).
5 LBJ/NSF/CF/VN/3/M6/61a (declassified July 1989).
6 See incoming telegrams from AMEMB Vientiane to SECSTATE and incoming telegrams from COMUSMACV to SECDEF, outgoing SECSTATE and JCS telegrams including LBJ/NSF/LAOS/268/C10/23 (declassified March 1988), 24a, 27 (declassified August 1988), 32 (declassified March 1989), 57 (declassified August 1988), 69, in which McGeorge Bundy personally approves YANKEE TEAM armed reconaissance missions 1155–1160 (declassified July 1989), 71, 72 (declassified July 1988), 74, 80, 80a (declassified July 1989).
7 LBJ/NSF/CF/V/54/SEA III/93, p. 2 (declassified June 1986).
8 LBJ/NSF/CF/VN/45, 46/Courses of Action SEA, 11-64/9, pp. 3–8. It is obvious that McNaughton is the only author of this document as may be seen from its first draft which bears only his name. See LBJ/NSF/VN/54/SEA IV/62 (declassified May 1989).
9 LBJ/NSF/CF/VN/201/SEA Meeting/1a, p. 1 (declassified March 1987).
10 LBJ/NSF/IMT/2/6/4–6; NSF/CF/VN/202/ Meetings of the Principals/5, 7a (declassified April 1987).
11 LBJ/NSF/CF/VN/201/SEA Meetings/1/1a (declassified March 1987).
12 LBJ/NSF/CF/VN/14/M30/131.
13 LBJ/Papers of Paul Warnke–John McNaughton Files/1/McNaughton Drafts, 1965 (1)/53, p. 1.
14 LBJ/NSF/CF/VN/54/SEA IV/66, p. 4 (declassified July 1986).
15 LBJ/NSF/CF/VN/10/M21/201a.
16 Ibid., p. 2.
17 LBJ/PPW, MF/1/McNaughton Drafts (1)/53, p. 2.
18 LBJ/PPW, MF/1/McNaughton Drafts (1)/54, pp. 10–12.
19 Ibid., p. 12.
20 LBJ/NSF/CF/VN/74, 75/Troop Decision/48, pp. 1, 2.
21 See as an example of McNaughton's statement of goals and implied definition of victory in significant transition, LBJ/PPW–MF/5/Drafts XIII May 1967/8. For an undiluted McNaughton view see CIA's Vietnam expert, George Carver's April 1966 draft memo on 'Option A,' a continuation of present US activities, LBJ/PPW–MF/2/Drafts II/62 (declassified February 1988).
22 LBJ/NSF/CF/VN/2/M5/73a, pp. 5–6.
23 LBJ/NSF/CF/VN/3/M7/59.
24 LBJ/NSF/CF/VN/10/M21/201a, p. 1.
25 Ibid., p. 2.
26 LBJ/NSF/CF/VN/54/SEA IV/62 (declassified May 1989).
27 LBJ/NSF/CF/VN/SEA IV/69, p. 1 (declassified July 1986).
28 Ibid., p. 3.
29 LBJ/NSF/CF/VN/54/SEA IV/85a, p. 23 (declassified June 1986).
30 Ibid., p. 37.
31 LBJ/NSF/CF/VN/10/M21/201a, p. 1.
32 LBJ/NSF/CF/VN/201 SEA Meetings (1)/1a (declassified March 1987).
33 LBJ/WHCF/Meeting notes/1/1 December 1964, pp. 8–9.
34 LBJ/PPW-MF/3/McNaughton Drafts VII/8, Annex A, p. 1.

35 Ibid., p. 2.
36 LBJ/NSF/NSC/1/T5/2, summary record of NSC meeting no. 548, 10 February 1965, p. 3 (declassified February 1988).
37 LBJ/NSF/NSC/1/T5/3 (declassified February 1988).
38 LBJ/NSF/NSC/1/6/2 (declassified February 1988). See also LBJ/NSF/NSC/1/ T6/4 (declassified February 1989) and NSC/1/T6/8 (declassified October 1987); NSC/1/T6/13 (declassified May 1987).
39 LBJ/PPW–MF/3/McNaughton Drafts VII/12 (declassified January 1989).
40 Ibid.
41 LBJ/NSF/NSC/2/T1/2, summary notes of NSC meeting no. 554, 5 August 1965, p. 2.
42 LBJ/NSF/CF/VN/Reprisal Program/44a (declassified October 1986).
43 Ibid., p. 1.
44 Ibid., p. 2.
45 Ibid., pp. 4–5.
46 LBJ/NSF/CF/VN/74/RP/43 (declassified October 1986).
47 Ibid., p. 7.
48 LBJ/NSF/CF/VN/20/M37/413a (declassified December 1985).
49 Ibid., p. i.
50 LBJ/NSF/CF/VN/16/M32/213, 213a.
51 Ibid., 213a, p. 1.
52 Karl von Clausewitz, *On War*, trans. J. J. Graham, 3 vols, London: Routledge & Kegan Paul, 1968, vol. I, bk I, ch. II, p. 26.
53 Ibid., vol. I, bk III, ch. I, p. 26.
54 FM 100–5, *Field Service Regulations–Operations*, Washington, DC: DA, 1962, pp. 4–5.
55 FM 7–10, *Rifle Company, Infantry and Airborne Battlegroups*, Washington, DC: DA, 1962, pp. 3–4.
56 Special Warfare Board (Lt. Gen. Hamilton Howze, Chair), *Final Report* (HQ USCONARC: Ft Monroe, VA, 28 January 1962), p. 140.
57 FM 31–16, *Counterguerrilla Operations*, Washington, DC: DA, 1963, p. 20.
58 Ibid., pp. 21–2.
59 Ibid., p. 31.
60 This was explicitly recognized and accepted by the Ad Hoc Study Group, Summary Report, p. V.
61 LBJ/NSF/CF/VN/20/M37/413a, p. F–4; Secretary McNamara had accepted this contention as early as May 1964. See LBJ/NSF/NSC/1/T4/2, p. 5.
62 Ibid., F–5.
63 Ibid., pp. F–6, G–28.
64 Ibid., p. F–17.
65 Ibid., pp. F–6, F–18.
66 Ibid., pp. G–25–28.
67 LBJ/NSF/CF/VN/78, 79/3 C NVN Infiltration into SVN/7 (dated 24 June 1965).
68 LBJ/NSF/CF/VN/20/M37/413a, pp. G–28, G–29.
69 Ibid., Summary Report V.
70 Ibid., Summary Report, p. III.
71 Ibid., Summary Report III, pp. I–1, I–3.
72 LBJ/NSF/NSCH/42/VII/T436/36a.
73 Ibid., pp. 1–2.
74 Ibid., p. 2.
75 Ibid., p. 2.

3 EVERYTHING IS PERFECT AND GETTING BETTER

1 *US Army Combat Operations in Vietnam (ARCOV)*, Saigon, RVN: ARCOV MACV, April 1966. The report consists of a summary and eight annexes.
2 Ibid., summary report, section IV-1; annex C, 'Firepower,' especially pp. C9–11 in which it is concluded that doctrine for use of artillery is sound and the only recommendations are for restructuring of Table of Equipment; annex B, 'Mobility,' especially pp. B16–17 in which major doctrine recommendation is that rifle platoons should be foot mobile after demounting from transport helicopters.
3 Ibid., summary report, I–8–b (5).
4 Ibid., I–7–8–2–b (1), (2), (3).
5 Ibid., pp. I–9/10.
6 Ibid., p. I–16.
7 Ibid.
8 Ibid., p. I–19.
9 Ibid., I–20/21/22.
10 Ibid., p. I–23.
11 Ibid., pp. II–2, II–4.
12 LBJ/NSF/CF/VN/25, 27/C45/74 (declassified July 1989).
13 Ibid.
14 173rd Airborne Brigade (sep.), 'Combat Operation After Action Report – Operation CRIMP,' 23 February 1966, p. 17.
15 Ibid., pp. 12, 18.
16 Ibid., p. 18.
17 Ibid.
18 Ibid., pp. 15–16.
19 Ibid., p. 16.
20 LBJ/Papers of William C. Westmoreland/7/V. 3/42, 173rd Airborne Brigade, Commander's Note Number 91, dated 22 January 1966, p. 4.
21 LBJ/Papers of William C. Westmoreland/7/V. 3/51, 173rd Airborne Brigade, critique of Operations MARAUDER and CRIMP, dated 24 January 1966, p. 12.
22 Ibid.
23 Ibid., pp. 12, 19.
24 Ibid., p. 19.
25 Ibid., p. 6.
26 3rd Brigade, 1st Infantry Division, 'Combat Operation After Action Report–Operation CRIMP,' 15 February 1966, p. 8.
27 Ibid., p. 9.
28 Ibid.
29 Ibid., pp. 2, 3, 7, 8.
30 3rd Brigade, 1st Infantry Division, 'Combat Operation After Action Report–Operation BUCKSKIN,' 3 March 1966, pp. 11–12.
31 Ibid., p. 12.
32 Ibid., p. 13.
33 Ibid., p. 4.
34 A total of ten weapons including one German Mauser, two US M–1s and six unidentified rifles were captured. Ibid., p. 11.
35 LBJ/NSF/CF/VN/26, 27/M45b/118.
36 1st Infantry Division, 'Combat Operation After Action Report–Operation MASTIFF,' 21 December 1966. This report includes the second-echelon

reports from the brigades and division artillery written in March. See pp. 15–18.

37 Ibid., p. 18.
38 3rd Brigade 1st Infantry Division, 'Combat Operation After Action Report–Operation COCA BEACH,' 3 April 1966.
39 ARCOV, *Summary Report*, Enclosure 1, pp. 20–8.
40 COCA BEACH AAR, p. 7.
41 The artillery employed in support of the operation delivered 2,334 rounds aggregating 590 tons while the Air Force provided 73 close air support sorties. COCA BEACH AAR, p. 2.
42 Ibid., p. 6.
43 LBJ/NSF/CF/VN/26, 27/M48/155.
44 LBJ/NSF/CF/VN/26, 27/M48/153.
45 1st Cavalry Division (Airmobile), 'Combat Operation After Action Report – Operation JIM BOWIE,' 8 May 1966.
46 Ibid., p. 5.
47 Ibid., pp. 14–15; 20–3.
48 Ibid., p. 18.
49 1st Infantry Division, 'Combat Operation After Action Report–Operation ABILENE,' 27 April 1966. Includes AAR from 2nd and 3rd Brigade.
50 Ibid., p. 3.
51 Ibid., pp. 3, 30.
52 Ibid., p. 3.
53 Ibid., pp. 3, 5.
54 Ibid., p. 21.
55 Ibid., p. 22.
56 Ibid., pp. 24–5.
57 Ibid., p. 26.
58 Ibid.
59 Ibid.
60 Ibid., p. 30.
61 Ibid.
62 Ibid.
63 Ibid.
64 Ibid.
65 Ibid., pp. 30–1.
66 Ibid., p. 35.
67 Ibid., p. 3.
68 Ibid.
69 LBJ/NSF/NSC Meetings/2/T2/2.
70 Ibid., p. 2.
71 Ibid.
72 Ibid.
73 Ibid., p. 3.
74 LBJ/NSF/CF/VN/15/M31/181a, memo for the President from Secretary of State Rusk dated 23 March 1965.
75 LBJ/NSF/CF/VN/15/M31/181e.
76 For the Embassy see LBJ/NSF/CF/VN/198/41 Point Program/25. For follow-up reports see as examples, LBJ/NSF/CF/VN/194/McCone's 12 Points/6, 6a; LBJ/NSF/CF/VN/198/41 Point Program/22f, 23, 23c, 30a.
77 LBJ/NSF/Memos to the President/6/McGeorge Bundy, V. 18/39a, Transcription of Saigon 2503, to the President from Lodge, 'Outlook for 1966,' dated 12 January 1966, p. 1.

78 Ibid., p. 2.
79 LBJ/Papers of Paul Warnke–John McNaughton Files/1/Drafts III/87.
80 Ibid., p. 2.
81 Ibid., p. 3.
82 Ibid.
83 Ibid., p. 5.
84 Ibid., p. 6.
85 For Bell's very perceptive assessment and advice to the President, see LBJ/NSF/NSCH/43/T5/5b.
86 LBJ/NSF/NSCH/43/T24/24a.
87 LBJ/NSF/NSCH/43/T33/33a.
88 LBJ/NSF/NSCH/43/T38/38a.
89 Quoted in the Administrative Summary, LBJ/NSF/NSCH/43/Honolulu Conference, p. 26.
90 See LBJ/NSF/NSCH/43/T39/39b for the record of conclusions and decisions for further action.
91 LBJ/NSF/NSCH/43/T41/41r.
92 LBJ/Papers of William C. Westmoreland/7/V. 4/42, memo for record, 'MACV Commanders' Conference, 20 February 1966,' dated 10 March 1966, p. 2.
93 Ibid., pp. 5–7.
94 Ibid., p. 8.
95 See for example the forty-five page report by Secretaries Gardner and Freeman LBJ/NSF/NSCH/43/T47/47a, or the Embassy reports, T48/48b, 48c and 48g; LBJ/NSF/CF/VN/27, 28/C49/63.
96 LBJ/NSF/NSCH/43/T48/48f.
97 Ibid., p. 4.
98 LBJ/Papers of McGeorge Bundy/12/Basic Political Position/6.
99 Ibid., p. 2.
100 Ibid.
101 Ibid., pp. 2–3.
102 Ibid., p. 4.
103 Ibid.
104 LBJ/PPW–JMF/1/McNaughton Drafts 1966/I, II/61., p. 1.
105 LBJ/PPW–JMF/1/McNaughton Drafts 1966/1, II/62 (declassified February 1988).
106 Ibid., p. 3.
107 LBJ/NSF/AGENCY/8, 9, 10/CIA II/22. Helms stated that the memorandum was not a 'formal coordinated paper' but that it represented a joint effort between the CIA and the Defense Intelligence Agency.
108 Ibid., p. 4.
109 Ibid., pp. 5–7.
110 Ibid., pp. 2, 8.
111 Ibid., p. 9.
112 LBJ/Papers of McGeorge Bundy/15, 16/Vietnam Intelligence/3.
113 Ibid., p. 1.
114 Ibid., pp. 5–6.
115 Ibid., p. 9.
116 Ibid., p. 6.
117 Ibid., p. 20.
118 Ibid.
119 Ibid.
120 Ibid., p. 23.

121 LBJ/NSF/CF/VN/31/52/207, 207a.
122 Ibid., p. 8.
123 Ibid., p. 11.
124 Ibid., p. 15.
125 Ibid., p. 26.
126 2nd Brigade, 25th Infantry Division, 'Combat Operation After Action Report Operation KAHALA,' 14 May 1966.
127 Ibid., p. 4.
128 Ibid., pp. 2–3, 9.
129 Ibid., p. 9.
130 Ibid., pp. 9–10.
131 Ibid., p. 13.
132 Ibid., p. 12, 14.
133 1st Infantry Division, 'Combat Operation After Action Report – Operation BIRMINGHAM', 15 June 1966.
134 Ibid., p. 3.
135 For a detailed intelligence appreciation of Viet Cong options see Ibid., p. 4.
136 Ibid., pp. 10–12.
137 Ibid., pp. 12–21.
138 Ibid., pp. 4, 6.
139 Ibid., pp. 21–3.
140 Ibid., pp. 72–3.
141 Ibid., p. 26.
142 Ibid., p. 28.
143 Ibid., p. 29.
144 Ibid., p. 30.
145 Ibid., pp. 30–1.
146 Ibid., pp. 32–3.
147 Ibid., p. 37.
148 173rd Airborne Brigade (Separate), 'Combat Operation After Action Report – Operation HOLLANDIA,' 15 September 1966.
149 Ibid., p. 2.
150 Ibid., p. 3.
151 Ibid., pp. 4 11.
152 Ibid., pp. 18, 20, 22.
153 Ibid., p. 22.
154 Ibid.
155 1st Infantry Division, 'Combat Operation After Action Report – Operation EL PASO II/III,' 8 December 1966.
156 Ibid., pp. 3–5.
157 Ibid., pp. 57–65.
158 Ibid., p. 64.
159 Ibid.
160 Ibid., p. 65.
161 Ibid., p. 3 gives the figure as 93 KIA (BC) while at p. 57 the KIA (BC) figure is given as 105.
162 Ibid., pp. 89 96.
163 Ibid., p. 90.
164 Ibid., p. 90.
165 Ibid., p. 91.
166 Ibid., pp. 101–8.
167 LBJ/NSF/Memos to the President/8/W. W. Rostow V. 6/21a, transcript of Saigon 879 dated 13 July 1966, p. 1 (declassified July 1988).

168 Ibid., p. 106.
169 In addition to the reports previously cited, see Goure's report of 1 August 1966 LBJ/NSF/CF/VN/35/M57/163a, particularly p. 4. This report went to W. W. Rostow and was marked for Presidential reading.
170 1st Infantry Division, 'Combat Operation After Action Report – Operation EL PASO II/III,' 8 December 1966, p. 106.
171 Ibid., p. 146.
172 Ibid., p. 249.
173 Ibid., pp. 44–5.
174 Ibid., p. 42.
175 Ibid., pp. 42–3.
176 Ibid., p. 8 gives the figure as two while p. 43 provides the lower number.
177 2nd Brigade, 25th Infantry Division, 'Combat Operation After Action Report – Operation SANTA FE,' 20 July 1966.
178 Ibid., pp. 8–17.
179 Ibid., p. 17.
180 Ibid., p. 18.
181 Ibid.
182 173rd Airborne Brigade (Separate), 'Combat Operation After Action Report – Operation AURORA I,' 15 September 1966.
183 Ibid., p. 3.
184 Ibid., p. 12.
185 Ibid., p. 13.
186 Ibid., p. 15.
187 Ibid., p. 16.
188 173rd Airborne Brigade (Separate), 'Combat Operation After Action Report – Operation AURORA II,' 15 September 1966.
189 Ibid., pp. 3–12.
190 Ibid., p. 13.
191 Ibid., p. 14.
192 Ibid., p. 8.
193 Ibid., pp. 14–15.
194 Ibid., p. 16.
195 1st Brigade, 101st Airborne Division, 'Combat Operation After Action Report – Operation JOHN PAUL JONES,' 28 September 1966.
196 Ibid., p. 4.
197 Ibid., pp. 4, 10.
198 Ibid., p. 26.
199 Ibid., pp. 5–6.
200 Ibid., p. 9.
201 173rd Airborne Brigade (Separate), 'Combat Operation After Action Report – Operation SIOUX CITY,' 15 December 1966.
202 Ibid., pp. 2–5.
203 Ibid., pp. 6–7.
204 Ibid., pp. 7–8.
205 Ibid., pp. 19, 22–4.
206 Ibid., p. 23.
207 Ibid.
208 3rd Squadron, 11th Armored Cavalry Regiment, 'Combat Operation After Action Report – Operation HICKORY,' 26 October 1966.
209 Ibid., p. 9.
210 Ibid., p. 14.
211 Ibid., p. 16.

212 Ibid., p. 21.
213 Ibid.
214 196th Light Infantry Brigade, 'Combat Operation After Action Report – Operation ATTLEBORO,' n.d.; 2nd Brigade 25th Infantry Division, 'Combat Operation After Action Report – Operation ATTLEBORO,' n.d.; 2nd Battalion 27th Infantry (The Wolfhounds) Operation ATTLEBORO, 28 April 1967; 173rd Airborne Brigade (Separate), 'Combat Operation After Action Report – Operation ATTLEBORO,' 30 December 1966.
215 196th Brigade, op. cit., p. 3.
216 2nd Brigade, op. cit., p. 2; 173rd Brigade, op. cit., p. 3.
217 196th Brigade, op. cit., p. 4.
218 2nd Brigade, op. cit., p. 3; 173rd Brigade, op. cit., p. 3.
219 196th Brigade, op. cit., p. 8.
220 Ibid.
221 Ibid.
222 Ibid., pp. 8–9, 17–18.
223 2nd Brigade, op. cit., pp. 8–13.
224 173rd Brigade op. cit., pp. 7–11.
225 The 196th Brigade reported a body count of 254 with 6 POWs, 60 suspected Viet Cong and 19 detainees. Thirty individual weapons were recovered. Eleven hundred tons of rice were captured or destroyed (op. cit., pp. 18–20). The 2nd Brigade reported 43 Viet Cong confirmed killed, one captured and 9 small arms recovered. Five hundred tons of rice were captured or destroyed (op. cit., p. 14). The 173rd Airborne Brigade reported 7 Viet Cong killed and 2 weapons recovered. A total of 248,800 pounds of foodstuffs were captured or destroyed (op. cit., p. 14).
226 4/503rd Infantry, 173rd Airborne Brigade, 'Combat Operation After Action Report – Operation WINCHESTER,' 30 December 1966.
227 Ibid., p. 23.
228 Ibid., p. 53.
229 Ibid.
230 Ibid., p. 63.
231 Ibid.
232 Ibid., p. 2.
233 Ibid., p. 31–2.
234 Ibid., p. 33.
235 Ibid., pp. 40–6.
236 173rd Airborne Brigade (Separate), 'Combat Operation After Action Report – Operation WACO,' n.d.
237 For a detailed account of how a battalion of the 173rd Airborne Brigade had developed and employed the concept of the Reconnaissance Commando (RECONDO) patrol in Operation VAN BUREN see LBJ/Papers of William C. Westmoreland/7/4, 42, memo for Record, 'MACV Commanders' Conference 20 February 1966,' dated 10 March 1966, Annex, 'RECONDO CHECKERBOARD Concept of Operations.'
238 Ibid., pp. 7–9.
239 Ibid., p. 9.
240 Ibid., pp. 12–13.
241 See Leo Goure's 1 August 1966 briefing to the JCS on Viet Cong morale, a copy of which went to the President with a very favorable cover memo by W. W. Rostow. LBJ/NSF/Memos to the President/9/WWR 10/72, 72a (cover memo declassified May 1989, Goure briefing declassified August 1986).

242 LBJ/NSF/NSC Meetings/2/Meetings with the President/25 (declassified January 1989).
243 See as examples Lodge weekly telegram of 28 September 1966. LBJ/NSF/-Memos to the President/9/WWR 10/28a (declassified June 1988) and 13 October briefing, memos to the President/9/WWR 11/34, 34a, 34c.
244 See LBJ/Papers of William C. Westmoreland/7/V. 5/29, memo to COMUSMACV from Colonel Scofield, Acting ACOS J2, MACJ234, 'The Threat in Northern I Corps.'
245 See JASON Study on VC/NVA Logistics and Infiltration plus cover memo form Ginsburgh to Rostow LBJ/NSF/CF/VN/190/VC/NVA Logistics – JASON Study/1, 1a.
246 LBJ/Papers of William C. Westmoreland/7/V. 10/47, memo to record, 'Assessment of the Situation In South Vietnam: October 1966,' n.d. but manuscript notation reads, 'Drafted during Manila Conference, Oct. 1966,' p. 3.
247 LBJ/NSF/NSC Meetings/2/T7/3.
248 Ibid., p. 1.
249 Ibid., pp. 2–3.
250 Ibid., pp. 4–5.
251 Ibid., p. 7.
252 LBJ/NSF/NSC Meetings/2/T7/4.
253 LBJ/NSF/Files of Komer/5/McNamara/Vance/McNaughton/47, 47a (declassified February 1988).
254 Ibid., p. 1.
255 Ibid., p. 5.
256 Ibid. Also see Office of Current Intelligence, Directorate of Intelligence, Central Intelligence Agency, intelligence memo, 'The Vietnamese Communists' Will to Persist,' 22 August 1966.
257 Ibid., pp. 6–7.
258 See National Security Action Memo no. 343, LBJ/NSF/Files of Komer/7/-NSAMS/3 (declassified December 1986).
259 LBJ/NSF/NSC Meetings/2/Meetings with the President/2.
260 LBJ/NSF/NSC Meetings/2/Meetings with the President/2b, p. 1 (declassified May 1987).
261 Ibid.
262 Ibid.
263 LBJ/NSF/Files of Walt W. Rostow/3/7, summary notes, 'Meeting with the President, Friday, December 17, 1966,' p. 2 (declassified January 1990).
264 LBJ/NSF/Memos to the President/11/WWR 15/8, 8a (declassified February 1990).
265 Ibid., 8a, p. 21.

4 THE OPERATION WAS A SUCCESS BUT THE PATIENT DIED

1 LBJ/NSF/CF/VN/210/Taylor Report/1, 'Report on General Taylor's Mission to South Vietnam,' 3 November 1961. Appendix F, p. 1 (declassified March 1967).
2 Ibid., appendix F, pp. 3–5 and summary report, p. 13.
3 Ibid., Unconventional Warfare appendix, p. 1.

4 LBJ/NSF/CF/VN/8/M17/90b, Joseph Zasloff, 'The Role of North Vietnam in the Southern Insurgence,' Rand memo, RM–4140 PR, July 1964, Table 10, p. 43. This report was prepared for the Air Force and was sent by Air Force Chief of Staff Curtis LeMay to the Joint Chiefs of Staff on 17 August 1964. A copy was forwarded to the National Security Council.

5 Ibid., pp. 74–81.

6 Ibid., pp. 2–3.

7 LBJ/NSF/NIE/1/14.3 NVN/3b, Special National Intelligence Estimate 14.3–64, 'The Outlook for North Vietnam,' 4 March 1964, p. 5 (declassified March 1987).

8 Ibid., pp. 6–7.

9 Ibid., p. 9.

10 Ibid., p. 8.

11 Ibid., p. 11.

12 Ibid., pp. 13–15.

13 LBJ/NSF/CF/VN/6/M14/23, State Department Bureau of Intelligence and Research, memo to the Secretary, 'Khanh's Claims of Increased North Vietnamese Infiltration,' dated 17 July 1964.

14 LBJ/NSF/CF/VN/2/M4/86, 'Situation in South Vietnam,' 20 February 1964; 2/M4/87, 'Situation in South Vietnam,' 28 February 1964; 2/M4/88, 'Situation in South Vietnam,' 6 March 1964; 2/C5/67, 'Situation in South Vietnam,' 13 March 1964.

15 LBJ/NSF/CF/VN/1/M3/111a, 111b, 111c, memo from William Colby to McGeorge Bundy, Dean Rusk, Robert McNamara et al., dated 11 February 1964, 'Increased Pathet Lao Military Activity,' and 'Further Comments on the Situation in Vietnam.'

16 LBJ/NSF/CF/VN/2/C5/55/a, memo for the President from Secretary McNamara, 'South Vietnam,' dated 13 March 1964, especially p. 2, note 'a'.

17 LBJ/NSF/NSC Meetings/1/T5/2 plus attachments, 'Summary Record of NSC Meeting No. 524.'

18 Ibid., particularly document #9, pp. 6–8, 15.

19 Summarized in 'Office of the Secretary of Defense, United States–Vietnam Relations, 1945–1967,' Washington, DC, 1971, IVc3: 2–3. See also LBJ/NSF/ CF/VN/4/M9/2a, memo to the President from McNamara dated 14 May 1964 in which he summarizes conversations with General Taylor and states the position of Ambassador Henry Cabot Lodge who 'wishes to carry out air strikes against the North . . . not only to cut off the supply of men and equipment from the North but also to destroy the morale of the North Vietnamese' (declassified May 1987).

20 LBJ/Papers of McGeorge Bundy/18/Meetings on SE Asia/42, CIA SNIE 50–2–64, 'Probable Consequences of Certain US Actions with Respect to Vietnam and Laos,' 23 May 1964, particularly pp. 12–15 (declassified May 1987).

21 Ibid., p. 16.

22 LBJ/NSF/NSC Meetings/1/V. II/T6/2, 'Summary Record of NSC Meeting No. 533,' 6 June 1964.

23 Ibid., p. 1.

24 LBJ/NSF/CF/LAOS/268/C10/48, 49, telexes to White House from [deleted] dated 2 September 1964 (declassified September 1988).

25 LBJ/NSF/NSC Meetings/1/V. II/T9/9a, 'Viet Cong Activity January through June 1964.'

26 See CIA weekly and monthly reports, 'The Situation in South Vietnam,'

LBJ/NSF/CF/VN/4/M8/35, 36, 37; 4/M9/36; 5/M11/8; 5/M12/9, 10; 6/M13/47, 48a, 49; 6/M13/47; 6/M14/233a, 234.

27 LBJ/NSF/NSC Meetings/1/V. III/T19, 20–2, 'Summary Notes of the 538th NSC Meeting,' 4 August 1964, p. 1.

28 Ibid.

29 Ibid.

30 Ibid., document #3.

31 LBJ/NSF/CF/VN/216/Reprisal Program/V. II/54c, 'Summary of Aircraft Strikes Against North Vietnam,' dated 1 April 1965 (declassified May 1988); LBJ/NSF/CF/VN/7/M15/123, 'The Situation in Vietnam,' dated 6 August 1965; USVR, IVc3: 3.

32 JCSM 639–64, memo for the Secretary of Defense from the JCS, 'Action Relevant to South Vietnam,' dated 27 July 1964; LBJ/NSF/CF/VN/7/C16/130, telex from CINCPAC to JCS, 'Planning for Cross Border Operations,' dated 19 August 1964; 8/C18/114, telex from CINCPAC to JCS, 'Cross Border Operations into Laos,' dated 21 August 1964; 8/C18/116, telex from COMUSMACV to JCS, 'Cross Border Operations,' dated 22 September 1964; 8/C18/117, telex from CINCPAC to operational elements, dated 20 September 1964.

33 LBJ/NSF/CF/LAOS/268/C10/57, telex from JCS to CINCPAC, 'Definitive Rules of Engagement Applying to Laos,' dated 28 September 1964 (declassified August 1988).

34 LBJ/NSF/CF/LAOS/268/C10/80, 80a, 80b, 80c, telex from COMUSMACV AIG 967 and from CINCPAC to JCS, 'Proposed Photographic Reconnaissance Routes for Laos, 2–15 September 64,' dated 31 August 1964 (declassified July 1989); LAOS/268/C10/74–79 inclusive, telexes from COMUSMACV to JCS dated 11 September 1964, 'Proposed Photographic Reconnaissance Routes for Laos, 16–30 September 1964,' White House clearance slips and execute order telex from JCS to CINCPAC (declassified March and July 1989).

35 LBJ/NSF/CF/LAOS/268/C10/22, telex from State Department to AmEmb Vientiane dated 25 September 1964 (declassified March 1989).

36 Ibid., p. 2.

37 Ibid. The RLAF finally did undertake attacks in the northern panhandle or the Laotian Corridor, see LBJ/NSF/CF/VN/9/M20/151, telex from USAIRA/ VIENTIANE to CSAF dated 12 October 1964 outlining forthcoming RLAF attack on the corridor scheduled for 14 October; 9/M20/150, telex from COMUSMACV to CINCPAC on same date and same subject.

38 LBJ/WHCF/Meeting Notes File/1/Memo for the record 9/14/64.

39 Ibid., 11b, p. 2.

40 Ibid.

41 LBJ/NSF/CF/VN/10/C21/90, telex from COMUSMACV to CINCPAC/JCS, 'Summary of VC Mortar Firing Against Bien Hoa Airbase,' dated 1 November 1964.

42 LBJ/NSF/CF/VN/10/C21/86a, telex transcript of Westmoreland Press Briefing dated 1 November 1964, Section I, p. 2.

43 LBJ/NSF/CF/VN/8/M17/103, intelligence memo, 'Communist Reaction to Increased US Pressure Against North Vietnam,' dated 9 September 1964.

44 USVR, IVc3: 4.

45 LBJ/NSF/CF/VN/45, 46/Courses of Action SEA/9, memo from William Bundy and John McNaughton to NSC members, dated 26 November 64, p. 2. See also USVR, IVc3: 4.

46 LBJ/Aides Files/2/Memos to the President 7/53, memo from the President to Secretary of State, Secretary of Defense, Director of Central Intelligence, dated 7 December 1964. LBJ/NSF/CF/VN/11/M23/116, intelligence memo, 'Infiltration of Military and Technical Personnel from North to South Vietnam,' dated 3 December 1964. This memo took the 'quality personnel' approach, arguing that leadership and specialist personnel as well as key supplies made up the bulk of the infiltration. The use of leadership cadre allowed Hanoi to continue control of the movement in the South while the provision of key supplies such as munitions, heavy ordnance and communication equipment greatly enhanced the military potential of the Viet Cong. It was believed that the rate of infiltration had increased.

47 LBJ/Aides Files/1/Memos to the President 7/53b, 'Position Paper on Southeast Asia,' dated 2 December 1964, p. 1.

48 Ibid., p. 2.

49 Ibid.

50 LBJ/NSF/CF/VN/11/M23/28b, intelligence memo, 'Communist Reaction to BARREL ROLL Missions,' 29 December 1964.

51 Ibid., pp. 1–2.

52 Ibid., p. 2.

53 See intelligence memo TS #185793, 'Probable Communist Reaction to US Option C or C–Prime Measures,' dated 27 November 1964. Copies went to both W. Bundy and John McNaughton.

54 LBJ/NSF/CF/VN/12M25/155, memo to McGeorge Bundy from Colonel Bowman, 'Southeast Asia Operations,' dated 5 January 1965.

55 LBJ/NSF/CF/VN/12/M25/122, memo to the President from McGeorge Bundy and Chester Cooper, 'Political Developments in South Vietnam (Fifth Report),' dated 4 January 1965; 12/M25/132, 132a, memo to the President from McGeorge Bundy with attached 'Summary of Conversation between Ambassador Taylor and Four Members of the Armed Forces Council,' dated 5 January 1965; 12/M25/117, memo to the President from Cooper and McGeorge Bundy, 'Political Developments in South Vietnam (Sixth Report),' dated 6 January 1965; 12/M25/113, memo to the President from Cooper and Bundy, 'Political Developments in South Vietnam (Seventh Report),' dated 8 January 1964; 12/M26/188a, memo to the President from Cooper and Bundy, 'Political Situation in South Vietnam (Ninth Report),' dated 18 January 1965; 12/M26/220, 220a, memo to McGeorge Bundy and the President from Cooper, 'Vietnam – The Present State of Play,' dated 26 January 1965.

56 LBJ/NSF/CF/VN/202/Meetings of the Principals/9, memo from James Thompson to McGeorge Bundy, 'Reflections on the Current Vietnam Experience,' dated 28 November 1964, p. 2 (declassified May 1987).

57 LBJ/NSF/CF/VN/13/C27/7, telex from COMUSMACV to JCS.

58 LBJ/NSF/AF/II/2, memo to the President from McGeorge Bundy, 'The Situation in Vietnam,' dated 7 February 1965. See also, USVR, IVC3: 23.

59 LBJ/NSF/CF/VN/216/Reprisal Program 2/43a, 'Summary of Air Attacks against North Vietnam,' dated 12 April 1965.

60 LBJ/NSF/NSC Meetings/1/V. III/T29/2, 'Summary Notes of the 547th NSC Meeting,' dated 8 February 1965, p. 1 (declassified February 1988).

61 Ibid., p. 2.

62 See for example LBJ/NSF/CF/VN/10/C21/154, telex to AIR INTEL OFF USMACV from E&P DIV INTEL which warned of possible mortar attack at Danang by imitators of Bien Hoa.

63 Op. cit., 547th NSC Meeting, p. 3.
64 Ibid.
65 LBJ/NSC Meetings/1/V. III/R30/2, 3, 4, 'Summary Record of NSC Meeting No. 548' including attachment, 'Meeting of the Principals,' both dated 10 February 1965 (declassified February 1988).
66 See in addition to Ibid., LBJ/NSF/CF/VN/13/M28/224, 224a, memo to McGeorge Bundy from Chester Cooper and Fred Ungar, 'Elements in a Program of Continuing Action Against North Vietnam' and 'Report of Meeting,' both dated 9 February 1965.
67 Consult the weekly and monthly CIA intelligence summaries, 'The Situation in Vietnam' for the period September 1964 through January 1965. LBJ/NSF/CF/VN/8/M17/131, 133; 9/M18/283, 285; 9M19/107, 108; 9/M20/170, 171; 10/C21/213, 214; 10/C22/110; 11/M23/184, 185, 187; 11/M24/238; 12/M25/178, 179; 12/M26/146, 148, 149; 13/M27/199.
68 LBJ/NSF/CF/VN/48/SEA V. I/Special Intelligence Material/4, CIA special report, 'The Hanoi Directed Front for South Vietnam Liberation,' dated 10 July 1964.
69 LBJ/BSF/CF/VN/12/M26/169, CIA special report, 'Communist Liberation Front in South Vietnam – A Progress Report,' dated 15 January 1965.
70 LBJ/NSF/CF/VN/48/SEA V. I/Special Intelligence Material/21, CIA special report, 'Trends of Communist Insurgency in South Vietnam,' 17 January 1964; 9/M20/157, CIA special report, 'Viet Cong Infiltration into Northern South Vietnam,' 23 October 1964; 11/M23/116, CIA special report. 'Infiltration of Military and Technical Personnel From North to South Vietnam,' 3 December 1964; 48/SEA V. III/Special Intelligence Materials/26, CIA intelligence memo, 'Communist Troop Movements in Laos,' 13 January 1965. On the question of using South Vietnamese intelligence sources to demonstrate infiltration, see LBJ/NSF/CF/VN/199/Briefing Materials/30, 'Summary Statement on Infiltration of Military and Technical Personnel from North to South Vietnam,' 23 January 1965.
71 LBJ/NSF/CF/VN/48/SEA V. III/Special Intelligence Material/26, CIA special report, 'Communist Troop Movements in Laos,' 13 January 1965.
72 LBJ/NSF/CF/VN/13/M27/104, memo for the United States Intelligence Board from Joseph Seltzer, Executive Officer, National Estimates, 'SNIE 10–65: Communist Military Capabilities and Near-Term Intentions in Laos and South Vietnam,' 1 February 1965.
73 LBJ/NSF/CF/13/M27/107, SNIE 53–65, 'Short-Term Prospects in South Vietnam,' 2 February 1965.
74 LBJ/NSF/CF/VN/M28/218, SNIE 10–3–65, 'Communist Reactions to Possible US Actions,' 11 February 1965. It should be noted that earlier drafts of this SNIE were circulated to McGeorge Bundy and the NSC staff.
75 See the FISHNET reports for February such as LBJ/NSF/Reprisal Program I/2/171; I/2/169; 168; 167; 166; 165.
76 LBJ/NSF/CF/VN/13/C28/6, telex from COMUSMACV to CINCPAC, 'Stepup of Military Pressures Against DRV,' dated 10 February 1965.
77 LBJ/NSF/CF/VN/13C28/51, telex from COMUSMACV to JCS, dated 19 February 1965; 13/C28/67, telex from COMUSMACV to NMACC, CINCPAC, dated 19 February 1965; 14/C29/4, telex from COMUSMACV to NMCC, CINCPAC, dated 20 February 1965; 14/C29/7, Telex from COMUSMACV to CINCPAC, dated 21 February 1965; 14/C29/10, telex from COMUSMACV To NMCC, CINCPAC, dated 21 February 1965.
78 LBJ/NSF/CF/VN/14/C29/49, telex from COMUSMACV to JCS/CINCPAC, 'Use of US Air Power,' dated 22 February 1965.

79 LBJ/NSF/CF/VN/14/M30/144, telex from COMUSMACV to CINCPAC, reprinted for President Johnson, 'Resume of US Jet Bombing Strikes within South Vietnam,' dated 2 March 1965. See also 14/C29/38, telex from COMUSMACV to CINCPAC, 'Use of US Jets in South Vietnam,' dated 24 February 1965 and Reprisal Program I/2/42, telex from COMUSMACV to NMCC, 'Jet Strikes in Phuoc Tuy and Pleiku Provinces,' dated 2 March 1965.

80 LBJ/NSF/CF/VN/49/SEA V. V/Special Intelligence Materials/4, 4a, memo to McGeorge Bundy from Ray Cline dated 22 April 1965 plus attached CIA/OCI intelligence memo, 'Results of US Air Strikes in South Vietnam,' dated 21 April 1965.

81 LBJ/NSF/CF/VN/216/Reprisal Program II/54c, 'Summary of Aircraft Strikes Against North Vietnam (as of 31 March 1965)' (declassified June 1987).

82 Ibid.

83 LBJ/NSF/CF/VN/216/Reprisal Program II/54b, memo to McGeorge Bundy, 'Summary of Rolling Thunder Operations,' dated 31 March 1965 (declassified May 1988). The White House received as well copies of the frag orders pertaining to every ROLLING THUNDER mission.

84 An evaluation of the effects of FLAMING DART I/II was available on 5 March. The CIA noted that as a result of the three attacks on the 304th PAVN Division headquarters at Dong Hoi, the troops of that unit had been dispersed along the DMZ, that construction in the region had been halted, civilians dispersed to rural areas and an internal security program initiated. At Dong Hoi, damage was moderate to heavy while at the other targets it was lighter. Casualties included 185 soldiers and 150 civilians killed. LBJ/NSF/CF/VN/14/C30/64, Intelligence Information Cable, dated 5 March 1965.

85 LBJ/NSF/CF/VN/15/M31/195, memo to the President from John McCone, 'Communist Reactions to US Air Attacks on North Vietnam,' dated 13 March 1965.

86 LBJ/NSF/NSC Meetings/1/V. III/T33/2, 'Summary Notes of 550th NSC Meeting,' 26 March 1965.

87 See LBJ/NSF/CF/VN/14/M30/134, 134a, memo from Ray Cline, DDI to McGeorge Bundy, 'Status Report After Seven Days in March,' dated 8 March 1965 and 15/M31/220, memo from Chester Cooper to McGeorge Bundy, 'Military Issues, Vietnam and Laos,' 9 March 1965.

88 Ibid.

89 LBJ/NSF/NSC Meetings/1/V. III/T33/2, 'Summary Notes of the 551st NSC Meeting,' 5 April 1965.

90 LBJ/NSF/CF/VN/16/M32/222, memo, 'Recent Indications of Communist Intentions In South Vietnam,' 8 April 1965, p. 5. A draft version had been circulated on 6 April.

91 LBJ/NSF/CF/VN/C32/141, intelligence cable, 15 April 1965.

92 LBJ/NSF/CF/VN/15/M31/199, Johnson 21–Point Program, dated 14 March 1965.

93 LBJ/NSF/CF/VN/16/M32/231b, memo to the President from John McCone dated 2 April 1965; 231c, memo to Rusk, McNamara, McGeorge Bundy and Taylor from McCone, dated 2 April 1965.

94 LBJ-Aides Files/Meetings of the Principals/1/10/198d, memo to the President from McNamara, dated 21 April 1965; see also CF/VN/16/M32/213, memo to McNamara from Harold Johnson, 'Actions Designed to Accelerate Stability in South Vietnam,' dated 12 April 1965.

95 USVR, IVc3: 74–80.

96 USVR, VIc3: 99–105.
97 LBJ/NSF/CF/VN/17/M33/120, intelligence memo, 'An Assessment of Present Viet Cong Military Capabilities,' dated 21 April 1965, p. 1.
98 LBJ/NSF/CF/VN/50, 51/SEA V. VIb/Special Intelligence Materials/20, 20a, 20b, intelligence memo, 'Status of the War in South Vietnam,' dated 12 May 1965, 20b, p. 1.
99 Ibid., p. 3.
100 LBJ/NSF/CF/VN/16/M33/92a, special memo, 'Current Trends in Vietnam,' 30 April 1965.
101 LBJ/NSF/CF/VN/217/Reprisal Program/V. II/54b, 54c, 69, 77, 83, 94, 99, 113, 114, 117, 118, 121, 128, 129, 146 (declassified June 1987); Reprisal Program/ V. III/21, 23; 41–9; 56, 57, 60, 65, 70, 71, 74, 80, 86, 91, 100–3; 148–58; 161–6; 169, 180–9; 191–7; 202a (declassified October 1986 and November 1988).
102 LBJ/NSF/CF/VN/217/Reprisal Program/V. III/197.
103 LBJ/NSF/CF/VN/18/M35/326, 326a, memo to McGeorge Bundy with attached CIA Monthly Report, 'The Situation in Vietnam,' dated 4 June 1965. Compare with LBJ/NSF/CF/VN/50, 51/SEA V. VIb/Special Intelligence Materials/20, 20a, 20b. See also LBJ/NSF/CF/VN/18/M35/320a, telex from Taylor to the President, dated 1 June 1965.
104 LBJ/NSF/CF/VN/18/M35/326a, memo to McGeorge Bundy with attached CIA monthly report, 'The Situation in Vietnam,' p. 3.
105 LBJ/NSF/CF/VN/19/C36/28, telex from Taylor to McNamara and McGeorge Bundy, dated 24 June 1965; LBJ/Aides Files/MP/3/11/38c, 'Agenda for 5:30 Meeting with the President,' 23 June 1965.
106 LBJ/NSF/CF/VN/49/SEA V. VI/Special Intelligence Materials/2, 2a intelligence memo, 'Developments in South Vietnam During the Past Year,' dated 30 June 1965.
107 Consult LBJ/NSF/CF/VN/207, 208/ARC LIGHT I; 209, 210/ARC LIGHT II.
108 LBJ/NSF/CF/VN/207/ARC LIGHT I/14, telex from MACV to DIA/NMCC, 25 August 1965. This was a typical formulation found repeatedly.
109 Ibid., 7, p. 2.
110 Ibid., 201/ARC LIGHT I/GEAR TRAIN/2 is an example. Chester Cooper gave telephone approval to a portfolio of three missions with less than one day turnaround. See also ARC LIGHT II/CAPE COD/2 where a package of eight strikes is perfunctorily approved.
111 LBJ/NSF/CF/VN/18/M35b/326, 326a, memo to Bundy from B. K. Smith with report, 'Effectiveness of B–52 Operations,' 10 January 1967.
112 Ibid., p. 1.
113 Ibid., p. 2.
114 Ibid., p. 3.
115 LBJ/NSF/CF/VN/49/SEA V. VI/Special Intelligence Materials/8, intelligence memo, 'Interdiction of Communist Infiltration Routes in Vietnam,' 24 June 1965, pp. 5–6.
116 Ibid., p. 7.
117 Ibid., Chart i.
118 Ibid., p. 10.
119 Ibid., p. 9.
120 Ibid., p. 11.
121 LBJ/NSF/18/M35/362, State Department, Bureau of Intelligence and Research, intelligence note, 'The Effects of the Bombings of North Vietnam,' 29 June 1965.
122 LBJ/NSF/CF/VN/190, 191/NODIS–MAYFLOWER/2, 2a; transcribed telex from Taylor with McGeorge Bundy cover memo, dated 11 July 1965.

123 Ibid., p. 6.
124 Ibid., p. 8.
125 Ibid., p. 21.
126 LBJ/NSF/VN/201/Special Meetings on SE Asia/V. I/20, 22, 24, 25 (declassified January 1987).
127 For an indication as to the trends in the ROLLING THUNDER program consult the following frag and execute orders: LBJ/NSF/CF/VN/201/Special Meetings on SE Asia/V. I/40, 42a, 50a, 60b, 62, 64, 70, 71b (declassified January 1987).
128 LBJ/NSF/CF/VN/50, 51/SEA V. VIII/10, USIB memo, 'Infiltration and Logistics – South Vietnam,' 28 October 1965, p. 1.
129 Ibid., p. 19. See also LBJ/NSF/CF/VN/78, 79/3C NVN Infiltration into SVN/48h, CIA intelligence memo, 'Construction of Roads Will Make Possible the Strengthening of Communist Forces in South Vietnam and Southern Laos,' 25 October 1965. This report details the impressive program of road and trail construction which the North Vietnamese had undertaken in the Laotian Corridor under the weight of the BARREL ROLL and STEEL TIGER attacks.
130 Ibid., p. 24.
131 Ibid., pp. 30–1.
132 Ibid., p. 11.
133 LBJ/NSF/CF/VN/18/M35/268a, memo to the President from McNamara, 'Evaluation of the Program of Bombing North Vietnam,' dated 31 July 1966, p. 2 (declassified November 1966).
134 LBJ/Papers of McGeorge Bundy/2/ V. 17/72, Eyes Only message to the President from McGeorge Bundy, 3 December 1965.
135 LBJ/Papers of McGeorge Bundy/2/ V. 17/86, memo to the President from McGeorge Bundy, 'Once More on the Pause,' 27 November 1965.
136 LBJ/Papers of McGeorge Bundy/2/V. 17/86a, memo to McGeorge Bundy from George Ball, 'Pros and Cons,' n.d. This memo was sent to the President by Bundy on 17 November 1965.
137 Ibid., p. 8.
138 LBJ/Papers of McGeorge Bundy/2/V. 17/72, op. cit. p. 2.
139 LBJ/NSF/CF/VN/83/3H (1)/4, 4a, memo to McGeorge Bundy from Ray Cline plus appended report, 8 November 1965, p. 2 (declassified July 1987).
140 LBJ/Papers of McGeorge Bundy/2/V. 17/68, memo to the President from Bundy, 4 December 1965.
141 LBJ/Papers of McGeorge Bundy/2/V. 17/55, memo to the President from McGeorge Bundy, 'Broodings on Vietnam,' 14 December 65, p. 2. See also Ball talking notes, 55a.
142 LBJ/WHCF/CF/Meeting Note File/1/Meetings of Foreign Policy Advisors, 12/17/65, 'Notes' by Jack Valenti, pp. 2–3.
143 Ibid., p. 1.
144 Ibid., p. 2.
145 Ibid.
146 Ibid., p. 4.
147 LBJ/WHCF/CF/Meeting Notes File/1/Meetings of Foreign Policy Advisors 12/18/65, 'Notes' by Jack Valenti.
148 Ibid., p. 6.
149 Ibid.
150 Ibid., p. 7.
151 LBJ/NSF/NSC Meetings/1/V. II/T2/2, memo to Rusk and Ball, 'Points you may wish to make at NSC 5:45 Meeting Today,' 5 January 1966.
152 LBJ/NSF/Memos to the President/6/McGeorge Bundy V. 18/84a, transcript

of Saigon 2376, to the Secretary from Lodge, dated 4 January 1966, p. 1.

153 Ibid., p. 2.

154 LBJ/Papers of Paul Warnke–John McNaughton File/1/McNaughton Drafts (III)/75a, 'Some Paragraphs on Vietnam–3rd Draft,' dated 19 January 1966, p. 2 (declassified March 1988).

155 Ibid.

156 Ibid., p. 5.

157 LBJ/Papers of Paule Warnke–John McNaughton File/1/McNaughton Drafts II (3)/79, McNaughton draft memo, 'Some Observations About Bombing North Vietnam,' dated 18 January 1966, p. 2 (declassified March 1988).

158 Ibid., pp. 3–4. See LBJ/Papers of Paul Warnke–John McNaughton File/1/-McNaughton Drafts (III)/83, Freedman, draft, 'The Future of the Bombing Program against North Vietnam,' dated 15 January 1966 (declassified May 1986).

159 Ibid., pp. 7, 11–13.

160 LBJ/WHCF/Meeting Notes File/1/Meeting in Cabinet Room, 24 January 1966.

161 LBJ/WHCF/CF/71/ND CO 312/2a, intelligence memo, 'Hanoi's Reaction to the Bombing Lull,' dated 18 January 1966, p. 1.

162 Ibid., p. 3.

163 LBJ/WHCF/Meeting Notes File/1/Meeting in Cabinet Room, 25 January 1966, p. 2.

164 LBJ/WHCF/Meeting Notes File/1/Meeting in Cabinet Room, 26 January 1966.

165 LBJ/WHCF/CF/71/ND CO 312/Situation in Vietnam, January–March 66, memo to the President from McGeorge Bundy dated 26 January 1966.

166 LBJ/WHCF/Meeting Notes File/1/Meeting in Cabinet Room, 27 January 1966.

167 Ibid., p. 4.

168 Ibid., p. 8.

169 LBJ/WHCF/Meeting Notes File/1/Meeting in Cabinet Room, 28 January 1966.

170 Ibid., p. 2.

171 Ibid., p. 9.

172 Ibid., p. 10.

173 LBJ/NSF/NSC Meetings/2/V. II/T2/2, 'Summary Notes of 556th NSC Meeting,' 29 January 1966, p. 2.

174 Ibid.

175 Ibid., p. 3.

176 LBJ/NSF/CF/VN/26, 27/C47/3, Office of National Estimates memo, 'Possible Effects of Various Programs of Air Attack Against the DRV,' 11 February 1966, p. 2 (declassified July 1989).

177 Ibid., p. 13.

178 Ibid., p. 12.

179 LBJ/NSF/Memos to the President/6/V. 20/15, memo to the President from McGeorge Bundy, 'CIA memorandum on alternative programs of air attack on North Vietnam,' 25 February 1966.

180 LBJ/NSF/NSC Meetings/2/V. II/T4/2, 'Summary Notes of 557th NSC Meeting,' 10 May 1966, p. 1.

181 LBJ/NSF/CF/VN/78, 79/3C NVN Infiltration into SVN/3, intelligence memo, 'Buildup of Communist Forces Continues After Resumption of Air Attacks,' 21 February 1966, p. 10.

182 LBJ/NSF/CF/VN/78, 79/3 C NVN Infiltration into SVN/2b, intelligence

memo, 'The Current Status of PAVN Infiltration into South Vietnam,' 9 April 1966.

183 LBJ/WHCF/CF/71/ND CO 312/intelligence memo, 'An Appraisal of the Bombing of North Vietnam through 14 May,' dated 21 May 1966 and intelligence memo, 'An Appraisal of the Bombing of North Vietnam through 14 June,' dated 20 June 1966.

184 'An Appraisal of the Bombing of North Vietnam through 14 June,' op. cit., p. 4.

185 See LBJ/NSF/Memos to the President/7/W. W. Rostow V. 3/32, memo to the President from W. W. Rostow dated 16 June 1966 in which he reported his conversation with UN Ambassador Goldberg regarding the low civilian casualties to be expected from the POL campaign and the means by which a diplomatic confrontation with the Soviets might be mitigated (declassified January 1989).

186 LBJ/NSF/NSC Meetings/2/V. II/T4/2, 'Summary Notes of 559th NSC Meeting,' 17 June 1966.

187 Ibid., p. 2.

188 Ibid.

189 Ibid., p. 3.

190 Ibid., p. 6.

191 Ibid., p. 8.

192 LBJ/NSF/Memos to the President/8/WWR V/41a, transcript of Lodge weekly report, 15 June 1966 (declassified March 1989).

193 LBJ/NSF/NSC Meetings/2/II/T7/2, notes of the President's meeting with the National Security Council, 22 June 1966.

194 Ibid., p. 3.

195 Ibid., p. 5.

196 LBJ/Papers of William C. Westmoreland/8/V. 7, telex MAC 5740 to Sharp from Westmoreland, dated 8 July 1966, p. 5.

197 Ibid.

198 LBJ/Papers of William C. Westmoreland/9/V. 8/6, telex MAC 6148 to Sharp from Westmoreland dated 19 July 1966, p. 1.

199 Ibid.

200 LBJ/NSF/NSC Meetings/2/II/T9/3, memo to the President from McNamara, 'Actions Recommended for Vietnam,' 14 October 1966.

201 Ibid., p. 3.

202 Ibid., pp. 4, 6–7.

203 LBJ/NSF/NSC Meetings/2/II/T9/4, memo to the President from the JCS, 'Actions Recommended for Vietnam,' 14 October 1966, p. 3.

204 LBJ/Papers of William C. Westmoreland/9/V. 10/11, memo to W. W. Rostow from Westmoreland, 'COMUSMACV's Comments on ROLLING THUNDER,' dated 24 October 1966.

205 Ibid., p. 5.

206 LBJ/Papers of William C. Westmoreland/9/V. 10/11, memo to W. W. Rostow from Westmoreland, 'COMUSMACV's Comments on ROLLING THUNDER,' dated 24 October 1966, p. 1.

207 Ibid., p. 3.

208 LBJ/NSF/CF/VN/221/CIA Report on Effectiveness of ROLLING THUNDER/1, 1a, memo to W. W. Rostow from R. J. Smith, DDI, dated 5 November 1966 plus attachment, intelligence memo, 'The Effectiveness of the ROLLING THUNDER Program in North Vietnam, 1 January to 30 September 1966,' dated November 1966 (declassified April 1986).

209 Ibid., pp. 5–9.

210 Ibid., p. 2.
211 Ibid., p. 3.
212 Ibid., p. 35.
213 LBJ/NSF/CF/VN/222/Effectiveness of Air Campaign/1, intelligence memo, 'The Effectiveness of the Air Campaign Against North Vietnam, 1 January–30 September 1966,' dated December 1966.
214 Ibid., p. 19.
215 Ibid., p. 20.
216 Ibid., p. 22.
217 LBJ/Komer–Leonhart, Files/24/Special Studies/3a, memo to Leonhart through Rogers from Rossom, 'Answers to Questions from Ambassador Leonhart,' dated 9 September 1966, pp. 8–9.
218 Ibid., p. 9.
219 LBJ/NSF/CF/VN/26, 27/C47/3, op. cit., p. 2.
220 Ibid., pp. E12–E17.
221 Ibid., p. C1.
222 Ibid.
223 Ibid., pp. C21–C27.
224 Ibid., p. 15.
225 It should be noted in this respect that the US air attacks had been delivered in a way which minimized civilian casualties. It was estimated for the year 1966 that ROLLING THUNDER had inflicted 15,700 casualties on the North Vietnamese of which only 5,000 were fatal. This was not a significant number considering 350,000 people died annually in North Vietnam from other causes and the accidental death rate was estimated to between two and three times that of ROLLING THUNDER-caused fatalities (Ibid., pp. 14–15).
226 LBJ/NSF/CF/VN/81–84/3F Memos on Bombing/35, Rand memo RM–5213–ISA, Oleg Hoeffding, 'Bombing North Vietnam: An Appraisal of Economic and Political Effects,' December 1966.
227 Ibid., p. 17.
228 Ibid., p. 32.

5 THE BIG WAR AND THE OTHER WAR

1 LBJ/WHCF/Meeting Notes File/1, meetings on Vietnam, pp. 1–43 and memos for record 23a, 23b, 24, 24a and 24b.
2 Meetings on Vietnam, 21–27 July 1965, op. cit., pp. 24, 31–33.
3 Ibid., p. 32.
4 LBJ/Papers of Paul Warnke–John McNaughton Files/6/McNaughton Drafts (XIV)/2, memo from Ungar, 'Status of Work of Planning Group,' dated 1 April 1966; 21, report from VNCC, 'A Settlement in Vietnam,' with appendices, dated 12 February 1966; 26, memo to Ungar from Kissinger, 'Alternative Approaches to negotiations,' dated 22 February 1966, constitute representative examples of the thinking on negotiations through spring 1966.
5 LBJ/Papers of Paul Warnke–John McNaughton Files/1/McNaughton Drafts (III)/73, memo to McNamara from McNaughton, 'A Barrier Strategy,' April 1966, p. 9 (declassified April 1986).

6 LBJ/NSF/Memos to the President/6/McGeorge Bundy V. 18/39a, transcript of Saigon 2503, to the President from Lodge, 'Outlook for 1966,' dated 12 January 1966, p. 1.

7 LBJ/NSF/Memos to the President/6/McGeorge Bundy V. 29/46a, memo to the President from McGeorge Bundy, 'Non-Military Organization for Vietnam – in Saigon and Washington,' dated 16 February 1966 (declassified March 1987).

8 Ibid., p. 3.

9 Ibid., p. 5.

10 Ibid.

11 LBJ/Komer–Leonhart Files/13/Leverage/3, NSAM 343, dated 28 March 1966 (declassified August 1986).

12 LBJ/NSF/Memos to the President/7/W. W. Rostow V. 1/69a, transcript of Saigon 4085 to the President from Lodge, dated 20 April 1966 (declassified August 1986).

13 Ibid., p. 5.

14 LBJ/NSF/Files of Komer/3/Backchannel Cables/115, telex to Komer from Porter suggesting a draft NSAM, dated 19 April 1966 (declassified June 1989).

15 Ibid., p. 2.

16 Ibid.

17 LBJ/NSF/Files of Komer/3/Backchannel Cables/109b, telex to Porter from Komer dated 20 April 1966 (declassified December 1988).

18 LBJ/NSF/Files of Komer/3/Backchannel Cables/101, telex to Porter from Komer dated 27 April 1966 (declassified December 1988).

19 LBJ/NSF/Files of Komer/3/Backchannel Cables/98, telex to Porter from Komer dated 27 April 1966 (declassified December 1988).

20 LBJ/NSF/Files of Komer/3/Backchannel Cables/97, telex to Komer from Porter dated 28 April 1966 (declassified June 1989).

21 Ibid.

22 LBJ/Papers of Paul Warnke–John McNaughton Files/1/McNaughton Drafts III/87, memo to Rusk, McNamara, McCone, Bell, Rowan, M. Bundy, Lodge from Porter and Ungar, 'Warrenton Meeting on Vietnam, January 8–11, 1966,' dated 13 January 1966, pp. 3–6.

23 LBJ/Komer–Leonhart Files/22/RD/Cadre/14, letter to Komer from McNaughton dated 27 April 1966, p. 2.

24 LBJ/NSF/Files of Komer/3/Porter to Komer/14, letter No. 5 from Komer to Porter dated 27 April 1966 (declassified January 1989).

25 LBJ/WHCF/CF/71/ND 19/CO 312/Situation in VN, April–May 66, National Security Council Meeting 10 May 1966, 'Lodge Agenda,' Items 6, 7, 9.

26 Ibid., agenda items 12, 13, 14, 15.

27 LBJ/NSF/Memos to the President/7/W. W. Rostow V. 2/10a, transcript of Saigon 4952 to the President from Lodge, dated 25 May 1966, p. 3 (declassified March 1988). The figure of ninety RD teams is confusing considering that the CIA reported the figure of seventy-six for the 'New Revolutionary Development Cadre' teams. See LBJ/WHCF/CF/71/ND CO 312/Vietnam Situation June 66, intelligence report, 'The Situation in South Vietnam,' dated 8 June 1966, p. 4.

28 Ibid.

29 LBJ/NSF/Memos to the President/9/W. W. Rostow V. 8/38a, transcript of Saigon 2041 to the President from Lodge, dated 27 July 1966, p. 4 (declassified July 1988).

30 Ibid.
31 LBJ/Komer–Leonhart Files/7/Economic Stabilization V. 3/30; LBJ/NSF/Files of Komer/3/Memos for Record II/4, 'Memorandum for Record,' dated 5 October 1966 (declassified July 1989).
32 LBJ/NSF/Files of Komer/3/Porter to Komer/1, dated 26 November 1966, p. 1 (declassified January 1989).
33 Ibid.
34 Ibid.
35 Ibid., p. 2.
36 Ibid., p. 3.
37 LBJ/NSF/Files of Komer/3/Porter to Komer/11, letter No. 8 from Komer to Porter dated 11 May 1966, p. 2 (declassified January 1989).
38 LBJ/NSF/Komer File/3/Porter to Komer/5, letter No. 14, dated 20 August 1966, p. 1 (declassified January 1989).
39 LBJ/NSF/Files of Komer/3/Porter to Komer/11, letter No. 2, dated 13 April 1966 (declassified January 1989).
40 LBJ/NSF/Files of Komer/3/Porter to Komer/9, letter No. 10 from Komer to Porter dated 27 July 1966, p. 2 (declassified January 1989).
41 LBJ/NSF/Files of Komer/3/Porter to Komer II/68, telex to the President from Komer dated 6 May 1966, p. 1 (declassified December 1988).
42 Ibid.
43 LBJ/NSF/Files of Komer/3/Porter to Komer II/12, telex from Wheeler to Johnson, McConnell, McDonald, Greene, Rostow, Rusk, McNamara, Vance, McNaughton dated 5 July 1966, p. 1 (declassified April 1987).
44 Ibid.
45 Ibid., p. 2.
46 Ibid.
47 LBJ/NSF/Memos to the President/9/W. W. Rostow V. 10/17, transcript of Saigon 3129 to the President from Lodge dated 10 August 1966, pp. 4–5.
48 Ibid., p. 6.
49 Ibid., p. 3.
50 See LBJ/Papers of William C. Westmoreland/8/V. 7/77, telex MAC 5740 to Sharp from Westmoreland, dated 8 July 1966, p. 9.
51 LBJ/Komer–Leonhart Files/22/RD Reports/4, memo to Komer from Timmes, 'Report of Finding Related to Revolutionary Development Program in Vietnam,' dated 12 October 1966, with attached report, p. 1.
52 LBJ/NSF/Files of Komer/3/Porter to Komer I/5, letter No. 14 to Porter from Komer dated 20 August 1966, p. 2 (declassified January 1989).
53 LBJ/Papers of William C. Westmoreland/8/T7/77, telex MAC 5740 to Sharp from Westmoreland, dated 8 July 1966, p. 9.
54 LBJ/NSF/Memos to the President/10/W W. Rostow V. 11/16a, memo to the President from Taylor, 'Concept of Military Operations in South Vietnam,' dated 30 August 1966 (declassified May 1989).
55 Ibid., p. 1.
56 Ibid., p. 2.
57 Ibid., p. 2.
58 LBJ/NSF/Files of Komer/6/Report to President I/77, 77a, memo to the President from Komer with attached report 'The Other War in Vietnam – A Progress Report,' dated 13 September 1966.
59 Ibid., p. 23.
60 LBJ/NSF/Files of Komer/7/Pacification/3, report, 'Giving a New Thrust to Pacification: Analysis, Concept and Management,' dated 7 August 1966, p. 10.

61 Ibid.
62 Ibid.
63 LBJ/NSF/Files of Komer/6/Reports to President I/80, FY 1967 Goals, dated 22 August, 1966.
64 LBJ/NSF/NSCH/Manila Conference/45/V. II/T30/64, memo to the President from McNamara, 'Actions Recommended for Vietnam,' dated 15 October 1966.
65 Ibid., p. 4.
66 Ibid.
67 Ibid., p. 5.
68 LBJ/NSF/NSCH/45/Manila Conference/V. II/T29/62, memo to W. W. Rostow from Komer dated 16 October 1966.
69 LBJ/NSF/Memos to the President/11/W. W. Rostow V. 15/8, memo to the President from Rostow, dated November 1966 (declassified February 1990).
70 Ibid.
71 'A Strategy for Viet Nam, 1967' op. cit., p. 2.
72 Ibid., pp. 8–9.
73 Ibid., pp. 11–12.
74 Ibid., p. 12.
75 Ibid., pp. 12–14.
76 Ibid., p. 21.
77 Ibid.
78 LBJ/NSF/Files of Komer/5/Helms/17b, memo to the President from Leonhart, 'Visit to Vietnam – August 1966,' dated 30 August 1966. Copies were sent by Komer to Rusk, McNamara, Taylor, W. W. Rostow, Moyers and McNaughton (declassified February 1989).
79 LBJ/NSF/Files of Komer/7/Manila/1, letter to Secretary of State Rusk from Komer dated 2 December 1966, p. 2 (declassified December 1988).
80 LBJ/NSF/Memos to the President/12/W. W. Rostow V. 15/96, 96a, 96b, 96c, memo to the President from Rostow with attachments including report by Lansdale, 'The Battleground in 1967,' dated 17 November 1967 (declassified January 1989).
81 LBJ/NSF/Files of Komer/7/Pacification/3, report, 'Giving a New Thrust to Pacification: An Analysis, Concept and Management,' dated 7 August 1966.
82 LBJ/NSF/Files of Komer/5/McNamara–Vance–McNaughton/63a, letter to McNamara from Komer dated 1 September 1966 (declassified December 1988).
83 Ibid., p. 2.
84 LBJ/NSF/Files of Komer/7/Pacification/1, letter to Maxwell Taylor from Komer dated 26 September 1966.
85 LBJ/NSF/Files of Komer/5/McNamara–Vance–McNaughton/58, memo to McNamara from Komer, 'Key Matters on Which October Decisions Needed,' dated 9 September 1966, p. 3 (declassified December 1988).
86 Ibid., p. 4.
87 LBJ/NSF/Files of Komer/5/McNamara–Vance–McNaughton/56, memo to McNamara, Rusk, Helms, Gaud and Marks from Komer, dated 29 September 1966 (declassified December 1988).
88 Ibid., p. 3.
89 LBJ/NSF/Meetings/1/Meetings with the President Apr 66–Jun 67/8g, telex from Katzenbach to SecState, Rostow and the President dated 18 October 1966 (declassified January 1988).
90 LBJ/NSF/Meetings/1/Meetings with the President Apr 66 to Jun 67/10d, memo to Rusk from Leonard Ungar, 'Ambassador Porter's Views on

Secretary McNamara's Proposal to Place the Viet-Nam Pacification/RD Program Under COMUSMACV,' dated 2 October 1966, p. 2 (declassified January 1988) together with document 10c, cover memo to the President from Rostow dated 4 October 1966.

91 LBJ/NSF/Files of Komer/5/McNamara–Vance–McNaughton/32, 32a, 44, memo to Vance, Katzenbach and Rostow dated 30 November 1966 (declassified December 1986); memo, 'A Strategic Plan for 1967 in Vietnam,' dated 29 November 1966 (declassified December 1988); memo, 'Vietnam Prognosis for 1967–68,' dated 28 November 1966 (declassified February 1988).

92 'Vietnam Prognosis,' op. cit., p. 1.

93 Ibid., p. 2.

94 Ibid., p. 5.

95 LBJ/Komer–Leonhart Files/2/Chieu Hoi (II)/7, Rand memo 4864–ISA/ARPA, by Lucien Pye, 'Observations on the Chieu Hoi Program,' dated January 1966; 57, memo, 'the GVN/US Joint Chieu Hoi Program, Psychological Operations,' dated 15 April 1966; 57a, JUSPAO/FDD, 'Guidelines to Chieu Hoi Psychological Operations: the Chieu Hoi Inducement Program,' dated April 1966; 51, USAID/FO/Chieu Hoi Section, 'The Chieu Hoi Program: Information and Guidelines,' dated June 1966.

96 LBJ/Komer–Leonhart Files/3/Chieu Hoi (III)/62a, report from M. L. Osborne, Chieu Hoi Project Manager, dated 15 December 1966.

97 Ibid., p. 6.

98 Ibid., p. 6.

99 'A Strategic Plan for 1967 in Vietnam,' op. cit. See also, LBJ/NSF/Meetings/ 1/Meetings with the President for Apr 66–Jun 67/2b, lunch with the President, 13 December 1966, draft NSAM, 'Strategic guidelines for 1967 in Vietnam,' dated 10 December 1966 (declassified May 1987).

100 'Strategic Plan,' op. cit., p. 1.

101 LBJ/NSF/Files of Komer/6/Gen. Maxwell Taylor/6, memo to Taylor from Komer, 'Matters to Look Into in Vietnam,' dated 13 January 1967 (declassified March 1989).

102 LBJ/NSF/Files of Komer/6/Gen. Maxwell Taylor/7, 7a, letter to the President dated 30 January 1967 and 'Memorandum for Record, Viet-Nam Visit, January 20–25, 1967,' dated 30 January 1967 (both declassified March 1989).

103 Ibid., 'Memorandum for Record,' pp. 2–5.

104 Ibid., p. 7.

105 Ibid., p. 8.

106 LBJ/NSF/Files of Komer/6/Gen. Maxwell Taylor/2a, letter to the President from Taylor dated 6 February 1967 (declassified March 1989).

107 LBJ/NSF/Files of Komer/5/McNamara–Vance–McNaughton/56, memo to McNamara from Komer, dated 29 September 1966 (declassified December 1988).

6 THE YEAR OF VICTORY?

1 LBJ/NSF/CF/VN/39/M63/96b, intelligence memo, 'The War in Vietnam,' dated 9 January 1967, p. 1.

2 Ibid., p. 20.

3 Ibid., p. 4.

4 Ibid., p. 15.

5 Ibid., p. 17.
6 Ibid., p. 2.
7 LBJ/Papers of William C. Westmoreland/10/V. 12 (I)/44, special communication to Sharp and Wheeler from Westmoreland dated January 1967, p. 2.
8 Ibid., p. 5.
9 Ibid. and LBJ/Papers of William C. Westmoreland/10/V. 12 (II)/77, telex to COMUSMACV from III MAF, 'Visit of COMUSMACV to I CTZ,' dated 20 January 1967.
10 Ibid., p. 8.
11 LBJ/NSF/CF/VN/81–84/3E (1)b/17a, memo to McNamara from JCS, 'Portions of a Draft DPM with Factual Corrections,' dated 29 May 1967, p. 7, citing memo from Wheeler, CM 2377.
12 LBJ/NSF/Files of Komer/5/W. W. Rostow/5, memo to Katzenbach from Komer dated 11 January 1967 (declassified August 1989).
13 LBJ/NSF/Memos to the President/16/W. W. Rostow V. 19/119, memo to the President from Rostow dated 19 January 1967.
14 LBJ/NSF/CF/VN/39/M63/111a, memo to the President from Leonhart, 'Visit to Vietnam – December 1966, Report and Recommendations,' dated 30 December 1966.
15 Ibid., p. 4.
16 Ibid., p. 8.
17 LBJ/NSF/NSC Meetings/2/T35/2b, NSC meeting of 8 February 1967, report by Wheeler, 'Air Campaign Against the North,' p. 1.
18 Ibid., p. 3.
19 LBJ/NSF/CF/VN/190/JASON Study/1, memo to Rostow from Ginsburgh, 'VC/NVA Logistics and Manpower,' dated 13 September 1966 and 'A Study of Data Related to Viet Cong/North Vietnamese Army Logistics and Manpower,' 81 pages, dated 29 August 1966.
20 LBJ/NSF/Meetings/1/Meetings with the President Apr 66–Jun 67/52b, 'Outline' n.d. (declassified June 1989).
21 Ibid., pp. 1–14.
22 Ibid., p. 15. Compare with the 60-kilometer figure given in LBJ/Papers of William C. Westmoreland/10/V. 12/12, 'Comments on the 7 December 66 Plan,' n.d. Incl. 2, 'SHINING BRASS,' para. 3d.
23 LBJ/NSF/Meetings/1/Meetings with the President Apr 66–June 67/52b, 'Outline' n.d. (declassified June 1989). Rostow annotation on cover page.
24 Ibid., p. 17.
25 Rostow annotation on cover page.
26 Ibid., p. 18.
27 Ibid., p. 19.
28 Rostow annotation on cover page.
29 Komer had met with Rostow prior to this trip and Rostow had briefed the President concerning it. The most important feature of this briefing was the strong agreement between Komer and Rostow concerning the necessity of US interference in the forthcoming presidential elections to assure that Ky and Thieu were not simply perpetuated and that Ky and Thieu should not oppose one another which would split the military and that regionalism be obviated. See LBJ/NSF/Files of Komer/5/W. W. Rostow/9, memo to the President from Rostow dated 4 February 1967 (declassified August 1989).
30 LBJ/NSF/Files of Komer/6/Supplement to Komer Report/2, memo to the President from Komer, 'Change for the Better – Latest impressions from Vietnam,' dated 28 February 1967, p. 1 (declassified February 1989).

31 In mid-January Komer had made it clear what sort of action the US should take to achieve useful goals within the South Vietnamese elections: take out coup insurance, send Thieu back to the Army, discourage sectionalism, limit factionalism. See LBJ/NSF/Files of Komer/5/W. W. Rostow/17, memo to Katzenbach, Vance, Rostow from Komer, 'Action Program to Promote a Favourable Political Evolution in Saigon,' dated 13 January 1967 (declassified August 1989).

32 Ibid., p. 3. See also as confirmation of Komer's appreciation of the growing status of land reform, LBJ/NSF/CF/VN/61/Vietnam Land Reform 1 D (2)/32, letter to Komer from James D. Rosenthal, land reform specialist, dated 14 February 1967.

33 Ibid., p. 5.

34 Ibid., p. 7.

35 Ibid.

36 Ibid.

37 Ibid., p. 8.

38 Ibid., p. 10.

39 LBJ/Papers of William C. Westmoreland/10/V. 12 (2)/89, memo for record, 'MACV Commanders' Conference, 22 January 1967,' dated 9 February 1967, p. 19.

40 Ibid., p. 20.

41 Ibid., p. 17.

42 LBJ/Komer–Leonhart Files/2/Chieu Hoi (I)/18d, memo to Komer from O. Williams–OCO/CH, 'The Chieu Hoi Program,' dated 17 February 1967, p. 6.

43 LBJ/NSF/CF/VN/61/Land Reform/32, letter to Komer from Rosenthal, OCO Saigon, dated 14 February 1967 with 32a, memo, 'Some Current Aspects of Land Reform in Vietnam,' dated February 1967 and 32b, memo to Porter from Rosenthal, 'Land Reform,' dated 13 February 1967.

44 LBJ/NSF/Files of Komer/3/Ambassador Bunker/12b, memo to the President from Komer, dated 6 March 1967, p. 2 (declassified June 1989). See also 12c, memo to the President from Ambassador Chet Bowles re land reform, dated 27 February 1967 (declassified July 1989).

45 LBJ/Komer–Leonhart Files/21/Private Channel Messages/55, telex to Porter from Leonhart, dated 16 March 1967 (declassified July 1989).

46 LBJ/Komer–Leonhart Files/11/IDA Project Packard/1, memo to Komer and Leonhart from Holbrooke dated 12 January 1967 with 1a, memo to Leonard Sullivan, Deputy Director Southeast Asia Matters, DoD from Joshua Menkes, Institute for Defense Analysis, 'Trip Report,' dated 10 January 1967. Project Packard was ongoing and would continue to influence perceptions at the command level.

47 LBJ/Komer–Leonhart Files/1/Agriculture (I)/7, 'Progress Report on Secretary Freeman's Recommendation for Vietnam Agriculture,' dated March 1967.

48 LBJ/Komer–Leonhart Files/1/Agriculture (I)/7c, 7d, 'Status Report of Actions Taken to Implement the Recommendations and Suggestions of HEW Secretary Gardner and his Staff Following their March 1966 Visit to Vietnam,' dated March 1967.

49 See LBJ/NSF/International Meetings and Travel/12, 13/Guam March 67 (3)/entire file.

50 LBJ/NSF/Meetings/1/Meetings with the President Apr 66–Jun 67/41, 'Lunch Meeting with the President, Tuesday March 7, 1967,' p. 2.

51 173rd Airborne Brigade (Separate), 'Combat Operation After Action Report, Operation JUNCTION CITY I,' dated 15 June 1967. Noteworthy was the very low level of Viet Cong or suspected Viet Cong captured or

detained, five, and the number of weapons recovered, 17 bolt-action rifles, 8 automatic rifles, 1 light machine gun and 2 B–40 launchers compared with the body count, 266 (pp. 12, 36). The intelligence catch of nearly 11,000 documents may have been significant.

52 LBJ/NSF/Meetings/1/Meetings with the President/41a, 'Agenda' for lunch with the President 7 March 1967 (declassified May 1987).

53 LBJ/NSF/Files of Komer/3/Ambassador Bunker/3a, memo to Komer from Holbrooke, 'Warning Flags on the Saigon Political Scene,' dated 11 April 1967 (declassified June 1989).

54 LBJ/Papers of William C. Westmoreland/11/V. 15 (I)/48, telex to COMUSMACV from CG II FFORCEV, 'Visit by COMUSMACV to II FFORCEV,' dated 16 April 1966.

55 LBJ/Papers of William C. Westmoreland/11/V. 15/44, telex to Sharp and Wheeler from Westmoreland, 'situation in I Corps,' dated 12 April 1967 (declassified January 1989).

56 Ibid., p. 2.

57 Ibid., p. 3.

58 See LBJ/Papers of William C. Westmoreland/11/V. 15 (1)/48, telex to COMUSMACV from CG II FFORCEV, dated 14 April 1967, particularly pp. 4–5.

59 LBJ/NSF/CF/VN/66/2A (1)/49c, intelligence memo, 'The Communist Build-up in South Vietnam's Northern I Corps,' dated 11 May 1967.

60 Ibid., p. 2.

61 Ibid., pp. 2, 11.

62 Ibid., p. 9.

63 LBJ/NSF/CF/VN/66/2A (1)/54, intelligence memo, 'The Communist Build-up in Northern South Vietnam,' dated 22 November 1966.

64 Ibid., p. 7.

65 Ibid., p. 9.

66 LBJ/Papers of Paul Warnke–John McNaughton File/5/McNaughton V. XIII/Memos 1967 (1)/1, untitled memo on strategies for Vietnam, May 1967 (declassified February 1986).

67 Ibid., p. 1.

68 Ibid., p. 5. On morale see also LBJ/WHCF/CF/72/ND19–CO 312, July to December 66/Rand report by Leon Goure, 'Quarterly Report on Viet Cong Motivation and Morale Project, October–December 1966,' dated 30 January 1967.

69 Ibid., p. 6.

70 Ibid., p. 8.

71 Ibid., p. 12.

72 Ibid. pp. 20–2.

73 Ibid., p. 22.

74 LBJ/Papers of Paul Warnke–John McNaughton Files/5/McNaughton V. XIII/19, JCS Study, 'Alternative Courses of Action for Southeast Asia,' dated May 1967, p. 2.

75 Ibid., pp. 2, 36.

76 Ibid., p. 43.

77 Ibid., p. 42.

78 Ibid., p. 45.

79 Ibid., p. 46.

80 Ibid., p. 48.

81 Ibid., p. 49.

82 See the arguments of ibid., pp. 56–61.

83 Ibid., pp. 62–3.
84 Ibid., pp. 77–81 comprise what passes for an assessment of the impact of the proposed escalations on the diplomatic community and US domestic opinion.
85 LBJ/NSF/CF/VN/81–84/3E (1)/Future Military Operations/18, memo to members of Katzenbach Committee from Cyrus Vance, dated 20 May 1967 with 18a, draft memo for the President from JCS, 'Future Actions in Vietnam,' dated 19 May 1967 (declassified June 1989).
86 Ibid., p. 2.
87 Ibid., pp. 1–5.
88 Ibid., p. 6.
89 Ibid.
90 Ibid., p. 8.
91 Ibid., pp. 8, 14.
92 Ibid., pp. 14–16.
93 Ibid., pp. 18b–18d.
94 Ibid., p. 18d.
95 LBJ/NSF/CF/VN/81–84/3E (1)/Future Military Operations/17, memo to SecDef from Wheeler, 'Future Actions in Vietnam,' dated 29 May 1967, p. 2 (declassified June 1989).
96 For the disclaimer of advocacy see LBJ/NSF/CF/VN/81–84/3 E (1)/Future Military Operations/17a, appendix, 'Portions of Draft DPM with Factual Corrections,' p. 10 note.
97 LBJ/NSF/CF/VN/81–84/3E (1)/Future Military Operations/18a, draft memorandum for the President, 'Future Actions in Vietnam,' dated 19 May 1967, p. 18a (declassified June 1989). This draft was sent by Cyrus Vance OSD/ISA to Katzenbach and the VNCC.
98 LBJ/NSF/Memos to the President/14/W. W. Rostow V. 27/147a, transcript of Saigon 24624 to the President from Bunker, dated 3 May 1967.
99 Ibid., p. 5.
100 LBJ/NSF/Memos to the President/12/W. W. Rostow V. 29/7a, 50a, 94a, transcript of Saigon 25260, dated 10 May 1967; transcript of Saigon 26566 dated 25 May 1967; transcript of Saigon 27204, dated 31 May 1967.
101 Op. cit., Saigon 27204, p. 3.
102 Ibid., p. 2.
103 Ibid., pp. 10–12.
104 See as examples, LBJ/Papers of William C. Westmoreland/11/V. 15 (1)/50, telex to Wheeler and Sharp, MAC 5994, dated 25 June 1967 and 60, telex to Wheeler and Sharp, MAC 6150, dated 1 July 1967 (both declassified May 1989).
105 LBJ/NSF/CF/VN/81–84/3E(1)A/Future Military Operations/14, memo to W. W. Rostow from Robert Ginsburgh, 'Future Military Operations in Vietnam,' dated 3 June 1967 with 14a, memo to SecDef from JCS, JCSM-312-67, 'Air Operations Against NVN,' and 14b, 'Appendix to Basic Report' (all declassified June 1989).
106 Ibid., 'Appendix,' pp. 45–46; 'Air Operations Against NVN, p. 7.
107 Ibid., 'Air Operations Against NVN,' p. 1.
108 LBJ/Papers of Paul Warnke–John McNaughton Files/5/McNaughton memos XIII (2)/33, memo to McNamara from DCI Richard Helms dated 1 June 1967 with 33a CIA memo TS 196752/67, 'Evaluation of Alternative Programs for Bombing North Vietnam,' dated 1 June 1967.
109 Ibid., p. 5.
110 Ibid., pp. 10–11.

111 Ibid., p. 12.
112 Ibid., pp. 16–17.
113 LBJ/Papers of Paul Warnke–John McNaughton Files/5/McNaughton XIII/41, memo to McNaughton from Brown dated 5 June 1967.
114 LBJ/Papers of Paul Warnke–John McNaughton Files/5/McNaughton XIII/39, memo to McNamara from Brown, dated 9 June 1967, p. 10.
115 Ibid., pp. 10–11.
116 LBJ/Papers of Paul Warnke–John McNaughton File/5/McNaughton XIII (b)/42, memo to McNamara from Brown dated 3 July 1967.
117 LBJ/Papers of William C. Westmoreland/11/V. 15 (1)/65, talking paper, 'Justification of Continued Bombing of NVN,' dated May 1967.
118 Ibid., p. 2.
119 LBJ/NSF/CF/VN/259/McNamara Trip, No. IX/1, memo to the President from Rostow, dated 13 July 1967 with 1b, 'Briefing by Ambassador Bunker,' n.d., p. 25 (declassified January 1986).
120 Ibid. p. 26.
121 Ibid., pp. 3–4.
122 Ibid., p. 5.
123 Ibid., p. 6.
124 Ibid., p. 11.
125 Ibid., p. 12.
126 LBJ/Papers of William C. Westmoreland/11/V. 15 (2)/4, talking paper for SecDef Briefing, 'Outline of Assessment of Alternatives,' dated 6 July 1967.
127 Ibid., p. 1.
128 Ibid., p. 2.
129 Ibid.
130 Ibid.
131 LBJ/Papers of Paul Warnke–John McNaughton File/6/McNaughton V. XIV (3)/27, MACCOC briefing, 'Current Operations,' dated 7 July 1967.
132 Ibid., p. 4.
133 Ibid., p. 7.
134 Ibid., p. 8.
135 LBJ/Komer–Leonhart Files/15/Memos to the President (WML)34, memo to the President from Leonhart, 'The New Civil/Military Organization in Vietnam,' dated 7 June 1967.
136 LBJ/Komer–Leonhart Files/21/Private Channel Messages/29a, telex to Komer from Leonhart, dated 29 June 1967 (declassified July 1989).
137 LBJ/Komer–Leonhart Files/11/ICEX/30h, memo to Bunker from Komer, 'Organization for Attack on VC Infrastructure,' dated 14 June 1967 (declassified July 1989).
138 LBJ/Komer–Leonhart Files/11/ICEX/30m, 'Phased Plan for Developing the Attack Against VC Infrastructure,' n.d.
139 LBJ/Komer–Leonhart, Files/11/ICEX/30k, 'ICEX Staffing Requirements,' n.d. (declassified July 1989).
140 LBJ/Komer–Leonhart Files/11/ICEX/30, memo to Leonhart from Volney Warner, dated 27 July 1967 (declassified July 1986) and 30g, 'A Concept of Organization for Attack on VC Infrastructure,' n.d. (declassified July 1989).

7 HOW DO WE KNOW IF WE'RE WINNING?

1 William R. Corson, *The Betrayal*, New York, 1969.
2 LBJ/NSF/CF/VN/78, 79/3C NVN Infiltration into SVN/49, letter to Director, DIA from Admiral Sharp, 'Intelligence Conference Report,' dated 21 February 1967, with 49a, 'Report of Intelligence Conference,' n.d.
3 Ibid., 49a, p. 1.
4 Ibid., p. 2.
5 Ibid., pp. 9–10.
6 Ibid., pp. 3, 14–15.
7 Ibid., pp. 4, 12–14.
8 Ibid., p. 21.
9 Ibid., pp. 5, 22.
10 Ibid., p. 24.
11 Ibid., p. 14.
12 Ibid., p. 15.
13 Ibid., p. 16.
14 Ibid., p. 16.
15 LBJ/NSF/CF/VN/187/MACV Report–O.B./1, MACV, OACS–Intelligence, 'Order of Battle Reference Manual–Strength,' dated 12 February 1967, p. i.
16 Ibid., pp. 21–7.
17 Ibid., appendices A and B.
18 See ibid., Charts 1–3.
19 LBJ/NSF/CF/VN/69/2C (1)b/General Military Activities/1, memo to W. W. Rostow from R. J. Smith, Deputy Director for Intelligence, CIA, dated 26 May 1967 with 1a, CIA report, 'Phases of the War in South Vietnam 1963–First Quarter 1967: An Analysis by Moving Averages.'
20 Ibid., 1a, p. ii.
21 Ibid., p. iii.
22 Ibid., pp. 6–8.
23 Ibid., p. 10.
24 Ibid., p. 11.
25 Ibid., figures 1–5.
26 Ibid., figure 5.
27 LBJ/NSF/CF/VN/68, 69/2C (1)a/General Military Activity/39, memo to Rostow from Ginsburgh, dated 28 October 1967, 'The Military Situation in Vietnam: Alternative Projections for October 1968.'
28 LBJ/Komer–Leonhart, Files/1/Blueprint for Vietnam/1, memo to Rostow from Leonhart, 'Blueprint for Vietnam,' dated 11 September 1967 (declassified August 1989) and 2, report, 'Blueprint for Viet-Nam,' n.d. (declassified February 1989).
29 LBJ/NSF/CF/VN/68, 69/2C (1)a/9a, memo to the President from Helms, dated 14 November 1967 with attachments.
30 Ibid., pp. 1–2, C–11, 2.
31 LBJ/NSF/CF/VN/81–84/3E (1)A 6/65–12/67 Future Military Operations/9, memo to the President from Rostow, dated 15 November 1967 (declassified October 1989).
32 Ibid., pp. I–2, C–11, 2.
33 LBJ/NSF/CF/VN/161/Helms Memos/1, memo to the President from Helms, dated 22 November 1967, p. 5.
34 LBJ/NSF/CF/VN/68,69/2C (1) a General Military Activity/50, memo to the

President from Rostow, dated 29 November 1967 with 50a, memo to Rostow from McCafferty, 'Body Count Verification,' dated 29 November 1967 and 50b, memo to Director, DIA from MJG Kerwin, MACV COS, dated 24 November 1967 including MACJ343 report, 'Enemy Body Count Survey Report,' dated 9 November 1967.

35 Ibid., report, p. 3.
36 Ibid., appendix, p. 2.
37 Ibid., appendix, p. 9.
38 LBJ/NSF/CF/VN/68,69/2C (1)a General Military Activity/48a, Saigon A–324, 'An Assessment of the Current Enemy Situation,' dated 25 November 1967, p. 1.
39 Ibid., p. II–3.
40 Ibid.
41 LBJ/Papers of William C. Westmoreland/13/V. 20 (I)/15, telex to Sharp and Wheeler from Westmoreland, 'COMUSMACV Monthly Assessment,' dated 11 August 1967, p. 15. A transcribed copy was forwarded to the President. LBJ/NSF/68, 69/2C (1)a General Military Activity/46, memo to the President, 'General Westmoreland's Military Assessment for July,' dated 11 August 1967.
42 LBJ/Papers of William C. Westmoreland/13/ V. 21 (I)/27, telex to Wheeler from Westmoreland, 'Assessment of Progress by CTZ,' dated 25 August 1967.
43 Ibid., p. 14.
44 Ibid., p. 2.
45 Ibid., p. 8.
46 Ibid., p. 9.
47 Ibid., p. 13.
48 LBJ/Papers of William C. Westmoreland/13/V. 21 (I)/65, telex to Sharp and Wheeler, 'Monthly Assessment,' dated 6 September 1967. A transcribed copy was forwarded to the White House. LBJ/NSF/CF/V-N/Memos to the President IV/51d.
49 Ibid., p. 29.
50 Ibid., p. 27.
51 LBJ/Papers of William C. Westmoreland/13/V. 21 (II)/71, telex to Acting Chairman JCS General Johnson and Sharp, dated 27 September 1967.
52 Ibid., p. 1.
53 Ibid., p. 7.
54 LBJ/NSF/CF/VN/68, 69/2C (1)a General Military Activity/44, memo to the President from Rostow with 41a, 'Summary,' and 41b, 'Text of General Westmoreland's Military Assessment for September,' dated 10 October 1967.
55 Ibid., 41b, p. 1.
56 Ibid., p. 14.
57 Ibid., p. 8.
58 Ibid., p. 4.
59 LBJ/NSF/CF/VN/58, 59/2 C (1)B–1/General Military Activity/2b, III MAF, 'Operations of US Marine Forces, Vietnam, September 1967,' with memos of transmittal 2, 2a.
60 LBJ/NSF/Memos to the President/22/ W. W. Rostow V. 45/29, memo to the President from Rostow dated 7 October 1967 with 29a, memo to the President from McCafferty, 'Viet Cong Difficulties in First Corps,' dated 5 October 1967.

61 LBJ/Papers of William C. Westmoreland/14/V. 24/51, telex to SecState from AmEmb Saigon, dated 7 November 1967.
62 Ibid., p. 6.
63 Ibid., p. 10.
64 Ibid., pp. 15, 20–1.
65 Ibid., p. 22.
66 Ibid., p. 26.
67 LBJ/NSF/Memos to the President/27/W. W. Rostow V. 50/62, memo to the President from Rostow, dated 10 November 1967 with attachment, 62a, transcribed texts of Saigon 7867 and Saigon 10573, 'Measurement of Progress,' dated November 1967.
68 Ibid., p. 1.
69 Ibid., pp. 3–19 gives a point-by-point rendition of the aspects of success to be stressed. As examples of the statistical approach to evaluating success see the State Department Bureau of Intelligence and Research weekly publication, 'Selected Military Statistics on the Vietnamese Hostilities.' Drawn from Mission MACV and DIA sources the numbers presented in this summary were widely circulated within the Administration as well as the Department of State. The statistical abstract was not interpreted by INR and thus allowed the user to employ the numbers which he liked to measure or demonstrate progress. As a result, purportedly neutral assessments were in fact highly colored. Examples of the series are scattered throughout LBJ/NSF/CF/VN/58, 59/2C, General Military Activity.
70 LBJ/WHCF/Meeting Notes File/2/Meeting with Foreign Policy Advisors, 2 November, 1967.
71 LBJ/NSF/CF/VN/68, 69/2C (1)a General Military Activity/48a, report, 'An Assessment of the Current Enemy Situation,' dated 25 November 1967.
72 Ibid., p. II–3.
73 Ibid., p. 11.
74 Ibid., pp. III–3, III–4.
75 LBJ/Papers of William C. Westmoreland/14/V. 25 (II)/64, transcript of General Westmoreland's speech before the National Press Club, dated 21 November 1967.
76 LBJ/Papers of William C. Westmoreland/14/25 (2)/104, telex from Westmoreland to Abrams, 'Concept of Situation Portrayed During Recent Visit to Washington,' dated 26 November 1967.
77 25th Infantry Division, 'Combat Operation After Action Report – Operation GADSDEN' including report of 196th Infantry Brigade, dated 22 March 1967. 3rd Brigade, 4th Infantry Division, 'Combat Operation After Action Report – Operation GADSDEN,' dated 10 March 1967.
78 25th Division AAR, op. cit., pp. 52–3.
79 1st Infantry Division, 'Combat Operation After Action Report – Operation JUNCTION CITY,' 8 May 1967 including Brigade Division Artillery, Aviation, Engineer and Support Services After Action Reports. 173rd Airborne Brigade, 'Combat Operation After Action Report – Operation JUNCTION CITY,' 15 June 1967, 11th Armored Cavalry Regiment, 'Combat Operation After Action Report – Operation JUNCTION CITY,' n.d., 3rd Brigade, 4th Infantry Division, 'Combat Operation After Report – Operation JUNCTION CITY,' 12 May 1967, 1st Brigade, 9th Infantry Division, 'Combat Operation After Action Report – Operation JUNCTION CITY,' n.d.
80 1st Infantry Division, AAR, pp. 13–14.
81 Ibid., p. 15.
82 Ibid., annex C, incl. 3.

83 Ibid., annex C, incl. 4. The body count was given as 609 which represented over a third of all enemy fatalities reported by the division for JUNCTION CITY.

84 Ibid., annex C, incl. 2.

85 Ibid., p. 18.

86 3rd Brigade, 4th Infantry Division, 'Combat Operation After Action Report – Operation FORT NISQUALLY,' 6 June 1967, p. 8.

87 Ibid., p. 20.

88 Ibid.

89 Ibid., p. 22.

90 1st Brigade, 101st Airborne Division, 'Combat Operation After Action Report – Operation PICKETT,' 15 February 1967.

91 Ibid., p. 12.

92 Ibid., pp. 13–14.

93 4th Infantry Division, 'Combat Operation After Action Report – Operation SAM HOUSTON,' 16 May 1967.

94 Ibid., pp. 19, 22.

95 Ibid., p. 19.

96 See ibid., pp. 42–4, 50–1 for implications of new enemy tactics.

97 Ibid., p. 51.

98 1st Brigade, 101st Airborne Division, 'Combat Operation After Action Report – Operation FARRAGUT,' n.d.

99 Ibid., p. 7.

100 Ibid., p. 14.

101 1st Brigade, 101st Airborne Division, 'Combat Operation After Action Report Operation GATLING I/II.'

102 Ibid., p. 6.

103 25th Infantry Division, 'Combat Operation After Action Report – Operation AHINA,' 16 July 1967.

104 Ibid., p. 5.

105 Ibid., pp. 5–6, 13.

106 Ibid., p. 14.

107 1st Infantry Division, 'Combat Operation After Action Report – Operation DALLAS,' 28 June 1967.

108 Ibid., p. 10.

109 Ibid., pp. 4–5. 1st Squadron, 4th Cavalry, 'Combat Operation After Action Report – Operation DALLAS,' 13 June 1967. The destroyed tank was not mentioned in the 25th Division COAAR.

110 2nd Brigade, 9th Infantry Division, 'Combat Operation After Action Report – Operation HOPTAC XVI,' 16 June 1967.

111 Ibid., p. 9.

112 See 9th Infantry Division 'COAAR – Operation AKRON,' n.d.; 11th Armored Cavalry Regiment 'COAAR – Operation AKRON,' n.d.; 11th ACR, 'COAAR – Operation KITTY HAWK,' n.d.; 11th ACR, 'COAAR – Operation MANHATTAN; 1st Infantry Division, 'COAAR – Operation PAUL BUNYAN.' In particular, see 1st Infantry Division, 'COAAR – Operation BILLINGS,' in which the division's three brigades reported that they had destroyed the 271st VC Regiment for the fourth time in just over a year. Compare with 5th Special Forces Group COAARs, PIKESVILLE, BLACKJACK 34, BLACKJACK 41, ARROWHEAD, BLACKJACK 42.

113 1st Brigade, 101st Airborne Division, 'Combat Operation After Action Report – Operation WHEELER,' 11 December 1967.

114 Ibid., p. 1–1.

115 Ibid., p. 12.
116 Ibid., p. 1–4.
117 9th Infantry Division, 'Combat Operation After Action Report – Operation SANTA FE I/II/III,' 20 January 1968.
118 Ibid., p. 38.
119 4th Infantry Division, 'Special Combat Operation After Action Report – "The Battle for Dak To,"' 3 January 1968.
120 Ibid., p. 19.
121 Ibid., p. 21.
122 Ibid., pp. 46–7.
123 Ibid., p. 24.
124 Ibid., p. 34.
125 Ibid., p. 35 gives the lower number for both US and ARVN KIA while p. 16 gives the higher.
126 Ibid., p. 66.
127 Ibid., p. 31.
128 Ibid., p. 31.
129 173rd Airborne Brigade, 'Combat Operation After Action Report – The Battle of Dak To,' 10 December 1967, p. 41.
130 Eighty-eight journalists and cameramen covered the 173rd Airborne Brigade alone including four teams from CBS and two from ABC. See ibid., inclosure 7.
131 LBJ/NSF/National Intelligence Estimates/5/14.3 North Vietnam/4, SNIE 14.3-1-67, 'Problems of Viet Cong Recruitment and Morale,' 3 August 1967, p. 4 (declassified March 1990).
132 Ibid., p. 3.
133 LBJ/NSF/CF/VN/59/1 C (2) Revolutionary Development Programs/19c, memo to Henry Owen from Sam Huntington, 'Comments on Bob Komer's Comments,' dated 15 January 1968 (declassified March 1990).
134 LBJ/Komer–Leonhart Files/1/Blueprint–Vietnam/2, report, 'Blueprint for Vietnam,' August–September 1967, p. III-1 (declassified February 1989).
135 LBJ/Komer–Leonhart Files/18/Pacification (3)/22, MACV Report, Project TAKEOFF, II, 'Assessment of Pacification,' June 1967.
136 Ibid., p. III-1.
137 Ibid., p. XII-1.
138 Ibid., p. XII-2.
139 LBJ/Komer–Leonhart Files/22/RD Combined Campaign/2, Report entitled 'Annex B (Military Support of Pacification) to Combined Campaign Plan, 1968, AB 143' (declassified July 1990).
140 As an excellent albeit typical example see, LBJ/Komer–Leonhart Files/22/-RD/Planning/12 memo to Leonhart from Richard Holbrooke, dated 29 August 1967 with 12b, memo, 'Special Joint Report on Revolutionary Movement,' dated 30 July 1967 (both declassified July 1990).
141 LBJ/Komer–Leonhart Files/11/Project PACKARD/4a, Menkes and Jones, IDA Research Paper P-340, 'Pacification in Vietnam,' June 1967. This draft report was sent to Leonhart by Sullivan in DoD. Copies were sent to Komer and others. The final, toned-down report was issued in December 1967. See LBJ/Komer–Leonhart Files/ 18/ Pacification (3)/ 20.
142 Ibid., pp. 49–50.
143 Ibid., pp. 27, 38, 40–1, 47, 50–1.
144 Ibid., p. 34.
145 Ibid., pp. 20, 29.

146 See as a typical example LBJ/Komer–Leonhart Files/18-Pacification (5)/59a, COMUSMACV NOFORN 41514, telex from MACJ01R to CINCPAC, JCS, DOD, DOS, CIA, 'Pacification in South Vietnam During October 1967,' dated 14 December 1967. This eleven-section, forty-six-page telegram from CORDS purported to demonstrate such 'facts' as the decrease of Viet Cong-controlled population from 19 per cent to 17.2 per cent as well as illustrate the impressive progress made in all sections of the country in all areas of pacification and revolutionary development. Not only was the report badly outdated by the time it arrived in Washington, but its statistical approach obscured all realities. Other examples of the monthly pacification report from Komer's shop include: LBJ/NSF/Komer–Leonhart Files/15/Memos to the President (WML)/18b, telex from COMUSMACV to CINCPAC and JCS, 'Revolutionary Development (July 1967),' 31 August 1967; 9b, telex from COMUSMACV to CINCPAC and JCS, 'Pacification in South Vietnam During August 1967,' 3 October 1967; 4a, telex from COMUSMACV to CINCPAC and JCS, 'Pacification in South Vietnam During September 1967,' 15 November 1967.

147 LBJ/Komer–Leonhart Files/17/Pacification (1)/3a, MACCORDS briefing paper, 'Pacification Program in Vietnam,' dated 23 October 1967, especially pp. 22–8.

148 See as illustrations NSF/Komer–Leonhart Files/18/Pacification (3)/19, MAC–RF–PF Briefing Paper, 'Role of RF/PF in Pacification,' 23 October 1967; Komer–Leonhart/3/Chieu Hoi (II)/26, CORDS Chieu Hoi Division, 'Sector Plan 1968,' 31 December 1967.

149 See as examples LBJ/NSF/CF/VN/68, 69/2C (1)B1 General Military Activity/2b, III MAF, 'Operations of US Marine Forces, Vietnam, September 1967,' pp. 34–49; Komer–Leonhart Files/11/Hamlet Evaluation (2)/47a, HQ III MAF Report, 'Quang Tin Completed RD Hamlet Inspection Report,' dated 30 October 1967 with memo of transmittal to Warner/Leonhart from Komer dated 10 November 1967.

150 LBJ/Komer–Leonhart Files/11/Hamlet Evaluation/31, JUSPAO research report, 'Nationwide Hamlet Survey: Second Interim Summary Report–II Corps,' dated 1 November 1967, p. 6.

151 LBJ/Komer–Leonhart Files/11/Hamlet Evaluation/35, JUSPAO research report, 'Nationwide Hamlet Survey: First Interim Report–I Corps,' 10 October 1967, p. 6.

152 Op. cit. II Corps and ibid., p. 7.

153 LBJ/NSF/CF/VN/58, 59/VN 1C (2) 11/67–12/67/Revolutionary Development/21a, MACV Combined Intelligence Center study, ST 67086, 'Effects of Pacification as Perceived by the VC,' 3 November 1967, with 21, memo of transmittal to W. W. Rostow (declassified June 1989).

154 Ibid., pp. 2, 3, 24.

155 As an example of the HES report and the comforting statistics of success see LBJ/Komer–Leonhart Files/17/Pacification (2)/13, MACV monthly pacification report dated 14 January 1968 covering December 1967, 57 pp.

156 LBJ/NSF/CF/VN/58, 59 VN 1 C (1) Revolutionary Development 3/67 to 10/67/12, telex from AmEmb Saigon to SecState, 'Measurements of Progress,' dated 7 October 1967, p. 1 (declassified June 1989). See also LBJ/NSF/Komer–Leonhart File/16/Monday Group (2)/25e, telex from AmEmb to SecState dated 20 October 1967 regarding the use of statistics to demonstrate to media how GVN control was being extended over a greater percentage of the South Vietnamese population which noted that the data

'cannot confirm' the percentages previously used so estimates by US Government will be employed as these are 'in line with President's most recent speech.'

157 LBJ/NSF/Komer–Leonhart Files/16/Monday Group (2)/22c, telex from AmEmb Saigon to SecState, 'Measurements of Progress,' dated 8 November 1967.

158 Ibid. p. 16.

159 LBJ/Komer–Leonhart Files/8/Econ Strategy/3b, OASD(SA) economics report, 'Inflation, Income and Incentives in Vietnam,' dated 6 November 1967 with memo of transmittal from Enthoven to Leonhart dated 16 November 1967.

160 LBJ/Komer–Leonhart Files/1/Blueprint for Vietnam/2, 'Blueprint for Vietnam,' n.d., p. 7 (declassified February 1989) together with 1, memo to Rostow from Leonhart, 'Blueprint for Vietnam,' dated 11 September 1967 (declassified August 1989).

161 Ibid., p. 7.

162 Ibid.

163 LBJ/NSF/CF/VN/66/2F (1)/29, INR research memo to the secretary from Thomas Hughes, 'Hanoi's Resolve to Statnd Firm on the DMZ Shows No Sign of Weakening,' dated 24 October 1967, p. ii.

164 LBJ/NSF/CF/VN/81–84/3H 2 Appraisal of the Bombing in NVN/4, memo to the President from Rostow, dated 29 August 1967 with 4a, memo to the President from Helms, 'Effects of the Intensified Air War Against North Vietnam,' dated 29 August 1967 (declassified November 1987).

165 Ibid., p. 1.

166 Ibid., p. 2.

167 Ibid., p. 5.

168 For a brief review of the process see LBJ/NSF/Files of Walt W. Rostow/ Pennsylvania/5, memo to the President from Rostow, dated 9 September 1967 (declassified September 1989).

169 LBJ/NSF/Files of Walt W. Rostow/Pennsylvania/3a, memo to the President from Acting Secretary of State, 'Negotiations with North Vietnam,' dated 26 September 1967, p. 2 (declassified January 1990).

170 LBJ/NSF/Files of Walt W. Rostow/9/Pennsylvania/8c, telex to Kissinger from Rusk, dated 12 September 1967 (declassified January 1990).

171 LBJ/NSF/CF/VN/81–84/3 H (1) Appraisal of the Bombing of NVN/2a, memo from A. C. Edmunds to General George Brown, 'CIA Evaluation,' dated 10 October 1967, p. 1 (declassified August 1988). Sent to White House by document 2, memo to Rostow from Brown.

172 Ibid., p. 4.

173 LBJ/NSF/CF/VN/81–84/3 H (1) Appraisal of the Bombing of NVN/1, memo to Rostow from Helms, 'Questions on Vietnam,' dated 24 October 1967, p. 1 (declassified November 1987).

174 LBJ/NSF/CF/VN/84/3H (2) 1967, Appraisal of Bombing NVN/8a, CIA/DIA Report S–2574/AP4A, 'An Appraisal of the Bombing of North Vietnam (through 16 October 1967),' October 1967 (declassified October 1987).

175 Ibid., p. 10.

176 Ibid., p. 11.

177 LBJ/NSF/CF/VN/127/Decision to Halt Bombing (1)/5, memo to the President from McNamara dated 1 November 1967 with 5a, draft memo to the President, 'A Fifteen Month Program for Military Operations in Southeast Asia,' dated 1 November 1967.

178 Ibid., p. 9.
179 Ibid., p. 7.
180 LBJ/NSF/CF/VN/127/Decision to Halt Bombing (1)/Tab J /22, memo to the President from McGeorge Bundy, 'Vietnam – October 1967,' dated 17 October 1967, p. 5 (declassified March 1986).
181 LBJ/NSF/CF/VN/127/Decision to Halt Bombing (1)/Tab K/–, memo to the President from Rostow, dated 2 November 1967.
182 LBJ/NSF/CF/VN/127/Decision to Halt Bombing/Tab K–1/26, memo to the President from Rostow dated 7 November 1967 with attached Clifford memorandum.
183 LBJ/WHCF/Meeting Notes File/2, meeting with the foreign policy advisors, Thursday 2 November 1967.
184 Ibid., p. 3.
185 Ibid., p. 8.
186 Ibid., p. 10.
187 LBJ/NSF/CF/VN/127/Decision to Halt Bombing (1)/Tab I/20a, memo to the President from Taylor, dated 3 November 1967, p. 2.
188 LBJ/NSF/memos to the President/25/WWR 49/6, memo to the President from Rostow with 6a, letter to the President from Taylor dated 6 November 1967 and 6b, memo, 'An Estimate of the Vietnam Situation November 1967,' n.d. (all declassified January 1988).
189 Ibid., 6b, p. 7.
190 Ibid.
191 LBJ/NSF/CF/VN/127/Decision to Halt Bombing (1)/Tab H/18, memo to the President from Fortas, dated 5 November 1967, p. 1.
192 LBJ/NSF/Memos to the President/25/ WWR 50/59, memo to the president from Rostow, dated 11 November 1967. Attachment, 59a, memo, 'Progress or Stalemate.'
193 Ibid., 59a, p. 3.
194 LBJ/NSF/CF/VN/127/Decision to Halt Bombing (1)/Tab E/12 memo to the President from Rostow, dated 21 November 1967; Tab F/14, memo to the President from Rostow, dated 20 November 1967 (both declassified March 1986).
195 LBJ/NSF/CF/VN/127/Decision to Halt Bombing (1)/Tab D/10, memo to the President from Rusk, dated 20 November 1967, p. 2 (declassified November 1986).
196 LBJ/NSF/CF/VN/127/Decision to Halt Bombing/Tab G/10a, memo to the President from Katzenbach, 'Vietnam,' dated 16 November 1967, p. 12 (declassified November 1986).
197 LBJ/NSF/CF/VN/127/Decision to Halt Bombing (1)/Tab L/28, memo of the President for the file, dated 18 December 1967, pp. 1–2.
198 LBJ/NSF/CF/VN/84/3 H (2) 1967/7a, CIA/DIA Report S 2607/AP4A, 'An Appraisal of the Bombing of North Vietnam (through 16 November 67),' dated November 1967 (declassified October 1987).
199 LBJ/NSF/CF/VN/68, 69/2 C (2) General Military Activities/1, memo to the President from Rostow, dated 13 December 1967.
200 LBJ/NSF/CF/VN/68, 69/2 C (2)/General Military Activities/1b, intelligence memo, 'A Review of the Situation in Vietnam,' dated 8 December 1967, p. VIII–1.
201 Ibid., p. VIII–6.
202 Ibid., p. II–1.
203 LBJ/NSF/CF/VN/68, 69/2 C (1) General Military Activities/2, intelligence

report, 'Questions and Answers Relating to Vietnam,' dated 8 December 1967, pp. 5, 6, 11.

204 Ibid., p. 11.
205 Ibid., p. 7.
206 Ibid., p 8.
207 Ibid., pp. 48, 49, 58.
208 LBJ/NSF/CF/VN/247/JASON Study/1, 2, 3, 4, Institute for Defense Analysis, JASON Study, 'The Bombing of North Vietnam,' vol. I, Summary, vol. II, Accomplishments, vol. III, Analysis, vol. IV, Evaluation of Various Interdiction Campaigns, dated 16 December 1967.
209 Ibid., I, p. 1.
210 Ibid., I, p. 7.
211 Ibid., I, p. 16.
212 Ibid., II, p. 82.
213 Ibid., II, p. 83.
214 Ibid., IV, p. 93.
215 LBJ/NSF/CF/VN/84/3 H (3)/4, memo to Rostow from Ginsburgh, dated 13 January 1968 with 4a, memo, 'JASON Study – The Bombing of North Vietnam,' dated 13 January 1968 (both declassified August 1989).
216 Ibid., document 4.

8 SHOCK AND REASSESSMENT

1 LBJ/NSF/CF/VN/68, 69/2 C 3 General Military Activity/85, memo to Rostow from McCafferty, dated 9 January 1968 with 85a, BG Philip Davidson, ACoS, J–2, extracts from November intelligence report, p. 12.
2 LBJ/NSF/CF/VN/68, 69/2 C 3 General Military Activity/92a, telex to JCS from CINCPAC, 'Year-end Review of Vietnam,' dated 1 January 1968, pp. 1–2. Sent to Rostow several days later.
3 Ibid., pp. 2, 5.
4 Ibid., pp. 24–5.
5 Ibid., p. 25.
6 Ibid., p. 3.
7 Ibid.
8 LBJ/NSF/CF/VN/68, 69/2 C 3 General Military Activity 213, DoS INR, research memo RSA–34.69, 'Selected Military Statistics on the Vietnamese Hostilities November 26 through December 2, 1967,' dated 11 January 1968; 82, DoS, INR research memo REA 34.71, 'Selected Military Statistics on the Vietnamese Hostilities December 10–16, 1967,' dated 12 January 1968; 250, DoS INR, research memo REA 34.72, 'Selected Military Statistics on the Vietnamese Hostilities December 17–23, 1967,' dated 15 January 1968.
9 LBJ/NSF/CF/VN/68, 69/2 C 3 General Military Activity/84, telex to the President from Rostow CAP80284, 'CIA Summary of a Longer Text on the Enemy Threat to Khe Sanh,' dated 11 January 1968.
10 LBJ/NSF/DSDUF/3/Memos to the President/ W. W. R. V. 57/62d, memo to the President from Rostow, dated 18 January 1968.
11 LBJ/NSF/DSDUF/3/Memos to the President/W. W. R. V. 67/62b, untitled and undated memo, p. 2.
12 Ibid.
13 LBJ/NSF/DSDUF/3/Memos to the President/W. W. R. V. 57/62, memo to the President from Rostow, dated 19 January 1968.

14 LBJ/NSF/DSDUF/3/Memos to the President/W. W. R. V. 57/9, memo to the President from Rostow dated 24 January 1968 with 9a, transcription of telex, Saigon 16851, dated 24 January 1968.
15 LBJ/NSF/CF/VN/68, 69/2 C 3 General Military Activity/77a, transcribed copy of MAC 01049 from COMUSMACV, dated 22 January 1968 sent to the President by Rostow by document 77, memo to the President, dated 22 January 1968.
16 LBJ/NSF/CF/VN/68, 69/2 C 3 General Military Activity/76, memo to the President from Rostow dated 6:20 p.m., 22 January 1968 with 76a, transcription of telex MAC 00967, dated 22 January 1968.
17 Ibid., 76a, p. 3.
18 LBJ/NSF/CF/VN/68, 69/2 C 3 General Military Activity/69, telex from COMUSMACV to PACOM/JCS, MAC 01333, dated 29 January 1968.
19 Ibid.
20 LBJ/NSF/CF/VN/68, 69/2C 3 General Military Activity/64, memo to the President from White House Situation Room dated 11:45 a.m., 30 January 1968 based on MACV situation report received 7:30 a.m.
21 LBJ/NSF/CF/VN/68, 69/2 C 3 General Military Activity/63, memo for record, 'Summary of Principal Enemy Activity in South Vietnam,' dated 1:08 p.m., 30 January 1968 (declassified June 1987).
22 LBJ/NSF/CF/VN/68, 69/2 C 3 General Military Activity/40, telex to Wheeler from Westmoreland, MAC 01438, dated 5:55 a.m., 30 January 1968, p. 3.
23 Ibid., p. 4.
24 LBJ/NSF/CF/VN/68, 69/2 C 3 General Military Activity/42, telex to DCI from Saigon, Saigon 7725 dated 1905Z, 30 January 1968. 1905Z would be 2:05 p.m. EST (declassified March 1988).
25 LBJ/NSF/CF/VN/68, 69/2 C 3 General Military Activity/44, CRITIC to DIRNSA from CIA stamped received by White House at 8:01 p.m. (declassified March 1988).
26 LBJ/NSF/CF/VN/68, 69/2 C 3 General Military Activity/43, CRITIC telex to DIRNSA from CIA, stamped received WHCA 2059, 30 January 1968 (declassified March 1988).
27 LBJ/NSF/CF/VN/68, 69/2 C 3 General Military Activity/45, telex to Bunker from Rostow, dated 30 January 1968 (declassified January 1989).
28 For an excellent summary of the MACV FONECONs of 30 January, some of which occurred at three-minute intervals see LBJ/NSF/CF/VN/68, 69/2 C 3 General Military Activity/50, memo for the record, 'Enemy Attacks in South Vietnam,' dated 1904 EST, 30 January 1968 (declassified June 1987).
29 LBJ/NSF/CF/VN/68, 69/2 C 3 General Military Activity/34, telex to Rostow, Rusk and Helms from Wheeler passing on telex to Wheeler from Sharp, dated 31 January 1968.
30 Ibid., p. 2.
31 Ibid. See also General Westmoreland's history notes for 1 February in LBJ/Papers of William C. Westmoreland/16/V. 29 (I)/3, History Notes (declassified January 1990).
32 LBJ/NSF/CF/VN/68, 69/2 C 3 General Military Activity/20, memo to Rostow from Ginsburgh, 'General Westmoreland's telephonic answers to the President's questions,' dated 31 January 1968, p. 1.
33 Ibid.
34 LBJ/NSF/CF/VN/68, 69/2 C 3 General Military Activity/14a, memo to Rostow from George Carver, '31 January Telephone Conversation with Saigon Station,' dated 31 January 1968, pp. 2–3.

35 Ibid., p. 3.

36 LBJ/NSF/DSDUF/2/Memos to the President W. W. R. V. 54/28a, memo to Rostow from George Carver, 'Papers on Viet Cong Strategy,' including appended field papers, dated 15 December 1967, with 28, memo to President from Rostow, dated 16 December 1967.

37 A virtually complete series of CIA spot reports is to be found in LBJ/NSF/ NSCH/47/March 31st Speech/Vol V/Tabs 86–99 inclusive. See as examples, LBJ/NSF/CF/VN/68, 69/2 C 2/5, 'Situation in South Vietnam, as of 4:30 p.m. EST,' dated 30 January 1968; 4, 'Situation in South Vietnam, as of 7:00 a.m. EST,' dated 31 January 1968; 3, 'Situation in South Vietnam, as of 12 Noon EST,' dated 31 January 1968; 2a, 'Situation in South Vietnam, as of 3:30 p.m. EST,' dated 31 January 1968.

38 See the all-too-heavily sanitized CIA intelligence report, LBJ/NSF/Memos to the President/28/W. W. R. V. 59/85a, CIA report, TDCS 314–01890–68, 'Account of Preparations for Attack on Chau Doc City,' dated 2 February 1968. Sent to President by Rostow memo, 85, in which he apologizes for having the President read an entire two-page report, dated 6:45 p.m., 2, February 1968. See also memos to the President/W. W. R. V. 59/92, 'Literally Eyes Only' to the President from Rostow, dated 10:00 a.m., 2 February 1968 which reports NLF broadcast as stating goals of 'general uprising' are overthrow of Saigon Government and replacing it with NLF-sponsored 'neutralist' regime.

39 LBJ/NSF/DSDUF/2/Memos to the President W. W. R. V. 59/96a, CIA spot report, dated 5:30 p.m. EST, 1 February 1968, p. 2.

40 LBJ/Papers of William C. Westmoreland/16/V. 29 (1)/17, 21, 33, telexes from Bunker to Rusk: Saigon 17361, dated 1 February 1967; Saigon 17363, dated 2 February 1967; and Saigon [date unreadable], dated 1125Z 2 February (all declassified June 1990).

41 LBJ/NSF/Memos to the President/29/W. W. R. V. 60/39b, transcript of Saigon #030, dated 6 February 1968. Sent to President by Rostow, 39, dated 7 February 1968.

42 Ibid., p. 4.

43 LBJ/NSF/Tom Johnson's Notes of Meetings/2/February 7, 1968 NSC meeting/47 ff.

44 Ibid., 48a, p. 2.

45 Ibid., pp. 1, 4.

46 Ibid., p. 4.

47 LBJ/NSF/NSCH/47/March 31st Speech/Vol V./100, CIA spot report 'Situation in the Khe Sanh Area,' dated 7 February 1968 (declassified February 1989).

48 Ibid., p. 3.

49 LBJ/Papers of Clark Clifford/2/White House (Vietnam War)/12, telex to Sharp from Westmoreland, 'Assessment of Situation and Requirements,' dated 12 February 1968, p. 1.

50 Ibid., p. 2.

51 Ibid., p. 3.

52 LBJ/NSF/Memos to the President/29/W. W. R. V. 60/49a, telex to Wheeler from Westmoreland, MAC 01754, 'Enemy Casualty Figures,' dated 8 February 1968. Sent to the President by Rostow on 8 February 1968. Located in DSDUF/3.

53 LBJ/DUSDUF/3/W. W. R. V. 60/80, memo to the President from Rostow, 'Increase in Enemy Forces in Vietnam Since December,' dated 11 February 1968. These were revised upwards on February but remained below the

December overall strength figure. See LBJ/DSDUF/3/W. W. R. V. 62/15, memo to the President from Rostow, dated 16 February 1968.

54 See LBJ/Papers of Clark Clifford/2/White House (Vietnam War)/8a, memo to the President from Maxwell Taylor, 'Further Reinforcements for Vietnam,' dated 10 February 1968, p. 1.

55 LBJ/Papers of Clark Clifford/4/2nd set of memos on Vietnam, February 1968/1, memo to the President from General Johnson, 'Validity of Present Strategy of Operations in South Vietnam,' dated 1 February 1968.

56 Ibid., p. 4.

57 LBJ/Papers of Clark Clifford/2/White House (Vietnam War)/8a, memo to the President from Taylor, 'Further Reinforcements for Vietnam,' dated 10 February 1968.

58 Ibid., p. 3.

59 Ibid., p. 4.

60 LBJ/Papers of Clark Clifford/4/2nd set of memos on Vietnam, February 1968/2, memo to the Secretary of Defense from Wheeler, 'Emergency Reinforcement of COMUSMACV,' dated 12 February 1968.

61 Ibid., p. 2.

62 Ibid., p. 5.

63 LBJ/Papers of Clark Clifford/4/2nd set of memos on Vietnam, February 1968/3, memo to the President from Wheeler, 'Reinforcements for South Vietnam,' dated 12 February 1968, p. 1.

64 LBJ/Papers of Clark Clifford/4/2nd Set of Memos on Vietnam, February 1968 3a, telex to Westmoreland from Wheeler, JCS 01695, dated 12 February 1968, p. 2.

65 LBJ/Papers of Clark Clifford/2/White House (Vietnam War)/3a, memo to the President from Taylor, 'Khe Sanh,' dated 14 February 1968. This constituted an expansion of the arguments he had employed at the reinforcement meeting of 12 February 1968.

66 The complete file of daily briefings is found in the LBJ/NSF/NSCH/47/31st of March Speech/Tabs 26–51.

67 LBJ/NSF/CF/VN/68, 69/2 C 4 General Military Activity/101a, CIA Operations Center memo to DCI, dated 17 February 1968, relayed to President by Rostow, 101 (declassified February 1989).

68 LBJ/Papers of Clark Clifford/2/Memos on Vietnam/2, 'Report of Chairman, JCS on Situation in Vietnam and MACV Force Requirements,' dated 27 February 1968.

69 Ibid., p. 1.

70 Ibid., p. 2.

71 Ibid., p. 3, Inclosure 1, p. 1.

72 Ibid., Inclosure 1, p. 3.

73 Ibid., Inclosure 1, p. 6.

74 Ibid., pp. 12–13.

75 Ibid., p. 4.

76 Ibid., Inclosure 7, p. 3.

77 Ibid., Inclosure 8, p. 3.

78 LBJ/NSF/CF/VN/50/1 C (3) B–2, CORDS/42a, memo to the President from Leonhart, 'The New Refugee Situation,' dated 10 February 1968, together with 42, memo to Rostow from Leonhart, 'Vietnam Refugees,' dated 13 February 1968 (declassified June 1989).

79 LBJ/Papers of Clark Clifford/2/Vietnam Alternatives/19, CIA memorandum, 'Communist Alternatives in Vietnam,' dated 29 February 1968.

80 LBJ/WHCF/Meeting Notes File/2/Meeting of Advisors on Vietnam, 27 February 1968.
81 Ibid., p. 2.
82 Ibid., p. 4.
83 Ibid.
84 LBJ/NSF/CF/VN/127/Decision to Halt Bombing (1)/T. K–1/26, memo to the President from Clifford via Rostow, dated 7 November 1967.
85 LBJ/Clark Clifford Oral History/AC 74–97/Tape 3/pp. 14 ff.
86 LBJ/Papers of Clark clifford/1/Alternative Strategies vis a vis SEA/25, Maxwell Taylor, memo, 'Viet-Nam Alternatives,' n.d.
87 Quoted in ibid., p. 1.
88 LBJ/Papers of Clark Clifford/2/Memos on Vietnam/3b, William Bundy draft memo, 'Introductory Paper on Key Elements in the Situation,' dated 29 February 1968.
89 LBJ/Papers of Clark Clifford/2/Memos on Vietnam/3d, Nicholas Katzen-bach, 'US Public Opinion,' n.d., but by context circa 1 March 1968.
90 Ibid., p. 3.
91 LBJ/Papers of Clark Clifford/2/Memos on Vietnam/3e–2, 'Probable Western European Reaction to Various US Courses of Action in Indochina,' n.d.
92 LBJ/Papers of Clark Clifford/2/Memos on Vietnam/3g, William Bundy draft memo, 'European and Other Non-Asian Reactions to a Major US Force Increase,' 1 March 1968.
93 LBJ/Papers of Clark Clifford/2/Vietnam Memos/9, Organization of the JCS, Plans and Policy Directorate, 'Analysis of COMUSMACV Force Require-ments and Alternatives,' 1 March 1968.
94 Ibid., p. II–3.
95 Ibid., p V–1.
96 Ibid., p. VI–1.
97 Ibid., pp. V–5, 8.
98 Ibid., p. VII–3.
99 Ibid., p. VIII–4.
100 Ibid., p. IX–3.
101 LBJ/Papers of Clark Clifford/Clifford draft memo to the President/1, DPM, dated 1 March 1968, p. 18.
102 Ibid., p. 26.
103 LBJ/Papers of Clark Clifford/1/Strategies vis a vis SEA/18, CIA memoran-dum, 'Questions Concerning the Situation in Vietnam,' 1 March 1968, pp. 8–9.
104 Ibid., p. 10.
105 Ibid., p. 3.
106 LBJ/Papers of Clark Clifford/1/National Objectives and Resources/10, memo, 'Public Affairs,' 3 March 1968, provides an excellent analysis of the difficulties involved in 'selling' the war to the public.
107 LBJ/NSF/NSCH/49/March 31st Speech/V. 7/T. 3, memo to the President from Rostow, 'The Clifford Committee,' dated 4 March 1968; LBJ/NSF/CF/-VN/127/Decision to Halt Bombing (1)/36, agenda, meeting with the President, Monday, 4 March 1968.
108 LBJ/Papers of William C. Westmoreland/16/V. 30 (I)/34, telex to Westmore-land from Wheeler, dated 8 March 1968, p. 1 (declassified January 1990).
109 Ibid., p. 3. See Papers of William C. Westmoreland/V. 30 (I)/36, telex to Wheeler from Westmoreland, dated 8 March 1968 for Westmoreland's response to the guidance [document declassified November 1989].

110 LBJ/Clark Clifford Oral History/AC 74–97/Tape 3/p. 16. Interview conducted 14 July 1969.
111 Ibid.
112 LBJ/NSF/NSCH/49/March 31st Speech/V. 7/83, CIA ONE memo to the Director, 'Communist Reactions to Certain US Courses of Action,' dated 13 March 1968.
113 LBJ/NSF/CF/VN/-60/1 C (3) A Revolutionary Development Program/1C, CIA Directorate of Intelligence, intelligence memo, 'Pacification in the Wake of the Tet Offensive in South Vietnam, dated 19 March 1968 (declassified June 1990).
114 Ibid., p. 22.
115 LBJ/Papers of Clark Clifford/1/Alternative Strategies and Strategic Guidance/ 3, memo to Clifford from Warnke, draft presidential memo, 2nd draft, dated 18 March 1968.
116 Ibid., p. 6.
117 Ibid., p. 7.
118 LBJ/WHCF/Meeting Notes File/Summary Notes, Advisors' Meeting 19 March 1968, luncheon meeting with the President, 22 March 1968.
119 LBJ/George Ball Oral History/Interview II/Tape 1, p. 13. Interview conducted 9 July 1971. LBJ/Oral History of William Bundy/AC 74–187/Interview I/Tape 4, p. 36. Interview conducted 2 June 1969.
120 LBJ/Cyrus Vance Oral History/AC 74–260/Interview III/Tape 1, p. 19. Interview conducted 9 March 1970.
121 Ibid., p. 20.
122 George Ball Oral History/Interview II/Tape 1, p. 14.
123 LBJ/WHCF/Meeting Notes File/'Summary of Notes,' dated 26 March 1968, p. 1.
124 George Ball Oral History/Interview II/Tape 1, p. 14.
125 Ibid., Interview II, Tape 2.
126 Ibid.
127 Ibid.

INDEX